Praise for *The Family Legacy* and *Vocation*

Brian Clark is renowned for his research and insight in this field. He is an experienced teacher and counsellor as well as a gifted communicator. We in Australia are fortunate to have had the benefit of his influence and inspiration for many years. *The Family Legacy* does not disappoint.

— Cate Whelan, *The FAA Journal*

For newcomers to astrology and intermediate students, *The Family Legacy* is an excellent doorway to learning about astrology and making leaps in personal growth. For advanced students, professionals, and teachers, you won't find a better reference on the astrology of family. *The Family Legacy* would make a great 'recommended reading' for any astrology class. This one is bound to be a classic and deserves a prominent place on any astrologer's 'favourite books' shelf.

— Chris Lorenz, *Dell Horoscope*

Here in southern Oregon, we talk of guides on the world-class rivers and rapids. Brian Clark is in that category: a very skilled guide for the interior terrain that ties us together with those in our blood lineage and the others with whom we are close.

— Mary Plumb, *The Mountain Astrologer*

When writers make their writing live, they have done all they possibly can. *Vocation* is fully alive; I can offer no higher praise or recommendation.

— Roderick Kidston, *The FAA Journal*

Brian Clark writes beautifully. His long experience as a teacher, practitioner, and student of the esoteric arts shines through the book. I would thoroughly recommend it for astrology students, for astrologers just beginning to engage with client work, and for experienced practitioners. I have certainly found that reading *Vocation* has provided me with some new, useful insights into my own wayward and diverse vocational journey.

— Anne Whitaker, *The Mountain Astrologer*

ISBN: 978-0-9944880-4-6

First edition published 2018 by Astro*Synthesis
PO Box 111
Stanley, Tasmania 7331
Australia
www.astrosynthesis.com.au

The author can be reached at: brian@astrosynthesis.com.au

Charts calculated using Solar Fire software
Cover Designer: Cat Keane
Proof-reader: Jane Struthers
Project Manager and Layout: Frank C. Clifford

Cover Image: Edward Burne-Jones, *Cupid Delivering Psyche*, 1867.
This version of Edward Burne-Jones's *Cupid Delivering Psyche* depicts the
moment in the myth when Psyche consciously recognizes Eros after the many
trials that Venus had ordered her to complete. While painting this, Burne-Jones
was engaged in a passionate affair with Maria Zambaco, his model for Cupid and
Psyche. Ironically it was Maria's mother who had commissioned Burne-Jones to
paint her daughter as Psyche, an interesting twist in Venus's mythic triangle.

FROM THE MOMENT WE MET

The Astrology of Adult Relationships

BRIAN CLARK

Astro*Synthesis

Acknowledgements

I am forever grateful for the opportunities I have been given to pursue my vocational course as an astrological counsellor and educator throughout my adult life. This path has interconnected with so many outstanding and distinctive individuals who I have had the honour of working with as clients, colleagues and students. My deep appreciation to all the students who have participated in our classes on Relationship Astrology and the clients who have willingly shared their relational anecdotes, their heartbreaks and their joys, as well as their beliefs and desires about relationship. These interactions have contributed valuably to my understanding.

I have been privileged to work with many colleagues who, over the course of planning classes, seminars or tours together, have become treasured colleagues. Verena Bachmann, Demetra George, Peter O'Connor, Tracey Potter, Melanie Reinhart, Anne Shotter and Mary Symes: my deep appreciation that our paths crossed. Over so many years I also have been blessed to have been encouraged and sponsored by many colleagues who have promoted and organized many wonderful educational adventures. My thanks for making me feel so special: Barbara Brackley, Narelle Macnamara, Clare Martin and Evelyn Roberts. My sincere appreciation to my Federation of Australian Astrologers (FAA) colleagues and co-workers for all your support and encouragement throughout the years.

I have been well supported by friends and colleagues who have read, proofread and assisted me to present the manuscript. My thanks to all those who have lent a hand; in particular Mary Symes and Barb Thorp for their much appreciated comments. Thanks to Frank Clifford for encouraging me to write and publish and Liliane Liou for making that possible.

And, to Glennys, my thankfulness for the fullness of our relationship,

Brian Clark
Stanley, Tasmania

TABLE OF CONTENTS

SOUL AND RELATIONSHIP

Relationship is essential to the soul, at the very heart of existence, and its labyrinthine path leads us into the mysteries of life itself. By its very nature, relationship is inevitable; it supports and contains each person throughout the stages of their life, while at other times may avert or be in opposition to their development. Embedded in every human being is an instinct to respond and attach, including the urge, desire and anticipation to relate. As an integral human pattern, relationship is an aspect of every individual's future, shaped by the familial, ancestral and cultural atmosphere of the times in which they live.

Relationship begins before birth, in the womb of the mother. Symbiotic, deeply felt and on the whole an unremembered passage, gestation is a primal image of intimacy and relationship. During gestation we experience the inescapable processes of dependency, bonding and attachment. At birth we inhale our first breath, initiating the unavoidable experience of separation through individuation, another integral aspect of human relating. Vulnerable, unable to survive independently, the newborn greets its caretaker – prospectively not only its first relationship, but also first love and first partner – while simultaneously experiencing its first separation.

These first independent moments are significant to relational patterning and commemorated astrologically by the Ascendant, the image of birth, and its polarity the Descendant. From earliest times, the soul has been associated with the breath of life and imagined as entering the body at birth through the first inhalation. Soul, as the breath of life, animates the natal chart, which becomes an ideal locus for contemplating soul and relationship as well as the mysteries of attachment and separation, intimacy and individuality.

From this experience we move forward into a variety of familial and extra-familial relationships. From birth through to childhood and adolescence, we forge sibling, parental and peer relationships, and it is these experiences that significantly inform and shape the path towards our adult relationships. My previous book *The Family Legacy*[1] focused on the astrology of our formative relationships and their impact on later adult attachments and partnerships. *The Family Legacy* serves as a prelude to this volume which focuses on adult relationships.

This book has organically grown out of the classes Glennys Lawton and I developed for our four-year teaching program *Astro*Synthesis*. Relationship patterns were explored in our first- and second-year classes as well as in an advanced unit called Synastry. Three student booklets prepared for those modules, called *Intimate Others: The Astrology of the 7th and 8th Houses; Soul Mates: The Houses of Relationship*; and *Synastry: An Astrological Anatomy of Relationship*, became the starting point for this book.[2] In addition, some of the interpretations such as Venus and Mars in the signs have been adapted from my report writer *Kindred Spirits*.[3]

Beneath the western examples and experiences in this book lies the archetypal nature of relationship which can be studied in all languages and all societies. Being a universal language, astrological images are cross-cultural; therefore, when using astrological symbols to understand individual, familial and social patterns, these images can have resonance across all cultures.

Relationship in and of itself is archetypal; that is, the experience of relating is common to the human condition. In addition, there are archetypal roles characterized by mythological gods and goddesses. While their names and narratives differ across traditions and civilizations, the spirit of each is similar, e.g. the spirit of archetypes such as 'king', 'queen', 'husband', 'wife', 'lover', etc., remains the same. Being archetypal, it is only their clothing, characteristics and interests that vary across cultures. Their essence is the same. From an astrological perspective this essence is expressed through the planetary archetypes, uniquely disseminated through their signs, houses and aspects in each horoscope.

On some level all planetary archetypes are concerned with love and relationship, yet three in particular can be identified for their strong association with love: the Moon, Venus and Neptune. The Moon is first love, mother love, and is indicative of early attachment, while Neptune is cosmic, universal love. Venus is identified with adult love and relationship, and her sign of Libra has become an enduring symbol for the qualities of union and partnership.

Each individual is born into a generation that has its own versions, values, attitudes and experiences of relationship. I was born with Neptune in Libra (1942–57), the war and post-war generation when seeds of idealism about love and relationship were implanted in the collective soul. Enormous change has taken place in the attitudes towards relationships, marriage and sexuality throughout my generation's lifetime. Uranus moved into Libra in 1968, and Pluto entered Libra in 1971. Those in my generation were still adolescents or in their twenties when the 'relationship revolution' began. Relationship institutions, traditions and boundaries were torn down; for instance, no-fault divorce laws in the US saw the divorce rate soar. The transformation of relationship attitudes and customs happened across the board, including women's liberation, gay rights and open marriages.

When Uranus entered Libra my parents were shocked at my generation's rejection of traditional marriage and our preference for living together or remaining uncommitted, rather than feeling obligated to marry. But by the time Uranus left Libra in 1975, some of my parents' friends were divorced and living unmarried with new partners. The three outer planets in Libra in the last half of the twentieth century altered the cultural approach to relationship, setting in motion new patterns and possibilities, so much so that it is often difficult for younger generations to imagine the conventional approaches that existed prior to this in the middle of the twentieth century.

Even so the archetypal innate processes of relating have not changed – e.g. attachment, separation, intimacy, individuality, dependence and independence. The essence remains the same but has adapted to grow with the times. The archetypal roles of the gods and goddesses have not changed; while they are ever engaged in relationship, it is their roles that have been updated to contemporary versions.

Throughout the book I share case examples to illustrate various aspects of relationship astrology, not simply to demonstrate techniques, but also to show countless archetypal possibilities. Some case studies I was already familiar with, having used these as teaching examples over the years. Others captured my interest and attention. My intention was to let the narratives reveal the astrology, rather than use the case studies to legitimize astrological techniques.

While the patterns of our relationships are not necessarily mapped out by the horoscope in literal ways, astrology offers insights and revelations when we openly participate with its symbols.

Astrology proposes a unique perspective into honouring the voice of the soul. A person's horoscope is created for the time of birth coincident not only with the soul's 'breath of life', but also with a person's first attachment–separation dynamics. Relationship patterns are innate to the human soul and at birth the relational template and tendencies are impressed upon the psyche and reflected in the horoscope.

Soulful relationships are experienced throughout the course of our lives and we are blessed when we find our soulmates. It does not guarantee that these relationships are trouble-free; in fact it is often the opposite, but the soul feels connected, at home and in the eternity of the moment when in the presence of a soulmate. As the ancients knew, the soul has its own reasons. Astrology assists us in reflecting upon these reasons.

– INTRODUCTION –
AN ASTROLOGICAL OVERVIEW OF RELATIONSHIP

When two souls form relationship with one another, so do their horoscopes.

Comparing the astrology between two individuals for compatibility is familiar to most people, even part and parcel of everyday life. In some ways astrology is the oldest typology of relationships. A common complaint is the incompatibility between Sun signs; for instance, a person who has the Sun in Taurus may feel their Aries friend walks too fast, while an Aquarian might not understand why their Cancer colleague is so emotional. Can a Sagittarian really understand why their Pisces partner would rather stay in bed than go out for an early morning jog?

Yet there's much more to chart compatibility than Sun signs. When working with two horoscopes, the amount of astrological information increases exponentially, as each individual's planets has a prospective interchange with their partner's planets. Therefore I have tried to present an approach to all the possible information in a sequential and in-depth way. Each practitioner will have their own personal style for this analysis, stressing some techniques that others may not. Like all professions and procedures there are variants and dissimilarities from which you will forge your own understanding and practice.

Throughout the book I concentrate on adult relationships; however, you can modify the astrological concepts to match a myriad of other partnerships. Different aspects of the horoscope are emphasized for distinct relationships such as parent–child, sibling–sibling, lovers, friends, marriage or business partners. As there are differing customs, conventions and codes of conduct for diverse relationships, the analysis needs to be tailored to suit the particular type of relationship, while keeping in mind that each and every relationship is inherently unique within itself.

The following is a synopsis of what we will develop throughout the book, beginning with Part 1 where we will concentrate on relationship themes and considerations in the natal charts.

Relationship Themes in the Natal Charts

The first step in relationship astrology is to study the natal chart of each individual, concentrating on the interconnecting patterns and possibilities. This includes being mindful of what the horoscope reveals about their family relationships, the parental marriage, the family atmosphere and the sibling system. We begin looking at the planets through the eyes of relationship, becoming accustomed to how they function in the sphere of relationship. Then we will focus mythologically on the gods of relationship and their symbolic presence in our horoscopes. As we are focusing on adult relationships we will concentrate on the planetary archetypes of Venus and Mars, as well as the terrain of the 7th and 8th houses. As friendship is another important adult bond we will open the door to the 11th house to amplify our connection to friends.

One of the seminal moments in any relationship is when each one crosses paths with the other. How does each one come to be at the same crossroads at the same time? This is a question that relationship astrology contemplates through its use of the angles and axes of the horoscope, astronomical circles that intersect with the ecliptic to bring two forces into the same plane at the same time. Therefore we will look at the Nodal axis as well as the Vertex–Anti-Vertex angle in this context of intersecting paths.

Temperament plays a significant role in relating; therefore we will consider ways to analyse each partner's temperament and the function it performs in the partnership. Since the horoscope is a vivid indicator of what the individual may attract to them by means of relationship, we also need to be aware of not only what is developed, but also what is lacking in the horoscope.

Synastry

In Part 2 we introduce synastry, the area of astrological analysis of two or more charts in the context of their relationship. Derived from ancient Greek, synastry suggests being together with the stars, recognizing the archetypal nature of relationship in the human experience. Synastry conjures up the image of a celestial guidebook to relating.

Synastry acknowledges the forces of human attraction, the synchrony of meeting, compatibilities and difficulties as well as the development of the relationship over time. It is a profound astrological tool for the amplification and exploration of relationships, a valuable guide in helping us to better understand relationships in general as well as the specifics of a given relationship. Some of the goals of synastry are to:

- *Address* specific questions and concerns in the relationship
- *Consider* each individual's style, attitude and approach to relationship
- *Delineate* the core issues within the relationship
- *Explore* the areas of potential conflict and compatibility
- *Honour* the authenticity of each individual and the relationship that is created
- *Reveal* the patterns, purpose and nature of the relationship
- *Review* critical and transitional times in the relationship

Synastry is about the study of more than one horoscope; therefore, the amount of detail and data that can be generated increases substantially. It is helpful to follow some steps and guidelines when analysing the relationship of two or more individuals. We will study each stage in synastry which develops the process of studying two horoscopes at the same time.

Chart Comparison
Chart comparison attempts to see how one individual's horoscope impacts on the other. This can be done in a variety of ways. One way to begin this process is to ascertain what is lacking in each horoscope and whether the other is fulfilling this lack. And if so, are the partners aware of this? What has the individual imported into their relationship experience? From a relationship point of view we are considering how one partner may be compensating for the other's lack, as well as exploring dynamics that the partners may be unaware of. Certain areas of the horoscope are more prone to projection, transference or distortion by one partner; therefore, by examining both horoscopes we are looking at how individuals impact one other, as well as areas of each horoscope that are susceptible to projection, compensation and idealization.

A technique highlighted by Stephen Arroyo in his book *Relationships and Life Cycles* is to place one partner's planets and angles over the other's horoscope, and vice versa. Using computer software, two bi-wheels can be created; each has their partner's planets on the outside of their chart. This gives us a visual image of the impact that the partner is making on the energy field and atmosphere of the other.

The Aspect Grid

One of the most dynamic techniques in chart comparison involves analysing the interaspects between each chart. Here it is necessary to understand the nature of each planet and how that affects the other, especially when there is a major aspect. Each planet in one chart is compared to each planet in the other to determine the most dominant and powerful aspects between the two charts.

The Composite and other Charts

When the two charts are thoroughly analysed, another chart can be created by combining the two charts. This is known as the composite or the Davison relationship chart. Each one attempts to delineate the energies of the relationship or the two individuals as one entity or system. Other charts which are also important, such as the marriage and/or meeting charts, will also be examined. Transits and progressions are important at the time of meeting, as they symbolize the founding energies of the relationship.

Each partnership will move through time; therefore, it is important to be aware of the transits and progressions that envision the evolution of the relationship. Not only transits and progressions to the natal charts are considered, but also to the composite chart. When considering relationship we are faced with stories and images of two individuals from two different family backgrounds, each having experienced their own unique life events. The time before they met is invested with memories, emotions, traumas, opinions, sentiments and experiences which infiltrate the relationship's present and future. The past that each one brings into the relationship is highly subjective and personal, yet is often unknown to the other. These influences will be present in the transitions the partners share together.

We will end with a reflection on the steps we've taken to understand the anatomy of relationship.

PART I

THE NATAL CHARTS

Possibilities and Potentialities of Relationship

Relationship astrology is not just a project about compatibility and possibility; it calls us to honour the mystery and soul of our attachments, not for what we want them to be, but for how they truly are.

Brian Clark

– CHAPTER 1 –
ARCHETYPES AND ATTACHMENT
Planets in Partnership

We start our exploration of adult relationships by reflecting on planetary archetypes in the context of adult attachment and relationship. *The Family Legacy* serves as a prelude to this book since it explores the astrology of family relationships which lays the groundwork for our adult ones. Yet, whether in childhood or adulthood, the patterns in the natal horoscope are always the same, although moderated through transits and progressions. What changes as we age is the consciousness we apply to these signatures, the development and experience of the self, as well as our own maturation.

Each planetary archetype has its own constant signification; it is the application of the planet's meaning that varies. The planetary archetypes are the gods of astrology. When they enter the arena of human relationship we become their surrogates: the divine force becoming entwined with the human life story. Before they were gods of astrology, they were alive in the Greek myths, and to a large extent the deity's character and personality were bequeathed to the planets.

The Inner Planets
Of all the planets in the horoscope, the five inner planets are the most individualized, characteristic of our personal needs, virtues, intelligence, values and desires. They also personify family members. For instance, the Sun characterizes the father; the Moon, mother; Venus, sister; while Mars represents the brother figure. When these planets are in relationship sectors or strongly aspected, the bond to this family member or their archetypal image may be highlighted. These planets serve as archetypal personifications of familial roles; for example, the Sun might suggest a paternal pattern in the context of a relationship; the Moon, a maternal one. Patterns associated with these planets are first evident in familial relations through childhood and adolescence before they emerge once again in adult interactions.

These planets are strongly shaped and influenced by the social and outer planets through dynamic aspects and transits. However, they are also reactive to and have an effect on planets in others' horoscopes. When attachment occurs or an intimate relationship develops, the planetary archetypes become more receptive and vulnerable to their partner's planetary temperament. How an urge, represented by each planet, seeks to be fulfilled through relationship is personal; however, since each planet symbolizes an archetypal orientation it has its own sphere of interest and attraction. In amplifying and reflecting on this sphere, insight into our relationship patterns and preferences is revealed.

With the exception of Mercury, the inner planets are also characterized by their gender; therefore, the Sun and Mars represent patterns in the ancestral and cultural past carried by males, while the Moon and Venus signify females in general, but also the patterns carried by women in the family. On a psychological level the inner planets are also characterized and differentiated by their masculine and feminine traits. Since the human psyche contains both, masculine and feminine characteristics feature in men and women. While masculine qualities are encouraged in men and feminine attributes are supported in women, each individual has their own temperamental mixture of these qualities.

In relationship astrology it has often been proposed that for a woman the Sun and Mars represent her inner masculine figure or *animus*; therefore, the condition of these planets will be strongly indicative of male partners. The Sun will be descriptive of the first relationship with father while Mars will be symbolic of what she desires in a man as a partner or peer. Similarly, the Moon and Venus for a man have been deemed the inner feminine qualities or the *anima*, which will be activated through relationship. His Moon is indicative of his first love, mother, while Venus will illustrate his feminine ideal perceived through the women he is attracted to.

To some extent this line of thinking is beneficial in relationship analysis due to familial and cultural traditions; however, all four planets are also archetypal and transcend gender descriptions. Therefore it is sensible not to be too fixed about assigning traits by gender. Even so, it is wise to recognize that the Sun and Mars for a woman, and the Moon and Venus for a man, become more available and conscious through relationships. Both the Sun–

Moon and Venus–Mars are natural pairs. They not only represent the masculine–feminine polarity but other dualities such as light and dark, assertion and passivity, confrontation and compromise, overt and covert. While they appear as opposites, they pair naturally and therefore are strongly attracted to one another beyond gender classifications. This dynamic also operates in homosexual relationships, due to the affinity of these archetypes.

In the context of early relationships the Moon and Sun play an important role that reflects their connection to mother, father and family members. But in an adult context Venus and Mars are referred to as the planets of relationship. Venus is the urge to be valued, loved and desired, while the impulse of Mars is to desire and chase what is wanted. Therefore, in relationship astrology, when analysing adult attachments and intimate relationships, Venus and Mars stand out. Their signatures by sign, house and aspect, as well as their interaspects to the partner's chart, are primary; therefore we will study these planets separately. But for now we will turn to looking at each planet through the lens of relating.

☉ The Sun

The heart has become the icon for emotive feelings, affection and love. It is often used to express tender feelings but as a symbol it reminds us of the enduring connection between the heart and love. As the ruler of the heart, the Sun is fundamental to the growth of a heartfelt relationship. It is central to the development of self-love and approval, a vital prerequisite for a healthy and equal adult relationship. Self-esteem develops through feeling loved and cherished in familial and early relationships, encouraging a healthy sense of self-worth. But when the solar archetype is underdeveloped it may veer towards egotism and self-centredness, which are divisive in adult relationships. In these cases the Sun seeks acknowledgment and gratitude from the mate rather than being able to offer praise and appreciation to their partner. Therefore, one of the Sun's central roles in relationship is to shine its light on the other through encouragement, support and recognition of their talents. In turn this provides a greater sense of achievement and personal satisfaction for the solar individual.

As the Sun seeks to be self-expressive and creative it is important that relationship not only supports the individual's aspirations and ambitions, but fosters their growth. In relationship, the Sun needs to feel it is being encouraged to do what it genuinely wants to do, no matter how arduous or seemingly impossible. It wants to be partnered in courage and creativeness. Since the Sun represents unique creativity, individuality and expression, it needs its partner to recognize and be aware of its importance. Depending on the nature of the charts and relationship, the mutual creativity of the couple may be utilized through common projects and work. A mythic image of the Sun is the Hero, and the course of the Sun through the zodiac is akin to the heroic journey. In relationship the Sun represents the need to encourage and support the heroic nature.

The Sun also symbolizes vitality and when this archetypal aspect of the individual is supported by their partner they feel more energized and alive. The Sun is acknowledgement, admiration and applause, and when these are felt in relationship the Sun is aglow, warming the individual and the relationship. In relationship astrology the Sun is challenged to become the centre of someone else's world by letting go of their own self-centredness and need for recognition or desire to be the leader or the one in charge. An active and warm-hearted relationship involves a system with two Suns.

By tradition, the Sun has always personified father; therefore, when the Sun is highlighted in relationship astrology it would be important to consider the father's attitudes to relating, familial patterns and images. Those who are confident and convincing or powerful and influential reflect the light of the Sun.

☽ The Moon

When the archetype of the Moon is highlighted, the themes of care, dependency, security and belonging are systemic to the relationship. The Moon in the natal chart represents our personal needs. From birth and through childhood we are dependent on others to meet our needs; however, as we mature, we can provide for some of these ourselves. Yet we always remain dependent on others for certain needs, such as companionship, support, learning and love. Therefore the Moon is indicative of how comfortable we feel when providing for both our own needs and the needs of others. For instance, contrast a Moon in Aries with a Moon in Cancer to reflect on how these needs might be expressed in a relationship.

Since dependency implies being reliant on others, it is often equated with vulnerability. However, vulnerability is not weakness, unless we use the word in the context of having a soft spot for someone. Dependency softens the boundaries between two people, creating a cooperative which is mutually beneficial. In childhood this relationship is not equal; therefore, we trust that others will fulfil our needs. If this trust was violated or abused, then the lunar propensity to bond may be compromised in adult life. Since the Moon is habitual by nature, the same pattern may unintentionally be repeated. In adult relationships we are the parent to our inner child and need to protect its vulnerability and secure a safe place for it in our relationships. Aspects to the Moon will be very revealing in exploring the individual's needs and potential patterns of emotional trust.

The lunar need to belong is strong. Its inclination in relationship is to feel attached and bonded to the other and to the relationship; therefore, each partner's attachment style or their capacity for closeness will be confronted in an intimate relationship.[4] The Moon is also suggestive of our habits, living style and emotional moods, all of which become evident as a relationship becomes more intimate or the couple spends more time together. The Moon reflects an individual's comfort zone, living style and habitual patterns such as eating, sleeping and relaxing. While a Moon in Sagittarius may crave a hot curry, jump out of bed early and enjoy backpacking through a jungle, this might not be well matched with their partner's Moon in Taurus needs.

Traditionally the Moon is embodied by mother; therefore, if the Moon is highlighted in the relationship analysis it is important to address the mother's relational legacy, the ancestral patterns in relationship as well as the mother's ease of affection and level of emotional closeness. Since the Moon is cyclical it is often associated with individuals who are inconstant or wavering; in other words, emotional and moody. In a relationship context it is important to recognize the moods and phases of the Moon by acknowledging without judgement the authenticity of feeling. The Moon brings the full range of emotion into any relationship and the lunar signatures will help to address the emotional spectrum in each individual and the relationship.

☿ Mercury

One of the most common complaints I hear from couples concerns the lack of communication in their relationship, or the feeling of being unheard or misunderstood. A simple suggestion turns into a heated argument or an observation is experienced as a criticism. Mercury's portfolio in the astrological pantheon is Minister of Communication. His sphere of influence is language, exchanging ideas, consulting on projects, communicating and listening: key aspects of the Mercurial nature highlighted in close relationships.

While Mercury is generally associated with verbal or written communication, he is also the trickster archetype so what is said or written may not be genuine. Communication in relationship is complicated by the influence of the unconscious. Unexpressed feelings, resentments and reservations may be conveyed by body language, changes in behaviour, disassociation or detachment which clog the access to direct discussion. The natal chart assists in confirming the natural modes of communicating while chart comparison will detail how this is activated in relationship. Familial patterns of communicating are brought into adult relationships, and it is in the intimacy of a mature relationship where the taboos and directives about what can be said, stated and shared are confronted.

Mercury's penchant for mobility, freedom of expression and portability needs to be honoured in relationship. Once this is acknowledged and experienced, the Mercurial journey moves from communication to communion. With practice, the facility for the two sides of Mercury to flow together is developed: as one talks, the other listens; or as one expresses, the other analyses. This close association develops empathy and understanding which are revealed through the language the couple uses when conversing. Over time this evolves into the couple's own dialect. Humour, wit and absurdity are also part of this dialogue. The Mercurial ability to laugh at life and not take it all so seriously is a positive side of the trickster that lightens and enlivens a relationship.

Mercury's duality, association with both the day and night world, and his access to both heaven and the underworld plays an important function in relationship. In an intimate relationship Mercury's role as the psychopomp or guide into the underworld becomes apparent. When Eros is awoken, Mercury finds many channels of expression through diaries, love letters, innuendo, arguments, fantasies, sweet talk. Intimacy requires Mercury to be faithful to the relationship; private words and thoughts need to be contained within the sanctity of the relationship.

Traditionally, Mercury is associated with learned types, either teachers or students, or others who live by their wits; therefore, relationship is a venue for this sense of curiosity. Mercury also has the urge to learn and be educated; therefore, when an attachment is made, the relationship becomes Mercury's campus. Mercury's association with the sibling archetype brings the images of companion, mate and fellow traveller into his relationships.

♀ Venus

In our examination of adult relationship Venus is paramount, as the archetype suggests the urge for love, union, connection and relationship. While the Moon is also the bonding instinct, it is representative of dependent and familial attachments, whereas Venus suggests more independent and equal relationships often forged outside the family's comfort zone. It denotes our personal values, tastes, likes and dislikes, as well as what we find pleasurable and beautiful. Therefore, underlying our passions, attractions and connections are our personal tastes, pleasures and values. While Venus is about the urge for a loving relationship, it also signifies the experience of self-love and self-worth.

Venus embodies the power to attract. In Greek myth the goddess had a magic girdle which when worn attracted the lover of her choice. In a vignette in *The Iliad*, the goddess Hera borrows Venus's magic girdle in order to seduce her husband Zeus after he has lost interest in their relationship. Venus is this magnetic quality which renders her irresistible. While fashion, style, adornment and taste go through collective trends, Venus is personal. One's tastes, pleasures and passions are highly subjective, for what one finds beautiful and alluring, another may not. Venus is the core of our own individual ideals and esteem.

Not only lovers fall under the goddess's spell: artists, singers, fashion and entertainment personnel, curators of museums and managers of bars, those enjoying festivities, gaming and other pleasures are also entranced by Venus. In other words, the inhabitants of Venus's domain are drawn to beauty, creativity, art, sensuality and pleasure, but it is also in her domain where love, sexuality and relationship are located. However, this domain is often fraught with other features of love and relationship, such as vanity, passion, jealousy and triangles.

The nature of Venus in each horoscope will reveal personal tastes, but will also reflect our attitude towards love and relationships, whether sexually intimate, emotionally close or friendly companionship. It is how we warmly respond to the other and the soulful quality that attracts us to someone else. Venus is our mode of expressing affection and the way in which we in turn receive it. Ultimately, it is the qualities we hold dear in ourselves and how we resonate to these qualities in others. Venus is the *anima* who connects us to the heart of adult relationship as well as the muse who draws us to the beauty in the world, not only in others but especially in ourselves.

♂ Mars

A vital masculine energy, Mars is often connected with the warrior archetype, evident since the early Babylonians associated their god of war Nergal with the red planet. This theme enters relationship astrology with Mars being representative of conflict, rivalry, competition and confrontation in human interactions. As an archetype Mars is also brave and courageous; hence relational images of heroes fighting for those they love or struggling against all odds to woo and win the one they desire. Representing motivation, desire and excitement, physically and emotionally, Mars is the archetype that inflames our passions. It increases our body temperature and produces rashes or flushes when we are physically attracted to someone. Instinctually, when we are possessed by Mars we are in heat and out of control.

When the warrior spirit possesses an individual they can stride fearlessly into battle, but when Martian desire arises, they can be disarmed and captivated. Mars's fiery energy is tamed through love. Mars's archetypal range covers a wide spectrum of emotion, from primitive urges for survival to the erotic urge to connect with beauty and pleasure, making him the ideal mate for Venus.

In the natal chart Mars is not only a barometer for what we desire or yearn for, but also for how we pursue our goals and go after what we want. In relationships it represents our pursuit of those we love, how we express our yearnings, as well as how we control our desires and passions, including anger. Through our emotional responses, Mars helps us consider whether our desires are able to be channelled or are blocked or impeded. When Mars is blocked it can be introjected, that is turned back on itself through self-blame or self-injury. In relationship a blocked Mars may explode in rage or separate from the conflict, severing the connection. Therefore in relationship analysis Mars is not only important as an indicator of passion and desire, but also as a gauge for the healthy expression of conflict and disagreements.

Mars traditionally has been linked to soldiers and athletes; those using knives such as surgeons, butchers and doctors; tradespeople; police; and individuals who are bold and brash. The Martian population is identified as strongly masculine. Along with the Sun, Mars is the animus in relationships, but unlike the Sun it is more instinctual, primitive and sexual. Mars's horoscopic nature involves the expression of potency and power, and, in relationship, desires and passions.

The Social Planets – Jupiter and Saturn
Jupiter and Saturn are thematic of the social strata of our lives and participation in systems outside our own family and culture. Together, their cycle is twenty years, a 'score' marking out the course of our lives through social customs, rituals and passages of the life cycle. In terms of relationship they are concerned with beliefs and traditions about marriage, divorce, sexuality, etc. Jupiter suggests the moral principles and ethics that we believe in, while Saturn represents the established traditions and laws that enforce these beliefs. Although seemingly opposite in their viewpoint they are a natural pair and together over the course of two decades they attempt to align the laws with what is deemed to be 'right'.

When Jupiter or Saturn enters one of the houses associated with intimacy, such as the 7th or 8th house, or when they aspect an inner planet, especially Venus or Mars, these archetypes are present in adult relationships. For instance, when a major aspect occurs between Jupiter and Venus or Mars, we are drawn to consider the philosophy and moral attitude underpinning the spectre of relationship and how that might liberate or inhibit relating. When Saturn is in aspect to Venus or Mars, we might reflect on the rules and regulations that either contain or obstruct relating.

Therefore we can regard Jupiter and Saturn as being both collective and personal ways of thinking about relationships. When Jupiter or Saturn is in a sign of relationship, such as Libra or Scorpio, we are alerted to the social climate in terms of relational patterns; however, we are also aware that individuals with planets in these relational signs will be undergoing a revision and analysis of their own relating patterns. It is also of interest to note that Saturn is exalted in the relationship sign of Libra. Are relationships a test, a trial or a reward?

♃ Jupiter

Jupiter influences personal relationships when occupying a house connected to relating or by aspect to an inner planet, especially Venus or Mars. When this occurs the archetype impacts relationships in many ways. Cross-cultural relationships are indicative of Jupiter; therefore the partner's beliefs and philosophies are leitmotifs. Jupiter's influence attracts foreign relationships or those beyond our social and familial background. The borders that Jupiter crosses are social, racial, cultural, economic, educational and religious; therefore a Jupiterian relationship is one that is intermixed, whether that is the intermingling of faith, social status or nationality. The motive underlying this highlights the attraction to what is foreign and the urge to learn and grow beyond the confines of the everyday and traditional. However, cross-cultural relationships can also criss-cross boundaries inappropriately, such as the line between a teacher and student, or be fraught with moral and ethical dilemmas.

What the archetype seeks through relating is freedom and adventure. In a natal chart a strongly placed Jupiter may describe a traveller, explorer or freedom fighter, aspects of a personality which will need to be supported in relationship. There is also an inclination to be open and optimistic towards intimacy; however, while the individual's positivity is an attractive asset, it is often balanced by a difficulty in accepting the challenging and negative times in relationship. Jupiter seeks personal growth through its interactions because the need for education and self-awareness is strong. Generosity in relating is admirable, but this can also be used as a defence mechanism against intimacy by always giving or being in control, so the person does not need to feel in debt or vulnerable to the other.

Jupiter's process includes the search for the divine and when transferred onto relationship this could become the search for the ideal other. Certainly this brings the issues of idealism, expectation, spiritual values and philosophical beliefs to the forefront of a relationship. It also suggests that when this archetype's presence is strong in relationship, the erotic and creative attributes of the relationship may be more focused on shared philosophical and spiritual ways of being.

♄ Saturn

Saturn is often representative of control, authority, obstacles and difficulties, but in relationship these can also be what keeps the couple bound together or what has been likened to the 'glue in the relationship'.[5] Saturn is commitment and maturity, as well as the intention to work and be responsible, all important attitudes in relationship. It also rules the process of ageing and longevity and together these qualities act as an adhesive for couples to work through difficulties and obstacles towards an enduring relationship. On a positive note the archetype embraces loyalty, steadfastness and tradition, having the potential to be reliable in relationship. However, Saturn can also be experienced as paternal and patronizing, even negative and controlling. In these cases relationships may endure through fear, domination and manipulation. In the natal chart Saturn represents self-control and personal responsibility. When an individual feels powerless or out of control, they may seek to manage and have power over others, bringing an authoritative and oppressive atmosphere to the relationship.

On the other hand Saturn helps to build authority and boundaries, and can be where we feel supported to be more responsible, serious and accomplished. Therefore in terms of relating, Saturn matures and develops through relationship. Saturn brings its fears to relating, often focused on not measuring up or not being good enough, which intensifies the dread of rejection and abandonment. Adulthood interactions often echo childhood neglect or lack of love and affection, which can undermine a relationship when not adequately addressed. Therefore Saturn confronts and reworks the issues of self-worth, autonomy and personal values in adult relationships. One way to sidestep being dependent or reawakening the pain of relationship is to be self-reliant, too busy or unavailable, all of which are Saturn's defences.

Saturn is strongly affiliated with work and achievement, and in the sphere of relationship this can translate to issues around status, ambition, money or time spent at work rather than shared time in relationship. Saturn rules Capricorn and is exalted in Libra so it excels in these areas, just not at the same time. Saturn addresses the juxtaposition of hierarchy and equality, so it is important to distinguish this boundary in relationship by agreeing on who has responsibility for what, as well as identifying the roles and expectations of each partner. The pattern of work versus relationship is thematic of this archetype, and when Saturn is in high focus in relationship astrology it is important that these themes be addressed.

Saturn is not identified as being demonstrative of love and affection, at least not publicly. This is a private matter. Rules and regulations about the display of love and affection are shaped in the family environs and met again in adult relationship where we have the opportunity to find our authentic way of showing tenderness. Standards of perfection and ways of being are challenged in adult relationships; therefore, with time, the rules, standards and routines in relationship mature in the individual and their relationships.

The Healing Potential of Relationship – Chiron

Chiron, while not classified as a planet, has taken an important position in the astrological pantheon since it was discovered on 1 November 1977. Since then it has had many reclassifications as a minor planet, asteroid and comet, and eventually found its place when it was once again grouped with other astrological wanderers known as the Centaurs. Considered transitory to our solar system, the Centaurs are small planets generally located between Jupiter and Neptune. As boundary crossers, they traverse the orbits of the giant planets. Like their mythological counterparts they were seen as outsiders, renegades and disorderly.

However, Chiron was one of the exceptions to the band of rowdy Centaurs fathered by Centaurus, the grandson of Ares. His lineage as the son of Philyra and Cronus meant he was half-brother to the three Olympian gods, Zeus, Poseidon and Hades, who by the modern era in astrology had all been named as planets. Chiron's demeanour was antithetical to the other Centaurs as he was wise, just and kind, but like the other Centaurs he was socially marginal and not part of the mainstream. Being half-human and half-horse, his divinity is compromised by his physical nature personifying the pain of incarnation, the suffering of the human condition and the angst of being marginal. His body must die before his divinity can be released, unlike immortals whose shape is eternal. Therefore in human relationships Chiron recognizes the inevitability of human suffering and pain as well as the shared experience of being human. Within each relationship the divine stirs and is experienced through the power of love, the pleasure of sexual passion and the sacredness of intimacy. Yet, for humans, pain and suffering is inevitable and Chiron addresses this profound mixture in each relationship. When prominent in an astrological relationship analysis it invites participation with the human yet soulful feelings of pain and suffering, so often rejected and feared by the human part of ourselves.

⚷ Chiron

Known popularly as the archetype of the wounded healer, Chiron is the paradoxical encounter with wounding and healing. The wound is the source of healing as it contains its own healing balm. In a psychological way of thinking, acknowledgement and acceptance of the wound quickens the healing process. In relationship astrology, Chiron suggests that wounds are reopened through the process of relating and intimacy.

Chiron is not a planetary archetype associated directly with relationship. His influence is felt when placed in an important house associated with relating or when Chiron is in aspect to an inner planet, especially Venus or Mars. When this occurs the astrologer will be alert to relationship themes which may manifest in many ways. We can begin to reflect on some themes in the context of Chiron's orbit. It spends its least time in the relational signs of Libra and Scorpio, remaining only 1–2 years in Libra and 1½–3 years in Scorpio; therefore these will represent more personal or cultural shifts in understanding relationships rather than the sweeping changes shown with the outer planets.

As discussed, a common Chironic theme is being marginal, outside the system or feeling disenfranchised. In relationship astrology this might suggest being involved in a non-traditional relationship, one that is outside the norm or atypical of the familial or cultural system of the individual. Perhaps the beloved is wounded or suffers in a way that is unfamiliar to others. Since Chiron represents this curious amalgam of wounding and healing, it may be through relationship or the partner that the wound is restored to health as a result of acceptance and understanding.

The Chironic wound of lacking worth, value or acceptance may be reawakened in relationship through feeling undervalued and marginalized by others. Ironically, partners can be agents of wounding but they may also be the angels of healing, as it is through their behaviour that difficult wounds are resurrected for conscious recognition and release. We may also be an agent of accidental wounding and through this awareness a more trusting and conscious relationship can be developed. In recognizing, honouring and accepting the scars in others as well as in ourselves we are able to become more intimate, creating a deeper soul connection. Chiron guides us to be gentle and patient with the vulnerabilities and limitations of one other, which changes our perceptions of these qualities, now able to be recognized as strengths and soulful virtues.

Chiron's philosophy teaches that our own pain is what makes us adept at healing others. In the wisdom of our own wounds we learn to recognize the pain and plight of others and develop compassion and understanding for what they suffer. Ironically, while we may not be able to fully accept and honour our own wounds, we can do that for others. This private paradox comes alive in relationship where we can do for our loved ones what we often are unable to do for ourselves.

Generational Differences and Trends in Relationship – Uranus, Neptune and Pluto

Having been discovered in the modern era, the next group of planets was not part of the ancient history of astrology. Symbolically their nature is not restrained by human concepts, laws, limits or morality. The outer planets reach beyond the human experience; hence they have often been referred to as transpersonal, collective, numinous, divine and supernatural. They are not instinctual to human perception; they have often been likened to a spiritual or supra-personal dimension, akin to Carl Jung's notion of the collective unconscious. By nature they bring something into the human experience that has not been conceptualized, planned, experienced, imagined or deeply felt before; perhaps this is why these planets suggest awakening, liberation, imagination, initiation and, always, change.

What takes place when the planets of change aspect the planets of exchange? When an outer planet has an effect on relationship, it suggests something unconventional, out of the ordinary or statistically on the outermost limits of the bell curve. The outer planets exert their influence on a private relationship when in aspect to an inner planet, especially Venus or Mars, or when placed in a house of relationship or intimacy. When the outer planets traverse through the 7th or 8th signs of Libra or Scorpio they influence the collective attitudes and ideas about adult relationship, intimacy and sexuality. Each of the outer planets traversed this segment of the zodiac from 1942–95, inevitably altering the human landscape of equal and adult relationship. These astrological epochs of enormous transformation in relationship are listed below in Universal Time (GMT):

Outer Planet	Average Time in Each Sign	Transit through Libra	Transit through Scorpio
Uranus	Uranus has a cycle of just over 84 years and transits each sign of the zodiac between 6½– 7½ years, spending 6½ years each in Libra and Scorpio.	28 Sep 1968 to 20 May 1969 24 Jun 1969 to 21 Nov 1974 1 May 1975 to 8 Sep 1975	21 Nov 1974 to 1 May 1975 8 Sep 1975 to 17 Feb 1981 20 Mar 1981 to 16 Nov 1981
Neptune	Neptune has a cycle of 165 years. Since the orbit is spherical, it will average nearly 14 years in each sign (generally 13½ –14 years in each sign).	3 Oct 1942 to 17 Apr 1943 2 Aug 1943 to 24 Dec 1955 12 Mar 1956 to 19 Oct 1956 15 June 1957 to 6 Aug 1957	24 Dec 1955 to 12 Mar 1956 19 Oct 1956 to 15 Jun 1957 6 Aug 1957 to 4 Jan 1970 3 May 1970 to 6 Nov 1970

| **Pluto** | Similar to Chiron, Pluto's orbit is elliptical. Its cycle of 248 years is not evenly spread throughout the zodiac, spending 12–13 years in Libra and 11–12 years in Scorpio, as compared to 29–30 years in Aries and 31–32 years in Taurus. | 5 Oct 1971 to 17 Apr 1972 30 Jul 1972 to 5 Nov 1983 18 May 1984 to 28 Aug 1984 *Transiting Pluto conjunct Neptune for the Neptune in Libra generation occurred during their late twenties* | 5 Nov 1983 to 18 May 1984 28 Aug 1984 to 17 Jan 1995 21 Apr 1995 to 10 Nov 1995 *Transiting Pluto conjunct Neptune for the Neptune in Scorpio generation occurred during their mid to later twenties* |

Because of the slow movement of the outer planets through the signs, individuals born within a few years of one another will have the outer planets in proximity.

♅ Uranus

This planet is the archetype of the unexpected so it is wise to suggest that we don't know what Uranus will bring into the relationship other than change, upheaval and a radical departure from what has been known before. Uranus is a circuit-breaker, altering the current between being connected and disconnected. An image I often use for a Uranus transit is: if the plug is in the socket, you pull it out; if it is unplugged, you reconnect it. Therefore it brings excitement, but also a high level of anxiety into relationships as it agitates what is known and certain. By nature it is anticipatory, which is both exhilarating and frightening, and can manifest as restlessness and worry.

One of the main themes of Uranus in relationship astrology is the fluctuation between autonomy and familiarity, often referred to as the freedom–closeness or approach–avoidant dilemma. This is especially apparent when Uranus is in aspect to the Moon or Venus, because then the planets of attachment are aligned with the archetype of detachment. This centres on the Uranian need for space and distance, and in relationship this might mean keeping the partner at arm's length to obtain the breathing space needed. In turn this ignites the fear of abandonment and being left behind which is often affiliated with the archetype. On the surface it may appear as if there are commitment issues; in truth, it may be an underlying need for liberty and autonomy. When freedom is available within the context of relationship the individual is more prone to be available or present.

Therefore the theme of individuality versus togetherness is highlighted. Space within the relationship, a room of one's own and being together while apart are common sentiments of a Uranian relationship. This can often lead to an 'open' relationship where there is a mutual understanding of being in a relationship without borders, or relationships that are open-ended rather than closed. Often friendship and companionship are more important than intimacy, echoing the classic break-up line of 'let's be friends'. Therefore when Uranus is in aspect to planets of intimacy, or in a house of relating in the horoscope, there is a strong indication that this pattern may emerge.

Because of Uranus's nature there is often a sudden engagement or break-up in relationship. While it looks as if the engagement comes from out of the blue or the divorce is unexpected, signs and symptoms have existed for some time. Uranus brings this pattern along with its far-reaching insight and intuition to relationship. When this archetype enters relationship a seat belt is necessary as it will be both exciting and undulating. A Uranian relationship is never dull.

♆ Neptune

In relationship astrology, Neptune is often thought of as either magic or tragic: the bliss of falling in love or the agony of unrequited love. Neptune symbolizes the diffusion and dissolution of boundaries; in relationship astrology the archetype promotes symbiosis and merger and its influence ranges from enchantment to deception, from confusion to inspiration. When unleashed between two lovers it is like a hallucinogen, altering their perception of themselves and the other. A veil descends and the couple find themselves captivated; that is, captive to the hypnotic power of the archetype. Neptune is akin to the divine madness often associated with falling in love. Plato emphasized that love brings us close to the divine; therefore it touches the eternal aspect of our soul.

Falling in love suggests the descent into the under or other world or the unconscious. And Neptune is one of the rulers of the subterranean worlds. When in houses, or is aspect to planets, associated with relating Neptune brings its archetypal flavour to bear on relationship. One of the common themes is its propensity to encourage sacrifice and surrender in relationship, often referred to as the saviour–victim pattern. This suggests the continual cycle of rescue; forgiving the partner when they promise never to do it again, rescuing them when they do, and forgiving them one more time. An endless cycle peaks with anticipation and hope, and crashes with disappointment and despair. Due to its boundlessness, Neptune encourages enmeshment where two partners can become so entangled in the lives of each other that they no longer know what they personally want or desire. Therefore the ability to be independent, separate or to leave is impaired.

The Neptunian ideal of surrender in relationship is akin to addiction; hence Neptune often equates with codependent relationships or ones which are anchored in addiction. One of the partners may literally have an addiction which stimulates the urge in the other partner to help, binding them to the addictive pattern. Neptune may also glamorize the pain of relating, equating being hurt with being loved. The other side of the archetype is the urge to share in spirituality and creativity, and often when Neptune is prominent in the relationship there is a highly spiritual or creative partnership.

Idealization of the other is also part of the Neptunian profile in relationships. However, idealization is often a defence that blocks out the pain of the missing, lost or unavailable partner, who may be unattainable or a fantasy. Neptune often brings unreal expectations into relationships and may be more in love with the ideal of love than with the reality of what might be.

♇ Pluto

Whatever sphere Pluto influences, it brings with it the process of confronting the truth, facing denials and digging up the past. This process is not to invoke shame or negativity, but to let go of what no longer promotes life. When this archetype enters the sphere of relationship it invites honesty and intimacy, but it also evokes an inevitable encounter with the depth of self through the mirror of the other.

Pluto's mythic narrative as the underworld god involves relationship. Unlike his brothers, he wants only one mate and with his brother Zeus's blessing he abducts Persephone into his underworld residence. Virginal, innocent and strongly bonded with her mother, Persephone is simply gathering flowers in the field when Pluto erupts out of the underworld to snatch the girl away from her familial surroundings. But through a process of transformation Persephone becomes the queen of the underworld and an equal partner to the lord of the dead. As an allegory of Plutonic relationships, this myth confirms the themes of obsession, power, transformation and initiation as well as equality and intimacy.

When Pluto is involved there is often a powerful encounter with others where themes of trust and betrayal dominate the relational landscape. Pluto awakens intense feelings of life and death, love and loss, as well as trust and betrayal. When an individual emerges from the deathlike encounter with betrayal, they are brought back to life, transformed in the awareness of themselves. Trust in Plutonic terms is the trust in oneself, not the other; trusting the self enough to know that it can survive any loss. For with Pluto, love and loss are intimately entwined.

Power and love are also entwined; either Pluto is the power of love or the love of power. When the relationship is focused on the power of love, Pluto suggests a deep level of intimacy and sharing. When the relationship is focused on the latter, then power issues, manipulation, jealousy, possession and control issues enter the relationship. In a Plutonic relationship power is often wielded either through money or sex, as it is these concerns that reveal the lack of intimacy and shared power. In this type of relationship, secrets become an issue because they keep the partners separate, whereas in an intimate relationship each partner is aware of the delicate balance between privacy and holding back something of themselves from the other.

Plutonic intimacy is an experience of being stripped bare. This can either be liberating or shameful, as there is no in-between or shades of grey with Pluto. When liberating, the individual feels met, understood and empowered. But when ashamed, the individual may begin to use sex as a weapon or defence to mask these unpleasant feelings. Either way, a Plutonic relationship has the potential to transform each individual. Pluto is 'therapy love': in this therapeutic relationship, the partner in your life may be your 'live-in' therapist.

CHAPTER 2

GODS OF LOVE, SEXUALITY AND RELATIONSHIP
Eros, Venus and Mars

Every culture has its legends of relationship, and in Greek and Roman traditions myths of love, sexuality and relationship flourish. In Greek myth, Zeus was known for his numerous liaisons, but it was Aphrodite who was renowned as the great goddess of love and beauty. She was embraced by the Romans as Venus, the eponymous planet in each horoscope that speaks of love and relationship. Venus entered the astrological pantheon with a rich mythological history informing her archetypal nature. In Greek myth, her constant companion is Ares, later integrated into the pre-existing Roman god Mars. The relationship between these iconic gods of love and desire is eternalized throughout astrological tradition.

Legends of Love

Throughout Greek myth Aphrodite and Ares are consistently paired together as companions, either deeply attached passionate lovers or siblings. In *The Odyssey* they are caught in a golden web woven by Aphrodite's husband Hephaestus, who crafted the fine filament in order to entrap his wife in bed with Ares. Aphrodite and Ares's relationship is erotic, passionate and timeless. In Homer's earlier epic, *The Iliad*, their relationship is depicted as less compelling, yet just as close. Aphrodite refers to him as 'dear brother'. When we imagine these gods, we think of them as eternal lovers, gods of beauty and battle, peace and war, enmeshed in a golden web of love and desire. Aphrodite is also mother to Ares's children: Harmonia, Phobos and Deimos, or Harmony, Fear and Terror. Another child is Eros, a personification of the magnetic power of love.

As soulmates their partnership has two layers. One is erotic, emotional and intimate while the other is friendship and companionship. In psychological terms they are archetypal representations of pleasure, desire and passion. In astrological terms they identify what qualities are attractive and appealing in others, what we value, what we want and crave. Physiologically, they embody our scent and libido; they are the instinctual, yet active, forces that draw us towards companionship and the other.

In Roman mythology Venus and Mars are the deities who preside over the Empire, parents of the two founders of Rome, Aeneas and Romulus. Aeneas, the son of Venus, fled the destruction of Troy and fathered a new line of kings who would eventually rule Rome. Romulus, the son of Mars, re-established Rome on the banks of the Tiber. Venus and Mars are archetypal foundation stones for the golden city of Rome which, like its benefactors, is known as being eternal and romantic.

But before we meet Venus and Mars and their Greek predecessors Aphrodite and Ares, let's return to a time before these gods emerged, a more primitive time before civilization flourished. Here we encounter Eros, one of the five primal deities of creation and the first personification in western mythology of intercourse and interconnection. In subsequent mythic accounts Eros becomes the son of Aphrodite and Ares, and by the later Roman period Eros is involved in a triangle with his mother Venus and his lover Psyche.

Eros's rich mythological tapestry begins to be woven at the dawn of creation. He is born prior to the differentiation of the other deities and it is his erotic qualities that warm and stimulate them, inspiring the gods to mingle together. Eros is a primal force, the desire for life, sexual attraction and union. Beneath the racing pulse of the heart, swept up in a passionate embrace, feeling a soulful connection, being abandoned or under love's dark shadows, Eros is there. As the driving force behind the initial procreation of the gods, his first impulse is to intermingle, come together and attach.

Later myths feature his attachment to his mother. In fact, mythic writers told a tale of Aphrodite and Eros being literally attached to one another. Typhon was a fearsome beast who confronted Aphrodite and Eros while they were relaxing on the banks of the Euphrates river. To escape the monster's fury, they disguised themselves as fish throwing themselves into the river. So that they would not be separated, they tied themselves with a bond that linked them eternally together. The gods praised Aphrodite and Eros by shaping the constellation Pisces in the image of the two fish whose form they had taken. In traditional astrology, Venus is exalted in Pisces, the sign of the fish.

Throughout western mythic tradition Eros has had many incarnations and transformations, from the primal god to the son of Aphrodite to Psyche's husband. The Romans knew his two faces of love and desire as Amor and Cupid. He is described as primitive, pornographic, passionate, instinctual and spiritual. But what is important to remember is that Eros existed before the other gods. Eros animates the gods by bringing them into relationship with one another.

> It is Eros who makes the gods – the archetypes – loving, creative, and involved. Only through Eros can the gods or archetypes be loving. As far as we mortals are concerned, gods are neutral, inhuman, distanced and cold. Only when they are combined with Eros do we sense their movement, do they become creative, intimate and stimulating.[6]

As the animator and stimulator of the gods it becomes apparent why Eros eventually becomes the husband of Psyche, as it is he, the personification of love, attachment and affection, who arouses Psyche, the embodiment of Soul.

Eros

There are varying accounts of the birth of the gods but the most complete narrative is given by Hesiod in *Theogony*, his epic of the late eighth century BCE. Chaos is the gap or yawning void through which creation emerges. Out of Chaos five deities materialize: Gaia, Tartarus, Eros, Erebos and Nyx. But it is Eros who arouses the others to mingle together and procreate. Eros is Love, a force that overpowers intelligence. When Eros is present life is full of extraordinary intensity, yet for little or no reason. Hesiod in the *Theogony* describes the deity as 'the most handsome among the immortal gods, dissolver of flesh, who overcomes the reason and purpose in the breast of all gods and all men.'[7] Eros's influence is heavenly and worldly, spiritual and bodily.

Eros symbolizes each human being's deeply embedded instinct towards union, propagation and creation. Being primal, its nature exists without reflection, thought or control. It is impulsive, seizes control and weakens the sensibilities. Two thousand and seven hundred years later Andrew Lloyd Webber, like Hesiod, expressed a similar theme in his song 'Love Changes Everything': 'Love bursts in and suddenly all our wisdom disappears.'[8] When Eros is unleashed, so is chaos. And as in the original mythic scene, wherever there is chaos, Eros emerges.

Eros is mentioned once again in Hesiod's *Theogony* as being an attendant at the birth of Aphrodite. Both seminal references to the god unite him with the process of sexual union and love. His nature of bringing opposites together to be creative and procreative is established very early in Greek myth, but over time his nature becomes more civilized and socialized. As the Olympian gods become established, Eros becomes boyish. Primitive instincts like unruliness and passion are being tamed and controlled by the Olympian gods. Eros's instinctual realm begins to be aligned with Aphrodite, an Olympian.

During the Archaic period the poet Simonides (556–468 BCE) portrays Eros as the son of Aphrodite and Ares, bringing his temperament to the province of the gods of love and desire. This is not the only reference to his rebirth and new parentage,[9] but from this point on Eros is aligned with Aphrodite in epic and poetry as her matchmaking son and partner. Together Eros, the primal power of love, and Aphrodite, the goddess of love and beauty, conspire to bring lovers together through the unleashing of powerful feelings of erotic desire.[10] Eros has various forms and Erotes refers to the multiplicity and plurality of love. As this erotic power became differentiated, the separate forms of Erotes were known as Anteros (love returned), Pothos (yearning) and Himeros (desire). Psychologically, the spell-binding experience of Eros was becoming known through his various appearances.

Eros and Aphrodite were always linked throughout antiquity. Later, in the second century CE, the novel *The Golden Ass* by the Latin author Apuleius contained the fable Amor and Psyche within the larger narrative; Amor was the Latin Eros, closely associated with Love. This story has been retold many times in many ways and never fails to stir the imagination. Because of its powerful imagery the fable is seen as a feminine initiatory story from Psyche's point of view. But what does the story tell us of Eros?

Psyche was the mortal counterpoint to Aphrodite, revered and adored for her physical beauty, so much so that she was often regarded as the second Venus. Jealous of Psyche's beauty and the attention devoted to her, Venus demanded that her son Eros make Psyche fall in love with the vilest of men. Eros agreed to his mother's demands, but when he glimpsed Psyche's beauty for the first time it was as if Eros's heart had been pierced by one of his own arrows. He fell in love with her. Without his mother's knowledge, Eros had Psyche taken to his golden palace. Instead of being wed to the vilest of men, Psyche becomes partnered with the love god.

Eros's attachment to his mother complicates the situation as he cannot tell Venus that he has fallen in love, nor can he reveal himself completely to Psyche. Therefore Eros is compromised; he enters into a clandestine relationship with Psyche, who promises to be with him in the dark and to never look upon his face, never to know who he really is. Spurred on by her jealous sisters, however, Psyche breaks her promise to Eros.

But when Psyche sheds light on the situation she finds herself staring into the face of the god of Love. But it is too late; the betrayal has occurred. Eros has taken flight, as love cannot live without trust. Ironically it is this betrayal that awakens Psyche to the authenticity of love. Bereft, Psyche prays to Venus for the return of Eros. Still vengeful, Venus sets four tasks for the young girl, attempting to destroy her spirit. These seemingly impossible tasks develop Psyche's strength and awareness, which prepares her for a more conscious marriage. Eros is the awakening agent that initiates Psyche's individuation process. Psyche's labours are the soul tasks that open up the mystery of union by consciously reclaiming her own Eros. Venus is the archetype that encourages the conscious union of Eros and Psyche through trials, suffering and initiation. In Jungian terminology, Psyche's trials to redeem her inner Eros are akin to her reclaiming her animus, her masculine spirit.[11]

The story reveals the tasks and suffering experienced on the way towards a more conscious union of souls. Psyche is pregnant during her trials and underworld journey which conclude with her heavenly marriage to Eros. Their child is named Voluptas and to the Romans she was the goddess of sensual pleasures and delights, the source of the word 'voluptuous', suggesting generous and pleasurable sensations. To the Greeks the personification of the goddess of pleasure and enjoyment was Hedone, the root of the English word 'hedonism', which suggests that virtue and morality are also attached to the concept of Eros.

Eros, later depicted as Cupid, adorns pictures of Catholic saints in blissful union with God, illustrating the devotee's passion. Eros stirs the divine in the human. In his primal form he exists before the splitting of heaven and earth, or symbolically before the separation of spirit and body, culture and instinct. Psychologically speaking, Eros is a primal god underlying the layers of consciousness that split opposites, and in him we find a sense of union, albeit often one born out of anguish and pain.

With the advent of psychoanalysis Eros is examined in the light of sexuality. Between Plato and Freud, Eros was viewed from two extremes: Plato's Eros is spiritual energy that descends to Earth, while Freud's Eros is instinctual energy sublimated upwards. Either way, Eros is the soulful function that embodies love, sensuality, pleasure, affection and sexuality. But it is not exclusively sex, as Carl Jung reminded us: 'people think that Eros is sex, but not at all. Eros is relatedness'.[12] Confusing Eros with purely the sexual instinct denies Eros's initiatory aspect that leads us into our own individuality and creativity. Jung describes Eros in the following way, illuminating Eros's dual connection to spirit and body:

> Eros is a questionable fellow and will always remain so, whatever the legislation of the future may have to say about it. He belongs on one side to man's primordial animal nature which will endure as long as man has an animal body. On the other hand he is related to the highest forms of spirit. But he only thrives when spirit and instinct are in the right harmony.[13]

When in the grip of an erotic compulsion an individual may unconsciously annihilate their former sense of self along with their current relationship. But an individual also has the capacity to reflect on their instinctual nature. Plato referred to Eros as a great daimon, neither human nor Olympian, but rather an intermediary between these two realms. When in Eros's domain we are transported to the realms of the gods. As humans experiencing Eros we can contact the eternal and pleasurable realm of the gods. On the other hand, the gods can touch the human delight of attachment and connectedness. The Christian absorption of this god is like the cherub, Cupid, the angelic guardian of the blissful state of union with God. Teresa of Avila's torturous rapture in her experiences with her love for God is erotic. Francis of Assisi's love for God and Poverty[14] is a joyously painful account of erotic love. In the Christian Eros, spirit pervades but where are instinct and body? As Jung reminded us, both aspects of spirit and instinct need to be in harmony or the lopsidedness may become pathological.

In 1898, an asteroid was discovered and named Eros.[15] It is interesting to note that, at the time of its discovery, this asteroid was the only known body, besides the Moon, to come so close in orbit to the Earth. In 1932 another asteroid, Amor, the Roman Eros, was discovered and this asteroid's orbit also comes close to Earth. Whereas most asteroids orbit between Mars and Jupiter, the two named Amor and Eros leave the Olympian heights near Jupiter and orbit in close astronomical proximity to Earth. The astronomical synchronicity of Eros's travels between the Olympian spirit and the body of Earth reminds us of Eros's quest to balance spirit and body.

In 1930 the planet Pluto was discovered and Eros was proposed as a name for the planet. However, as it had already been catalogued as an asteroid, the name could not be used again. Interestingly, the astrological Pluto personifies facets of Eros when aspecting the inner planets, especially Venus and Mars. The 8th house, the environment associated with Pluto, is also symbolic of many of the initiatory rites of Psyche and Eros.

These astronomical discoveries were synchronistic with the development of psychoanalysis and the acknowledgement of the erotic archetype. Freud brought sexuality into focus and articulated the various stages of sexual development. He named Eros as one of two basic instincts; Thanatos, or the death instinct, is the other.[16] Freud revived Eros by addressing sexuality, biological development, sexual perversion and bodily issues. Freud's Eros theory discusses infantile sexuality and needs, differentiating these by age, gender and personal development. His discussion centred on primal instincts, self-discovery, pleasure, desire and repression, returning the focus to the child, the Eros in us all. Freud had Mars and Venus in mutual reception: Mars was in Venus's sign of Libra and Venus was in Mars's sign of Aries. Both were in aspect to Pluto: Venus was conjunct and Mars was quincunx Pluto. Of interest was that the asteroid Amor was conjoining Pluto; therefore it repeated the aspects to Freud's Venus and Mars.

Eros is visible in the struggle on both sides of the gender line for equality, emancipation of sexuality, gay marriage debates, sexual deviance and abuses. Eros is the force that allows us to know ourselves through all types of human relationship. As the primal god of love, he is unlike any other god. Eros lives in all emotional attachments from sexual to platonic, familial to foreign. It is the force that brings archetypes together; therefore this power is active in every astrological aspect. We might think of Eros as the force behind the aspect which mingles the planetary archetypes together. When looking at adult relationships Eros is particularly vibrant when considering the aspects to Venus and Mars.

Eros is the transforming power of love. Marie-Louise von Franz says: 'Love with its passion and pain becomes the urge toward individuation, which is why there is no real process of individuation without love, for love tortures and purifies the soul.'[17] It is this process of Eros and love that accompanies the urge to wholeness through coming to know the 'other' in ourselves. But it is mainly through the astrological archetypes of Venus and Mars that Eros enters into our lives.

Venus is embodied in each horoscope as passion, affection, beauty and relationship. In the astrological pantheon Venus encompasses the erotic dimension and is informed by the primal and instinctual energy of Eros as well as her heavenly and spiritual side.

Venus
Venus, goddess of love, sexuality and beauty, has her origins in the Near East in the land between the Tigris and Euphrates rivers. In the Mesopotamian myths she was the great goddess of erotic love, fertility and war. From the Sumerian tradition she inherits aspects of Inanna, the queen of heaven; in the Akkadian tradition she was called Ishtar; while the Assyrians referred to her as Mylitta. To the Phoenicians she was known as Astarte. In all these traditions her beauty was linked to the bright planet.

The bright star personified the goddess. When she was close to the Earth she infused humans with sexual and passionate longing in their bodies and hearts. This bright and unifying disposition was imported into astrology, because Venus is classified as a benefic, a supportive and stabilizing planet. The evening star in the western sky became known as Venus Hesperus, while Venus Phosphorus was the bright, morning star visible in the east before the Sun rose. Like the planet Venus, the great queen of heaven Inanna descended into the underworld and rose again. Some believed the goddess came to earth and walked amongst the common people when she disappeared from the heavens. Venus was often envisioned as a dual goddess of heaven and earth. Her two dominions are Taurus, which represents her sensual and bodily aspects, and Libra, her spiritual and mystic ways.

It was the trade winds that most likely brought the goddess to Greece. To the Greeks she was Aphrodite, whose cult was continuous and universal in the ancient world. Aphrodite's earliest cult of worship in Greece was at Paphos in Cyprus. Her cult image and worship were probably brought to the island by the seafaring Phoenicians. Throughout *The Iliad* Homer refers to her as 'the lady of Kypros'. Hesiod describes the first land to gaze upon the goddess as the island of Kythera, at the foot of the Peloponnese. It was here that Aphrodite rose out of the foam and was transported to Cyprus. The Phoenicians also brought her to Corinth where shards of seventh century BCE pottery, with the goddess name of Astarte on them, have been discovered.[18]

Aphrodite may have been amalgamated with other indigenous local deities; however, throughout Greek myth she clearly retains her eastern heritage. While her cult may have been imported, she developed into a uniquely Greek goddess whose independence, passion and morality often conflicted with the emerging culture. To put Aphrodite's sexuality and freedom in the context of classical Greece, we can reflect on the life of an Athenian woman in the fifth century BCE. Women did not vote and were physically separated from the men. Women remained at the back of the house and rarely enjoyed the freedom of movement in the agora or outside the house unless accompanied by a man. Athenian etiquette suggested that 'a woman who travels outside the house must be of such an age that onlookers might ask, not whose wife she is, but whose mother'.[19] The exceptions were the prostitutes and the courtesans known as the *Hetairai*, Aphrodite's women who were intellectual, socially and erotically skilled and free to choose their own life. Aphrodite is neither maternal, domestic, nor housebound; she is free to be who she is.

Other Greek goddesses who were part of the Olympian pantheon had well defined roles influencing specific spheres of daily life.

Their spheres of influence were often defined in terms of a male or the masculine, whereas Aphrodite does not define herself in these terms, except perhaps as the lover of men. Hera was defined by her role as the wife of Zeus; Athena was the daughter of Zeus; and Artemis was the sister of Apollo. These characterizations are culturally situated in time, whereas archetypes are timeless and culturally unbiased.

Aphrodite is the goddess of sexual desire, love and beauty, independent, not defined by the customs and traditions of the times. As such she is outside convention. Like Eros she can burst into a conservative life and alter it forever. She can influence the other goddesses except the three virgin goddesses, Artemis, Athena and Hestia, who are not overwhelmed by Aphrodite's sexual passions.[20] Their erotic quality and passion is directed elsewhere. Artemis adores nature and animal welfare; Athena is passionate about the city and democracy; and Hestia is devoted to the inner and spiritual life. Aphrodite's ability to constellate desire for another is a force that the other gods cannot control, a passion that is often destructive and/or life-altering. Hence she was often marginalized or manipulated because of her magical seductive powers.

Aphrodite's genealogy is not consistent in Homer and Hesiod. According to Homer, Aphrodite is the daughter of Zeus and Dione. In Homeric tradition Zeus was the supreme Olympian and therefore every god was under his jurisdiction. However, Hesiod in the *Theogony* portrays a very different and primitive birth myth.[21] When Cronus had severed the sky god Ouranus's testicles with his sickle, he threw them into the sea. From this act the sea became impregnated and bore Aphrodite. The great goddess of sexual love was fathered by the severed genitals of the sky god and brought into creation out of the womb of the sea, ostensibly a goddess without parents. Aphrodite represents a force that is not easily parented, nor tamed.

It is curious that Venus is born from the dismemberment of her father. Ironically, love is often born from the disempowerment of oppressive and domineering forces. Love never seems to enter life without commotion. Venus's marriage to Hephaestus, the lame and unappealing god of the forge, is both intriguing and psychologically truthful. Hephaestus is the creative craftsman and wounded artisan, the reflection of beauty mastered through vocation and exertion.

It is evocative of a deeper beauty that underpins appearance and personality, the theme often replayed in romantic relationships and fairy tales like Beauty and the Beast.

The goddess's ancient link to war was preserved in Aphrodite's involvement in the Trojan conflict, referred to as the Judgement of Paris. On Mount Pelion the great wedding feast of Peleus and Thetis, the parents-to-be of the great hero Achilles, took place. Mortals were invited to join all the gods and goddesses in the celebration, all except one: Eris, the goddess of strife. As we can imagine, Eris arrives in the midst of the celebrations in a furious rage. In her hand is a golden apple with 'to the fairest' engraved on it. She rolls the golden apple down the length of the banquet table until it finally rests in the midst of the three goddesses Aphrodite, Hera and Athena, each goddess claiming the title of the fairest as hers. Handsome Paris is given the heroic task of being the judge in the beauty contest that will take place amongst these three powerful goddesses.

Paris was one of the many children of the Trojan dynasty of King Priam and Queen Hecuba. On the day he was born he was exposed on Mount Ida behind Troy, as his mother had experienced a frightening vision that this child would be the ruin of Troy. Paris survived, maturing into a young man known for his skill of judgement. Hence Zeus chose him to resolve the argument which had broken out amongst the three goddesses.

To convince Paris to choose her, Hera offered him great wealth and power. Athena offered him heroic status and, finally, Aphrodite offered him the most beautiful woman alive, Helen. Paris chose relationship over wealth, power or fame. However, as with the fate of many Venusian choices, there were dire consequences. Helen was already married, yet with Aphrodite's help Paris was able to seduce his bride-to-be away from her husband, her family and her homeland. Beautiful Helen is the prize Aphrodite awards to Paris for choosing her over Athena and Hera. However, Aphrodite's scheming ignites a major conflict that erupts into the Trojan War and the ultimate destruction of Troy. Besides underlining the inevitable theme of conflict, the narrative highlights other Venusian themes, such as the necessity of choice, the declaration of values and her involvement in love triangles.

She was known as Venus to the Romans who claimed her as their patroness, being the mother of their ancient founder, Aeneas.

Vestiges of the eastern goddesses and Aphrodite's archaic traditions were integrated with the Roman goddess who inspires the planetary archetype that characterizes the erotic themes of love and sexuality. Venus is erotically attached to beauty and pleasure and is given dominion over the signs of Libra and Taurus.

Mars

To the Greeks he was Ares. His name is derived from the root 'to destroy' or 'to be carried away', and the deity has always been associated with war or in psychological terms the aggressive and sexual masculine instincts. The Babylonians called him Nergal, an 'angry fire god' who was a god of the netherworld as well as their war god. Mars's penchant for conflict became an enduring aspect of astrological tradition, being categorized as a malefic planet or one tending to be destructive and separate.

The Romans embraced him as Mars, amalgamating the Greek god of war with an indigenous agricultural god; hence he was associated with spring or the rising of the sap, fertility and new growth. Our month March (march or marching, beating the drum, etc.) is named after the Roman god Mars, as is the constellation of Aries, also associated with the Northern Vernal Equinox. Sacrifices were made to Mars to help avoid natural calamities, such as inclement weather or the destruction of grain, and to promote a bountiful harvest and encourage prosperity amongst their herds.

The Romans saw Mars as protective, bestowing a much more elevated position upon him than he had in ancient Greek myths. As the father of Romulus, the founder of Rome, he was revered as both their founder and champion. He was a patron of the Roman army whose conquests spread throughout most of the known world. Augustus proclaimed him as Mars *Ultor,* 'the avenger', for avenging the assassination of Julius Caesar through his victory at Philippi in 42 BCE as well as avenging the disaster suffered by the Romans at the hands of the Parthians. Along with Venus the mythic couple served in the transformation of the Roman Empire. To the Romans, Mars was the defender of their empire; psychologically, Mars is the defender of our ego and individuality.

However, in Greek myth Ares was not always portrayed as a victorious war god, but often as a coward and oaf, especially in Homer's *The Iliad.* Ares is referred to in the epic as violent, man-slaughtering, bloodstained, huge and bellowing. Ares was the battle god, the god of dreadful war and the overseer of the storms in human affairs. He is one of the most unpopular gods in Greek myth, reflected in Homer's view of him in *The Iliad.* Wounded and ridiculed by Athena, rejected by his mother Hera, he was also scorned by his father Zeus. He is a rejected son of the sky father, as these lines from the epic suggest:

> To me you are the most hateful of all gods who hold Olympus.
> Forever quarrelling is dear to your heart, wars and battles.[22]

The Greeks favour Athena as the patroness of war, a goddess who is more logical and rational. Athena's strategy and logic triumph over Ares's irrationalism and lust for battle; rationalism overpowers chaos. To the Greeks, violence was not sanctioned. While the war against the Trojans was idealized by the Greeks, it was not their war god who was heroic. In fact, Ares took the side of the Trojans at Aphrodite's request, setting him against his mother Hera who supported the Greeks.

Other mythic vignettes also suggest that he is often bound and injured. The Aloidae, the giant sons of Poseidon, declared war on the gods by trying to attack Mount Olympus. However, before they did they captured Ares and interred him in a bronze vessel where he remained for nearly thirteen months until Hermes intervened and released him. Heracles was also responsible for injuring Ares more than once. Early Greek writers seemed to prefer Heracles as a heroic image to Ares. The war god was also unsuccessful at attempting to bring his brother Hephaestus back to Olympus. His brute strength could not persuade Hephaestus to relinquish his place; it took Dionysus to loosen Hephaestus's attachment to his internal hideaway.

The discrepancy between the depictions of Mars in Greek and Roman culture illustrates differing cultural approaches to the archetype. Mars's instincts, such as aggression and sexuality, as well as human responses such as anger, fighting and fleeing, and the way we assert our desire and will are strongly influenced by the atmosphere of our families of origin as well as our cultural traditions and beliefs.

Ares is the son of Zeus and Hera. Both parents reject him, as they do his brother Hephaestus, yet both abandoned brothers are aligned with Aphrodite. Ares and Aphrodite's passion often exploded in jealous rages. Ares was responsible for killing Aphrodite's lover, Adonis, by enraging a wild boar so it would attack and kill him. However, Aphrodite was also enraged when Ares and Eos, goddess of the dawn, became lovers. Perhaps we might see these two brothers as being representative of different aspects of relationship: Aphrodite and Ares are passionate while Hephaestus and Aphrodite represent the value of companionship.

Ares is marginal to the civilized culture of classical Greece. His origins are in Thrace, a northern part of Greece considered to be wild and uncivilized. Its climate was severe and fierce and its people warlike. Due to the harshness of the climate it was also believed to be the home of Boreas, the North Wind. Thrace was also the home of the Amazons, the race of warrior women that Ares was credited with fathering. His daughters, the Amazons, also fought on the side of the Trojans during the war with the Greeks. *The Iliad* refers to Eris as Ares's marching companion and his sister. Like her brother, Eris was a bringer of conflict and discord. Priapus was sometimes mentioned as being a tutor to Ares, linking the ithyphallic fertility god with the war god and thereby connecting the masculine instincts of aggression and sexuality with fertility, as the Romans did with Mars. Hera directed Priapus to tutor Ares in the art of dance before the art of warfare. From Priapus, Ares learned to dance first and wage war later.[23]

The *Homeric Hymn to Ares* was a relatively late composition. It is uncertain whether this really belongs to the Homeric hymns or is a later composition, especially since Ares is portrayed positively. To these Greeks the planet Mars was known as the Star of Ares and in the hymn the war god is described as whirling his 'fire-bright orb amongst the portents of heaven that wander along the seven paths'.[24] This red, fire-bright orb is the planet Mars. But the hymn also depicts some of Ares's positive attributes that underpin the Martian archetype, such as being a champion of the righteous, a saviour of cities, superior in force and a tyrant against the rebellious.

Unlike the other Olympians, Ares had few cults or sanctuaries of worship. While the battlefield may have represented his sanctuary, these battlefields were often on cultivated land. Hence in Roman myth Ares became aligned with the indigenous agriculture god. As the war god he enters the astrological pantheon as the will to survive, to fight for the self, defend the ego and be potent. Even though he may have been depicted as clumsy and crude, he was unshakeable in battle and unbeatable in sport. He is erotically attached to the preservation of the self physically, psychologically and emotionally, hence his rulership of the astrological domains of Aries and Scorpio. In relationship astrology Mars brings his passion, flair and fight into the ring of relationships.

Feminine and Masculine, Yin and Yang, Anima and Animus
Although poles apart, in many ways Venus and Mars have always been paired together. Whether sister and brother, passionate lovers, wife and husband, mother and father, they personify pairing and partnering. Being feminine and masculine, passive and assertive, cold and hot, wet and dry, they are complements of one another. Astrologically, they rule the opposite signs of Libra and Aries, Taurus and Scorpio, and their glyphs are modern symbols for the biological polarity of female and male. Opposites attract; yet the truth underpinning this cliché may well be that the attraction is to becoming whole. The other completes the unlived, unconscious parts of ourselves in a way no one else or nothing else has, explaining why relationship is a major part of the individuation process, fuelled by the powerful forces of Eros and love.

Astrology addresses polarity in a variety of ways. From an astrological point of view, polarities are natural opposites that are complementary by nature and when combined together create a whole system. Astrological oppositions occur in the natural zodiac. Fire is always opposite Air, and Earth is always opposite Water. These oppositions are relatively compatible. We might think of each set of oppositions as a polarity. While visibly opposite one another, the signs in an astrological opposition are partners in a similar polarity. Astrological oppositions invite compromise and awareness of difference; however, when the astrological opposition is stretched to one extreme, the polarization may become so unbalanced that one energy eclipses the other.

Similarly, when two partners come together they create a new system through their relationship. In relationship analysis, it is important to keep polarities and oppositions in mind. For instance the twelve signs are six astrological pairs that form their own system. Venus and Mars rule two of these polarities which influence the interplay between me and the other and my physical resources and the other's.

The twelve signs are naturally categorized as masculine and feminine. The masculine signs are Fire and Air while the feminine signs are Earth and Water. These polarities are also referred to as yin (feminine) and yang (masculine), anima (feminine) and animus (masculine) or soul (feminine) and spirit (masculine). As the following table shows, astrological oppositions occur between masculine or feminine signs. Their ruling planets form natural pairs: Venus and Mars; Mercury and Jupiter; and the luminaries and Saturn.

Opposite Signs	Keywords for Polarity	Planetary Rulers
Aries–Libra	Me–You Self–Other	Mars–Venus
Taurus–Scorpio	Mine–Yours Forming–Transforming	Venus–Mars
Gemini–Sagittarius	Word–Symbol Familiar–Foreign	Mercury–Jupiter
Cancer–Capricorn	Home–Work Unconditional–Conditional	Moon–Saturn
Leo–Aquarius	Personal–Impersonal Singular–Collective	Sun–Saturn
Virgo–Pisces	Order–Chaos Secular–Spiritual	Mercury–Jupiter

Using the concepts of masculine and feminine often gets us entangled with the gender assignments of male and female. Masculine and feminine refer to ways of being, qualities and characteristics. Unfortunately these concepts can become limited by social stereotypes. Although they can be fairly gender-specific they refer more to a mode of being than an actual being. For instance, Aries is a masculine sign and a woman with planets in Aries may carry some of its masculine traits, such as assertiveness and independence, but this does not translate to her being aggressive and competitive. Cancer is a feminine sign and a man with planets in Cancer may be sensitive and caring, but this does not make him effeminate or unmanly. Due to familial and cultural stereotyping these natural contra-sexual characteristics may not be easily developed, or even acknowledged. Masculine and feminine is not a statement about gender but the recognition of opposites within the self and how becoming more aware of them creates a more conscious experience of wholeness.

Anima and Animus
Anima is the Latin word for 'soul' while animus in Latin has several meanings gathered around the idea of mind, reason and thought. Anima and animus were defined as archetypes by Carl Jung. Through his own personal experiences, Jung imagined an inner feminine authority and influence which he proposed was an aspect of all men's inner life projected out onto the world. Through engagement with these projections and by applying consciousness to the situation, he felt a man could become more familiar with his own feminine qualities, his own inner partner.[25] When in the grip of the anima a man may be flooded by moods and feelings while blaming his partner for his reactions.

Similarly, Jung felt that women have a masculine counterpart which he named 'the animus'. Through the projection of the animus some of the woman's masculine qualities are able to be reflected back through the mirror of the partner. When gripped by the animus, a woman can become opinionated and controlling, blaming her partner for these qualities that she sees reflected in the mirror of relationship. It is important to remember that the anima and animus are symbols, not facts, and when used imaginatively their images can be very useful in considering relationship complexes. Their images are not limited to heterosexual relationships. In homosexual relationships the interplay of these archetypes is equally as strong.

Psychoanalytic thought suggested that the inner contra-sexual image for a man was first shaped by the mother, then by sisters and in adolescence by the sister's friends and other females. The anima is modelled on females and the first experience of mother makes a strong impact. If there is a sister she becomes an intermediary figure who facilitates the anima's partial withdrawal from mother out into the world of the sister's friends and other women. Anima is the feeling, intuitive and receptive guide that accompanies the male on his descent into his unknown. Astrologically speaking, the anima can be thought of in terms of the Moon and Venus personally, and of Neptune in a collective sense; therefore these planetary placements become extremely evocative in a man's horoscope of his tendency towards relating.

Similarly, the animus is influenced through the first male experience of the father, but the brother becomes an agent to facilitate its partial withdrawal from father onto the world of the brother's friends and other men. Animus is the thinking, judging and assertive guide that accompanies the female into the world. We can think of the animus astrologically as the Sun and Mars personally, and as Uranus collectively. These planetary strengths, signatures and aspects play a defining role in a woman's orientation to relating.

Venus	Mars
Eros as Connection	Eros as Separateness
Feminine	Masculine
Anima	Animus
Taurus–Libra	Aries–Scorpio
Cold	Hot
Moist	Dry
Beauty	Courage
Love	Desire
Peace	Conflict
Attract	Assert
Compromise	Endure
Compare	Act
Culture	Instinct
Mirror	Sword
Perfume	Sweat
Bedroom	Battlefield
Eros	

– CHAPTER 3 –
INTIMATE ARCHETYPES
Venus and Mars by Sign

Venusian themes in relationship focus on shared values, feeling loved and appreciated, money and pleasure, affection and sensuality; while Mars brings themes of sex and desire, independence and individuality, plus dealing with conflict and expressing the self openly. In this chapter, I delineate each planet separately by sign to offer possible facets, features, attitudes, styles and characteristics of each of the twelve configurations. Consider these as points of departure for your own contemplation about individual preferences in adult relationships.

But first, let's briefly consider Venus and Mars from the points of view of polarity, planetary sect and retrograde direction.

Polarity and Partnership

As illustrated in the last chapter, astrological oppositions occur between masculine or feminine polarities. Aspects between a masculine and a feminine sign create squares or inconjuncts (semi-sextile and quincunx).[26] A different intensity of Eros is implied; for instance, an opposition occurs between two similar qualities, whereas squares and inconjuncts happen between opposing ones. For relationship analysis we might classify the conjunction and opposition as aspects of attachment whereas the squares and inconjuncts suggest separateness; together, these are two essential components of relating.

Masculine Signs	Planetary Ruler	Feminine Signs	Planetary Ruler
Aries	Mars	Taurus	Venus
Gemini	Mercury	Cancer	Moon
Leo	Sun	Virgo	Mercury
Libra	Venus	Scorpio	Mars
Sagittarius	Jupiter	Capricorn	Saturn
Aquarius	Saturn	Pisces	Jupiter

Each planet, except the Sun and Moon, rules both a masculine and a feminine sign. For instance, Venus rules the feminine sign of Taurus and the masculine sign of Libra, while Mars rules the masculine sign of Aries and the feminine sign of Scorpio. The signs that Mars and Venus rule are opposite one another, yet the signs that each planet rules separately are quincunx one another, i.e. the Mars-ruled signs of Aries and Scorpio are separated by 150°. Venus is in its detriment in the Mars-ruled signs of Aries and Scorpio, whereas Mars is its detriment in the Venus-ruled signs of Taurus and Libra. These interchanges suggest that each fulfils the other. Astrologically, these four signs of Aries, Libra, Taurus and Scorpio, along with their designated houses 1 & 7 and 2 & 8, describe the astrological territory of self and other, and their interrelational dynamics.

Nocturnal Partners
One of the primary cosmological polarities is night and day. Our astrological ancestors developed an astrological way of thinking about night and day through the technique of **planetary sect**. The word 'sect' comes from the Latin root which suggests to cut or to make a division. In context of the Hellenistic tradition the term proposed an astrological system whereby the traditional planets were grouped into a diurnal (day) sect led by the Sun, and a nocturnal (night) sect led by the Moon.

The day group consists of the Sun, Jupiter and Saturn, as well as Mercury when it rises before the Sun. The ancients placed Saturn here because his coldness would be warmed in the light. The night team consists of the Moon, Venus and Mars, plus Mercury when he sets after the Sun. Mars was placed on this team because his dryness could be moistened by the night dews. The night team are the personal planets and it is night time when pleasure and desire may reign without social judgement. Venus and Mars are on the same team, a more subjective, personal and inner orientated side.

It is of interest in relationship astrology that Venus and Mars were identified by the ancient astrologers as being nocturnal. By belonging to the night, both planets are more individual, private, sensitive and responsive to their environment. Out of the glare of the Sun they are free from scrutiny and authority. At night, they can be uncovered, open to the elements and free from the constrictions set by the day's agendas. At night, Venus and Mars find their shared connection, engagement and Eros. Here they are able to come together. Perhaps this is why we can never really know what happens in other couples' relationships. We can form an opinion, gossip and comment about their incompatibility in the day, but we do not witness their night union. It is only in the intimacy that we can know the mystery of that union.

Directions and Differences – Venus and Mars Retrograde

As individual planets, Venus and Mars are important guides in relationship. As they cycle around the Sun they form patterns in the heavens. True to her archetypal nature, Venus's cycle is especially beautiful and symmetrical, tracing out a pentagram in the sky.[27] At one point in their cycle the planets appear to change direction and move backwards, a visual distortion due to the fact that we are viewing the planets from our vantage point on Earth, which is also cycling around the Sun.

When Venus or Mars are retrograde, their direction reverses to retrace a previous zodiacal period. From a relationship perspective the retrograde route alters the expression of the archetype as it focuses retrospectively and reflectively on its own itinerary. During this backward-looking time the archetype reveals itself in a unique and private way.

Venus is retrograde for 6 weeks every 19 months or for about 7.5% of its cycle. This suggests an atypical attitude; therefore we might expect an unusual or uncommon pattern in relationships. Whether this nonconforming pattern manifests through sexual orientation, being solitary, highly aesthetic or unusually creative, the relational course faces a different direction. Venus retrograde highlights the issue of self-esteem and worth, along with atypical personal values which are confronted in social development.

Mars is retrograde for 58–81 days every 2 years or for between 9 to 10% of its cycle. During this period, desire and yearning are experienced more feverishly. In relationships this might manifest as being distinctively passionate and erotic or having desires that cannot be satisfied through a traditional relationship. There is often a high degree of competition between partners, yet this frequently remains unexpressed or unstated. Anger and frustration might be difficult to express and may be channelled into work, health issues or sexuality; if anger is triggered, it may be directed towards the self.

When Venus or Mars is retrograde at birth I find it enormously valuable to find the year when the planet changed direction by secondary progression. This will be before the age of forty-two for Venus and eighty for Mars, depending on how long the planet had already been retrograde when the individual was born. If the planet changes direction in the adult years it is symbolic of a major change of direction in their relationship patterns and preferences. Equally, I always check to see if Venus or Mars will turn retrograde by secondary progression and note the year when it changes direction.

Two of the women in our case examples have Mars retrograde. Virginia Woolf had Mars retrograde at 27♊23 which was notable in many ways in her life, perhaps foremost in her passionate desire to be a writer. Both her parents had children from a previous marriage so she grew up in a household of three blended families. The symbol of Mars retrograde is observable through her diverse experiences with her brothers. Her two natural brothers were loving and supportive of her longing to write, but her two half-brothers traumatized and sexually abused her. As part of the Bloomsbury Group she was also involved in a hoax when she dressed as a male. Though happily married, Virginia had a sexually intimate relationship with her female friend Vita Sackville-West. Of interest is Vita's Mars which was at 27♐17, exactly opposite Virginia's. Mars turned direct when Virginia was eight-and-a-half.

Anaïs Nin had Mars retrograde at 16♎13. Like Virginia Woolf, it is evident in her passion for writing; not only her erotic writing, but in her numerous journals which revealed her liaisons with many celebrities. Her relationships were distinctive and nonconforming. Besides her passionate relationship with Henry Miller and her obsession with his wife June, she had a relationship with her psychotherapist Otto Rank, and was also married to two men at the same time. By secondary progression, Mars remained retrograde throughout her lifetime.

Bobby Brown, whose chart is presented in the next chapter, was born with his Venus direct, but it turned retrograde when he was forty-one, two years before his ex-wife Whitney Houston died. In this year he became engaged to his manager Alicia Etheredge. Venus turning retrograde signals the possibility of a more introspective relationship to his inner feminine as well as with other women.

The Twelve Gestures of Venus

As mentioned, Venus enters the astrological pantheon with many mythic qualities, becoming aligned with self-love, self-esteem, what we value and appreciate. Venus symbolizes what attracts us to others, the value we place upon our relationships, what we need to feel partnered as well as our own inner sense of worth and value that wants to be received, honoured and respected. Through the agency of the two signs that Venus rules, she appreciates beauty in both its bodily and spiritual forms. As the golden goddess she became associated with material values like jewels, money and precious objects; as the heavenly one she was assigned spiritual values like peace and love.

Venus love begins with self-love, not a narcissistic love but one that values innate qualities. It includes the love of one's own solitude, self-respect and patience. Love is a choice and also a promise; therefore it is a process, a commitment and a discipline that involves discrimination and decision. While we often talk about the object of our love, it is subjective. Our Venus sign is a metaphor for the qualities that we value, appreciate and cherish most in ourselves, others and relationship. It is these virtues and characteristics that we will be attracted to in others, yet it also describes our process and commitment to loving.

As Venus's orbit is enclosed by the Earth, we view it in our skies as being close to the Sun. In an astrological chart it is never more than 48° away; therefore, it is limited as to the signs it can occupy. It is either in the same sign as the Sun or in one or two signs either side. When in the same sign it shares the qualities of the Sun sign, but it enhances the sign by bringing its archetypal nature to the Sun's domain. When in the adjacent sign the elemental qualities of the Sun and Venus are stressed and a more conscious attitude is needed to align the Venusian values with the identity. When two signs away, the elemental qualities are more compatible. Even though the differences may be subtle, nonetheless, the Sun and Venus occupy different terrains. Therefore when reading the Venus sign it is of interest to keep the Sun sign in mind as well.

♀♈ Venus in Aries

Traditionally, Venus is in its detriment in Aries; perhaps because it is difficult to rush pleasure. When you are attracted to someone you heat up; when they return your attention you become intensely focused on them and wildly romantic. However, when they turn away, you might bristle with anger. You're passionate and emotional, and where there's passion, there's anger. Mars rules the sign of Aries, so how you express your passions is fiery. You do not hold yourself back when you feel close and connected. When you are attracted to someone you are direct and identified, which is enormously refreshing. You take others at face value, as you accept that what you see is what you get. While you know this is naïve, you still enter your relationships with enthusiasm and gusto because that's who you are. You want a relationship that's alive and cutting-edge, and you want your kindred spirits to be co-adventurers and to share your enthusiasm for life.

Being independent, free and spontaneous are potent values. Therefore it is important that your partners appreciate these qualities too. Being positive about life, you tend to also be idealistic, romantic and full of hope. Your spirit of being upbeat and meeting life challenges is attractive and makes life with you exciting, but when the passionate fires die down, you may find it difficult to continue the romance. Separating, or moving on to another relationship may be more attractive. Venus in Aries values the excitement of living and loving and she might rush to experience it all. Over time, the right relationship moderates these urges.

♀♉ Venus in Taurus

Venus rules Taurus. Through this earthy sign her sensual qualities come alive. When you are attracted to someone you feel it in your body – a tingle, sometimes a torrent. She values quality and time in relationship. Functional aspects of life can be dealt with quickly, but the pleasures of life cannot be rushed; therefore, time to build up the relationship is valuable. The sensual world is where you find pleasure and you need to share tastes, sights, smells, sounds and feelings with those you love.

Being sensual also means being comfortable, so you prefer luxury and quality to bargains and quantity. While this takes money, it is not the motivating factor in relationship. Money is one of the resources ruled by both Venus and Taurus, so it does play a major role in your relationships, but what you value most are the qualities of tenderness, loyalty, consistency and stability. Perhaps money becomes the issue when these qualities are lacking. You invest a lot in your relationships and you want to be sure it pays off. This signature is often described as possessive; therefore it is worth considering what you can and cannot share in a relationship. You don't want to be pushed into relationship, as it takes time to know if the prospective partner feels the same, is compatible and shares the same passions. With Venus in Taurus you take your time to appreciate the delights of close attachments. On the other hand, you may also hold onto relationships when it is time to let go.

♀Ⅱ Venus in Gemini

Naturally sociable, you veer towards companions who are communicative, who understand your ideas and are easy to talk to and spend time with. But you can be easily bored and feel the need for change if things are becoming repetitive or dull. You value variety in relationship, such as different restaurants, joining new courses and changing routines. Being involved with you means learning the quick step, but not everyone is as agile as you might want him or her to be. You know when you are attracted to someone, because you might stumble over your words and be awkward. Your nervous system runs amok as it is a monitor for your level of attraction. Mobility and versatility in any relationship are important. Love and communication are intertwined and you need to communicate how you feel, light or dark. Some might not be able to listen, but kindred spirits will love your aerial acrobatics and sense of humour. A valued relationship is one where you can communicate without fear of judgement or reprisal.

Venus in Gemini suggests that love and companionship are united. This might be a close bond with a sibling, or in a wider context, you value companionship and friendship in your intimate encounters. Your values are not fixed; in fact you can be quite changeable about what you like, experimenting with feelings and relationships before you can reach a decision. You need space and distance to make up your mind. When you are pinned down, you panic; therefore commitment is much easier when there is no pressure. You value someone who gives you the space to go through the changes you need to go through. You like to be connected but don't want to be present all the time; a Facebook post, a text or a tweet are ways to stay connected.

♀♋ Venus in Cancer

Love and nurturing are intermeshed for Venus in Cancer. You love to care for others, be needed by them and offer your emotional and physical support. You may do this professionally, but you value this mostly in personal relationships. Some astrological reports suggest you are prone to mothering your partners and companions or that you might be an orphan looking for a foster home. This applies when there is inadequate self-nurturing or when nurturing others becomes unbalanced. When you provide enough care for yourself, those you love value your warmth and depth of feeling. You value kindness, tenderness and empathy; qualities that need to be returned for you to feel loved.

Emotional tides will be a regular feature in your relationships. It is very painful when the ones you love don't respond or reciprocate. You are hurt fairly easily and are accustomed to dealing with mood swings. Bad moods develop when you start ruminating over being left out, misunderstood or taken for granted. While you value closeness and kindness, you cannot appreciate your emotional breadth when you are distressed. Kinship and family are also valued, but love and family can collide when choices need to be made between lovers and family. Venus in Cancer does not necessarily guarantee a loving family, but it does suggest that you need to make your soulmates your family. In adult years your family circle embraces your friends, workmates, kindred spirits and loved ones. A sentimentalist at heart, you make tradition and family values romantic.

♀♌ Venus in Leo

Venus concerns self-love; in Leo this becomes most apparent. What makes you attractive and desirable to others is important and so coming to know your own reflection and what others find appealing is of interest to you. Even if you're not extroverted you still like to be complimented. You blossom when the person you love displays affection. Why be modest when you can be remarkable; why be dull when you can be sensational? Leo is the fixed fire that rules the heart, so the flames of your love burn brightly and constantly. You value fidelity and strength and you are attracted to those who are proud and passionate as well. You know when you meet someone you are attracted to, as you feel your heart skip, your temperature rises and you are already imagining what it would be like to be together.

You value romance and passion and they are what you hope to find in your relationships. When you do, you flourish. Being fiercely loyal, devoted and proud of those you love you can lavish praise, gifts and approval on them. When you love someone you are their biggest fan. But it needs to be a two-way mirror. If you feel defrauded or treated badly, you can be quite unforgiving. So it pays to be discriminating, because feeling used or discarded cuts deeply. You are generous and big-hearted, but if the fire is put out you can be cold and disapproving. Loyalty is so important. Devaluing yourself leaves you open to projecting worth and values onto others, exchanging your lack of esteem for someone else's inflation. When you waver about your sense of worth you overestimate others. Soulmates value your warmth and generous heart, and when you are with them you feel cherished.

♀♍ Venus in Virgo

Virgo's essence is enigmatic, synthesizing the wildness and beauty of nature with aloofness and distance. Something about Virgo is unknowable; not unapproachable. Therefore Venus in Virgo is very appealing and mysterious to others. You value your privacy, time to yourself, your rituals and your lifestyle so you need others to respect and value these qualities as well. You love to be of service and helpful; therefore you make a great helpmate. Kindred spirits respect and appreciate this about you. You know when you are attracted to someone because you become shy and self-deprecating, which can be quite endearing.

When you are in that sacred space with someone else, it can approach perfection; however, in our busy and complex lives this is never easy. You may be critical when you're stressed or overly analytical when you're not happy. You value working on your relationships and trying to improve the quality of your encounters. With a committed partner who values this, you feel that you are growing together. Loved ones value your healing and helping qualities and share in the magic of your everyday life. When your soulmate appears you will be well prepared. Classical astrologers see Venus in Virgo in its detriment, because human love and divine perfection are uneasy partners. You value excellence, yet it is the flaws and imperfections of human relationship that render it meaningful. From a psychological point of view it is the limitations of love that make relationship soulful, a paradox you learn in relating.

♀♎ Venus in Libra

Venus rules Libra, so she is at home here and her home is beautiful. Instinctively, you value harmony and aesthetics because you have a natural affinity with beauty. Whether it's a Pre-Raphaelite or a Monet is not that important; what matters is its beauty. From an early age you have appreciated art, sculpture and all things sophisticated. Unfortunately, people aren't works of art or museum pieces and you learn to accept that sometimes those you love are tired, dishevelled and even rude. Being people-orientated, social skills are important but they can also disguise the true nature of your feelings. While you may have to be nice to the public, you do not need to be pleasant to loved ones if you are angry. You can swing between being too accommodating and then counterbalancing that by being aggressive. It's hard for you to create waves, which means you might say yes to something unsuitable for you because you do not want to offend someone. It is difficult for you to be confrontational or to show your displeasure.

You are romantic but you also need your own space, which sometimes gets a bit crowded because you've agreed to do so many things with so many people. You need to learn that intricate balance of saying no when you do not want to be involved, and yes when you truly do. You value relating and are genuinely interested in others, but you also need to balance that with your own time and space, which you often forget. You seek equality and spirituality in your relationships, which encourage you to also find that in yourself. Venus in Libra also finds her home in relationship.

♀♏ Venus in Scorpio

It is evident to others that you have the capacity for deep and abiding relationships; however, you may fear loss or betrayal if you were to become intimate. Therefore, you are challenged to love in spite of these anxieties. While you value your capacity for depth of feeling and being emotionally available, your integrity and sincerity render you vulnerable in relationship. Hence, you may be inclined to conceal your feelings while privately longing for the depth of connection that intimacy can offer. Loving the passion and intensity that closeness brings, you may mistake emotional crisis and pain for connection, or passion and emotion for love. You come alive in emergencies. In dangerous situations or at critical junctures you are fully present; therefore, it is wise not to confuse love with crisis, as you may become the therapist to partners in constant crisis.

Venus in Scorpio is in its detriment and is often delineated as being jealous or possessive. Because you have the tendency to connect deeply and are vulnerable, trust is always a relationship issue. Emotional control, jealousy and possessiveness, whether encountered in yourself or others, guard the heart from being broken. With the capacity to love so deeply, this sensitivity needs armouring. Secrecy is another way to defend against vulnerability, as are money and sex when used as a defence against personal disclosure. Reflect on how you might unconsciously build defences against feeling vulnerable; probably you are still nursing a relationship wound or memories of betrayal. It's hard for you to let go and open up again, but incredibly therapeutic when you do. At heart you value being a loyal, honest and trusting partner but you need this to be mutual.

♀♐ Venus in Sagittarius

Your heart longs for the freedom of wide-open spaces and is fascinated by foreigners, teachers, philosophers, metaphysicians and explorers. Some projection might be going on here. You value visionaries and change agents because you too are one. When caught in the guru projection, try spelling the word slowly out loud: *G U R U gee, you are you.* You have been known to go overseas just when you start a new relationship, or fall in love with someone who is on the road. Before you can settle into relationship, you need to quest and travel. You do want freedom in your relationships but you also want to adventure with your partner. Woven into the fabric of your associations are cross-cultural, foreign and sometimes exotic themes. You find your kindred spirits in foreign places, different cultures and other communities, challenging you to bring different beliefs, new customs and philosophies into your relationships, which keep you stimulated and engaged in the connection. Without this stimulus you can get easily bored. Your kindred spirits encourage you to diversify and grow beyond the familiar traditions of your youth.

Your Venus sign is ruled by Jupiter, which graces you with generosity and openness in your relationships, but sometimes you might be overly generous. This usually occurs because the relationship has not been equal. While losses due to relationship can be recovered, being so optimistic can be problematic. It is not easy to accept the negativity and difficulty that relationships can bring. Remember, you can't be optimistic with a misty optic so better that you face the challenge to see clearly before you shower others with generosity and abundance. You value openness, honesty and meaningful interchanges. Laughter and tears, playfulness and seriousness, idealism and realism all combine to make a soulful relationship. More than anything you value those in your life who walk the spiritual path with you and understand your philosophical yearnings.

♀♑ Venus in Capricorn

Let's be frank: you are probably successful at what you do and looking for quality in your relationships. Given the choice, you are going to choose items of good taste and value, ones that are expensive, rather than ones that are on sale. Therefore, in a partner, someone who is highly skilled, accomplished and has a good reputation does have appeal. When projection is at work, your feelings of not measuring up have a tendency to credit others with the worth and quality you feel is lacking in yourself. You are self-critical, often expecting too much of yourself. You value tradition, commitment and responsibility; therefore, you are someone we can count on. Rules and regulations are important too but not at the expense of connection and rapport.

Because you are accomplished and capable it is never easy for you to rely on others. You can be autonomous and self-reliant. However, this can get in the way of relating and is a good defence against the fear of being let down or the dismissal of your request for assistance. Demonstrating love or being affectionate does make you feel vulnerable so you often hold back. You may fear rejection, but it's more important to be in relationship than to be alone in complete control. You might also try to take charge of your partner when you're feeling vulnerable, so it is important to recognize the urge to organize and manage them. Your Venus sign is ruled by Saturn which brings the themes of work and relationship together, so issues of status, money, time or occupation could disturb relationship. You might meet your soulmate through work or you might work together. What if your boss was your partner? How do you deal with hierarchy and equality at the same time? You have a healthy sense of boundaries and are a supportive companion; therefore, you can manage the disparity by utilizing your dedication, dependability and trustworthiness.

♀≈ Venus in Aquarius

Even though you can be conservative, you are drawn to the original and the unusual, especially in relationships. Freedom is important to you and you value your own time and space. You are attracted to free spirits, identifying as one yourself, so much so perhaps that your ex complains about your lack of commitment, being too cool and distant, or of your sudden engagement and then abrupt disengagement. You might feel smothered in close relationships; you want a close relationship but not all the time. Many Venus in Aquarius people have explained it this way: 'When I am on the other side of the world I am madly in love and can't wait to be with my partner, but as I approach home and them, I begin to panic. I can't breathe and feel like fleeing.' They ask me 'What's going on?' This is the fated dilemma of wanting to be close and non-committal at the same time: an impossible match. So it is best to take responsibility for taking your own space, doing your own thing and finding enough time to satisfy your interests. Then you don't need to push others away to get space. When there's enough space, you don't panic and are wonderfully friendly, open and companionable.

You value your independence and friendship. But friendships and intimate relationships do not necessarily have the same expectations. Friends can support your adventures and escapades, but intimate others might feel that you are not spending enough time with them. You often confuse friendship and relationship and still expect your ex to be a friend even after a bitter break-up. So relating usually brings a learning curve of emotional intensity. At first, you disengage from it. Next, you might try to avoid it. But soon you learn that darker emotions pass and they pass more quickly when you engage them, not separate from them. The irony is that emotional intensity is somewhat attractive. You don't see it coming beneath that breezy welcoming personality! Equality, openness and truthfulness are guiding principles for you in relationship and your humanitarian and considerate character attracts soulmates who share your worldview and human values.

♀♓ Venus in Pisces

Being romantic at heart you have probably been told many a time to be more realistic about relationships. Or to steer that energy towards your own creativity, sing your own songs or rescue your own inner child. You are prone to idealization and projecting your enchantment out into the world, but probably it lands more productively on a canvas than a person. Your heart is imaginative and inspired, best expressed through creativity. In close relationship you may be prone to idealizing the other, then becoming enmeshed in their world. Perhaps you can't help helping or falling in love. But sometimes you are in love with the ideal and possibility of love, rather than the person. You are also prone to surrendering yourself to these possibilities before they have been tested or had a reality check. Sensitive to sacrificing aspects of yourself in order to help others leaves you feeling adrift, lost to yourself. Neptune is the modern ruler of your Venus sign and with this nebulous planet standing behind the curtain of your relationships you are susceptible to fantasy and to reading much into situations that are influenced by your own desires. It is magic, but could also be folly.

You value the spiritual and unseen. With intimate others you are able to part the veil between the worlds and be in a timeless space together. Therefore, in your close relationships it is wise to create time and space away from routine so that you can enter into this enchantment together. You have a gift of great compassion and understanding but relationship teaches you how to contain and shape this in the best possible ways.

The Twelve Expressions of Mars

Mars is heat, passion and desire. Whether spiritual, physical, intellectual or emotional, Mars symbolizes the instinctual way that desire, anger and frustration are channelled and expressed. It is emotive. Since many of this archetype's impulses can be antisocial and uncivilized, we learn restraint, refinement and moderation to express its unprocessed emotions. Mars symbolizes the urge to compete and win. Mars wants its own way and is ready to do battle for that. While fundamental in each relationship, it can be divisive; therefore, it is crucial to know our own Mars and its effect on others. In terms of relating, it describes how you assert yourself, deal with conflict and make your yearnings transparent. Your Mars sign describes how you go after what you want. In essence it is a symbol of how your life force naturally seeks expression.

For many years, as part of the Astro*Synthesis program, we conducted a Mars–Venus workshop to augment our classes. One day was experiential. Various exercises on Venus and Mars were used to evoke a lived experience of the archetypes. One exercise on Mars was fascinating, as no matter the size of the teams, the results were always consistent. This exercise was a tug-of-war which demonstrated how differently each Mars element approached competition. The outcome of this task was always a surprise and always an illuminating lesson. The participants were divided into four groups based on their Mars sign; then a tug-of-war between the four groups was facilitated. The masculine signs would first compete against one another, then the feminine signs. The winners of each would compete in the final. Mars prefers individual challenges, not necessarily a team effort. However, the exercises still evoked the Martian spirit of competition.

No doubt when dealing with physical strength and stamina, Mars in Earth has enormous resources and power while Mars in Fire has abundant spirit and drive. However, Mars also illustrates how we channel and direct that energy and whether we will be initiating or competitive. If the outcome is desirable and we want to go for it, then Mars's will concentrates on what we want. If the desire is not strong, then Mars may not be fired with the competitive spirit, enthusiasm and drive that are needed to actively pursue its goal and to accomplish its task. Time after time our experience of the groups was similar, as follows:

Mars in Air loses first round
Mars in Air was always the first group to be out of the competition, due to the scattered approach of the participants and their inability to concentrate. There was a lot of discussion and arguing over how best to approach the game. All the unfocused energy distracted the players from the task at hand; therefore they were pulled across the line very quickly. Mars in Air probably would compete better in strategic games such as chess or an intellectual debate where

the mental process, not physical stamina, is required. Mars in Air individuals can scatter themselves too thinly and do not always enjoy physical competition or confrontation. Mars in Fire went through to the finals.

Mars in Earth also loses first round

Mars in Earth was strong, but the members of the team did not apply themselves, nor pull their weight. When discussing this later, most of the members agreed that as there was no pay-off or reward at the end of the game, it was not really worth it. Since it was just a game, they could not see the value in it; therefore they held back from applying themselves and did not summon the drive to be present with the task. Mars in Earth is very robust and often has enormous reserves of power and stamina, yet needs to be committed to the process and the outcome. Mars in Water continued on to the final.

Mars in Fire – restless or victorious

Mars in Fire was very strong and enthusiastic. The team had lots of fun competing and playing. However, they became bored easily and were restless after the first burst of enthusiasm about their initial victory waned. Restlessness overcame them and they looked forward to the next activity, rather than concentrating on the present and completing the task at hand. Winning was not as important as getting on with the next activity; therefore, the energy needed to win was compromised by the momentum to move forward. Mars in Fire is very energetic but their commitment wanes and their drive diminishes when they become bored or there is not enough stimulation.

Mars in Water – depleted or tenacious

Mars in Water just kept hanging on. The invisible strength of Water is its tenacity and ability to hold fast. While appearing passive, its great strength and resource is to overcome obstacles through endurance. Therefore it always proved to be the winner, which gave the participants a great insight into the hidden power and strength of Water. However, if it were an emotional situation or one that had been contentious, the team's strength would have been depleted due to emotional undercurrents. If there are emotional overtones or personal attachments, Mars in Water may withdraw, holding on to wounded feelings. As this was just a game, there was not a lot of emotional investment, so they hung on with great reserves of strength and always won.

Like an engine, Mars is started by turning a key. Its force, will and power are motivated by the object of its desire; when hot and focused it is a powerful competitor and campaigner. When hot and uncontrolled it can be dangerous. But when the key is not turned, the engine of Mars remains cold and stalled. One of the keys to switching on Mars is its quality of sign. Let's examine this in terms of relating.

♂♈ Mars in Aries

How you assert yourself and are your own person in relationship is the domain of Mars, and in Aries it is in the sign of its rulership. So when stimulated it can be straightforward, up-front, enthusiastic, positive and goal-orientated. Being a natural warrior and champion you go into battle for what you want. Your learning curve is how you forge a way to meet your partner halfway. Being a self-starter and independent, you tend to take your own advice and create your own opportunities rather than depend on others. Comfortable in the leader's role or at the head of the pack, you may be more inclined to coaching or motivating rather than compromising or collaborating. Because you live spontaneously, it is frustrating to wait while others get ready or make up their mind; therefore impatience and autonomy become tempered in your relationships. You learn to control the urge to run away when your independence is threatened or you feel the relationship is not going anywhere.

It's great that you are able to express yourself, but with intimate others you also need to listen to their side of the story and manage your anger when you don't get your way. You love the chase and the heat of the moment. But relationships have middles and ends as well, and those need a little more work. You bring passion and excitement to your relationships; you desire a stimulating opponent who challenges you to be the best you can. But time is the key, as rushing does not let the alchemy of the relationship bring out its full flavours.

♂♉ Mars in Taurus

In a way the images of Venus and Mars intersect because Venus rules your Mars sign. But Mars is inclined to rush and this does not suit Taurus who desires to take things more slowly. Therefore, when in Taurus Mars needs to take its time, getting acclimatized to the terrain before it can feel comfortable enough to stay and make a commitment. Being in a sign of its detriment, Mars's urge for action is slowed down. Impatience can become frustration. If you're pushed or told to hurry, then you just go slower, becoming immovable or inflexible. With time the stability and pleasure you want in a relationship can mature.

In forging relationships you need time to familiarize yourself. After a while you may be surprised that an attachment has developed slowly. But familiarity can become boring unless you remain motivated. You can stop trying once you have accomplished the labour or won the prize; therefore it is worthwhile considering ways to enliven your intimate relationships to keep the fires burning. With Venus ruling this sign, one of these ways might be sharing sensual pleasures. In an Earth sign, Mars's desire is embodied and channelled through physical energy and application, whether that is cooking a meal together, listening to music or massaging your partner. Sharing is the key, whether delighting in a bottle of Merlot, a night at the theatre or the pleasure of the garden. When you are free with someone you love and you still feel secure, you feel more able to love.

♂♊ Mars in Gemini

When the god of action is channelled through the mutable and quick energy of Gemini, we imagine someone who is mobile, yet not always sure of the direction they want to take, as it could change at any moment. Because you are interested in so many things, it might feel as if a serious relationship is destined for later, not now. However, if you are fascinated in the moment, you leap in. Mars in Gemini is often portrayed as fickle. That does not suggest you are inconstant in relationship; however, it does highlight a tendency to unsettled feelings when it comes to making a commitment.

Trickster Mercury rules your Mars sign, and when he drives your impulses you may be temperamental and tricky to deal with. Is it sleight of hand or is it natural for things to vanish into thin air and feelings to change so quickly? So what happens when you are attracted to someone? Do you wait for this urge to pass or do you leap in? Like all Gemini energy, there are two sides to the story. One side is that you are very sensitive to loss and this anxiety drives you towards non-commitment. Yet a deeper side yearns for a more intense connection. Therefore, the more you are able to express your anxieties, talk through your concerns and be participatory, rather than anticipatory, the more at peace you feel. You are prone to panic and a simple remedy is in the breath. Focus on your breathing and relax. You bring a youthful and playful energy to your relationships and what you are longing to find is your other half, who you feel is missing and is searching for you.

♂♋ Mars in Cancer

Being opposite Capricorn, its sign of exaltation, Mars in Cancer was seen in traditional astrology to be in a weakened position. While this Mars sign may not have the forthrightness or spontaneity of other zodiacal signs, it does have tenaciousness and emotional force. The will is aligned with feeling; action is the response to emotions. Anger, aggravation and frustration often push you to act out your feelings. Passions are deeply felt, but finding ways to express them in personal relationships is not that easy. But you know how intense these feelings are when someone you love is in danger. If a member of your family is exposed to harm, a child is at risk or a small animal is in need, you can be forceful and courageous. You vigorously defend and protect those in your care. However, when someone asks *you* what you want, you can feel overwhelmed and withdrawn.

Being instinctively empathetic, your impulse is to fulfil others' needs. You are energized by helping others. However, expressing your needs is not as easy, especially if you sense they might be met with resistance. When you sense that what you want will be disapproved of, you tend to withdraw. While you might feel that you are protecting yourself against possible hurt, you're also closing a door on intimacy. Feelings run the spectrum from light to dark, kindness to anger, love to hate and they are all better out than in. Rather than acting out you may turn the anger back on the self. Being so strong yet so sensitive is both difficult and very appealing. People are attracted to you because of this mix; they feel they can be safe with you because you can be caring and vigilant, loving and sheltering. They may not necessarily know that you are overwhelmed with feeling, so it's best to find the courage to let them know.

♂♌ Mars in Leo

Mars is akin to fire so in Leo, warmed by the Sun, it suggests that you are masterful at expressing yourself with charm and charisma. With this brilliant light in the background it is hard for you to see your own shadows. Sometimes a comment is taken as a criticism or a suggestion is seen as a shortcoming. You yearn to be desired. You might not realize it, but you are powerfully persuasive. Your appeal can disarm the most difficult opponent; therefore you might be fast-tracked into prominence or positions of power. Some crushes and a few broken hearts have even occurred without your knowing. However, this also feeds an arrogant and stubborn streak that can create conflict in personal relationships.

When you desire someone you produce an incredible stage on which you are the hero or heroine. It is quite irresistible, but what happens when the lights fade and the curtain falls? What you will find is that the fires of the heart can be contained, burning steadily, not just ferociously. Your desire and passion are constant. Even though you like to play with others, you are loyal to those you love. You bring a great deal of fun, flair and warmth to your relationships and what you receive in return are fidelity and applause. The Greeks knew this as *philia*, the recognition of ourselves in the face of others and the playful awakenings that love and friendship make happen.

♂♍ Mars in Virgo

Having the forceful god in Virgo suggests that you are circumspect and discriminating about where you focus your energy. Before you exert yourself you analyse the situation. Being so prepared means you can be shrewd and critical, which serves you well in your everyday life of work and well-being. But perhaps these qualities are not as effective in terms of personal relationships. Unfortunately, people aren't as methodical, rational or organized as you had expected. The good news is that there is lots of room for improvement and that's where Mars in Virgo goes to work. You are the person to call to fix what's not working, analyse a problem or challenge a hypothesis. Therefore it is important that you work on your relationship, not your partner. You desire to feel that your close encounters are improving with age and that they fit in with the scheme of your life. You do have a tendency to make sure everything fits into your schedule and plans; unfortunately, relationships tend to be a bit more chaotic than you might be prepared for.

Your dedication to work, well-being and lifestyle allow you to enjoy the routines you have created. You are stimulated when a kindred spirit shares a similar health regime, work routine or lifestyle. Even though you may not physically occupy the same space during the day, at the end of the working day you want to share the highs and lows with someone who listens and understands. You have a drive for perfection and are quite comfortable on your own, but in reality you have been rehearsing for an intimate relationship for a long time. With Mars in earthy Virgo you also bring your sensual side and your pent-up passion into an intimate encounter.

♂♎ Mars in Libra

Being in the sign ruled by Venus, Mars's desires are influenced by what others want or value. Therefore, what motivates you is filtered through what others are doing, which often leaves you feeling unsure of what you want. Your ambivalence is confusing for others, especially when they are clear about what they want. You can be skilful at mediation and reconciliation when uninvolved, but when your heart is engaged with someone special it is difficult to express your desires if theirs conflict with what you want. Traditionally, Mars is in detriment here, since the urge to act for the self is compromised by the quality of conciliation. Your desire is for peace, balance and fairness.

Your loved ones might complain that you have been more charming to your enemies than to them. You subscribe to the adage of keeping your friends close but your enemies closer. When confronting an unpleasant situation you try to find a resolution that is pleasant, rather than one that is decisive. Therefore, in relationship you may act submissively when you need to be more assertive. You might express your anger by showing up late or ignoring those trying to get your attention. Your difficulty in confronting an unpleasant emotional truth leaves you feeling disconnected. On the other hand, being in relationship with you is extremely rewarding, as you are able to anticipate what others want. You know what they like to wear, want to do and where to go. You might be in two minds about what you want, but you are fairly clear about what others want. And herein is the redemption. You do desire a relationship and strive to be a considerate, caring and romantic partner. You're just learning to be more direct.

♂♏ Mars in Scorpio

As its ruler, Mars soars to the heights and scours the depths of Scorpio. In terms of relationships, this suggests both powerful love and intense desire. It's been said that Mars in Scorpio doesn't get angry, it just gets even, referring to the propensity for revenge when trust is broken. Trust is a central issue; when hurt or feeling betrayed you can become cold and untouchable. Unlike his other domain of Aries, Mars in Scorpio conceals these feelings, so few would know if he were in pain or even feeling elated. You too are intensely private and contain your feelings. Some say you might hide your feelings. And sometimes you do, as you are acutely engaged in what you do. You need time to be with yourself and process your feelings, otherwise you feel overwhelmed by others.

You offer a high degree of emotional integrity and honesty in your relationships, but you demand loyalty in return, wanting to share at the most intimate levels. And when you become emotionally or sexually engaged, the waters aren't tepid, they're hot! However, you often expect others to have your depth of understanding and to intuitively know what you need without your revealing anything. Be aware that not everyone has this silent understanding or is able to read subtleties like you can. Emotional and sexual engagement equals trust. To you, close relationships are sacrosanct. When a relationship ends, it is done. No more chances. You've grieved, you've railed, you've cried and now it's time to move on. And you do. When you emotionally commit to a relationship you are there 100%, offering a treasure chest of love and resource which you are willing to share. But it is not a one-way street and you expect a return on your investment. You bring integrity and honesty to your relationships and expect to find this passion and trust reciprocated.

♂♐ Mars in Sagittarius

Metaphorically, Mars in Sagittarius is like an archer or perhaps a rifleman shooting from the hip. It is second nature for you to be straightforward and confrontational. When there is difficulty you can be far-sighted, able to see beyond personal agendas and reactions into the symptom and the truth. But, as they say, 'truth hurts'. While it's natural to be impulsive, you are learning that a little discretion might be wiser. But to be fair, you add excitement and adventure and your warmth, generosity and optimism brighten up all your interactions. By nature you are an explorer and your desire for learning and cross-cultural experiences is high. You are called by a faraway horizon; therefore, in terms of being in relationship, it is important that you find the way to assimilate being connected and present with your urge to be free and impulsive.

You have a vital spirit which is a good barometer for how you are feeling. When you feel lethargic or depressed, it's because you feel trapped. You might be inclined to try to rationalize your position but the truth is that you need to move and express yourself. The more energy you expend, the more you seem to get. This works well in terms of personal connection too, since you need to express your restless energy without fear of judgement. You love stimulation and variety in all your endeavours and you need your intimate partner to be open to that as well. You bring a great deal of vitality and excitement into any relationship and what you hope to find in return is an accomplice who shares your search for meaning. It is vital that you share your life path, your religious and philosophical quest with those you love.

♂♑ Mars in Capricorn

Mars in Capricorn suggests that you strive to be the captain of your own ship. Mars being in its exalted sign adds determination, willpower, grit and commitment to the will to succeed. Saturn as the ruler of Capricorn brings his age-old wisdom and experience to what you desire. As a young person this might have been more difficult but with adulthood comes the opportunity and wherewithal to focus your ambition. These are highly valuable traits to use in your professional life, but what about the personal arena? How do you express your desires in your private life? In a calculated way you might choose partners who support your professional goals;

however, more than likely, you take your time, assess the situation and hold back until you know that you are respected for who you are, not what you do. Your intimate others might complain about your authoritarian nature as you straddle that fine line between controlling and sharing.

You want things to work and to work well; therefore, you might have to make some room for human frailty, irrationality and emotionality, as these are bound to show up at some point in your personal relationships. You want to work hard and be accomplished, and you want those you love to be on board as well. So it's possible you may start a business together or work in the same profession. Desire for success at work might clash with relationship responsibilities; hence time management is essential in satisfying the demands of a busy life. You bring dignity and worldly wisdom into your relationships and strive to find those who can share your goals and ambitions.

♂♒ Mars in Aquarius

With Mars in Aquarius you might be motivated by high ideals, humanitarian concerns and altruistic outcomes. Even though you are drawn to explore the unusual or are fascinated by the cutting-edge, you can have fairly fixed opinions and ideas. You have the opportunity to meet others through your communal concerns and projects; therefore, you could work alongside others on important projects or be sought after because of your innovative approach. But how do you translate an impersonal relationship into a personal one? How does an acquaintance become a soulmate? This could be problematic for this Aquarian energy.

Personal love might be more of an ideal than an emotion for you. The Greeks had the concept of *agape* which was an impersonal love, one not bound by human feeling. With Mars in Aquarius personal feelings are often rationalized or conceptualized. What you may think is separateness or individuality might be experienced by your partner as emotional distance. Hence your emotional clarity may be more of a defence against closeness than a statement of your desires. While you crave independence and freedom, your learning curve is concerned with how to maintain these goals when you are in an intimate relationship. The dilemma between wanting to be free yet being passionate about someone can be frustrating for you and your intimate others. You need the permission to be free, to explore and do your own thing, and the idea of freedom itself is often enough for you to stay. If there is a back door and it's always accessible, there is no reason to leave.

♂♓ Mars in Pisces

Mars in Pisces aligns action with spirituality, sensitivity and empathy like the archetype of the spiritual warrior or the compassionate athlete. With this placement you may move with a sense of grace, similar to a dancer or fencer, volunteer to help others or be a leader spiritually or creatively. You forge your own understanding about the human condition and reach out to improve the plight of those who are less fortunate than you. But sometimes your own desires drown in the seas of charity and compassion. Therefore, the task is to hold firmly on to your personal desires while still being loving and considerate. Overwhelmed or easily influenced by others, your desires and goals might be sacrificed for someone else's. Being romantic, tender and idealistic makes you captivating, but you can also become captive to your own altruistic self-sacrifice. You strive to be selfless, which is a commendable spiritual goal, but you are also a human being with deep feelings and desires. Your spiritual urge can dampen your personal drive; perhaps you might think of asserting yourself as being a spiritual practice.

Activity and passivity are interconnected, suggesting you might be passive about what you want, giving up on your passions or being underhanded in order to get them. Anger is difficult, so too is confrontation. You are inclined to forgive others too quickly, to spiritualize the disagreement, or sometimes you just forget it happened. But the repressed anger can slowly unravel the links between you and the ones you love. You may have a tendency to lack boundaries in intimate relationships, which might leave you feeling used or unmet. So while it may be difficult to set boundaries, they help your inner world of romance and passion to find an outlet. You bring poetry, diversity and spirituality into your relationships and want to be as creatively involved with others as possible.

– CHAPTER 4 –
THE LOOK OF LOVE
Venus and Mars by Aspect

Aspects are fundamental to astrology.[28] An archaic meaning of 'aspect' suggests 'regarding' or 'appearing'; the Latin root of 'aspect' means 'to look at'. Apropos the planets, aspect was how they looked or appeared to the other; therefore we could imagine aspects as being how planets might see or witness each other. The nature and condition of the planetary archetypes that are 'looking at' each other determines whether their interchange is supportive or not. Some aspects or 'looks' are favourable, whereas others are challenging.

Embedded in the Greek grammatical tradition was a way of reporting actions as either continuing or completed. This category was known as 'aspect' and it differentiated ways of viewing the temporality of a situation. Underpinning a Hellenistic astrologer's imagination of an aspect may have been whether the dialogue between the planets was complete, ongoing or perhaps wavering between both states.

Literally, an aspect measures the geometric distance in celestial longitude between planets, points or angles. In medieval and modern astrology, particular specific mathematical distances (their geometric separation, e.g. 90°, 120°), are considered 'in aspect', whereas other distances are not. Sometimes aspects are decided by sign only, but generally a defined orb of allowance creates an aspect (e.g. 95° is 'within orb' for a 90° aspect).

An aspect between two planets is the relationship formed between one another at a particular moment in their cycle; therefore, aspects are like natural tones of life, sounding out the beginning, middle and end of a particular planetary cycle. We could think about planetary aspects as being discourses or dialogues between two archetypal presences at a particular stage in their relationship.[29] An aspect is erotic in that it invites the archetypal images to mingle together as a creative force, 'seeing' or 'communicating' with each other at a particular evolutionary moment in their cycle. In relationship astrology, it is essential to examine aspects because they invite interaction. In chart comparison, the interaspects between the partners' charts illustrate the spirit of the relationship, while aspects in a composite chart embody the possibilities when the couple are in alignment with each other.

Natal aspects come to life in relationship astrology. The partner exists outside of our self, but is a witness to our archetypal temperament. They are able to see our make-up because they share in similar dynamics. Aspects that are ignited in relationship can be 'seen' when the other person's planetary energy stimulates the same zodiacal field. An astrological analysis of relationship is compelling because it visually reveals where a couple engages and separates.

Faces of Love – Ancient Greek Classifications

When considering the many 'looks of love' that are possible between astrological archetypes, let's turn to the early Greeks who distinguished various aspects of love in their language, recognizing a full spectrum of love's variations. In English, 'I love you' conveys a wide range of attachments. We use it for our parents, our children, our friends, our playmates, our lovers; even inanimate objects are loved. We rely on subtleties, social mores and common sense to grasp the level of love that is being acknowledged. Eros, as we have seen, first personified love at the very beginning of mythological time. The many faces of love that the early Greeks classified are often categorized into four or six types; however, each word is a symbol of a special nuance of love and it is important to find our own way of thinking about these subtle differences astrologically.[30]

Eros is often thought of as being sexual passion and desire, the force of love that ignites our instinctual and wild side. As an overpowering passion accompanied by powerful physical and emotional reactions, it can diminish the capacity for reflection and rational thought. Sensually-and/or sexually-based love does not exclude spirituality, as Eros can also be the medium that awakens the sacred. Eros was primal and divine; as human surrogates we find the depth of intimate love through our passions, whether sexual or sacred or both. Erotic love is not always sexually-based, but centred on the arousal of the inner and instinctual self: that which is deeply personal and soulful. It is an intimate love bound by what is sacred to each partner.

Platonic – In Plato's *Symposium*, Eros plays a part in understanding beauty and spiritual truth; hence *platonic* has come to suggest a deep and blessed love.

Epithumia – The word *epithumia* refers to desire, passionate longing and lust, which are aspects of Eros but not the full spectrum of erotic love.

Agape suggests a selfless love. It articulates a universal love for others, a form of compassion or the love between God and man. Often it is described as the noblest word for love in the Greek language. It is altruistic; in personal relationships it is generous and sacrificing, deriving pleasure from giving to the other. Agape is love that is deeply concerned for the other: patient, forgiving and understanding. In Latin it is known as *caritas*.

Philia was honoured by the Greeks as the profound love of friendship and mateship. It is with our closest friends and allies that we can reveal the depths of our soul without judgement or shame. Philia suggests the love of companionship, loyalty and the honour of sacrifice for those we love dearly. Philia is mutual, a sharing as well as a receiving of love. It is sisterhood and brotherhood, as evoked in Philadelphia, the city of brotherly love.

Philautia referred to the love of the self. The Greeks knew one side of self-love as narcissism through their myth of Narcissus, the young boy who fell in love with his own reflection. However, the other face of self-love promotes the capacity to love more freely without inhibition.

Ludus – In Latin the word *ludus* referred to a game or play and when used in tandem with love it referred to its playful side, such as the affectionate teasing or flirting that is part of young love.

Storge is similar to friendship, a love based on familiarity, common interests and a commitment to relationship; a familial love or utilitarian relationship.

Pragma, the root of 'pragmatic', when used in the context of relationship suggests a long-standing love based on compromise and tolerance. Not necessarily romantic love, Pragma is practical, based on shared values and focused on common goals. It is the love that couples experience after many years of combining their resources, skills and talents to accomplish the tasks of the relationship.

Aspects: Planetary Relationships

All aspects are vital, but we could think of the conjunction and opposition as being essential in relationship astrology because they are representative of the harmonics 1 and 2. These harmonics underpin the foundation of all relationships, blending the images of union or oneness and separation or twoness.

Ptolemaic and Later Aspects

The five traditional aspects of astrology are known as the Ptolemaic aspects. These were based on either the triplicities, aspects which embraced the elements, or the quadruplicates, those based on modalities. Ptolemy used the analogy of aspects as harmonics, like the ratios of the musical scale. The Ptolemaic aspects are the five principal aspects of the conjunction (0°), the opposition (180°), the trine (120°), the square (90°) and the sextile (60°).

Johannes Kepler used harmonic theory to propose new aspects such as the quintile (72°), bi-quintile (144°) and sesquiquadrate (135°). Since then other astrologers, starting with William Lilly, have proposed many other aspects including the vigintile (18°), the semi-sextile (30°), semi-quintile or decile (36°), novile (40°), semi-square (45°), septile (51.43°), sesqui-quintile (108°) and quincunx (150°).

In this book I am using the five Ptolemaic aspects plus one of the modern aspects, the quincunx, as I have found this to be a significant aspect in relationships. Of the five Ptolemaic aspects the conjunction might be considered neutral, the square and opposition complex, and the sextile and trine advantageous. In modern astrology the squares and oppositions are often labelled challenging or difficult, while the trine and sextile are referred to as easy or flowing. However, the nature of the planets involved also needs to be considered. For instance, Jupiter and the Sun will glance at each other very differently than Saturn and the Sun. Their relationship, no matter what the aspect, will be informed by their archetypal compatibility; therefore it is wise not to be too judgemental about the nature of an aspect before it is considered and reflected upon.

The Quincunx – Recognition and Reconnection

The quincunx, along with the semi-sextile, belongs to the 12th harmonic family of aspects and it is also referred to as an inconjunct.

From its Latin roots, 'inconjunct' literally means without conjunction or not joining together; in other words, unconnected. In traditional astrology the quincunx was not recognized as being connected to the Ascendant–Descendant axis, unlike the five classical aspects. As aspects suggested a line of vision or being able to see the other, the quincunx reveals archetypal energies that may be unseen or misread by the other, or where the partner needs to take a different viewpoint to what is natural to them. Therefore a quincunx in relationship astrology suggests where our vision needs to be adjusted so we can see the other more clearly. Although the archetypal combination seems unfortunate or unfavourable, if we look at it from another perspective we may see an underlying affinity between the planets involved in this aspect.

Prioritizing Major, Minor and Orbs
With the number of aspects cited in modern astrology, it is best to have a reliable and logical approach to using them. Aspects can be differentiated between major and minor ones. How one applies an orb of influence is also very important as there are different points of view about this. What is most important is consistency, not rigidity, because each horoscope presents its own unique condition. Relationship astrology involves comparing and combining two natal horoscopes with their progressions and transits; therefore, the amount of information increases dramatically from when we consider the natal chart on its own. This makes it imperative to prioritize the aspects used and develop a way of evaluating which planetary aspects are most significant. I have found the semi- and sesquiquadrate to be noteworthy; however, in most case examples, I am using only the Ptolemaic aspects plus the quincunx in order to control the amount of information that is generated.

Aspect	Exact	Orb
Conjunction	0°	+/– 10°
Opposition	180°	+/– 10°
Trine	120°	+/– 8°
Square	90°	+/– 8°
Sextile	60°	+/– 6°
Quincunx	150°	+/– 5°

Interaspects are the key when considering a relationship between two individuals because they symbolize how each one looks at or regards this facet of their partner. Astrology demonstrates the synchrony between horoscopes through shared astrological signs and signatures. Let's start with an example to demonstrate how aspects are triggered by others in relationship astrology. Then we will describe the potential of the aspects to Venus and Mars.

Case Example – Whitney Houston and Bobby Brown

Whitney Houston had the Sun–Venus conjunction in Leo in the 6th house. This opposed Saturn in Aquarius in the 12th and all three planets squared Neptune in Scorpio in the 8th house.

An aspect pattern is forged when three or more planets are involved by aspect. In Whitney's case four planets form a T-square with Neptune as the apex of the pattern. The opposition of Venus to

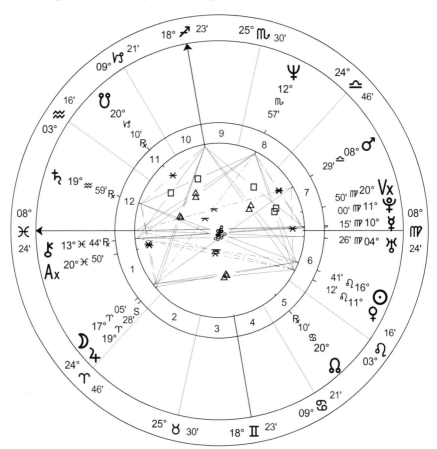

Whitney Houston, 9 August 1963, 8.55 p.m., Newark, NJ, USA

Saturn could be perceived as Whitney's vulnerability to authority and control, perhaps a self-critical perfectionist streak, or the potential for self-discipline and traditional values. Saturn square to Neptune challenges her ability to sustain firm boundaries and self-control. Neptune forming the square to Sun–Venus promotes creativity, enchantment and idealism. The Sun personifies father. He was a theatrical manager; therefore she was born into an atmosphere of drama and song, inheriting the solar appreciation of performance. Her relationship with her father reflected the archetypal gap between Neptune and Saturn, as it swung between her feeling adored and then rejected by him. As Venus is involved in these aspects the themes inherent in this aspect pattern will probably be encountered in Whitney's adult attachments and love relationships.

In an interview with Oprah Winfrey,[31] Houston described her complex relationship with her husband, Bobby Brown, as addictive

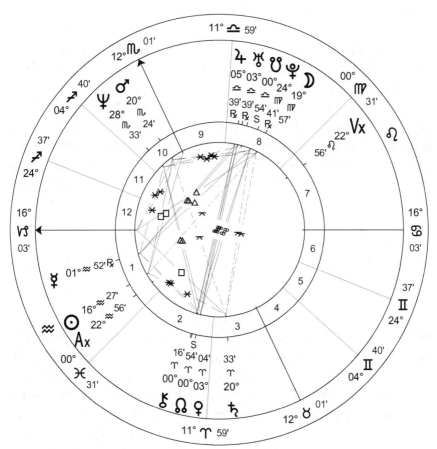

Bobby Brown, 5 February 1969, 5.21 a.m., Boston, MA, USA

and controlling, demonstrating the relational movement back and forth between the archetypes of Saturn (control) and Neptune (addiction). While the relationship started with passion, respect and shared creativity, it encompassed the themes of drugs, rejection and control, also evident in the aspect pattern. During the interview Whitney also described her popularity and fame as overpowering her relationship and disturbing Bobby, who responded with power and domination.

Bobby's Saturn in Aries controlled Whitney's buoyant and charismatic Moon–Jupiter conjunction. From an adult perspective her relationship with Bobby became the vehicle that exposed her conflicting needs and urges as reflected in the natal T-square. Synchronistically her Sun was exactly opposite her husband's, while her Neptune matched his Midheaven, creating enough overlap for the pattern to be ignited.

Bobby has a Jupiter–Uranus conjunction in Libra opposite Venus. Both freedom-loving planets are 'regarding' Venus, bringing the issues of travel, freedom, separation and abandonment to his relationships. Whitney's Mars in Libra inflames this opposition with passion and obsession.

How the other planets 'look at' Venus and Mars will be key aspects of adult attachment, especially in relationships where love, connection, desire and passion are aroused. When a planet makes a strong aspect to Venus or Mars[32] the themes of love and attachment become activated in adult relationships. Eros is activated in both the aspect and its archetypal resonance with Venus and Mars.[33]

The Look of Love: Aspects to Venus and Mars
Before we study the planetary engagements with Venus and Mars, let's imagine them in aspect with each other.

♀♂ Venus–Mars
When the two mythological lovers Venus and Mars aspect each other, there is a potent drive to express Eros whether that is creatively, sexually or personally. Creatively suggests the urge to beautify or be directed to the pleasure of performing or producing. The combination suggests magnetism which can be expressed through the personality, an art form or a relationship. It combines two fundamental forces of the human experience: the longing

to connect and the drive to be independent. This can range from passionate involvement through to ambivalence.

When expressed through relationship there is ample passion, pleasure and excitement. If this is a romantic relationship then this might lead to adventure and exploration on physical and emotional levels, suggesting a relationship where passion abounds. Sexual desire, devotion, jealousy and anger may feature in the relationship landscape. Venus and Mars play out the archetypal 'battle of the sexes' or in Jungian terminology the encounter between the anima and animus. Equally, this suggests delight at relating to the opposite, something foreign or not known. When the passion is uncontained or the relationship is unable to address its inherent conflicts, then there can be high drama, sometimes created though a third party. Wherever we find Venus, triangles are an option. In aspect to Mars, romantic triangles and affairs could be acted out when the relationship is no longer stimulating. Money can also be the other area of high drama in the relationship. Financial difficulty or conflict arises when the partners lose value in their relationship.

Note that in Whitney Houston's horoscope Venus in Leo is sextile Mars in Libra. In Bobby Brown's horoscope, both are in Mars-ruled signs: Venus in Aries forms a sesquiquadrate (135°) aspect with Mars in Scorpio. His Venus in Aries is opposite her Mars in Libra, revealing a strong mutual attraction between them; however this link also ignites their own creative passions held in their Venus–Mars aspects. It is Bobby's Venus or anima image that aspects Whitney's Mars, her masculine animus image, suggesting that the passionate attraction will awaken inner and soulful images for each of them. Both planets are in detriment so the aspect represents a challenge; nonetheless, it is highly charged and magnetic.

Planetary aspects to Venus and Mars are at the forefront of a relationship analysis. When either planet is in aspect to other inner planets, relational patterns will have been strongly influenced by familial and ancestral patterns and prejudices. In *The Family Legacy* we looked at these aspects from the perspective of the family. We will now summarize how these might be carried into adult relationships. Venus or Mars in aspect with social planets suggests that cultural and generational influences have shaped relationship attitudes. The outer planets aspecting Venus or Mars introduce new discoveries into the pattern of one's relationships.

☽♀ Moon–Venus

The two potent archetypes of the feminine are in dialogue here, suggesting that values from the family, including the likes and dislikes of the parents, are impressed upon the child. The Moon inclines towards dependency while Venus is more independent; therefore, relating swings between caring and loving, being public and private, and reacting subjectively and objectively. Sentiment and romance can become confused. Home and place are important parts of any relationship, as are family values and traditions which are different for each partner. The relationship with mother has influenced the pattern of relationship. For a male this might suggest being in a triangle with his partner and mother, or psychologically split between the image of mother and lover. Or it suggests a man loved by women, but how does the man respond to the demands of the partner? For a woman this might suggest the struggle between mothering her lover and feeling independent enough to care for herself.

☽♂ Moon–Mars

Active and passive principles become aligned in an uneasy combination here, which can express itself through fiery emotions or emotional conflicts. Mars is desire while the Moon is need; when these urges clash, the individual could go after what they don't need, or attack what is nurturing; a difficult combination for relating. This conflict between wanting to assert their desires but not hurt anyone can lead to passive-aggressive behaviour. This may have been experienced in the family where anger may have been equated with 'you do not love me'. For men this often suggests that the line between caring for someone and sexual feeling is blurred. Or anger about those we care for can be inappropriately expressed. For women, it can be learning to express what they want in an adult relationship and still feel loved. When harnessed, there is a supportive strength in the face of adversity. For both sexes the lunar emotions are heated up by Mars's passionate flames, leaving smouldering, moody and often erotic feelings exposed.

Let's look at another couple whose chart examples we will be using throughout the book – Brad Pitt and Angelina Jolie. Brad has a Moon–Venus conjunction in Capricorn. This aspect was literalized through the conflict between his wife and his mother over his mother's public stand on gay marriage.[34] This aspect symbolizes the tension between the roles of son and lover, father and husband, carer and partner; roles that may be on a collision course in intimate relationships. It might also describe a paradoxical need for closeness alongside an appreciation for autonomy that may become problematic in relationship.

Angelina Jolie has the Moon–Mars conjunction in Aries. Her parents divorced before her first Mars return and she continued to have an estranged and conflicting relationship with her father. Brad's Venus and Angelina's Mars each are conjunct their Moons, which suggests the probability that their familial patterns concerning love, care, desire and anger will be imported into their present relationship. As their relationship becomes more familiar and family-focused, volatile feelings from the past may surface. Interestingly, their Venuses oppose each other, while each Mars

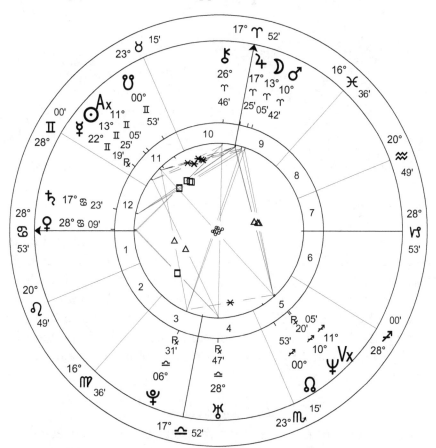

Angelina Jolie, 4 June 1975, 9.09 a.m., Los Angeles, CA, USA

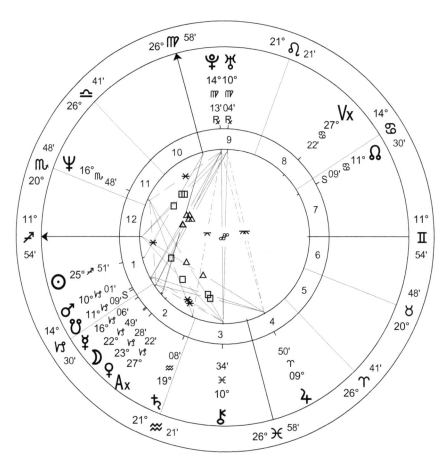

Brad Pitt, 18 December 1963, 6.31 a.m., Shawnee, OK, USA

forms a tight square with the other. Although an erotic link between them is highlighted, their values and desires are in conflict.

Angelina and Whitney share an optimistic Moon–Jupiter conjunction in Aries. As this aspect suggests, both experienced their mother as being dynamic, courageous and faithful, perhaps even regal. Brad was born in the same year as Whitney, twelve years earlier than Angelina. His Jupiter in Aries is more likely to 'fire up' Angelina's Moon–Jupiter unlike, as mentioned previously, Bobby's Saturn in Aries which restrains Whitney's Moon–Jupiter conjunction.

☉♀ Sun–Venus

Venus can only be 48° away from the Sun so aspects between these two are minimal. The possible aspects are the conjunction, semi-sextile and semi-square. Of these, the conjunction is the most potent and important. In terms of relationship patterning, the archetype of father is influential. Father's attitudes towards self-worth and his displays of affection and love will have been significant in the individual's development. The Sun shines its light on the area of relationship and wants to feel favoured and cherished in adult partnerships. With a Sun–Venus aspect, the pursuit of beauty, peace, pleasure and cooperation is significant in the context of relationship.

☉♂ Sun–Mars

When these two masculine archetypes combine, the roles of father and males in general are highlighted. Attitudes towards competition, adventure and risk-taking that were first modelled by father and other males in childhood are taken into adult relationships. Since the healthy expression of rivalry, confrontation, anger and sexuality are integral to the individual's vitality, it is essential that there is enough space in adult relationships to express these fiery emotions and still feel loved and supported. The partner needs to stand up to the confrontation and challenge. If not, the other may be quick to leave. This aspect implies courage against the odds and this nerve is applied when leaving abusive relationships or ones that are not equal, nor supportive. On the other hand, it is also the courage to take on an 'impossible' relationship.

☿♀ Mercury–Venus

Mercury and Venus are in a confined arc geocentrically; therefore, the most potent aspect to consider here is the conjunction. When Mercury is conjunct Venus there might be a sibling story surrounding relationships in the family history, such as an unrequited or unacceptable love, a love amongst kin or the legacy of love letters that remind us of the necessity to communicate love. How love is conveyed is important in relationship. Therefore, the need to express the language of love, share the sense of beauty or converse about shared values is fundamental to being in relationship. Companionship is at the heart of every relationship, whether that is sharing the love of the road, the fondness of literature or an opinionated debate. Trickster Mercury makes sure there are enough twists and turns to keep the relationship stimulating.

☿♂ Mercury–Mars

Attitudes towards rivalry, envy, anger and competition are shaped by the early interactions with siblings. If the familial background was argumentative the individual may have learned to be silent about their ideas or opinions. When a relationship is forged, these themes arise again; therefore, the way in which we express our personal thoughts and views in an adult context is important. As this aspect often synchronizes with an agile and alert mind, it seeks to be partnered. In order to feel met, it needs to feel free enough to be impatient, annoyed, even angry. In the context of relationship it needs to speak its mind, sometimes sharply, but mainly to communicate a desire to be connected. In partnership it may be the one to say what is not being said. And often what is not being said is obvious: 'Yes, there is an elephant in the room.'

♀♃ Venus–Jupiter

Venus–Jupiter aspects look at relationship from a cross-cultural perspective. Themes involving education, religion and race or social and economic standing are introduced into relationship. In relationship, spiritual values, the value of education and the search for meaning are central. This might literalize as a partner from a foreign country, different race, religious persuasion, financial standing or educational background. What is erotic is these cultural differences. The constant learning in relationship about the different ways of being in the world is exciting. The themes of education and religion, language and beliefs that are embedded in the relationship can either divide or bring the partners closer, depending on the depth of love and development of generosity in the partnership.

Jupiter is involved in the search for God, and in aspect to Venus this can become enmeshed with the search for a partner. Idealism might propel the individual into constantly searching for the ideal other. Or the belief in positivity and eternal optimism may lead to difficulty in accepting negative feelings in the relationship. Relating to another challenges and broadens the individual's belief system and lifestyle if they are willing to engage in and appreciate what is unfamiliar and foreign to them.

♂♃ Mars–Jupiter

Here, two potent masculine archetypes combine. Adventurers, competitors and trailblazers are images arising from this merger. There is a lot of energy to be channelled. All this dynamism can be focused physically through sports, exciting activities, travel or ambitious entrepreneurial pursuits. If not, it might seep out angrily. How anger, frustration and hyperactivity are conceptualized in the family forges how we react in adult relationship. Family myths might include taking the 'right action' or 'doing the right thing', setting a precedent by rationalizing or denying anger and ambition. This aspect is inflammable and prone to inflation, so it would be of interest to know how the family handled volatile emotions like desire and anger or the urge to compete and succeed, as these will influence adult relational patterns. The combination also indicates abundant desire for adventure and experimentation. This might manifest as being sexually adventurous and playful without commitment. Perhaps the urge for sexual and relational experimentation needs to be satiated before the urge to commit can be contemplated; hence there may be multiple liaisons before this energy can be focused on one relationship.

Both Brad and Angelina have a Mars–Jupiter aspect. Brad has Mars in Capricorn tightly square to Jupiter in Aries while Angelina has Jupiter conjunct Mars in Aries. Brad has a list of former relationships and a previous marriage. Angelina was also experimental in relationships, having been married but also sexually involved with male and female lovers. Angelina's Mars is within 1° of Brad's Jupiter, bringing adventure and altruism into their partnership; however, the mutual aspects also bring conflict in prioritizing the larger picture and what is important.

♀♄ Venus–Saturn

When the symbol of authority and conditionality looks at love, the combination might result in feeling unloved, not worthy of being loved or not attractive enough. What is 'enough' is strongly influenced by the prevailing conventions and attitudes towards love, affection, sexual and gender roles in early family life. Love may have been conditional, only shown when the rules were obeyed, creating a feeling of not being loved for self but for what one achieved. As the family folklore about the feminine may inhibit the development of self-worth, there may be a fear of intimacy or commitment in relationship. Issues around self-esteem, self-criticism and the demonstration of affection are brought into adult relationships. This can manifest as a lack of intimacy to extreme control in relating. But Saturn also governs time and it is over time, along with persistence and hard work, that relating becomes more comfortable as the sense of self-worth improves.

This archetypal combination suggests that issues of work, status, money, time, parental authority, rules, traditions and standards enter relationships. In early years, love and achievement may be enmeshed, but in adult life this alliance can unravel through a committed and supportive relationship. This arrangement echoes the Greek concept of *pragma*, a realistic love comfortable with the practical routines necessary to achieve a stable, long-lasting relationship.

♂♄ Mars–Saturn

The Martian impulse for an individual to be assertive and champion their desires can be restrained by Saturn. This aspect suggests that the individual's willpower may be dominated by an authority embodied as a parent, teacher or boss. However, the figure can also be internalized, manifesting as a critical voice that puts down any attempt to assert or go forward. While both archetypes can be autonomous, they conflict in the way they achieve their goals. Mars goes it alone in an independent way, while Saturn strives to find autonomy within the system. Individuality (Mars) and hierarchy (Saturn) conflict; therefore, clashes with authority figures may arise when the individual feels out of control. On the other hand, this combination becomes masterful when mentored and coached. How the father figures dealt with anger, violence, separations, work and control will impress the child with either a certainty or doubt about their own ability to control their desires.

Control, aggression and domination, which are often symptomatic of deeper fears of inadequacy and impotence, as well as shared goals and ambitions are potentially on the landscape of adult relationships. Mars is virility, courage and competition, and when chastised by Saturn, it can feel powerless and ineffectual, a recipe for rage. Adult relationships confront this pattern and those who love us give us permission to be assertive, to express our ambition and champion our desires. Note that Bobby Brown has Mars in its ruling sign of Scorpio exactly quincunx Saturn in its fall in Aries. Of the multiple offences he has been charged with, one is resisting arrest, a potent metaphor for this aspect. He also brought well publicized violence into his marriage with Whitney.

♀⚷ Venus–Chiron

When Venus is in aspect to the slower-moving planets, the erotic amalgamation of love and suffering becomes more evident. This planetary relationship combines the archetype of wounding and healing with love, probably first experienced through the family atmosphere. The attitudes towards love, beauty, sexuality and gender roles may have dishonoured the feminine in the family. For a woman, this may leave a scar of not feeling valued or being wounded by the envy of others. For a man, the mark of this aspect wounds his internal feminine, influencing the way he perceives women as the healer or the helpless.

Through adult relationships the re-engagement with this archetypal combination evokes the healing power of love. But love is not found in familiar places; it flourishes in non-traditional, foreign or marginal areas where the freedom to be outside the system places a value on differences and accepts peculiarities as soulful. Venus–Chiron energy can appreciate beauty where others cannot or can see beyond suffering into the soul. Therefore, there may be an attraction to the wounded artist, the suffering musician, the disenchanted therapist or the excommunicated cleric, all images of the capacity for love to prosper and relationships to develop beyond the system's constraints. In friendships and romantic relationships this combination evokes *philia*, the deep acceptance of the other.

♂⚷ Mars–Chiron

With Mars–Chiron, the impulse to act is tempered by the fear of being injured. This fear may have first emerged in the family where the parental messages associated spontaneity and risk-taking with being hurt. This punctures the child's natural curiosity and impulsiveness, leaving a scar on the development of willpower. Alternatively, the expression of anger and fighting in the family may leave the child feeling marginal to the family unit, aware that they are an outsider to the system. However the archetypal arrangement was experienced, it leaves its impression on adult relationships, because desires may be held back for fear of wounding the other. To no longer be identified as the injured one takes an act of courage.

In adult relationships this suggests repairing the split between what you desire and its harmful potential. Mars is the warrior and this aspect personifies the hero who was trained in the art of healing and warfare by Chiron. Rather than shying away from the inevitable conflict that arises in intimate relationships, healing occurs by participating with the instrument of wounding. For both men and women this also suggests the courage to be intimately involved with others who are marginal to the system.

♀♅ Venus–Uranus

A thread of unconventional women and/or relationships is woven through the family fabric; however, we do not know how this was valued or respected in the ancestral atmosphere. The family legacy of femininity, sexuality and attitudes to money and resources is unorthodox, but how this manifested and impacts adult relationships is what we need to consider. Forging adult relationships will awaken the themes of individuality versus togetherness as well as the dilemma of integrating the urge for the bizarre and the unusual into relationship. Uranus is mythologically personified as the disengaged sky god; therefore he brings his temperament of being distant and separate into relationship, generating the predicament of wanting to be in love versus wanting to be free.

Wherever we find Uranus we often find an 'oppositional disorder'; that is, the urge to know the self through rebellion or opposition. Therefore, expect the unexpected with Uranus; in relationships this often manifests as a sudden engagement or an abrupt break-up, neither one anticipated. Lovers may enter or exit in unusual ways at peculiar times. Often this can leave severed and incomplete feelings that are reawakened in subsequent relationships. Breaking with tradition often brings excitement and stimulation into the relationship, but at other times it may feel like a roller-coaster ride. Uranus tends towards *philia*, the love of friendship, whereas Venus desires *eros*; hence the task of an intimate relationship is moving between companionship and intimacy by making sure there is enough space, distance and freedom to do one's thing. With enough breathing room there is more space to move towards the other.

♂⛢ Mars–Uranus

Both archetypes are masculine in orientation, symbolizing the attitudes towards masculinity and male roles that were passed down through the family. The archetypal mixture is combustible, as both planets are combative and separating in their own ways. Both are quick and eager to get going, to taste the excitement and feel the adrenalin that risk-taking brings. However, living dangerously is not always so interesting to others who might prefer to be settled and have a routine. Therefore, Mars–Uranus individuals can have a dilemma in relationships as their urge for independence and excitement often collides with others who seek stability. As a result, Mars–Uranus individuals often live outside the box, involved in unconventional and non-traditional relationships, emotionally and sexually.

When the archetypes are well combined there is originality, brilliance and uniqueness; however, when the pair are dysfunctional there can be reckless and bizarre behaviour. There is often impatience coupled with a defiant will which is not always easy to accommodate in a relationship. Mars–Uranus is often cited as being accident-prone; however, this is more symptomatic of fixity and wilfulness. Mars is physical while Uranus is more cerebral. Both are focused on the future or what is possible, rather than what is. This anticipatory attitude, along with a highly charged nervous system, often keeps them from fully participating in the present, leaving their adult partners and companions feeling disconnected.

♀♆ Venus–Neptune

Neptune is often described as the 'higher octave' of Venus, while Venus is exalted in Pisces, the sign that Neptune rules. Astrologically there is already an interchange between the planets. They find their common ground in the sphere of love as Neptune aligns itself with universal love. Neptune is akin to *agape* and in its highest expression yearns to be selflessly dedicated to the partner's well-being. But Venus is not as altruistic; her domain is personal. *Eros* wants intimacy, connection, to feel met, not necessarily idealization and devotion. Therefore the urge towards divine and human love can become entangled, resulting in enmeshment, confusion, fantasy and disappointment. One partner might sacrifice what is valuable or be caught in a co-addictive pattern of constantly forgiving their partner's bad behaviour.

When Neptune's vast and somewhat abstract love is channelled through Venus, an individual may feel able to be impersonally compassionate and forgiving, yet overwhelmed by feelings on a personal level. Part of the overwhelming feeling is affected by fantasy, expectation, idealization and romantic notions, leaving the individual dreaming of an intimate relationship rather than actually experiencing one. However, when the two archetypes are creative together, the divine is made manifest through beauty, art and music. When the muse is unleashed it can bring compassion and consideration to the personal bond. The sharing of creativity and spirituality helps the archetypes find their balance in relationship. The urge to lose oneself in the other is strong; therefore this energy needs to find functional ways of expression. While it is difficult to refrain from giving and forgiving, this is part of the nature of relating. The task is to create a relationship where this is mutual and equal.

♂♆ Mars–Neptune

Mars is aligned with erotic love; Neptune with *agape*; hence this amalgam blends the force of personal will with the urge to be selfless and sacrificial. The outcome swings from being a compassionate warrior to an abused victim. Most experiences fall somewhere in between. In adult relationships the struggle might be between feeling sensitive and being strong, being sympathetic but not surrendering, or being receptive but not passive. Ironically, for this archetypal pairing strength is derived from vulnerability, understanding and sympathy. The family patterning of anger may have been to sacrifice it or forgive others in order to avoid confrontation, leaving the expression of anger in a childlike, immature state. This is confronted again in adult relationships when there is a disagreement or misunderstanding. Since Neptune erodes psychic boundaries there can be confusion between what the individual wants and what their partner wants, leaving them unsure about their own desires.

Having macho Mars in aspect to Neptune also suggests the confusion surrounding the masculine and the experience of being male. For a man, this confusion may focus on his sensitivity and receptivity, making him highly seductive and approachable, but inwardly unsure of himself and what he wants. For a woman, the masculine may be idealized, leading her into relationships which are ultimately disappointing. The cutting edge of Mars is eroded by the romantic and unrealistic images supplied by Neptune. For both sexes, sexual fantasy and romantic desire can align to offer the relationship a creative or spiritual sanctuary.

♀♇ Venus–Pluto

Venus and Pluto are both erotic by nature and the combination creates an intense coupling between the archetypes of power and love. In the family legacy the feminine narratives of sexuality and control, love and desire, beauty and power, influence the extent to which the individual is comfortable with adult relationships. Pluto is generally all or nothing; therefore, relating can be intense, passionate and transforming or cold, calculating and torturous. It is black or white, so you love intensely or hate intensely. The feeling life is forceful, often seductive and compelling. While love and trust are woven together through all relationships, with Venus–Pluto it is a dominant theme; therefore, strong feelings might be unleashed through jealousy, envy or betrayal.

The level of intimacy in relationship is dependent on the individual's level of self-worth, which has often been damaged through familial secrets or love denied. Therefore, there can be a tendency for the depth of passion and love to be expressed through affairs or relationships which do not demand a commitment. Intimacy issues might surface through the control tactic of withholding sex and money or through debt which keeps a couple bound together. However, the alchemy of the planetary mixture suggests that relationships are therapeutic and it is through sorrow and crisis that the individual finds their strength of self-love. There is often a fear of loss of the beloved and it is true that one day this will happen, but we never know when; so Venus–Pluto in relationships invites us to love genuinely and passionately in the face of loss.

♂♇ Mars–Pluto

This powerful combination alerts us to the relationship between the polar instincts of survival and death. By nature the combination is critical, suggesting that the power of life is often resurrected from an encounter with loss or death. Hence in early years this aspect often manifests as a compulsion to be triumphant or a drive to win in order to overpower the dread of loss. However, in later years when loss is inevitably confronted the individual finds an authentic power and strength in the participation with grief rather than its denial. When brought into adult relationships this ability to accept death allows more intimacy and authenticity.

As the traditional and modern rulers of Scorpio, both planets share an instinctual understanding of the underworld. In experiential terms this suggests the encounter with the taboo of what has been repressed and buried. It is the nature of Mars–Pluto to excavate this territory and flush it out to confront what is forbidden. In relationship this is often threatening, as the energy can often take a primitive or savage form, yet it is in facing this fear that life is renewed. Pluto invests Mars with power which needs to be used wisely and discriminately for the masculine to be therapeutic and transforming rather than controlling and dominating. The masculine sagas of competition and triumph, aggression and direction, fight or flight, are also important to consider in the context of relationship.

– CHAPTER 5 –
INHABITING RELATIONSHIP
Places Where We Meet

Astrologically, houses represent place, whether that be an outer location or an inner landscape. While the houses were moulded from the twelve signs, they differ in that they represent place, locale, environment and atmosphere, the 'where' of the life experience. The twelve houses of the horoscope reflect the ecosystem of our life; therefore, the horoscope is a manual of how we might learn to live in accordance with our environment by understanding the layered meaning of the houses. As we excavate the houses we discover a deeper resonance with the provinces of our lives, such as our personality, our talents, our language, our home, our creativity, our employment, the other, intimacy, meaning, vocation, community and spirituality. Each of these provinces has its own planetary rulerships and correspondences. When looking at the houses of the horoscope through the eyes of relationship we can differentiate many meeting places.

Places
A house is an archetypal symbol of shelter, a place to feel safe, at home. When we feel at home, we are grounded, centred and closer to the core of who we are. In dream imagery a house can represent different layers of the psyche from the exterior, suggesting the persona and outer appearance through to the basement, which is a symbol of the unconscious.[35] Similarly, each astrological house represents psychic layers, from the literal to the soulful experience.

The twelve houses are also where the planetary gods reside. For instance, the house where Venus resides is where we locate our personal values, likes and dislikes, our attitudes towards love and patterns of relationship. Mars's location signals the landscape of our desire, where we feel challenged, motivated, conflicted or threatened. The astrological houses are symbolic of our environment and where our urges, longings and goals are placed. On the deepest level they reveal the place where the archetypal longings of our lives find solace and meaningfulness.

As a dominant feature of the human experience we can expect to find different houses associated with the diversity of relationship. In *The Family Legacy* I focused on relationships with parents, siblings and extended family members as seen through the trinities of houses known as the Houses of Endings and the Houses of Relationship.[36] In this book I look in detail at the houses concerned with adult relationships: the 7th and 8th houses. These houses are placed in the interpersonal sphere of the horoscope (houses 1–4 being personal; 5–8 being interpersonal; 9–12 suggesting a transpersonal setting). The foundations of these houses are built on the personal and familial development of the 3rd and 4th houses. The 11th house is another important realm in adult relationships as it is the place of friendship. The four 'interpersonal' houses from 5–8 inclusive trace the development of adult relationships from the first love or love affair experienced outside the bounds of the family to an intimate relationship. In adult development, each house assists in developing the capacity to relate.

The Houses of Relationship: 3, 7 and 11
Underpinned by the element of Air, the Houses of Relationship are founded on mutuality, sharing, equality, exchange, communication, objectivity, openness and separateness. While the word 'separate' implies distance, the capacity to be independent and detached is essential in the formation of adult relationships, as it engenders consciousness, objectivity and individuality. Each of these houses locates important partnerships throughout life: the sibling, the spouse and the friend, witnesses to our course throughout life, but also reflectors of our self and our soul. In these houses we find our patterns, attitudes, phobias and preferences for relating.

Developing Relating Skills in the 3rd House
The 3rd house locates our early encounters with those who shared the environment, mainly siblings, but also other familial peers such as cousins, neighbourhood friends and schoolmates. For this reason the 3rd house is critical in developing relating skills, as it suggests how we encounter peer relationships and the impact this has upon subsequent relationships. We test the response from the world

through the reaction of our first peers, using them as mirrors to how we are received. Our encounter with our first social circle occurs in our 3rd house. Expectations we have of relationships, patterns repeated with our adult partners or even our choice of mate may be more influenced by the 3rd house sibling archetype than we realize. The sign on the cusp of this house, the ruler of and planets in the 3rd house illustrate the primary bond with our sibling or sibling surrogate, which contributes to the potential pattern that is brought into adult relationships.

Committing to Relationship in the 7th House

The 7th house was traditionally known as the house of marriage and questions pertaining to legalities and contracts. Marriage was viewed as a contractual relationship; therefore the ground of the 7th house was also pragmatic, arranged in some way. In traditional astrology the symbols of the 7th were utilized to profile the partner and the conditions of the relationship. In a contemporary context the 7th is viewed as the house of a committed relationship, whether or not the vows are sanctioned by an outer authority. From a modern perspective the 7th house not only characterizes the partner but the qualities that we are attracted to in our mates. These characteristics are often unobserved aspects of the self that the personality has not yet owned. However, the personality perceives them in someone else positively and negatively, hence the open enemy. Inhabiting our 7th house are our life partners, or at least an illustration of their qualities.

Meeting Kindred Spirits in the 11th House

The 11th house is the place in which we hope and wish for a better future, not only for us and our loved ones, but the world family. Friendship is one of the keynotes of this house and while we feel we have more choice in creating our friendships, we may discover leftover sibling rivalries or incomplete feelings with partners intruding on our adult relationships. The ideal of the 11th house is to participate and contribute to our community. Friendship helps to expand our boundaries, encourages growth and exploration. The relationships of the 11th house are forged outside the family circle, away from what has been familiar. These are our kindred spirits, bonded by spirit, not blood. In the 11th house we are citizens of a community, individuals in a collective and belonging to a larger family. The 11th house is the sphere of democracy; however, impinging upon its success is our trust in human relationships and our unconscious expectations of others. The houses of relationship mark the journey from fraternity to democracy, which come together in the 11th house.

Outer planet transits through these houses have a prolonged influence on our experience of relationship, as well as shaping the patterns of relating throughout our life. Their transits through these houses take considerable time; therefore they exert a strong influence on our equal relationship, especially when transiting these sectors early in life. In the progressed Moon's first cycle (0–27 years), its journey through these houses records the emotional effect and reaction to relationship. The progressed Moon's second cycle (27–55 years) through the horoscope remembers these earlier reactions.[37] Transits through these houses in adult life focus on relationship patterns, bringing more consciousness to bear on the experience of relating.

The Interpersonal Houses: *Myths of the Heart*
Included in this category are the 5th to 8th houses: this sequence of houses outlines a developmental process from self-love to intimacy, autonomy to interdependency. These houses track our psychological maturation and the formation of adult partnerships beyond the family system. As part of a developmental process each house locates important initiations in relationship, and the following myths contextualize these initiations.

The Fifth House: Narcissus and Echo
The cusps of all the Fire houses – 1, 5 and 9 – suggest a type of rebirth or initiation into a new phase of existence. The 5th house cusp is an intermediate zone between what is familiar and what is unknown. It is a metaphor for the dawn of discovery into the world beyond family. Our first experience of relating to someone outside familial territory is often passionate and exciting, at times upsetting and frightening. In traditional astrology Venus rejoiced in the 5th house, which is an appropriate image to begin our journey through the interpersonal houses.

In a developmental way the transition between the 4th and 5th houses separates the individual from the refuge of the family matrix.[38] This is the hero's emergence into the world to quest for his birthright. A common heroic motif is of exile. Similarly, the 5th house speaks of the separation from the primal place of belonging, home and family, so as to consciously continue with the larger task of individuating. A latter phase of the heroic motif is to return home, but first the hero must leave to claim the inheritance of his ancestry.

Our early relationships are often a means of self-reflection, not necessarily equal or committed. The partner is a catalyst to encourage the creative quest; hence the 5th house is branded as the sphere of 'love affairs'. A love affair exists outside another emotional attachment and/or is the reflection of the heroic part of the self attempting to emerge. In the 5th house, romance is not just a love affair but it also evokes the intensity of sexual love, being fascinated and inspirited with adventure. Romance is a story of love. Whether that is first love, heartbreak or an unrequited love, the terrain of the 5th house reveals how we create romance and write the scripts for our love stories. In the 5th house we discover our reflection through relating; however, the process is not yet equal. Love enters our lives and challenges us to leave the familiar, redirecting our emotional attachments away from the family. Relationship is focused on supporting or denying creativity and self-expression, and not always on equality. *Philautia* to the Greeks referred to the love of the self, and their myth of Narcissus considered its moral consequences.

The 5th house is where we develop self-love through our discovery of our differences from others. When the other is seen as separate from self, a healthy self-love can model and reflect back qualities we admire. But when the reflection is the vain admiration of the self to the exclusion of the other, this is narcissism. Keywords such as creativity and self-expression are founding principles of the 5th house. Herein lies our imagination and ingenuity that want to be shared. But to share our creative and original self, we need an audience. The word 'audience' stems from the Latin *audentia*, meaning a hearing, listening. The 5th house initiation suggests that in being heard we can internalize the audience as part of our self. In doing so, we are capable of admiring our specialness and that of the other. Perceiving the audience as being external perpetuates the myth of Narcissus or that our specialness needs to be reflected, not shared. Therefore it is interesting to me that the ancient mythmakers paired Narcissus with Echo, the image of being reflected but not heard.

Liriope was Narcissus's mother. When she became trapped in torrential flood waters, the river god took advantage and ravaged her. Because of the rape she fell pregnant, giving birth to a beautiful boy child named Narcissus. When he was young his mother consulted the seer, Tiresias, to ask if her son would live a long life. Tiresias suggested that Narcissus would live a long life only 'if he does not come to know himself'. But this fate was not to be. As an adolescent he became inflated with his own beauty. Being so enamoured with his own magnificence he was not interested in relationship; no other youth could inspire Narcissus's heart to love.

One day while hunting, Narcissus became lost in the woods where he encountered the nymph, Echo. Juno, the goddess of marriage, cursed Echo for her incessant chatter. Her punishment was that she could only repeat a portion of what had been said, rendering her unable to express her own self. When Echo saw the beautiful boy, she threw her arms around Narcissus. He became cold and unresponsive and cruelly rejected her: 'Away with these embraces! I would die before I would have you touch me!' But all Echo can reply is: 'I would have you touch me!' Rejected, she remained mesmerized by Narcissus, infatuated by the addictive power of his attractiveness.

Another spurned lover petitioned Nemesis, the goddess of divine retribution, pleading: 'May he too be unable to gain his loved one!'[39] The rest is mythological history: Narcissus finds the reflecting pool, falls in love with his own likeness and dies from the consuming fires of self-love. The myth details the devastating power of unrequited and unequal love. The 5th house locates the love we are able to express to others through our creative self. But if we cannot participate with others' projections, we risk remaining transfixed by our own reflections. The 5th house initiates us into the process of self-awareness through the internalization of our projections as well as contemplation of the images reflected back by others. It is up to us to monitor and become conscious of how we manage the reflections and projections placed upon us by others.

Planets in the 5th symbolize the natural ways in which we might leave home and confront the transfer of loyalties from our family to those outside our family. They characterize our creative talents, our urges that seek a response and our romantic and passionate narratives.

The Sixth House: Hestia and Hermes

The 6th house, while often referred to as a sphere of 'unequal' relationship, is where a more conscious process of self-reflection can occur. This sphere symbolizes the psychological processes that take place before we are ready consciously to enter an equal relationship. The daily rituals of the 6th create a coherent experience of the self that pave a way for sharing our daily life. The work and service of the 6th is directed to the maintenance of our well-being, which is strengthened through the process of self-reflection. This contributes to being conscious of our sense of self within relationship. Here, we are engaged in the sphere of the goddess Hestia.

The 6th house is Hestia's territory of sacred space where the focus is on our internal self. Of the three Olympian sisters, Hera, Hestia and Demeter, it was Hestia who was not violated by her brothers. Her threshold is sealed and within her precinct the focal fires of the self are kept sacred. Hestia is the image of the hearth and no god can move across her threshold unless invited. She personifies aspects of self that cannot be violated. She is the only one who does not get caught up in familial dramas and remains uncontaminated by the family bickering. One sister, Hera, is identified with her brother–husband Zeus, while the other sister, Demeter, is identified with her daughter, Persephone. Hestia is not identified through another family member, but with the internal core of her own self.

Hestia represents the focused tasks of day-to-day living. In her domain of the 6th house we filter what is exclusively personal from what is familial and collective. The process of discrimination is awakened and the boundaries between our private self and the other become conscious. Hestia is sacred space focused on the hearth. Around this hearth of our interior self gather the guests and ghosts that we welcome across our psychological threshold.[40]

The 6th house process of relationship development supports finding our inner core, exclusive of another. Like Hestia we may find our own hearth not violated by familial toxicity. Hestia's tradition brings the coals from the hearth of the mother to the new bride's home, honouring the legacy she is to bring into the marriage, reminding us that the 6th house is a preparation for union in the 7th.

Hermes is the guide of souls to the door of Hestia. He is the outer traveller; Hestia is the inner voyager. Hermes is the patron of the sibling, and in sharing our daily lives with siblings we learn to be private. In the 6th house we learn to honour our privacy in adult relationships. Sharing the daily rituals of preparing food, eating, cleaning and housekeeping influences our ability to differentiate successfully between our private and public selves. Similar to the 6th house connection between Hermes and Hestia, our siblings and/or our adult partners may be the guide to our interior world. Mercury (Hermes) rules both Gemini and Virgo, and therefore is associated with the 3rd and 6th house imagery.

Sibling themes are replayed in our adult day-to-day relationships with co-workers who inhabit this house. Relationships in the 6th are focused on work and those with whom we share our daily life. They also include those who serve us, such as our grocer, our doctor and our vet, or those we serve, such as our clients or patients. We learn the art of discrimination and boundary, and in a way the 6th house represents 'a kind of rehearsal for the relationships of equality we form in the 7th house.'[41]

The 6th house has many levels, including our urge for fitness and health and the integrative well-being of body and mind, the outer and the inner. While the 5th house is one of creativity and imagination, the 6th is one of craft and technique. In traditional astrology this is the house of disease, but from a contemporary perspective we strive to acknowledge and work within our limitations. The 6th house polishes, purifies and prepares the self.

The Seventh House: Hera and Zeus
Astrologically, this is the quintessential house of relationship and its process involves the experience of being with equals in committed and intimate ways. From the soul's point of view, this is the arena where mutuality, reciprocity and respect for individuality fashion a soulful relationship that embraces the uniqueness in each partner. Traditionally, the 7th house is the house of marriage. Today we understand this to mean a contractual, equal and committed relationship, whether or not it is sanctified by the Church or

legalized by the State. It also suggests our parents' marriage and the patterns of their partnership. As it is our first encounter with adult relationship, our parents' marriage has a profound impact on the way we respond to relationships in our adult years. Cultural and familial myths about marriage can pollute the atmosphere of the 7th house.

In Greek mythology Hera was the goddess of marriage, yet Hera's marriage to her brother Zeus would hardly qualify as a happy or peaceful union. They had heated arguments which often turned physical; with help, Hera tied Zeus up so tightly that he could not escape and had to be rescued. In retaliation, Zeus hung Hera from the rafters of heaven. Although Hera moaned in pain, she was not set free until she vowed to Zeus that she would never rebel against him again. Zeus was a womanizer and, while Hera did not resist, she sought her revenge with his lovers. And when Zeus fathered Athena, Hera evened the score by giving birth to Hephaestus. The ancient Greeks were not ones to romanticize marriage, and embedded in their myths were motifs of deceit and discord. The marriage partner was also the antagonist.

Horary tradition identified the 7th as the house of 'open enemies', differentiating these adversaries from the secret foes of the 12th. Since the 7th is observable from the querent's 1st house vantage point, the enemy was silhouetted against the 7th house background. While this may manifest as a literal individual, in a contemporary context the 7th house 'open enemy' is our own shadow material. The 'enemy' is differing or conflicting ideas, different values, uncomfortable personality traits, maybe the discordant beliefs of our partner. In a way we partner our problems, which is sometimes an apt description of the 7th house equal other. The open enemy could also be our unresolved rivalries, leftover anger or unfinished challenges with our siblings that rearrange themselves with current partners, who become the target for unresolved hostilities that siblings cannot confront with each other. In modern astrology the 7th house not only profiles the outer partner, but the inner one as well.[42]

The arrival of a partner is analogous to the birth of a sibling, who often ignites conflicted feelings of love and rivalry, fascination and anger, closeness and separateness. But this is the nature of intimate relationships. Astronomically, the 7th house is where the Sun prepares to set. It is twilight, when the light elongates the shadows and we prepare to meet the dark. Partners evoke a deeper stratum of psyche where unresolved and incomplete issues and patterns from previous relationships permeate the present. Whether these are from our own experience or those of our ancestors, myths of marriage are re-imagined and reworked though our relationships.

Marriage is a myth. In a contemporary context traditional marriage is dying or nearly dead; however, it is not marriage that has died but the institutionalization and organization of it. In the 2010s the support for gay marriage is an example. The people agree but the Church does not. Marriage is a vow, a contract and agreement between two people, whether that is socially sanctioned or not. It is part of the individuation process and a rite of passage which brings an individual in contact with the other and demands sacrifice, compromise and cooperation without the loss of one's self. This task becomes conscious in the 7th house.

The Eighth House: Eros and Psyche

In the 8th house we enter territory in which we risk exposing the deeper aspects of our self. We return to a mysterious sphere where love penetrates our strongest defences and we are rendered vulnerable, at risk of being betrayed or abandoned. The first time we were vulnerable and exposed to the powerful bond of love and betrayal was with our caretakers, the custodians of our 4th house. This realm of relating confronts us again with the possibility of the loss of the beloved.

The 8th is a burial ground where the ghosts of previously incomplete relationships may haunt us. Ancestral ghosts, the undertow of the parental marriage and the fragments from each partner's relational past continue living beneath the 8th house union. The 8th reconnects us back to the inherited 4th house family complexes that are ready to surface. The 8th house is where the resources of the family are shared with our equals, our partners and our sibling/s.

The 8th house evokes the *catabasis*, the journey into the underworld. One of the final labours of any heroic or heroine's journey was the descent into Hades's realm to retrieve an essential aspect of their past which bestowed on them the ability to move forward into life and relationships. Psyche's final task set by

Venus was to take back the beauty box that was in Persephone's possession. Persephone herself had been a young maiden abducted into the underworld. Now she was regent over this place, an equal to Hades, the lord of the territory. Her beauty box was iconic of her journey from abduction to equality. Through her journey to the underworld, and by retrieving the beauty box for Venus, Psyche was free to marry Eros, her beloved.

In the beginning Psyche was in an unconscious relationship with Eros, as she did not have permission to look at him. His mother, Venus, still haunted their relationship because he had not separated from her to be with Psyche. In not being permitted to fully know her lover, Psyche cannot completely participate in an authentic relationship and betrays Eros in an attempt to become aware of who he is. Ironically, betrayal allows Psyche to become conscious and know the truth of her marriage. The triangle formed between Psyche, Eros and Venus is reminiscent of 8th house triangles that defend intimacy. When betrayal breaks the triangulation, the truth is revealed. The descent begins and, along with it, the journey towards a more honest and authentic relationship.

The interpersonal houses describe the process of the development of relationship from the narcissistic experience of self-love through to the dynamic and moving experience of intimate love. These houses mark our departure from our family of origin to the place where we risk recreating the familial patterns once again in our own adult lives, within our relationships and our families of choice.

CHAPTER 6

THE SETTING PLACE
The Other Half's Horizon

In traditional astrology the 7th house cusp or the Descendant was known as the setting place, locating where the planets descended below the horizon and opened the gate to the night world. 'Setting' implies that they were transitioning from being seen to unseen. Opposite is the Ascendant where planets rise out of obscurity, surfacing into the light. As the Ascendant is the emergent self, the Descendant is associated with the dying self, metaphoric of what is mysterious and unknown. The Ascendant portrays the persona or mask we present to the world; therefore, we might think of the Descendant as the place where the mask is taken off and where awareness turns to the not-self, the other, focused on relationships rather than personality. As the setting place, the sign of the Descendant is evocative of unknown qualities in us that are often seen in the mirror of another. It is a soulful place because it is unknown, mysterious and focused on depth. As the western portal of the chart, the 7th house could be likened to the Hesperides of the horoscope. The Hesperides are the daughters of the evening when the dying light is at its most colourful. At twilight shadows are elongated and we are preparing to meet the dark. Here in this golden light that lasts only a short time we can see the shadow of the other.

The 7th house is the astrological site where individuality and relationship converge. Metaphorically, this place symbolizes the end of the light when the transition to night begins. What we can see is muted and not always as clear as we would like it to be. Yet in these shadowy images of the 7th house are likenesses of our own qualities. When its mystifying and shadowy nature is brought into intimate contact with another, a genuinely soulful relationship becomes possible. Like the Ascendant, the Descendant or 7th house demarcates a boundary between the upper and lower worlds, symbolized by polarities such as light and dark, known and unknown, inner and outer. At the cusp of the 7th house the horizon opens up a sphere of relationships. This is not the first house to engage us in relationships, but it is the house that supports equality and choice. The 7th house is where we encounter others who are different, yet familiar enough to complement what we sense is missing in ourselves. There is mutuality and reciprocity. Seventh house partners are not only marriage or life partners, but also business partners and others engaged in relating at this equal level of exchange. There is a sense of kinship, congeniality, familiarity, yet not from a system we have known previously.

'Partner' contains *part*, the sense of being separate – apart, yet also able to join together. Partners are no longer only muses to our creative being or a mirror for the self, but companions. In the 7th house narcissism is challenged and egocentricity is exposed. Without relinquishing our solar-centric view of self, we cannot participate in the fullness of relationship. Crossing the Descendant marks the halfway point in our journey and the relinquishing of our self-centric view of the world. The 7th house engages us in the act of cooperation and compromise and invites us to stretch ourselves into another's world view. Although this is the house of cooperation, conflict also arises when we relate to those who oppose our world view. With Venus as the natural custodian of the 7th house, our values and self-worth are examined and questioned when we encounter those whose values differ from ours.

Psychological astrology stresses the propensity to project the 7th house qualities on to the partner. All the while we remain unconscious of these energies, we assume they belong to someone else, generally the other. Projection, as Jung explained, is an unconscious mechanism; therefore the task is an eternal one. As we become more aware of qualities we disown, a greater facility to be authentic in relationship develops. The 7th house mystery is that what appears in our partners as being opposite and different from us is really a partial reflection of what is still unconscious within us. The partner of the 7th house stimulates us to reunite with these missing parts of ourselves.

The sign on the cusp of the 7th house represents important qualities; therefore it is often very prominent in our partner's horoscope. It is these attributes that we seek in our long-term partners, qualities that we need to be happy. The planets in the 7th house personify archetypal patterns constellated in the exchange between partners. Generally they are embodied in the partner before they can be consciously and successfully integrated into our own lives.

The Inner Partner

At the Descendant, both the visible outer and the invisible inner faces of the partner are constellated. What is invisible to a man is often his feminine face, and, to a woman, her masculine side. Jung named these two opposites the anima and animus respectively. He suggested that the anima/animus was balanced by the persona, the face turned towards the world. By nature the anima/animus is more deeply embedded in the psyche. As their images are brought to consciousness through the auspices of the other, shadow qualities are also drawn to the surface. The 7th house addresses both archetypes of shadow and anima/animus.

The Ascendant or persona is what is visibly rising in the world while the Descendant, the shadow, is what is setting. Intimate relationships confront who we appear to be, exposing foreign and submerged parts of our self; therefore 7th house partners awaken an awareness of deeper aspects of the self. When we encounter these submerged parts of our self (hopefully the 6th house has prepared us) our ego strength prevents us collapsing into the other or allowing them to live out these facets for us. This can happen when relationships are premature, or when we abdicate responsibility, bringing about a co-dependent relationship where the partner embodies what is necessary for us to complete. We can become 'hooked'. While we may be carried away by the enormous charge of released potentials within our own being, we may continue to let them live through someone else, rather than through ourselves. The partner then becomes inflated with our unlived 7th house potentials, which we eventually come to blame them for.

Planets in the 7th house have been used to literally describe the partner. For instance, if Saturn were in the 7th, the qualities used to describe the partner might include being cold, authoritative, controlling, disciplined and responsible. The partner may be described as being older, an expert or a mentor, along with the statement that we will probably marry later in life.

While this may be true, it is equally as true that these are unlived aspects of self. With Saturn in the 7th house, there may be incomplete issues regarding responsibility, authority and autonomy, which we unconsciously seek through our partners. With Jupiter in the 7th, the partner was described as a generous, optimistic adventurer, but psychologically this points to our innate wisdom projected onto others, hooking teachers, gurus and pseudo wise men.

The 7th house offers us the opportunity to meet these foreign aspects of self, both positive and negative, cloaked in the partner's persona. In the 7th, we begin to learn to tolerate differences. In experiencing the tension created by the polarity of opposites we realize some of our own unconscious behaviour. This is the arena where we are able to begin to objectify who we are by placing our self in someone else's shoes. This is the beginning of adult relating and commitment to exploration of the 'not self'. But as Carl Jung, born with the Sun on the Descendant, reminded us in his paper 'Marriage as a Psychological Relationship': 'Seldom or never does a marriage develop into an individual relationship smoothly or without crises.'[43]

Patterns of Relating
The Ascendant symbolizes birth and our emergence into the world; the Descendant symbolizes a rebirth into the world of the other. It is our readiness to relate. The qualities and energies of the 7th house are more prone to be experienced in early adulthood when the narcissism of adolescence subsides, creating more space to explore other facets of self in the context of a relationship. Our experiences of the parental marriage and other significant relationships make their mark upon the topography of the 7th house. Therefore 7th house planets may first be triggered in response to the dynamics of a significant relationship in our childhood environment. Before the formation of adult relationship, many patterns of relating are established, moulded by the parental marriage, the sibling system and early experience of close friendship.

Symbolically, adolescence emerges in the 5th house after the childhood of the 4th. By the time we reach the 7th house, we are ready for relationship after the experience of self-obsession. What passes for an adult relationship may still be a 5th house experience of loving in a narcissistic way. In the 7th we engage in an equal adult relationship that aids in the process of becoming whole.

A psychological cornerstone suggests that we recreate our parents' marriage in our own relationships. Unwittingly, the partner may be reminiscent of our opposite sex parent, or our relationships may echo some themes from our parents' marriage. Since the 7th house is where we encounter equal relationship, it may also be where the earlier patterns of relationship are constellated. Surely one of the foundations that the 7th house is built upon is the archaic pattern of relationship, not only from the parents, but also from the culture itself. This may be especially relevant if the Sun, Moon or Saturn is in the 7th or if the rulers of the MC or IC are placed here. Parental experience is linked with the experience of relationship; therefore the messages that we received about our parents' relationship will echo through the 7th house just as their intimate connection informs our 8th house.

The intention of the 7th house relationship is commitment, unlike the 'love affairs' or 'first love' of the 5th house. The commitment is generally ritualized through the act of living together, marriage, a contractual agreement or an engagement. This also marks the willingness to engage in adult responsibilities and prepare oneself for a deeper examination of the self. The Descendant is a sensitive angle with regard to transits or progressions when commitments to others take place. Transits and progressions to the 7th house synchronize with important developments in the sphere of equal relationships. It often is a time when outmoded patterns of relationship are revealed, constellating the need for change in our relationships.

The Astrology of the 7th House
Astrologically we can begin to interpret the 7th house through the sign on the Descendant. This sign is the gateway to relating. Since it is opposite the Ascendant, it is often experienced as foreign, as we are more inclined to live out the qualities of the Ascendant, leaving its polar characteristics at the Descendant to drift out into the world. Any denial of Ascendant qualities may also exaggerate the qualities of the Descendant. The Descendant sign is symbolic of qualities we are attracted to in others, perhaps still unaware that they are also part of ourselves. Therefore it is no surprise that the Descendant sign is often that of the Sun, Moon or one of the angles of our partner. If

not, then the partner often displays the qualities of that sign. The ruler of that sign also plays a role: if it is well aspected or supported in the chart, then the 7th house area may be more accessible, while a poorly aspected ruling planet may have difficulty in sustaining 7th house features such as commitment in the relationship, a feeling of equality in partnership or compromising and cooperating.

Planets in the 7th are archetypal patterns encountered in the process of relating. They may actually be visible traits that we are attracted to in others, only to find out later that they are untapped potential within our own self. They symbolize our attitudes to relating and the partner. These planets are often projected, but, once recognized as our own qualities, these energies become more available to us. Due to the nature of the 7th house this may not take place until well into our adult years. For instance, with Mars in the 7th house we may find ourselves drawn to enterprising, independent and active individuals. This prompts us to reflect on how we use our own Martian energy: how competitive are we willing to be? How do we assert our own needs? How do we express our anger? All these are potential issues that arise out of the arena of relationships once Mars is activated through the partner. However, Mars also addresses patterns and themes in relationship, such as competition, anger and independence.

More than one planet in the 7th house presents a complex picture of the psychic activity that may be stirred by the partner. Because of the intensity, the individual may become aware of one archetype at a time. For instance, Susan, a client with Saturn–Pluto in the 7th house, entered therapy because of her relationship difficulties. She described her husband, a school principal, as dominating and controlling. Through the therapeutic relationship she discovered her own dormant ambition and returned to the work force, having given up her career as a teacher when she married. However, she also discovered her erotic power and transferred these feelings onto the therapist. This is when I first met Susan. We were able to use her 7th house planets to imagine the process that was unfolding, and she could clearly see that she was projecting her Plutonic side onto the therapist in a similar manner to how she had projected her Saturnine features onto her husband.

Seventh house stelliums are complex by nature. One way to handle the complexity is to polarize the energy into the 1st house, mobilizing a strong sense of self that defends against relationship and intimacy. Another is to work through the complex slowly, unravelling one planetary archetype at a time. Often different relationships embody these differing themes. Like Susan, we can often see each planet in the 7th house as being personified by different partners or the different facets of one partner.

When there are no planets in the 7th house, then the sign on the Descendant and its ruler provide information regarding this area of our lives. This certainly does not lessen the impact of the partner, but perhaps it does suggest that the archetypal patterns may not be as potent. If there are no planets in the 7th house but there are planets in the 8th house, the process of establishing a relationship may be sacrificed for the passion and drama of relationship. In other words, the 'getting to know you' phase is relinquished for the impact that intense emotional bonding brings. In these instances the relationship does not have anything to fall back on and may deconstruct as quickly as it began. Planets in the 7th develop footholds for the relationship; therefore, it is wise to allow time for relationship.

Seventh house planets which are not integrated are often uncontained and undeveloped in other areas of our life. For instance, an individual with Mars in the 7th house may appear overly aggressive or highly competitive in other areas of life, yet in their relationship they are submissive and directionless. In the presence of their partner, Mars is inaccessible, as it has been surrendered to the partner. Outside the territory of the partner Mars pours out of its container, often in an uncontrolled or compulsive fashion. The individual is out of touch with the repercussions of their behaviour and oblivious to how they are using this energy.

In a synastry workshop the students and I had a clear example of this. Throughout the weekend one of the participants had been totally uncontained verbally. She interrupted, talked incessantly and had an example for everything that was presented in the teaching. My efforts to contain her were mostly unsuccessful and we continued on with the endless interruptions. It was also clear that she did not recognize the frustrated reactions to her behaviour. Each time she spoke, the group became agitated and restless. When exploring 7th house planets, she declared 'I have Mercury in the 7th house.' The group tensed once again. She continued, 'And my husband thinks he's so intelligent, I can't get a word in edgewise.' The group fell silent, mistrusting what they had heard. As the story unfolded, we found out that she was extremely intimidated by her husband's ideas, intelligence and knowledge. He was a university professor and clearly her Mercury was lived out through him, leaving her own Mercurial process disorganized and disconnected. Unable to move past the shadowy aspects projected onto her partner, her Mercurial function remained virtually split off from her personality, leaving it to unconsciously act out in other areas of her life. A group discussion assisted her to see the unconscious process that she was engaged in. She withdrew into a sombre and reflective mood.

Projecting our 7th house planets excludes them from the rest of our life. They have no animation or character because that is being lived out through the partner. When we meet an individual outside their relationship, at work, study or a social group, and then experience them with their partner we are often surprised by the change in their personality. We are often shocked to realize that the gregarious individual is quieter when their partner accompanies them or the carefree, extroverted friend becomes concerned and timid in the atmosphere of their partner.

An interception in the 7th house adds another layer to the relationship. The intercepted sign symbolizes other qualities that emerge through the process of the relationship and these are often at odds with what has already presented itself. An interception also disturbs the connection between the Descendant and the 8th house cusp that is so important in the development of the relationship. While the Descendant describes the qualities that attract us, the 8th house cusp represents our way of establishing emotional closeness and intimacy. When Fire is on the Descendant, then Earth is on the cusp of the 8th, and so on. In the natural wheel the transition to the 8th is always at odds with the visible qualities of the 7th. With an interception, this will not be so and some of the issues arising in the 7th house may delay the 8th house process of establishing emotional closeness and intimacy.

Because the delineation of 7th house placements depends a great deal on whether we are projecting these qualities or beginning to marry and integrate them into our self, it is helpful to look at the phenomenon of projection and how this pertains to the 7th house. It is most probable that in our early adult life we are still getting to know the complexity of who we are through this process of projection.

Projection

Projection is the mechanism that illuminates unconscious qualities or characteristics of our selves through the process of perceiving and reacting to them in another person. Projection is common. As a defence mechanism it attributes feelings, emotions, thoughts and behaviour onto others or objects in order to defend our unconscious impulses or desires that are still inadmissible or unacceptable. When aspects of the self are disowned, they can be projected onto the world; therefore, when used as a constructive process, projection is a method of becoming more self-aware.

Projected qualities or attitudes can be either positive or negative. For instance, we may be in denial about some creative aspect of self and project this unlived potential onto those living out their creativity. If this becomes entrenched, the person carrying the projection can become the scapegoat for our inadequacies. We blame others for what we cannot tolerate in ourselves. Qualities that are unconscious distort our perception; therefore, the more unconscious our motivations or urges, the more exaggerated the projection becomes. The view is filtered through a distorted lens regulated by the ego that feels threatened if these urges are permitted into conscious perspective. When others constantly display exaggerated characteristics and we are strongly reactive, this becomes an opportunity for reflection on the projection. We recognize projection when there is a continuing pattern of emotional reactions to exaggerated characteristics in others. Constantly blaming others or situations is also a signal that we may be projecting because we are unwilling to recognize our part in the process. The unconscious is constantly projecting so it is psychologically naive to imagine that there is an end to this process; however, the awareness of projection allows us more space in a relationship to truly be ourselves.

The following diagram shows how projection operates. Our attitude A is unknown to us and we have no direct access to it; however, this characteristic becomes conscious through its reflection AOX by the other person who demonstrates a similar quality. When we become conscious of the attitude X, we are inclined to perceive this as being part of the other person, A1, not part of us, A. Most often the other person has similar attributes to the unlived aspect of our nature, so it is easy to 'hook' the blame or projection onto them. Consciousness develops as we recognize our own unconscious attitude A and begin to withdraw its projection. When we start to own these qualities the other individual becomes less distorted by these projections that emanate from our own unconscious perspective.

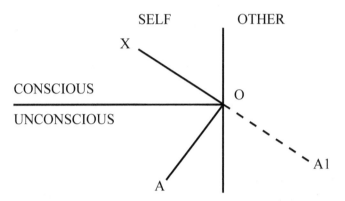

In a natal horoscope, projection occurs throughout the horoscope. Houses are the psychological arenas where projection occurs. Since the houses differentiate where we locate others (siblings, the 3rd; children, the 5th; workmates, the 6th; partners, the 7th, etc.), planets in houses or the rulers of the houses are prone to projection. The house placement gives us the clue as to who might hook these projections. Projection is a process akin to Air; therefore, the houses of relationship (the 3rd, 7th and 11th houses) are areas where projection is prevalent. The houses of relationship are territories where consciousness can surface because of another. In relationships, projections onto the partner are clearly indicated by planets in the 7th house and qualities associated with the sign on the 7th house cusp.

   Projection with partners generally has recognizable phases. We can classify the process of 7th house projection into three stages.[44] First is the numinous stage: the bright side of the archetype is embodied in the individual to whom we are attracted. The qualities shine and we are in awe. When we first experience the quality we are projecting, it is magical and vivid. Since it is still unconscious, the planetary energy is exaggerated or idealized and has an archetypal potency, hence it feels transcendent, perhaps divine. For instance, we may first meet the 7th house Mercury as the brilliant and witty genius; Saturn, the success story; or Pluto, the magnetic and intriguing therapist. If the Sun were projected onto your partner you would first experience them as being magnetic, confident, warm and creative. In fact, you may never have met a person with whom you were so enchanted, who was so vital and original. The first phase is marked by enchantment, fascination and the attribution of special qualities to the individual.

Next is the waning stage: the very qualities that were once mesmerizing are now annoying and uncomfortable. The negative undercurrents of the qualities that were irresistible are beginning to surface, as the shadow of the archetype becomes unleashed through relating. Qualities once divine now seem demonic; the contrast is striking. At this stage the projection can be recognized through our disappointments, emotional reactions and blame. As the shadow side of the projected complex begins to emerge, the Mercurial projection is now seen as someone who knows it all. You are complaining that you can't get a word in edgewise because the person never draws a breath. Mercury has become superficial and noncommittal; Saturn is now patronizing and cold; while nowadays Pluto is obsessive and controlling. And the solar person, once so charismatic and productive, has become egotistical, arrogant and self-serving. The 7th house planets reveal both sides of the archetype through the same partner. While integration of the presenting shadow material is possible, regression may occur by choosing another partner with whom the magical first stage can be re-experienced.

The last stage holds the tension between the opposite sides of the archetype, which we come to recognize as aspects of ourselves. The integrative process begins when we acknowledge these qualities in our self. We struggle to balance the bright and dark aspects of this complex, both in our self and in our partner. For instance, with the projected Mercury, we begin to challenge the partner's ideas, to form our own opinions and communicate more confidently. Our own Saturn becomes more authoritative, disciplined and directive. And the Pluto in us respects its own power, depth and intensity. And when we begin to claim more of our own solar potential we make contact with our own creativity and self-expression. This stage is characterized by confrontation, a struggling towards equality and greater self-reflection.

Reclaiming some of the projections we have cast onto the partner helps to release authentic aspects of ourselves. It strengthens the relationship; however, it is possible that we painfully discover we have inflated another's character through our own projections. Reclaiming our projections creates a psychic disturbance because dynamics in the psychological relationship are changing; when one partner changes, anxiety is unleashed in the other. When we withdraw projections we also leave behind our idealization of the partner, so they often feel cold and unsupported. In actuality, they too are ready to develop in a more authentic way.

Following are some examples of what we may give away in relationships based on qualities represented by the sign on the cusp of the 7th house, the Descendant. Remember that the individual may have become cognizant of his or her projections and the pattern of attracting these energies may have lessened. The individual is then freer to claim the potential of the planet or sign for themselves rather than living it through others. As projection is often exaggerated, what we are attracted to may be distorted if we are in the grip of a projected quality. The following table is a simple way to introduce the profound dynamic of projection in an intimate relationship.

Projection in Relationship: Sign Scenarios

Sign Projected	First Stage Idealization	Second Stage Denigration	Third Stage Integration
The sign on the Descendant	Qualities in others that attract us	Shadows emerge as the projection weakens	What I need to recognize about myself
♈	Assertiveness, directness, independence, courage, entrepreneurial skills, being confrontational, self-reliant and a self-starter.	Selfish, arrogant, angry, volatile, weak, cowardly, unwilling to cooperate or share, taking flight from intimacy and relating.	My need to be independent and assertive. My desire to be adventurous and risk-taking. To be myself and follow my own choices.
♉	Easy-going, a love of comfort, pleasure and beauty, simplicity, resourcefulness, capability and generosity.	Lazy, dull, stubborn and unwilling to shift, a 'couch potato', materialistic, possessive and fixated on money and belongings.	My need for self-esteem and personal worth. To appreciate beauty, to value stability and security. To be worthy of love.
♊	Fun, light-hearted, variety of interests, good sense of humour, a wide spectrum of ideas and knowledge, good conversationalist.	Avoiding anything serious, superficial, contradictory, trickster, changeability of beliefs, lack of commitment.	My need for variety in my life. To be free enough to change my ideas and express myself in different ways.

♋	Unconditional, caring, nurturing, feeling safe and protected, security of emotional expression and kindness.	Moody, heightened sensitivity to feelings, being hurt, sulking, pouting, hanging on and dependency.	My need to nurture myself and develop emotional security. To feel I belong and am accepted for just being myself.
♌	Confidence, excitement, magnetism, big-hearted, vibrant, bright and warm, and centre of attention.	A star, a show-off, demanding and seeking attention, narcissistic, big ideals and a big mouth.	My need to express myself creatively and confidently. To be proud of who I am and what I create.
♍	Practicality, urge to serve, thoughtfulness, work ethic, order and coherence, privacy, neatness and an analytical approach.	A perfectionist, a critic, a workaholic, an inability to let go, splitting hairs and being picky, a nag and a pessimist.	My need to create order and continuity in my life, to be purposeful and contribute to others' well-being.
♎	Equality, romantic, charming, artistic, cooperative, caring and peaceful.	Indecisive, not able to take a stand, moody, selfish, rude, detached, peace-at-any-price attitude.	My need to be peaceful, equal and appreciated in relationship. To value my own imbalances.

♏	Intensity, passion, honesty, trustworthiness, emotional strength, charisma, in-depth understanding.	Power plays, emotionally controlling, possessive and jealous, secretive, suspicious, withdrawn and emotionally cold.	My need to be emotionally open, honest and intimate with others. To be met on the deepest level in relationship.
♐	Optimism, faith, wisdom, worldly-wise, visionary, uplifting, optimistic, convincing and a broad base of understanding.	Know-it-all – the guru, opinionated, dogmatic, spiritual short-sightedness, manic behaviour and restlessness.	My need to know and develop my own set of beliefs. To question and search for truth in all my relationships.
♑	Security, predictability, committed and dutiful, reliable, patient, fatherly, protective and organized.	Patronizing, dominating, stern and cold, work before play, controlling and autocratic.	My need to own my own authority and seek my own counsel. To acknowledge my ambition and goals.
♒	Unique, futuristic, open to change and new ideas, alternative, stimulating, inspiring, independent and friendly.	Ungrounded, detached, overly independent, individualistic, chaotic, rebellious and politically militant.	My need to be unique and independent and live more alternatively. To be an individual and feel free in all relationships.

♓	Gentle, loving, sensitive, selfless, compassionate, giving, spiritually attuned, artistic and creative.	Overly sensitive, confused, vague, self-victimization, caring for everyone else but me.	To feel magic and creativity in all relationships. To pursue spirituality and creativity.

It is important to remind ourselves that projection is an unconscious process designed to protect the ego from uncomfortable psychic qualities, whether positive or negative. As we begin to recognize these as our own qualities, we empower our self with their unlived potential. Carl Jung pointed out that it was the unconscious that projects, not the individual; therefore, reclaiming projections is a conscious act. It also is an ongoing process because the unconscious is continually projecting.

– CHAPTER 7 –
THROUGH THE LOOKING GLASS
Delineating the Descendant

No matter how we conceptualize our life partner, whether it is the significant other, a committed companion, the soulmate or our spouse, their image hovers over the threshold of our Descendant. Our 'other half' is an image embedded in the horizon since birth. As the sign opposite your Ascendant it complements your personality, like another half of the self available as you step through the looking glass into the shape-shifting world of relationship. This other half is often more recognizable in others than in yourself. Sometimes you want to embrace it, sometimes reject it; certainly the qualities that you find both appealing and annoying are symbolized by the reflection. The sign on the 7th house cusp is often prominent in your partner's horoscope, but whether you marry or divorce, your 7th house is essentially always a part of who you are. For example, in Brad Pitt's horoscope Gemini is on the cusp of the 7th house, which is Angelina's Sun sign. Angelina has Capricorn descending and Brad has four planets, including the Moon and Venus, in Capricorn. Angelina's Sun is conjunct Brad's Descendant while Brad's Moon is conjunct Angelina's Descendant. In the horoscopes of Whitney and Bobby, similar interchanges occur. Whitney's 7th house cusp is Virgo and Bobby has the Moon in Virgo; Bobby has Cancer on the Descendant, and Cancer is the sign of Whitney's North Node.

In the 7th we enter into the mystery of relating. What we are attracted to appears to be opposite and different; yet it is also the partial reflection of what is not yet conscious in us. The 7th house is an amalgam of what is seen and what is in shadow. We sense kinship, congeniality and familiarity with our 7th house partners, yet these feelings do not arise from a conscious memory.

Our partners are our companions, kindred spirits and intimate others. Human nature inclines towards styling our partners from the clay of our own unresolved patterns and complexes. The materials we use for this are our own projections, fantasies and ideals, as well as earlier patterns of relationship that we have internalized from our parents and siblings. The 7th house is an area of equality; therefore, our partners will share in our characteristics and qualities. Not only a house of union, the 7th house is also one of separateness and individuality. Rainer Maria Rilke, who wrote eloquently of love and relationship, could have been referring to the 7th house when he wrote 'two solitudes protect and border and greet each other'.[45] In this place a partnership is created between separate individuals who are equals.

Signs of the Partner: On the Cusp of the 7th
Here are general descriptions of Descendant signs. They are not intended to profile the partner, but to actively imagine the qualities in us that respond to the other. Along the floor of the Ascendant–Descendant axis, a dance happens between our ascending personality and the setting qualities of the self held by our partners. This axis plays an important role in relationship astrology as it so often intersects with the partner's horoscope in significant places. By reflecting on your own Descendant you can become more conscious of underlying patterns which allow you to be less focused on the past and more anchored in the present. The 7th house qualities may seem to be at odds with your ascending personality, but in reality they are companionable characteristics of your own nature.

Aries Descendant (Libra Rising)
Qualities that attract you to others include assertiveness, directness, independence, courage, fearlessness and self-reliance. You may first respond to the other's vitality and outspokenness, but if these qualities remain projected, then the free-spirited, courageous entrepreneur you admire will eventually reveal his or her wilful, uncommitted, self-centred side. Through light and shadow Aries on the 7th draws you into a relationship that helps you to be more daring and take more risks, encouraging you to assert your values and desires.

Relationships teach you that your independence and fiery spirit are at risk when trying to please others; therefore, being yourself in all encounters is the key. While it is natural for you to support others' aspirations and goals, your partners teach you about your own will and desire and how to assert yourself in the face of adversity.

Metaphorically, you marry your own courage and conviction. Your natural tendency is to be spontaneous, engaging in relationship quickly with verve and dynamism, but you find the fires die down quickly if there is commitment but no freedom to explore and take risks. Therefore you need to be in relationship with those who are able to accept and meet your need to be your own person.

Taurus Descendant (Scorpio Rising)

What you are first attracted to in others may be personified through their patience and reliability. You are warmed by their determination, heartened by their ability to be on time, charmed by their generosity and comforted by their ability to savour the good things in life. Wanting to be balanced by a stable and grounding partner, you are attracted to those who can support your life but who are also self-contained and resourceful. When the placid, security-loving financier proves to be possessive and inflexible, projection is apparent. If what was once pleasurable now feels self-indulgent, or what you first felt offered you permanence now feels tedious, then you are invited to reflect on your own relationship to security, assets and resources.

Physicality, sensuality, affection and pleasure are important elements of an enduring relationship. Relationships teach you to discriminate between 'mine' and 'yours', because sharing resources could become an area of conflict. How you manage to exchange resources is directly proportional to how bonded and trusting you feel in the relationship. Your ability to share what you have and your ability to be intimate are entwined. Ironically, once you find your own inner rock of stability you are free to enjoy a variety of relationships and friendships.

Gemini Descendant (Sagittarius Rising)

Youthfulness, versatility or the way someone makes you laugh when they mimic your friends or tell a joke is very appealing. You are drawn to those who win your attention or make you think about things. Adaptability, communication skills, wit and fun are qualities you admire. Through relationship you find meaning and your own intellectual and storytelling talents begin to emerge. But most importantly you find the ability to navigate duality by being separate and in relationship.

You might be comfortable with the idea of equality, sharing and the theory of relatedness, but not as relaxed in the sphere of intimacy and emotional constancy. It is natural for you to experiment with a range of possibilities in any relationship, because you like to satisfy your curiosity and inquisitiveness. You need a great amount of space, emotionally, physically and psychologically, before you are comfortable enough to 'settle down' or undertake commitment. Qualities you admire and are attracted to in others, such as intellect, communication and adaptability, are the very qualities that a partner helps you to find in yourself. You meet others who help you to find the missing pieces of your theories. Through interacting with others' beliefs and concepts, you are better able to know your own narrative.

Cancer Descendant (Capricorn Rising)

Your own sensitivity, nurturing qualities and family patterns are part of the fabric of relating. You respond to others who are emotional and warm-hearted, protective of their loved ones, but also sympathetic and responsive to your needs. When the shadows emerge, what once felt protective may now feel smothering and troublesome, or what once was sensitivity is now anxiety. Care could be misread as love, and concern mistaken for passion. Emotional inequality is enormously painful, yet sometimes necessary for you to learn the difficult task of separateness and discrimination with others. Your relationship with your mother, other family members and the childhood pattern of love and care present themselves again in adult relationships.

Tenderness, kindness, caring, nurturing and emotional expression are attractive qualities. Once you bond with a mate you would like it to be for keeps, perhaps with all the traditions that come with family life. Through your relationships you learn not to be so tough on yourself and find a place to belong. Relationships help to instil an inner sense of security so you feel anchored in the world.

Leo Descendant (Aquarius Rising)

What you are first attracted to in others is their flair and positive outlook, their playfulness and fascination with their own creativity. You admire the way they are able to be spontaneous, charming, broad-minded and expansive. The shadow of these qualities is damaging to relationship if it is only focused on the self, not the other. When the talented, fun-loving actor you once admired becomes egocentric and arrogant, projection reveals the necessity to become more self-focused and have confidence in your own creativity and self-expression.

Leo on the 7th suggests that you know to impassion your relationship when it becomes dull. Your natural tendency might be to wear your heart on your sleeve or become weary and disinterested when the initial glow fades. Therefore you need to be in relationship with someone who is able to draw out your spontaneity, creativity and inner child, who can equal your passion and enthusiasm for life. Being attracted to the confident and creative qualities in others helps you to become connected to your own unique talents. It is important that you do not get stuck being the admirer of others' talents and skills, but that you are inspired to discover your own. Others will help you to find your own creative flair as well as the urge to improve and work with it.

Virgo Descendant (Pisces Rising)

Qualities you admire in others include modesty, self-control, work ethics and an awareness of well-being. Because the ability to be practical and centred is appealing, you are attracted to those who help you become more focused, but when shadows emerge the partner may seem overly critical rather than one who accepts your imperfections. Ritual and routine are important in relationship, as you like to share the daily tasks with your partner. At the end of each day your partner can help you to debrief and make sense of what happened. Partners listen, attend and help you to empty out the residue of the day.

Adult relationships invite you to explore the intermediate space between your own private world and the inner world of others. Through relationships you learn the art of discrimination and how to order the chaos that arises in your life. Relating and communicating with others helps to prioritize what is important. Even though you are sensitive to the criticism of others they are never as critical as you are with yourself. What first attracts you to someone is their diligence and focus. You feel drawn to their modesty, sensing that there is much more beneath what is visible. That hint of sensuality and the allure of unavailability attract you.

Libra Descendant (Aries Rising)

What you are first attracted to in others is sophistication and their easy-going charm and sociability. Probably you are attracted to the romantic ideal, a hint of fantasy and the idyll of tender passion. While you may attract these qualities, you could also unearth their shadow, so the charming socialite becomes self-centred, not you-centred as you first thought. Underneath the urbane chic might be a lack of refinement or rudeness. Eventually you are drawn into a relationship that helps you to find a balance in life, someone with whom you can share both your heavenly and devilish sides.

Your ideal of relationship is very familiar to you, but the reality of commitment can be very foreign. Like other Air signs, you need space and distance in any close partnership. Qualities you admire and are attracted to in others include fairness, diplomacy, the appreciation of aesthetics and art as well as the ability to relate. Venus, in her heavenly face, rules your Descendant, so it is important to integrate the spiritual and platonic aspects of relationship with the mundane and erotic.

Scorpio Descendant (Taurus Rising)

Attracted to what is intense, you are drawn to the force of character, depth of emotion and passion of others; something mysterious, unknown, even dark, draws you towards the other. But the felt experience of white-hot passion can chill to an icy frost when you feel unmet or deceived. You may be torn between the excitement of passion and jealousy, the intensity of closeness and the possessiveness that follows. But through light and shadow, relationships help you to understand the complexity of feelings, the depth of union and the possibility of intimacy. Scorpio on this house cusp brings your intense, complex, even negative feelings to the surface of your relationships.

Qualities of honesty, integrity and intensity in others are attractive; therefore, you are suited to partners who relate profoundly and passionately. You want to be deeply engaged, but not possessed. Being attracted to the therapeutic aspects in others, you yearn to create a sacred place for your relationship to mature and transform. You are able to create something in a partnership far greater than you or the other could do on your own; therefore to be in a relationship where you know you are honoured as a valued equal allows a deep renewal of resources to take place.

Sagittarius Descendant (Gemini Rising)

An independent, freedom-loving optimist who inspires you to see the larger picture is very appealing. Someone who can make sense of all your ideas, who is honest and inspires hope is very attractive. But often behind the wise teacher lies dogma and prejudice that need to be confronted. Therefore, while you might meet a lot of wise ones in your life, you encounter a lot of know-it-all's as well. Sagittarius on the 7th draws you into a relationship that inspires you to cross many borders, move further afield and see a wider horizon to life; therefore it is quite possible that your partner is from another country of origin, a different generation, or a completely foreign background to you. You are attracted to the cultural, social and educational differences in their upbringing.

Qualities you admire and are attracted to include expansiveness and visionary thinking, idealism, freedom, ethical and moral behaviour, but especially their independence, passion for life and search for truth and meaning. These qualities are dear to your own heart and relationship teaches you how to find your own truth and believe in yourself.

Capricorn Descendant (Cancer Rising)

Stability, patience, maturity and a respect for tradition are qualities that are symbolized at the setting place. Others' ambition, dedication to work and, surprisingly, a quirky sense of self-deprecating humour all inspire you. But behind that disparaging side might also be pessimism and cynicism. Your ambition, urge to excel and that delicate balance between autonomy and aloofness gets played out in your relationships. A relationship that helps you to find your own authority, set your own limits and be worldly is attractive.

Discipline, commitment, economy, patience, authority, competence and those practical tips for being successful in the world are all part of your caring personality. You want to be able to share a successful life with a partner, rewarded by the hard work you both do and acknowledged for your achievements. Therefore it is possible that you form a close relationship later in life, or perhaps choose a partner who is older. Another way to describe this is to say that you bring a maturity and value to your relationships which must be respected and acknowledged. And therefore the perfect relationship appears with age. Capricorn setting suggests that you attract authoritative and capable people who teach you to manage and structure your life more successfully.

Aquarius Descendant (Leo Rising)

Openness, friendship, inquisitiveness, independence and equality are important virtues which you value in others. Friendship and marriage align and the subtle difference between friends and lovers is important to differentiate. Companionship and commitment, as well as independence and togetherness, are important in a relationship. Through friendship and relationship you learn to respect individuality, and also different opinions and viewpoints in yourself and others.

You admire others' independence, humanitarian spirit, intellectual curiosity, uniqueness, their refusal to be pigeonholed, and the way they don't seem to care what others think. You like their ability to live outside the system. When these qualities are projected, the once-appealing rebel may turn out to be reckless, and what was once inventive and experimental may be too cutting-edge or revolutionary for your liking. Aquarius on the 7th suggests that relationships help you to explore your individuality and independence and demonstrate how to claim your own space without pushing others away or cutting them off. By relating with peers and partners you find your own originality and uniqueness.

Pisces Descendant (Virgo Rising)

With Pisces setting you probably encounter chaos and a lack of clarity in others. Partners and close friends accept that life does not run on schedule, nor is it as ordered as you might like. While your commitment to relationship is with a sense of deep connection, inspired by feelings of closeness, there may be a lack of boundaries. When it is important to separate or be alone, it may be difficult. You have an ability to feel your partner's feelings, serve their needs and to care for their insecurities, but this can eclipse emotional separateness and personal needs, fostering enmeshment and a sense of being misunderstood.

What you are first attracted to in others is their sensitivity and poetry, the gentle way they approach life and their compassion and concern for other living creatures. But human nature is not always that perfect and the shadow of the real world is often revealed through the cracks. The dreamy, creative genius you admire may also be confused, lacking direction and unable to cope with life's constant demands. What was perceived as a great imagination now seems to be escapism. But this is a necessary part of the experience of relationship that helps you to discover the authenticity of your own spiritual and creative self. Your own quest for the sublime, as well as your creativity, will become better known to you through the seasons of your relationship and the influence of your partner.

– CHAPTER 8 –
ENCOUNTERING OTHER
Planets in the Seventh House

Your 7th house planets were setting or preparing to set when you were born. Their transition between the visible or objective 'day' world and the unseen subjective 'night' world was underway. Being between worlds, these planets are liminal, refocusing their vision and intention, becoming sensitized to a different mode of being. Metaphorically, this is a 'twilight' phase; these planets are more receptive to the shadows cast by the fading light, the shifting colours and the intense otherness of their experience.

The ancients recognized that when we are in a liminal space we are on a crossway between two ways of being. On a threshold, there is a likelihood that a divinity might appear; therefore in transition we are more likely to be alert and receptive to the signs and symbols that mark our way. As the atmosphere of the 7th house is transitional, any planet in this territory is watchful and sensitive to the divine crossing its path. When someone who embodies the planetary archetype is on the horizon, there is a reaction, sometimes an attraction, perhaps a revulsion, but nonetheless a response from our inner self. Something is awoken in us by the stranger in the shadows of the place. Like an epiphany, when the outer image reflects the inner situation, a sudden recognition of something occurs. The divine in us stirs.

The 7th house contains both the poetry of enchantment and the lament of disappointment with others who walk on the path of our life. They stir the unawakened gods in us. Astrologically, these are personified by the planets in the 7th house setting place. Imagine setting a place at the table for an unknown visitor: who would it be?

Planets in the 7th house are prone to being projected onto the partner or an equal other, which can inhibit the contact with them in ourselves. Since the horoscope symbolizes qualities in our self, not others, it is wise to try to honour our 7th house planetary energies in ourselves as well. When left projected they tend to empower and inflate others at our own expense. When equilibrium between the inner and outer situation does not exist, a power struggle between ownership can become apparent. Planets in the 7th house that are utilized by their owner are powerful and effective because they are on the horizon, opposing us and challenging our identity. This horizon represents the quest for selfhood through relationship and engages us in the polarity of self and other.

The Sun in the 7th House

You were born as dusk approached, so the Sun was lowering on the western horizon. Metaphorically, this suggests that your personal identity is reflective, aware of the interplay of shadow and light and prone to identify with others, seeing your reflection in their light. By nature, the Sun is bright and shining but here it is preparing to withdraw its light. The sunlight is still warming and illuminating but now it is on an internal and creative level.

The Sun in the 7th responds to the magnetism, creativity and charisma in others, attracted to the self-assured personality you might like to be. While drawn to the star quality in others, you may also feel eclipsed in their shadow. When your own identity and confidence are being eclipsed, you tend to see your partner as more creative, more vital and certainly more self-assured than you. Unconsciously, you may empower your partner with the qualities of strength, heroism and great accomplishments, leaving your own sense of self weakened, uncertain and insecure.

When you relinquish your solar right to shine, you may become disenchanted with your partner until you reclaim some of your own charm and appeal. Resentment and blame accumulate when your partners live out what has not yet become conscious in yourself. Once the shadow of self-absorption and narcissism appears, the necessity to regain your own creativity and confidence becomes apparent. At best you learn to share the stage equally, stressing your right to be recognized and appreciated. The Sun in the 7th finds creativity and identity through the process of relating. Since the Sun is also the archetype of the father, this placement also suggests that questions about father may enter the sphere of relationship. The partner may constellate your incomplete father issues, especially issues of favouritism and the need to be seen and acknowledged. When you find the balance between acknowledging and supporting your identity with the creative pursuits of your partner, your relationship is centred on the support of each partner's creative projects.

The Moon in the 7th House

You were born with the Moon setting, a symbol of care and concern, sensitivity and empathy for others. Those you are attracted to draw out your caring and nurturing qualities. However, you may be caught in the ebb tide of protector and nurturer or the one who is protected and looked after, eclipsing your psychic urge for independence. The Moon in the 7th house suggests the issues of dependency, symbiosis and caretaking subtly enter into your relationships. Ultimately, you want an interdependent relationship where you feel supported and emotionally protected, but not to the extent of feeling smothered or helpless. Unconscious of the emotional weight of your Moon, your partners may express the emotions that you do not, leaving you feeling unsupported and unloved.

The archetypal image of the mother is influential, and incomplete issues with the personal mother may dominate your current relationship. Unbeknownst to you, you might be unconsciously recreating mother's pattern of relating in your adult relationships. With the Moon in your 7th house, perhaps a worthwhile reflective question might be: 'How can I mother and nurture my own needs rather than projecting these onto my partners?' Your Moon in the 7th house is well attuned to knowing what others need before they do, leaving you susceptible to taking care of others. The shadow emerges when you feel either totally dependent on your partner or you have become the emotional provider. This is when you begin to demand more emotional support and interdependence.

When you are supporting yourself emotionally and financially, you are more capable of seeing your true partner. When you meet your partner you will know because he or she feels so familiar, as if you've known him or her all your life. Your close companions care for you and they are supportive in every way they can be; they are family.

Mercury in the 7th House

Mercury personifies partnering on the mental level, someone to communicate with who has varied interests and is ideas-orientated. In the 7th it is like a meeting of minds. When Mercury is projected you may attract bright, verbal people who always appear more intellectually superior and stimulating than you, encouraging you to become aware of your communicative skills and intellect. When a Mercurial individual appears, they are clever, witty, gregarious, bright, spirited and a courier of exciting new ideas. When the attraction wanes you see someone who is scattered, illogical, verbose and nervous. Perhaps somewhere in the middle is the truth; however, you cannot find that truth until you begin to share your ideas, communicate equally and be heard by your partner. You want variety and mental stimulation in your relationships but might attract partners who appear to be versatile but ultimately may be superficial, who cannot be pinned down or are the 'jack of all trades and master of none'. Mercury needs to be shared so that each partner can express their own ideas, have opportunities to verbalize them, and take turns being the critic.

Mercury also represents the sibling and the sibling bond. Placed in the 7th house, Mercury suggests that incomplete sibling issues may be drawn into adult relationships. Our partners may remind us of the early patterns established in the sibling system and we need to be alert to early patterns of communication between our siblings which could infiltrate our current relationship. Uncannily, there could be duplication between our partner and our sibling – similar mannerisms, the same name or Sun or Moon sign, doublings of some form. But it also suggests that we look for a sibling and a peer in the midst of our relationships.

Venus in the 7th House

At home in your 7th house, Venus suggests that relationship, or at least the idea of relationship, comes naturally to you. You might have a few ideals, expectations and standards about relating, but ultimately you value beauty, harmony, peace, companionship, fairness and above all sharing and equality. Being out of touch with your own sense of self may attract others who do not express themselves for fear of disrupting the harmony, or who have physical beauty but lack a depth of character. Eventually, Venus projected onto surface beauty fades, as there is not enough soul to nurture the interior ideals of love and beauty. The motif of Beauty and The Beast underpins an undervalued Venus who looks to what is beautiful to redeem itself. Once Beauty has compassion for the Beast equality is restored.

Unresolved issues with sisters or girlfriends may permeate adult relationships, or perhaps your partner's sister is entangled in your relationship. You could be caught up in relationship triangles as a defence against intimacy, but when you excavate your own self-worth you value yourself more to openly deal with the relationship's difficult feelings. You aspire to forging a relationship where co-operation and compromise are its cornerstones. Your ideal of a social and beautiful relationship is where both partners are equally supportive in creating a harmonious and aesthetic environment.

Mars in the 7th House

Feisty and competitive Mars is awkward in the 7th. A steep learning curve about co-operating, sharing and compromising takes place as you form relationships. You might attract competitive and independent partners who evoke an edgy response. Anger and hostility are difficult in relationships, but this placement suggests they are part of the territory. You might find yourself reacting in a variety of ways when confronted by aggressive behaviour:

- For instance, you could give up, believing that the other person has all the power.

- You might be quick to be competitive in any relationship, making sure you get in first.

- Finally, you could retreat so that others cannot threaten you.

All these scenarios are reactive and ultimately keep you feeling isolated within your primary relationships. Since anger and competition are a natural part of relationship, you learn that your own desires and independence contribute to, rather than take away from, relationship.

All the while you only see your partner's anger, not your own, you fail to see how you may have provoked the situation or colluded with them to express your anger. This leaves you feeling powerless, with no will to redirect the situation. When you overlook your own drive and determination, eventually you become frustrated. Healthy competition, where you and your partner can compete together, win sometimes, lose sometimes, is therapeutic. Your partner is your rival but he or she is also your best friend. You may have unresolved conflict with a brother or masculine figure that might affect your current relationship. Your partner wants you to go after whatever it is you want, so let them know what that is and how they can help.

Jupiter in the 7th House

With Jupiter setting, ethics, morality, philosophy and spirituality are highlighted in relating. Faith and truth are major relationship themes. If the wise and philosophical side of your own nature remains unexamined, you may be drawn to an expert who has all the answers, not realizing that the answers lie within you. Rather than finding truth in yourself or for yourself, you may unconsciously be attracted to prophetic partners in the tradition of a priestess or guru. As you begin to become more learned, more travelled and more conscious, your partner's knowledge becomes less spectacular. A classic example is the student who falls in love with the teacher, only to find that the teacher depends upon them for advice and understanding.

You might feel attracted to free spirits or you may dart in and out of relationships; therefore, eternal students, vagabonds, travellers and free spirits may populate your relational landscape. Your spirited urge to grow and expand finds it hard to settle in a relationship until you have travelled and explored on your own. You are attracted to the foreign so you might travel with a partner, live overseas with a soulmate or marry someone from another country. You need the stimulus of your partner to move beyond the beliefs that you inherited from your family. Rather than blandly adopting your partner's traditions, beliefs and rituals, you need to quest for your own.

Through partners and intimate others you find your own philosophy and spirituality, discovering how to rely on your own inner guidance and truth. You need enough space in your relationships to tolerate differing beliefs and cultures, other religions, alternative truths and complementary realities. If not, the shadows of dogma, entitlement and prejudice enter through the cracks. It is important that your relationships encourage your search for meaning and allow you to continue to develop and grow. When you are with your soulmate you feel the expansiveness of life, being content in knowing that it is unfolding as it is meant to be.

Saturn in the 7th House

Security, stability, organization and control are embodied by your partners. Your partners might be described as authoritative, limiting, cold, too responsible or controlling, which they often are if you are trying to live up to their standards and not your own. If you feel restricted by your partner and blame them for being so rigid, you may unconsciously be letting your partners set the rules and establish the boundaries, leaving you feeling dissatisfied and unfulfilled. When you encounter others who you feel are more worldly or competent than you, the Saturn archetype is evoked, reflecting your need to become self-regulatory and in control of your destiny.

When you feel that the controlling behaviour of others inhibits you or does not allow you to be as free as you want, the answer is not to work on the relationship, but to work to find your position in the world. Ultimately, your feelings of a lack of control or knowing what is right for you are exaggerating the restrictive behaviour of the partner. One accomplished role you could play is that of a business partner, but first you need to be sure it is an equal playing field. You are astute at helping your partner become successful, but it is important that you are acknowledged as an equal partner. As a silent partner, you may feel that your work is being undervalued and unacknowledged.

You might feel anxious when meeting others, expecting them to criticize, control or dominate you. This might delay the process of relating and the establishment of a secure relationship. But ultimately, your partner mirrors the older and wiser aspects of your soul. Time allows you to honour and respect your own authority and soul wisdom. Saturn represents linear time; therefore, it might take longer to ensoul your relationships, but it is over time that they become solid, secure and supportive.

Chiron in the 7th House

Chiron setting suggests you may be vulnerable to individuals who need help. Whether they are marginal, displaced, wounded or despairing, you find refuge for them in your heart. Chiron himself was homeless, knowing how it felt to be abandoned and left; therefore he was highly empathetic to the refugees who sought shelter in his care. In Chiron's cave-home young men learnt to be heroic, rising above their misfortunes to find their calling. A pattern of fostering those who may be wounded or abandoned is innate, but it is important that the roles of helper, healer or administrator do not overshadow being an equal partner. You might need to learn the balance between being a helper and a partner or hold the tension between your urge to help others and take care of yourself.

You may be drawn to the mentor or healer type, individuals who appear wise and caring. Yet underneath they might be damaged in their ability to relate to you on a personal level. Or you may be prone to recreating your role of healer and helper by administering to your partner's wounds. Therefore it is necessary to reflect on equality and exchange in the relationship, because the astrological pattern suggests that you may be prone to confusion between helping and partnering. Earlier wounds of not belonging or primitive feelings of abandonment may emerge in an adult relationship so they can be healed. Chiron in the 7th locates the heroic act of healing your feelings of exclusion and marginality in the sphere of relationship. This is done by relating to a gentle partner who helps to soothe your sores and allows you to belong to a relationship system where you do not feel excluded or excommunicated. And, like true hermits, your kindred spirits may dwell on the outskirts, not at the centre of your community.

Uranus in the 7th House

Uranus opens the gateway, more like a causeway, into new and unexplored worlds. When this energy is personified, individuality, uniqueness and separateness are enhanced. Distinctive individuals may enter your life suddenly and unexpectedly. Uranian energy comes like a bolt out of the blue and in the 7th you just might happen to meet that electrifying person unexpectedly. But events don't just happen, so perhaps you might not be living out your urges to be radical and independent; hence your unconscious urge to be different may be projected onto extraordinary and unorthodox people. These restless urges and desire for adventures need to be satisfied before you feel ready to take on a commitment.

A common theme is your need for space – physical, emotional and psychological. If you disown this need, you might attract those who are overly noncommittal and willing to give you as much space as you need. Or you may keep repeating the theme of engaging, then disengaging, in your relationships. As soon as you feel close, you need to flee; yet when your partner is far away you yearn for closeness. You may feel unable to reconcile your need for freedom with your need for relationship. This freedom–connection dilemma could be a defence against the fear of being abandoned. Another manifestation of this defence is hyper-vigilance and anxiety. Themes of abandonment often underscore anxiety in relating. Fears of separation and alienation may be echoes of earlier experiences; however, it is also the authentic nature of Uranus to desire separateness. Relationships teach you the difference between being separate and being left.

Balancing individuality and freedom implies the acceptance that your relationship may be unconventional; nonetheless, it is still a marriage in the truest sense. Your relationship allows the space and freedom to be an individual. Your intimate others might be unorthodox, but they are exciting and adventuresome, inspiring you to become the individual you know you can be.

Neptune in the 7th House

Under Neptune's spell we seek otherworldly, sensitive and idealistic souls, yet they are often elusive or unavailable. Neptune's world is creative, magical and romantic, filled with inspirational sounds and vibrant colour, yet it is also a world of mirage and fantasy, and a fine line separates imagination from illusion, creativity from chaos. Being drawn to the creative and spiritual qualities in others, you may also feel the urge to rescue and actualize their unlived potential. Since this experience is often mistaken for romantic or spiritual love, you may be prone to trying to rescue the soulful qualities in others, only to lose contact with your own.

As the energy of selfless service, when Neptune becomes entangled in relating it often denies the self and loses identity and creativity. At this stage of the relationship you will become aware of your own need to return to your creative and spiritual self. Being on a pedestal suggests it is only a matter of time before you or your partner falls off.

Your sensitivity and spirituality are heightened through relationships but can also leave you vulnerable to becoming enmeshed in others' dramas. You might fall into the hopeless feelings of trying to help the partner who doesn't want to be helped, or love the partner who cannot yet love themselves. How can you be more realistic in your expectations of relationship without killing off your romantic side? You desire romance without the unhappy endings and come to realize that perfection on the spiritual level is not found in someone else, but in your own creativity and spiritual pursuits. These become more real to you as you reflect on your own soul qualities. Neptune is boundless; the 7th is an area of equality. Therefore this combination is difficult, as your lack of boundaries can render you vulnerable to others. While you may face a psychological challenge, you also have the capacity for a deeply loving and spiritual relationship through your own self-examination and acceptance.

Pluto in the 7th House

Attracted to mystery and unexpressed depths in others, your relationships assist you to explore your own emotional depths. Therefore you are likely to be attracted to deeply intense individuals. You may be drawn to a therapeutic individual, who reveals your deeper and more passionate sides. Feeling controlled, manipulated or drawn into a mystery that captivates you is a warning that you may be giving your power away to someone who may not know how to be equal or intimate. During the course of your relationships, you learn how the darker and repressed feelings of both partners can be brought to light. Learning to share power is necessary, especially in dealing with shared resources like money or sex.

Pluto was the god of the underworld, so it might be beneficial to reflect on whether the motif of his relationship with Persephone underpins yours. Have your innocence and naiveté been abducted by compulsive feelings aroused in relationship? Partners may bring your dark and uncontrolled feelings to the surface or you may see these darker feelings in your partner, not realizing that they reflect your own. When you allow the underworld god into a trusted relationship by honouring your dark feelings, you also invite in transformation, honesty and intimacy. In the sharing of these deeper and vulnerable feelings you become more intimate.

The theme of trust and betrayal is evoked through your relationships. While a partner's betrayal may feel devastating, it awakens you to your own authentic feeling life where you discover your emotional strength. You might try to control negative feelings, but burying them only unleashes obsessive and controlling reactions which may surface through your partner. Summoning your emotional courage to express your deepest feelings and risking vulnerability with your partner is when you will discover intimacy. Persephone, innocent and virginal, was abducted by Pluto, yet she became his equal. By honouring your own underworld, you have a greater opportunity for equality within your relationships. Pluto demands integrity, honesty, vulnerability and trust, and Pluto in the 7th house suggests honouring these traits in intimate relationships.

– CHAPTER 9 –
INTIMACY
The Eighth House

Astrologically, the house of death follows the house of marriage; not necessarily the best combination for romance, but certainly good fodder for many bar-room jokes about marriage. In the marriage liturgy, 'till death us do part' was the wedding partners' vow to remain together for life. Death, being the force that would separate the partners, highlighted the serious commitment to marriage. Attitudes and approaches to marriage have altered significantly since this was widely used, but what has not changed is the complex nature of intimate relationships whose atmosphere is symbolized by the 8th house of death.

This mysterious amalgam of intimacy and death is not easy to comprehend. Neither are the depths of the 8th house. In traditional astrology, this house was one of four houses deemed 'bad', not that these houses were bad or where bad things happened, but that the places were not aligned by Ptolemaic aspect with the life force of the Ascendant.[46] Quincunx the Ascendant, the 8th house is in conflict with our personality. The topography of the house of death is not easily mapped nor recorded. Its history is kept in private journals, confidential records and undisclosed affairs. While this corner of the chart and the psyche has always been enigmatic, modern astrology has found different ways to convey the challenges.[47]

The ancient astrologers' view of the 8th house was mainly about death and questions concerning loss, especially gains from loss, such as inheritances or debts. The house referred to other people's money and assets, and to inheriting or gaining from others' death or misfortune. Death and debt are still linked through our words such as *mortgage* and *amortize*. While the modern usage of 'amortize' is a gradual payment of debt, in earlier usage it meant withholding property after death. *Mort* in 'mortgage' and 'amortize' refer to death, but *amor*, also a part of 'amortize', is love. This mysterious amalgam between death, debt and love is carried into modern astrology through the 8th house connection between intimacy and prosperity. Psychological astrology delineates the taboos of the 8th house and draws the link between the death of the ego and intimacy, sex and power, as well as love and loss. The transformative process of death is related to changes that partners experience in an intimate relationship: 'Each of the partners is changed individually, and a third entity, the union is formed.'[48] Death is not a literal death, but a turning away from life as it has been known, a turning inward towards the soul. The 8th house is a house of soul-making through the initiations of intimate relationships.

As the traditional house of sharing or withholding resources, the 8th house reveals an individual's level of emotional comfort with intimacy. Our attitude to being emotionally open or closed is a barometer of how we share our resources with those we love. Known as the house of STD or sex, taxes and death, there is another version of these key initials for this house. STD could be 'sexually transmitted debt', as it is in the 8th house that love and trust get entangled with sex and money. When the seal of trust is broken the joint finances are too! In my experience many 8th house signatures reveal this cementing or rupturing of resources, whether that is a lucrative joint business, an unexpected inheritance or a significant divorce settlement. The 8th is opposite the 2nd house, forming a natural polarity between what is mine and what is ours. What is mine is physical, economical and emotional, and how that is shared makes it ours.

The 2nd house explores the relationship we develop with our bodies; therefore the 8th is how we share our sensuality and physicality with others. While traditional astrology located sexual activity in the 5th house, in contemporary astrology it is also part of the 8th. The 5th house is an arena of recreation and procreation; sex is pleasurable and fun. Since the 5th house also rules children, sex is also seen as reproductive. The 8th house is an intimate environment where sex is a means of communion, a soulful exchange. Intercourse does not solely refer to sexual union, but also to a spiritual one. Equally, sex can be a means of domination or exchange for money. In the 8th house, sex and death/debt are fused. Orgasm is a symbol of this, as in this state there is a temporary collapse of conscious awareness, a complete surrender before return to conscious life. The French call orgasm 'le petit mort', which translated literally means the 'little death'.

Grant was a client some time ago who demonstrated this quandary. He had Libra on the cusp of the 8th house; Neptune was conjunct the Sun in the 8th. Venus, the 8th house ruler, was conjunct Saturn in Scorpio in the 9th. Grant had been celibate for most of his adult life as a spiritual practice. His urge towards transcendence was reflected in his chart in many ways, but the identification with celibacy as a tool for purification echoes the 8th house Sun–Neptune conjunction. The Neptunian urge to sacrifice and surrender intimate encounters with others had been channelled into the spiritual ritual of celibacy. In his celibate spirituality he did not have to face the painful feelings of indifference or abandonment that he had experienced in his childhood. He had perfected a practice of transcending the sexual, hence emotional, contact; however, wounded feelings from the past still lay dormant.

Progressed Mars was conjunct his Sun–Neptune conjunction when I saw him as a client. Grant was feeling out of control with his desires and his tremendous urge to act out his sexual and emotional feelings towards a woman he had known for some time in the ashram. He felt bewildered at how intense these feelings were, given his spiritual practice. Guilt and anger became intertwined with his sexual desires. At times he was overwhelmed with rage at not being able to control his compulsion and infuriated at not knowing how to proceed.

Leading Grant back to the primal understanding of the 8th house process was very helpful, enabling him to understand that his spiritual practice may have been avoiding rather than entering the sacred realm. Now a deeper part of himself called him to another initiation to explore sexual relating, which had been denied by his spiritual practice of celibacy. His Venus–Saturn in the 9th house became a rigid philosophy of love, focused on the love of God. Even though his commitment to spirituality was a natural inclination it was used defensively to avoid intimacy. Ironically, his exploration of 8th house intimacy was the initiation needed for a more authentic encounter with the divine.

The 8th house is a house of mystery and mastery in being true to your deepest self while participating in the world and engaging in relationships. When representative of place, the 8th house depicts dark and ominous locations on outer or inner landscapes. In the 8th house the primal fear of survival is stirred through intimacy, and often experienced as a fear of loss or abandonment. But the pain of loss is connected with attachment. Eighth house relationships are dependent on trust and integrity. They are not solely between life, love or sexual partners, but can also symbolize business relationships where the union takes each one into the shared territory of mutual resources, or the therapist/client relationship where privacy is sacred.[49] Intimacy involves loss. Loss implies discovery. Discovery leads to transformation; a sacred wheel that turns in the 8th house.

Intimacy and Integrity

The word 'intimate' comes from the Latin, *intima*, and is defined as being inward, innermost, intrinsic or essential; intimacy, as a student once said, was 'into-me-see'. It refers to a close association. An intimate relationship provides an inner experience of knowing oneself, as the innermost dimensions of the self are engaged. Intimacy begins with the relationship to oneself.[50]

What is opened through intimate sharing has been locked away, well sealed in one of psyche's vaults. Even though its contents are precious, they are vulnerable, often damaged, secretive and reluctant to be shared again. Dane Rudhyar suggested that three main factors are implied in all 8th house matters and one of these is trust.[51] Intimacy relies on integrity and trust. As this is a house of exchange, trust is essential at all levels. For instance, when you place your resources in the Stock Exchange you trust that they will not only be returned, but will have increased. Similarly, when you place your love in a partnership you trust that it will be shared and will grow in value. The 8th house domain is sacred and primal, and its potential is fully awakened when we are once again intimate, vulnerable or exposed.

Life is punctuated by separations. Birth itself is a severance from a transcendent, symbiotic oneness into an experience of separateness. Other primal separations and losses occur as we mature, and intimate contact in adult life reawakens these dormant memories; therefore, the feelings of being intimate are coloured with fears of separation. What can accompany this primal sense of loss and separation is sadness; hence we can feel neglected even if there is no conscious recall of this occurring. This can also explain why at the height of feeling bonded and intimate we can also feel painfully separate and sad. Through emotional and sexual closeness we discover the residue from earlier feelings of aloneness, sadness and abuse.

Being intimate runs the risk of betrayal. In many ways betrayal is an embedded but vital aspect of an erotic union, as it allows an individual to unleash the primal wounds that have left them helpless and dependent. Betrayal can be a transformative process, an opportunity to push through powerless feelings towards an independent adult perspective. When used as an agent of reflection, betrayal leads to consciousness. Betrayal is a deathlike feeling, yet in the 8th house initiation it reconnects us to our inner strength and resources. We learn to trust ourselves, to know we will survive and, ironically, to be stronger because of the process. Through facing death something irrevocably changes. The change cannot always be articulated, but it is always felt. The underworld is no longer as fearful.

The 8th house keywords that we are all familiar with, such as betrayal, death, emotional closeness, jealousy, love, passion, possessiveness, power, rage, rebirth, sexual intimacy, shared resources, transformation, trust and union, are all aspects of the 8th house developmental process. The primary stage includes the awakening of emotional closeness, love, passion, sexual intimacy and sharing resources. When the fusion is still unconscious there is a stage when betrayal, deathlike feelings, jealousy, possessiveness, power plays and rage will erupt. By consciously working through these powerful emotive states, another stage is reached with images of rebirth, transformation, trust and union. Intimacy is now an authentic union of inner and outer.

My experience is that there is often a cluster of 8th house episodes; for instance, this is evident in many situations where there are multiple deaths in the family around the same time. A gathering of death and betrayal might occur when defences are broken down and unconscious contents spill out. This has been evident to me many times in my practice. Janet was an early example of this; her set of circumstances always reminded me of this 8th house theme.

Janet had Scorpio on the cusp of the 8th house. Mars, the ruler of the Ascendant and 8th house, was in Scorpio in the 8th. Pluto, the modern ruler of the 8th house, opposed the Moon in Aquarius and both formed a T-square to Mars. Venus was in Sagittarius in the 8th as well. Both Mars and Venus were like bookends, close to the cusps and images of guardians on the thresholds of this house. When Pluto transited Mars and rekindled the natal T-square, a series of losses and betrayals occurred. All happened within such a short period of time that Janet spent the following three years in a state of loss, grief and depression, trying to separate out the tragedies.

Janet's mother and a close female friend died within weeks of Janet's hospitalization for a hysterectomy. Simultaneously, her husband confessed that he was having an affair and wanted to leave her for the other woman. Grief for her mother became entangled with feelings of betrayal, rage and lethargy; depression and disbelief were the hallmarks of her next few years.

Janet described her abusive father as a tyrant. Mother was described as a server and giver. This legacy had permeated Janet's marriage to the point where she was totally dependent on her husband serving and supporting his pursuits at the expense of her

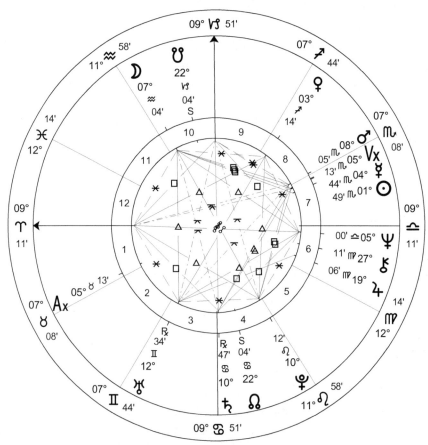

Janet, 25 October 1944, 4.45 p.m., Perth, WA, Australia

own. Her own vitality and independence had been closeted away with the painful memories of her parents' abusive relationship and father's abuse of the feminine. But as Pluto transited her 8th house Mars, and squared both her Moon and its own natal position, the complex erupted. While the constellation of losses was tragic, through this period Janet transformed her attitude to the archetype of Mars, becoming more independent and assertive of her own needs.[52] This manifested in increased vitality, the courage to do her own thing and an enormous desire to follow her own truth. Janet's experience confirmed the powerful impact of the parental legacy, not only financially but emotionally and morally as well.

Legacies

Inheritances are another aspect of the house of death. What we inherit might be at odds with who we are, but through the process of confronting our legacy we find the authenticity of our birthright. As the house of inheritance, the 8th house territory is where we claim our familial legacy, whether psychologically, emotionally or financially. Unearthing the ancestral inheritance of the 8th house is not straightforward because the inherited attitudes towards money, sex and love are rarely examined. The 8th house is associated with the landscape of the underworld, metaphoric of the unseen inheritances and legacies from the past; hence we can imagine the 8th house as where we might communicate with the dead. This sphere is where we encounter some skeletons in the family closet that help us to reclaim our legacy. It is wise to remember that in antiquity the underworld was the source of buried treasure.

Hidden in this house might also be family issues and legacies about money, wills and desires. Issues in the familial past might include emotional manipulation through money, debt, disputes regarding inheritances, the loss of family money or deep-seated feelings towards financial control. What was the attitude towards debt or borrowing money that we inherited? What was the familial approach towards sharing resources?

The 8th house is the place where the two sides of a family merge into one. Psychologically, the 8th house reveals the capacity for, or the lack of, familial intimacy and closeness; therefore, planets here will not only describe the family inheritance but secret alliances and taboos in the family. Interred in the 8th house are the familial gains and losses which are passed down. These gains and losses might be financial, as in monetary bequests and inheritances, or they might be a familial story of debt. In many cases the gains and losses are emotionally based.

As a barometer of closeness, the 8th house refers to the degree of parental intimacy experienced when growing up. We observe our parents' trust of one another over money and resources. Arguments about money are often never really about money but the sense of feeling unloved, unacknowledged or unmet. How we might share our personal resources with others we love is influenced by the family atmosphere and affects our feelings of financial and emotional trust in adult life. The attachment, emotional security and parental issues of our early life, if not yet resolved, will be prone to being re-experienced in an adult way through intimate relationships. We also 'marry' into or relate to our partner's psychological, emotional and financial composition.

The will and testament of those who have passed exert their influence on the emotional well-being of those in the present, and issues concerning legacies, wills, inheritances, shared resources and family trusts are all part of this terrain. Wills of the 8th house also refer to the will of those who have passed yet still exert emotional and financial control. While people may die, relationships do not, as their desires live on through their will.

Taboos

The word 'taboo' was coined by Captain Cook from the Tongan *tabu* and it means 'prohibited', usually because what it protects may be of danger to the uninitiated. A taboo is consecrated or keeps something restricted to a special purpose; it honours a mystery. A taboo is devoted to a sacred purpose, dedicated or sacrificed to something larger than what we can know consciously. Psychologically, the taboo we are most familiar with is the incest taboo whose function is to steer the course of psychic energy away from the regressive desire for the parent. A taboo propels the psyche towards individuation, as without the taboo the psyche may remain inert, stunted or regressive.

Taboos are essential to psychic life. There is often an unconscious taboo against intimacy, since intimacy exposes personal secrets, familial shame and cultural prejudices. But intimacy is part of the individuation process and therefore cannot be avoided. In the 4th house, the incest taboo encourages the image of the heroic self to be developed away from the family. In the 8th house, intimacy potentially unlocks the transcendent self. Intimate encounters are sacred because we are authentic and stripped bare in the presence of another. Intimacy is didactic and unconscious by nature, unlike closeness which is more conscious or systematic;[53] a helpful distinction between the equality of the 7th and the dependency of the 8th house. To be intimate implies a return to instinctual feelings of desire and rage, love and loss, union and death. In adult relationships these dangerous opposites can be consciously addressed.

Instinctual or unprocessed feelings lie below the surface of the 8th house. Since they feel dangerous they are controlled and managed, but erupt when emotional pressures wear down their defences. Negative feelings are an authentic part of this territory. When judged they cannot be heard or witnessed, a necessary act for their release and transformation. Judgement keeps them at bay yet only delays their inevitable advent. One of these feelings is jealousy.

Jealousy is an authentic feeling in relationship. When jealous or raging feelings erupt in a present-day relationship they may often be in response to what our partner shared intimately in a previous relationship. Alimony payments, child support and phone calls from an ex may activate our fears of being left or loved less. However, what are also triggered are earlier feelings of helplessness, fears, even memories of abandonment or images of being left. The present intimacy exposes the past, not as a prophecy or prediction of the future, but as an attempt to rework closeness in an adult context.

Triangles emerge out of the depth of union that intimacy brings. It echoes the triangular relationships in our families and early friendships, and few couples are untouched by triangular situations, whether that is another person, child, work, an outside interest or a project. This does not always have a disastrous ending, as relationships can be transformed and each partner strengthened in their love for one another. Sometimes 'the other' in the triangle may be a fantasy figure and when these images and feelings can be shared with the partner, they can enhance the intimacy of the relationship.

Love, Death and Power: Eros and Thanatos

Freudian psychology brought the two mythic figures of Eros and Thanatos together to personify two powerful instinctual human drives. Thanatos was the death or self-destructive drive as opposed to Eros, which was the tendency to survival, sex and creative life. Both gods meet in the 8th house. Sigmund Freud had the Moon and Saturn in Gemini in his 8th, an apt image of the life–death opposition that inspired his thinking, as well as the sibling intrigues that he brought into his adult relationships.[54]

Thanatos is the death instinct. It is through Thanatos's suffering that our differences and separateness become illuminated. What feels like death can be the beginning of reclaiming our individuality and accepting life's opposites. Thanatos in his positive face illustrates our aloneness and separateness. Although this is painful by nature, it is liberating. His negative face is fear of loss. The experience of Thanatos is inevitable since it is archetypal by nature and we experience this archetype in a variety of ways: despair, depression, withheld rage, loss of libido, all processes that remove us from union.

Eros's nature is passion, yet where passion exists so does its companion, suffering. The extent of the pain is often the catalyst that allows a more authentic love to emerge. Entering Eros's domain is to enter into the land of opposites. Eros's urge is to unite these opposites, not to destroy them. To lose one's identity through merging obliterates opposites and eventually the relationship becomes static: nothing is risked, hence nothing is gained. To unite the opposites is the work of Eros and the 8th house transformational experience.

Sex and power are aligned with intimacy in the 8th house. Sexual activity can be an expression of love or power. Sexual activity united with emotion moves us towards surrender, not to the other, but because of the other. Power and sex can also be used to avoid intimacy. Perversion is a denial of the union of opposites that keeps us detached from the possibility of intimacy. Perversion, sexual dysfunction, impotence, masturbation, promiscuity and abstinence may all be power-based attempts to avoid intimacy. In these ways sex can become aligned with Thanatos rather than the loving and intimate sphere of Eros.

Like sex, money and possessions are powerful defences against intimacy. An intimate relationship implies sharing – it is our car, our house and our bank account. Once an intimate relationship is established, it is the relationship that earns the money and worth in the world, not the individual partners. Refusal to lose control of our private assets, gained before or during the relationship, can be problematic for maintaining intimacy. Refusing to enter into sharing our resources may be symptomatic of a refusal to share the self.

Debt is another way we can ensnare ourselves in a power struggle. If we fear the exposure that intimacy brings we may be more inclined to re-enact our infantile dependency with the bankruptcy court or tax collector than to enter the world of adult relationships. The powerlessness of debt often masks a fear to enter intimate relationships. No surprise that our society has little understanding of intimacy, but a great regard for debt.

Malcolm has Pluto, Venus and Mars in the 8th house. Because of his underworld dealings he has been remanded on drugs charges. The police do not allow him to travel out of state without surveillance and he is in considerable financial debt. He feels like a powerless prisoner of the police and bankruptcy courts. Malcolm has always felt he could not survive in an intense and close relationship. Instead, his concentration and power took him into the literal underworld. But those he trusted and formed illicit business partnerships with in this world betrayed him, just as he feared any intimate relationship might. Malcolm had hoped to escape the pain of exposure in relationship by subversive activity; however, this path actualized his fear of powerlessness.

Love and Transformation

The wedding ceremony is a ritual that addresses each partner's urge to find the divine. The wedding ring, the sacred vows and the other symbols, depending on the culture, are part of the rites in the marriage initiation. In alchemy the mystic marriage was the *coniunctio*, or the conjunction. This represented the chemical fusion of opposites that gave form to a new possibility. But before union could occur, the opposites had to be melted down so their conflict or oppositeness could fuse together as one.

The transformation available in intimate relationships is through the outer union to the inner one. Eros's transformation heals earlier wounds and helps us to recognize that the figures of the beloved, the soulmate, the lover and the kindred spirit are also internal. When the urge to share is anchored in a deeper sense of love and we are able to trust ourselves, we can give freely without the fear of loss.

The Idle Place: The Astrology of the 8th House

In traditional astrology the 8th house was known as the idle place, as planets here were seen as ineffective. In terms of their place in the sky, these planets were beginning to fall, to be dragged down to the Descendant, turning away from their prominence above the horizon. The 8th house symbolized the place of heroic descent. The dying of the Sun's power was metaphoric of the dying of the 'day' self or ego. While 8th house planets may appear idle they certainly are not inactive, perhaps more internal or interior, but not inoperative.

Entering the 8th House

At the door to the 8th house there is a steep descent. For those who cross into this sphere it is wise to tread carefully, as there is a possibility of falling. However, falling may also be necessary in order to have a felt experience of the terrain.

The sign on the cusp of the 8th house symbolizes the attitudes that unlock, open and shape intimate relating. It also suggests qualities that may be magnetic or mesmerizing in others as well as what others find charismatic in us. Our attitudes towards sexual and emotional closeness will also be constellated around the cusp. These are inherited qualities, but ones that may not have been acknowledged or successfully used in the familial past.

The sign on the cusp can also be used as a defence against intimacy. For instance, the Water signs might unconsciously apply their caring nature to protect them from deeper involvement: Cancer's nurturing, Scorpio's intensity or Piscean compassion could replace authentic intimacy. Or Air might employ their ideologies to fend off relating at deeper levels; Gemini's curiosity, Libra's questions and Aquarian opinion can effectively safeguard against exposing the self. Fire's enthusiasm and generosity can be an effective defence against closeness; for instance, Aries' independence, Leo's narcissism and Sagittarian beliefs can not only lead an individual into intimate relationships, but also keep them away. Earth's pragmatism and need for structure can impede intimacy; for instance, Taurus's resistance, Virgo's analysis and

Capricorn's economy might block intimacy rather than invite it. The sign's virtues, whether they be courage, patience, kindness or generosity, can be mobilized as a defence against equality, sharing and, ultimately, intimacy.

As the 7th and 8th houses focus on the area of adult relationships it is of interest to note the sign combinations of the two house cusps, because what may be more apparent on the 7th house cusp becomes veiled on the 8th. If there is no interception in the 7th house, the sign on the 8th house cusp is elementally incompatible with that on the 7th. This implies that the terrain of the 7th house relationship is organically different to that of the 8th. Alchemically, the two individuals in relationship are submerging themselves in the waters of the unconscious.

Imagine each sign on the cusp of the 8th house as both a key to what we desire, yet also a lock to defend a vulnerable part of our self. The sign is a metaphor for the qualities we need in intimate relationships as well as what will be brought to the surface through intimacy. The sign's symbolism is double-edged in that it attracts us but also evokes a deeper fear in us. Reflect on the sign on the 8th house cusp as a natural progression from the sign on the 7th.

Once we have entered the 8th house we uncover the archetypal urges, represented by the planets. Planets in the 8th house are the urges and potential complexes that may be carefully disguised from conscious awareness. Intimate encounters awaken these strong needs and urges, along with their shadow sides. Eighth house planets were activated early in life through bonding and the intimate encounter with Mother. They are brought to life once again in personal relationships, remembering the early attachment, whether that was functional or not.

Planets in the 8th house express their need for close encounters and also reveal the intricate way we can dodge intimacy; for instance, Jupiter in the 8th house could be generous so as to avoid intimacy. When we are always giving we can prevent the partner from getting too close to us. Perhaps the Moon's caring touch may be also defending against the very realm that they want, yet also fear. While we are caring for the partner we do not have to have an equal relationship. Nurturing can be a defence against being open and vulnerable to the other. Perhaps Mars in the 8th is always doing, competing or leading. All this action and energy may be an unconscious defence against exposure and vulnerability. A planet gives us ample symbols for starting to explore the way in which we engage union, sexually, emotionally and financially. An 8th house planet gauges the trust we place in others and ultimately how we embrace our personal identity and separateness in the merger.

The 8th house belongs to the trinity of Water houses which symbolizes our ancestral inheritance as well as the impact of our partner's ancestry. An 8th house union involves the mutual task of transferring loyalties from the family of origin to the partner. The 8th house may also describe the level of intimacy in our parents' marriage or relationship, and planets in this house will characterize the intimacy issues we have inherited from our parents' relationship. Familial secrets and patterns often emerge into consciousness when we transfer our loyalties from the parent onto our 8th house partner.

Therefore I would not feel that planets in the 8th house are idle in the way that we understand the word today; however, they are mysterious, reserved and guarded, perhaps secretive. When considering 8th house planets in the context of a relationship it is important to remember that while they may be deeply felt and imagined, they may not be easily articulated.

The Sun in the 8th House

With the Sun in the 8th we would consider the nature of the inheritance – emotionally, psychologically and financially – that is passed down through the father's line. We might also consider any secrets or denials connected to father or his familial past, because the relationship to father has a bearing on our ease and experience of intimacy in adult life. The Sun is beginning to lose its brightness as it descends through the 8th house, a metaphor for the merger with darker sides of the self that are identified through intimacy. The focus of identity shifts from the self to the other and the creation of a deep connection.

The Moon in the 8th House

The Moon in the 8th house symbolizes a deep and almost basic need for intimacy. However, since the Moon evokes symbiosis in relationship, this dependency might be transferred onto the partner, with a desire for the partner to recognize their needs and to fulfil them. The Moon in the 8th may be extremely sensitive and emotionally reactive to the partner, intuiting and feeling every move, just as a mother feels towards her child, yet the developmental task is caring for their own needs. The Moon in the 8th house has the difficult task of finding intimacy out of the ruin of many maternal and familial feelings. Stability and security in adulthood are found through intimacy and sharing. Sigmund Freud, the author of the Oedipus complex, the psychological tale of the boy's marriage to his mother, had the Moon in the 8th house.

Mercury in the 8th House

Respecting privacy and showing consideration for personal feelings begins in the early relationships with family members and either develops or denies the capacity for intimacy. With Mercury in the 8th house, listening authentically and communicating honestly are first modelled in the parents' relationship; therefore the levels of sincerity and integrity in the parental patterns of interaction influence the individual's capacity for open and honest relationships. By nature Mercury was a guide to the underworld and in this house he is curious about what is not said or expressed in the relationship. In the 8th house Mercury's communication becomes communion as it develops the capacity for intimacy. Mercury is a metaphor for the love letters we write to ourselves.

Venus in the 8th House

Venus is aligned with the 2nd house in traditional astrology and finds herself accidentally debilitated in the 8th. While this sounds ominous it only suggests that Venus's nature now turns its attention to what is not innately comfortable. Venus aligns herself with peace, but now she needs to uncover the discord and darkness associated with her being. Venus in this house suggests that she may have inherited incomplete images of union, severed relationships, betrayals, affairs and triangles from the family history; therefore the avoidance or difficulty with intimacy may be linked to a family complex. In the 8th Venus's journey takes the individual into the underworld of self and others in order to disinter the legacy left from past familial relationships and inheritances. Through the intrigues and complexities of relationship, Venus discovers intimacy and love.

Mars in the 8th House

The expression of desire and sexuality in the parental marriage has an impact on the comfort level that an individual feels in their adult relationships. With Mars in the 8th house, desire and independence, sex and intimacy are woven together and the first place we may look for clues in dealing with these themes is the parental relationship. Mars is competitive and confrontational, striving for outcomes, and can be divisive when it does not get its own way. In the 8th Mars is invited to share at the deepest levels and place the relationship before personal desires. Personal goals and ambitions cede to the deeper needs of the relationship.

Jupiter in the 8th House

In the 8th house, Jupiter tells a story about a cross-cultural familial legacy. Underpinning this placement, I have often heard a family story of loss of inheritance. However, in another way there is an abundant inheritance when the individual follows their own desires. In mysterious ways an inheritance arrives; in most cases it is not only resources but ways of thinking, philosophy and optimism. Generosity is tested and the individual must often reach beyond the limits of the family's values to find their own. The partner's resources, whether they are financial, emotional or psychological, are highly beneficial. Intimacy is often found with a foreigner or in a place beyond the country or culture of origin.

Saturn in the 8th House

Saturn in the 8th house could suggest that the family inheritance is an issue; perhaps unfairly divided, mismanaged or fraught with parental control. On an emotional level this might suggest a difficulty in expressing closeness or affection; perhaps this was first experienced in the parental marriage. The consequences of how the family has expressed emotional closeness and financial values over time are highlighted. The fear of intimacy, sex, sharing resources or emotional closeness eases over time. Intimacy belongs to the adult years when the hard work and commitment in a close relationship mature. The need for control and authority is now focused through the intimate relationship.

Chiron in the 8th House

Chiron's legacy may have been affected in a variety of ways; however, the underlying symptoms would be due to familial displacement and upheavals. Perhaps emigration, divorce, separation and bereavement may have contributed to emotional and financial losses within the family. In the 8th house, Chiron's felt experiences of being estranged or disenfranchised enter intimate relationships to be heard and healed. This could also be experienced through the partner's wounds. No matter which partner exposes the pain and suffering, intimacy is where healing can occur. The relationship may be marginal, outside tradition and unconventional, yet it offers hope and solace to others.

Uranus in the 8th House

Uranus, an astrological archetype of liberation, independence and separation, is not comfortable in this sphere of intimacy. There may be an early experience of separation or tension in the parental marriage or a pattern of avoiding intimacy. When integrated into a partnership Uranus can bring an unusual and exciting atmosphere to the relationship, an abundance of passion and extraordinary experiences. But when disconnected, Uranus in the 8th can be cold and disassociated. Uranus defends emotional and sexual closeness through its ability to cut off quickly and detach. Therefore intimate relationships may be unpredictable; they need to incorporate enough space, freedom and distance so each partner's unique spirit can emerge.

Neptune in the 8th House

Neptune yearns for the divine and in the 8th house may transfer this desire into relationships by seeking an ideal other. But for various reasons the ideal other may be unavailable or unattainable. Keeping the other in an imaginary realm is a defence against the disappointment of everyday relationships. There may be mystery and intrigue in the family background or a feeling that something is lost or absent, and this otherworldly sense that something is missing is imported into adult relationships. Neptune's urge to merge and psychic openness can be satisfied in the 8th house through emotional contact, sexual activity, spiritual relationships and creative partnering, but disappointment follows when it cannot be sustained. Without adequate emotional, sexual and psychological boundaries, the boundlessness of Neptune may leave an individual feeling betrayed, taken advantage of or deceived. Intimacy is found in a mutually committed spiritual, creative and boundaried relationship.

Pluto in the 8th House

In the 8th house, Pluto might suggest a past family secret, a mystery or an inheritance that affects the individual's capacity for closeness. Betrayal, debt or loss may have been a cornerstone of the parental marriage. However this symbol manifests, there may be taboos and skeletons in the family closet that are reawakened with intimacy. Like Persephone or Psyche, an underworld journey may be triggered by a loving relationship. It is an underworld journey to find truth and authenticity. Passion and pain, all or nothing, love and losses are all part of forging a passionate and poignant relationship. Trust, love and intimacy are not givens but are found through the courage to face the truth about the self and be unmasked in the presence of the partner.

Transits to 8th House Placements

When 8th house placements are transited, wounds are often reopened and the resulting pain and uncertainty often prompt a client to seek an astrologer's advice about the complexity and confusion of the feelings. When an astrologer is entrusted with their client's story, able to listen to their pain and meet them emotionally with care and without judgement, an intimacy is forged and the relationship enters the territory of the 8th house.

The transits of the slower moving planets (Saturn–Pluto) to 8th house planets potentially bring the underbelly of the archetype to the surface. When a personal planet is transited by one of these outer planets the issues of trust and betrayal, possessiveness and jealousy, loss, death and bereavement, sexual dysfunction, secrets, shame and triangles may emerge into consciousness. The transit is an opportunity to recognize and transform some darker infantile feelings. The raging infant may be released to find his or her path of individuation.

If we see transits as times when potentials are uncovered, then transits to the 8th house bring our potential for intimate union to the surface. However, this transformation is often accompanied by painful feelings of grief and loss.

I believe that the potential of the 8th house cannot be fully appreciated until our adult years when we have reached some level of maturity. In our younger years the 8th house may represent our fascination with the mysteries of life and transits may lead us into exploring the occult and examining what lies underneath the surface of things. In the adolescent years the 8th house is synonymous with the awakening of our sexual desires, becoming powerful and influential; therefore transits to the 8th house at this time can intensify these feelings. In later years, 8th house transits transform the infantile wounds of aloneness and loss. In the 8th house we meet the powerful figure of Eros that moves in each one of us. He is the god that is awakened when love is ascending, but also leads us into the painful land of opposites in order to internalize our missing half.

Progressions of the 7th house personal planets – the Sun, Mars and Venus – into the 8th house are also potent indicators of self-development. Because of their slow movement the progression into the 8th house lasts for a long time. These developmental planets focus on the area of intimate encounters and the psychic transformation that takes place within them. The secondary progressed Moon through the 8th focuses the emotional development on the area of loss and letting go, so we can be more fully available in adult relationships. During these 2 to 2½ years there is an intense encounter with what has been repressed or unacknowledged. Coerced into letting go of what can no longer be a part of our lives, the progression of the Moon through the 8th house is a descent into the emotional depths of ourselves.

Progressions into the 8th house in adult life bring the self-conscious issues lingering from childhood into the present relationship. This may synchronize with the maturing and deepening of an intimate relationship. Transits may also be synchronous with the development of a close relationship that is helpful in transforming our life into a more lived experience. In opening and working with the painful death-like wound of infantile separation, the life force and libido are awakened. Opportunities for new growth lie under the surface.

– CHAPTER 10 –
FORTUNE AND FRIENDSHIPS
The Eleventh House

Traditionally, the 11th house was known as the place of the 'good daimon', a positive spirit who inhabited its landscape. It was seen to be a favourable house where the spirit of goodwill prevailed. On the wheel of fortune this place was ascending and its atmosphere encouraged a sense of trust and comfort in life. The good spirit that inspired this house was doubly fortunate in that Jupiter rejoiced in this area and blessed the goals, hopes and wishes of those who petitioned him.[55] I imagine friends, who are occupants of the 11th house, as being the surrogates of this good spirit.

The Spirit of Friendship
The ideal of the 11th house focuses on the power of the community and relationships forged outside the family circle, bound not by the bond of blood but by the similarity of spirit. Here we find our supporters, our allies, our benefactors and our friends, who observe who we are. They see through us, and in doing so they help us to see who we truly are. Friendship expands our boundaries and encourages growth and self-discovery. Perhaps the 'good daimon' of the 11th house is the hope that friends bestow upon us when they see in us the best that we can be.

> Communicating friendship's gift is hope. Friends who witness our own signatures on our lives help us believe there is something in us of the best that people can be. And a society with hope is a society that can believe in itself....[56]

While we have more choice in creating our friendships, these connections still can unearth the residue from previous relationships with siblings, childhood chums, even adult partners. This house is where we meet our kindred spirits in the world and where we have the opportunity to heal earlier wounds through the affection of friends. The roles and positions that have already been forged in our sibling and other relationships are instinctively taken into our relationships in the broader community. Our impact on society and society's impact upon us is interconnected with our primary experiences of relationship. In the 11th house we become citizens of a larger community where we meet our soul friends.

Across the polarity of the 5th–11th houses we encounter *philia*, the profound love of friendship where the depths of our soul can be revealed without judgement or shame. The 5th house was coined the house of good fortune. Through transitional relationships, play and creativity, a potential space is opened to share our originality with others, reflected and witnessed through our friends. It can be a place of both solitude and communion.

Carl Jung prefaced his biography *Memories, Dreams, Reflections* with a commentary that his life story was focused on his interior world, remarking that the only events and travels worth telling were those of his inner life. When remembering relationships with others, he commented:

> Similarly, other people are established inalienably in my memories only if their names were entered in the scrolls of my destiny from the beginning, so that encountering them was at the same time a kind of recollection.[57]

When we meet a soulmate we remember, as their signature is already a part of us. Eleventh house relationships feel familiar, as they are kin, allies who are soulmates. The shared spirit that infuses us is the bond to our friends and colleagues. In this house we find the sense of belonging to a larger family, being individuals in a larger collective.

In ancient Greece the polis was not just the city but also the spirit of the city-state; hence democracy flourished, the rights of citizens were respected and the early experiments at sharing power and influence were attempted. The 11th house is a political sphere as it links the individual to a collective spirit of equality, forging a democratic, peer and co-operative relationship with others. Impinging upon the success of 11th house relationships are earlier experiences of relating, our trust in human relationships and our expectations of others. Here we meet our kindred spirits in the world, those who share our passions, witness our successes and share our burdens: colleagues, rivals, competitors, companions, acquaintances and treasured friends.

Friends dwell in our hearts. Among Marsilio Ficino's ingredients for the recipe of a good life was the 'seasoning of friendship'.[58]

Signs on the Cusp

Like all cusps, the sign is an entry point to the house. It helps to open the front door. The ruler of this sign is also significant as it is a custodian of the threshold. Here are some short sketches to help you reflect on the qualities of your 11th house that may be witnessed through your friends and social others. These are the virtues and ideals that we hope to find through our friendships.

Aries on the 11th House Cusp

Friends dare you to try new things and travel new pathways, challenging you to make every effort to get what you want. Therefore you want to share your explorations and enterprises with them. When you were a child, your gang may have taken risks; as an adult, your friends are active and entrepreneurial. Friends bring out your confidence and allow you to be courageous. Even though you cannot see it in yourself, your friends are able to see your code of honour and they award you the medal of bravery.

While friends encourage your fighting spirit, they might also ignite your competitive streak. This is great as long as you are honest about it and able to find healthy ways of competing. Friends inspire you to find the place where you can meet as equals and revel in the enjoyment of competitive games or challenging adventures. So, whether they are competitive on the golf course, tennis court, dance floor or Scrabble table, it is important to recognize that this is how you engage and meet. Winning might be the goal, but engagement and mateship are the outcome. The energy created through this contact might inspire you and your friends to form a team, create an enterprise or begin an adventure together.

Taurus on the 11th House Cusp

Through your friendships you develop a sense of worth, coming to appreciate your reliability and constancy which contributes to you being a valued and trusted friend. Friends are a precious commodity, priceless in terms of the security and resources they offer and provide. Although your circle of friends is not your family, they are close to the inner circle of your valued relationships. Friends are your touchstone to security as they provide a solid support network, trusty advice and a fixed point of reference. When things get rough you look to friends for solace because they provide a secure harbour for you until the storm passes.

Because you form such strong attachments to your friends and you invest your sense of self and resources in them, you might feel shocked when they need to move on or develop new associations, but true friends value and appreciate you, even at a distance. Taurus is about possessions and ownership, and so you bring these to the arena of friendships; perhaps this echoes the wisdom which warns against the risk of lending money to friends. Or at least it alerts you to the complexity of lending valued treasures and hard-earned resources to friends who might not value these as much as you. It is your friends who help you to see what is valuable and of interest to you.

Gemini on the 11th House Cusp

Friends are similar to brothers and sisters; perhaps you nickname a friend 'Brother John', or use such expressions as 'she is like a sister to me'. You may feel a close bond with a friend that you were not able to feel with your literal brother or sister. Many community programmes acknowledge the universality of the attachment underlying the sibling relationship. Organizations that use volunteers to help the disenfranchised and underprivileged often model their names on the sibling bond, for example Big Brothers or Brothers and Sisters. Your friends become the link to your sibling relationships, helping you to heal them and celebrate them.

Gemini on the 11th house cusp suggests that you have a variety of friends and acquaintances and that community participation comes naturally to you. Your friends support your need to be free to explore all possibilities. You engage with many others in a friendly and open manner; therefore you create a wide network of friends and allies. Friends are playmates and fellow performers on the stage of life. They know how to communicate in a way that makes you feel known and understood, and they share your love of interaction, conversation and curiosity about life.

Cancer on the 11th House Cusp

Nurturance and protection are Cancer traits which are brought into the arena of friendship. True friends are those who you can depend upon, who help you to feel that you belong and who offer a safe shelter from the insecurity and randomness of life. You can be instinctively aware of your friends' needs and be there when they need a helping hand, a strong shoulder or a refuge. However, this might not always be helpful. While friendships are built on interdependency, they also need equality and individuality. You have a sense about others, and often that is a gut feeling that you need to honour. However, another feeling that you might experience is butterflies in the stomach because you are also shy and anxious about meeting new groups of people.

Family and friends intersect. In a social situation you might take on the role of caring for others in the group. Your task is to belong to the group, not to take on the sole parenting role. You bring warmth and personal openness into your encounters. You don't need a large social circle, just an intimate handful of friends who are like family, a circle you feel you belong to. Friends support you and make you feel safe without demanding that you take care of them. It is these friends who touch your soul.

Leo on the 11th House Cusp

Leo rules the heart, an evocative symbol of what your friends admire in you. Your warmth and generosity are appealing to others. As a youth, popularity might have been more important than it is as an adult because you know the true value of friendship. As you reflect on the past you appreciate that approval and acclamation from others was vital, but what is important now is your friends' recognition of creativity and their willingness to play and be engaged. Friends encourage your confidence, applaud your achievements and give you a very high approval rating.

Your true friends are your co-creators in life and the ones who share the labours, witness the triumphs and debrief about the reviews. When you need friends to boost your fragile sense of self you may collude by living out their projections of an unlived life. Therefore it is important to recognize that friends are companions who share the drama and together you create the scripts. Your first romance might bloom within your circle of friends, as you express yourself through your interactions and friendships. Friends help you to make important transitions in your life, because they remind you of what is important and where you need to place your loyalties. When you entered school, when you left home, when you got engaged or had your first child, friends were present. Friends witness the creation of your life.

Virgo on the 11th House Cusp

Friends need to respect your privacy and understand that you retreat and withdraw from the crowd from time to time. In earlier years your need for time alone may have been mistaken for aloofness. Therefore, socializing might not have come as easily to you as it did for others, which might have contributed to you being critical of yourself in social situations. Yet there is a strong sense of service to others, but a true friend is also one who attends to you in your time of need. Hence it is necessary to let friends know what you need them to do for you.

Your friendships are based on integrity, trust, respect, confidence and faith. In a way we could suggest that true friendships are sacred. While being a loyal and attentive friend, you also need solitude. Without that, relationships might feel suffocating, even when they are supportive and encouraging. True friends will respect your need for privacy and it is trusting and respectful friendships that help you to feel whole. It is important to establish continuity in your friendships and let your friends share your day-to-day activities and experiences. They are great at helping you to relax and debrief on the trials and tribulations of the world.

Libra on the 11th House Cusp

Partnership and friendship: are they the same? That's a question to ask yourself, because you could partner your friends and befriend your partners. No doubt there's a huge overlap, but the question of compromise, the level of commitment to time and resources, as well as lifestyle issues, will be different. Therefore, it is important for you to consider this difference and create the appropriate boundaries between the two. Being a natural at relating, you find yourself drawn to the social life. Your friends encourage your instinctive gift for hospitality and your ability to bring people together without taking advantage of your innate urge to please others.

Being adventurous, you may have many social engagements. But how, in the midst of all your social activity, do you satisfy your need for space and distance? For all your love of people you also like to follow your own programme, and so a great learning curve in friendships is balancing time and space for yourself with time for friends. Friendships teach you how to be in relationship, yet separate enough to do your own thing without feeling selfish or rude. Friends collaborate with your adventures and witness your travels, your growth and your life experiences.

Scorpio on the 11th House Cusp
Still waters run deep, and intensity, depth and intimacy colour your friendships. Your true friends are there when you need them, as you are for them in critical times. Being reserved and trustworthy, you will tell your friend the truth when they ask you to be honest. Friendship is sacred territory and you respect the mystery and intimacy of your close companions. On the other hand you can get caught up in triangles or intrigues with friends. Therefore it is wise to use your faculties of discrimination when you give your trust to friends.

A handful of close friends is more appealing than a clique of acquaintances. You have a great capacity for deep and personal friendships that are enduring and supportive. Sharing personal crisis and tragedy, as well as the successes and accomplishments, with friends binds you even closer to them; hence your friendships are ultimately a very private affair. Sometimes it is difficult to draw the line between intimacy and friendship. A friend and a lover are not necessarily the same; therefore you've learned that emotional boundaries between friends and lovers are essential.

Sagittarius on the 11th House Cusp
When young you were probably drawn to those who were foreign to you. Anyone exotic seemed so much more interesting. Your early friends supported your wanderlust and curiosity about life. Today that means your friends might be from distant parts of the globe or different cultures and backgrounds. It is important that your friends are an eclectic congregation who share your philosophy, ideals and values. They need to be far-sighted, broadminded and big-hearted. Prejudice and a lack of ethics leave you feeling despairing, but also

steer you into raising community awareness on human issues. You need your friends to share the bigger picture of life with you, to help to answer the larger questions and to journey through life together.

Community is important to you, especially the social groups that advocate human values and morals. However, you are also drawn to groups that defend ethics, stand for philosophical ideas, demonstrate spiritual ideals and pursue intellectual knowledge. You are welcomed into the community because you are outspoken about your faith and you act on the spirit of what you believe in. Whether friendship is shared in the religious community, in the university, through travelling together or being on the same team, your spirit and optimism are boons for others.

Capricorn on the 11th House Cusp

In a confusing and chaotic world it is great to know that you can rely on someone: a friend, a colleague or a teammate who won't let you down. True friends are responsible and committed to you. Therefore, you might not feel the need for many friends; what is important are dependable and reliable companions. From a young age your friends may have been older or more mature, because you were attracted to their worldly experience. In adult life these friends share your values, goals and ambitions.

Although you might feel dutiful towards others, this sense of obligation can impede friendship as you become a parent rather than an equal. It often takes an act of conscious awareness for you to realize that you are taking responsibility for others when they should be doing that themselves. When you strike the balance between friendship and duty you experience the loyal and indelible connection of friendship. At times you might be defensive, due to your high expectations of yourself in relationship. With friends you learn to be authentic, not perfect.

Aquarius on the 11th House Cusp

Aquarius is known for its liberal and innovative ideals, so you are probably attracted to individuals who are not part of the herd. Friendships are an adventure and are worth taking a risk for. You need friendships that give you the freedom to be who you are, enough space to experiment without judgement and permission to break the rules. When these conditions are met you are a true and devoted friend. When you feel someone's expectation to conform, you might react by disengaging and becoming distant. You need to feel free enough to be who you are, even if that means being unavailable for a while. The irony is that the more permission you feel from your friends to be unavailable or distant, the less inclined you are to be that way. Paradox and difference are hallmarks of your friendships.

Your fate may be politically orientated, to become involved in groups or organizations whose focus is humanitarian or focused on the future. Your mantra is to help build a more enlightened world, and your associates and comrades share this world view. Friendships need to have this openness and breadth of vision otherwise you feel stifled, escaping by making a run for it. You also seek an intellectual exchange in your friendships, as you need to explore and discuss your ideas and insights.

Pisces on the 11th House Cusp

Ideals, creativity and spirituality are important in your friendships. You may have high expectations of friends, although they are often met with disappointment. Yet on the other hand, when having no expectations, you are sometimes elated by your friends' small acts of kindness. Friendship is an area of your life that contains a full range of feelings. Whether those feeling are closeness or hurt, sympathy or envy, they are an indication of the soulfulness that you bring to friendships.

Your compassion, sensitivity and gentleness need to be acknowledged and returned by your close circle of friends. By being consistent and providing enough space for your creativity and spirituality, you become more widely known by others. Being so intuitive, you are in tune with your friends, often aware of their heartbreak before they are, administering healing thoughts and comforting words. Your sensitivity is sought out as a helpmate, healer and life coach. Your perceptiveness makes you a valued friend; therefore, among your social circle you will find some deep and lasting relationships based on depth of care, empathy and compassion.

Planets in the Eleventh House

Planets in the 11th are encountered through social activities with others. They seek to be equal and participate in communal ideals and goals; therefore, they also represent our hopes, aspirations and wishes for society, as well as the role an individual plays in the community. An 11th house planet symbolizes the patterns and needs that are apparent in social involvements and contacts. These archetypes are also embodied by our friends, and through projective identification we come to know these aspects of our soul through our intimate friendships. Here is a brief summary of the planets in the 11th house to begin considering the value and fortunes of friendship.

The Sun in the 11th House

With the Sun in the 11th house, friends and colleagues are part of your identity. It is important to be a good companion, as well as to have loyal friends. You want to be accepted by your peers, acknowledged by your colleagues and favoured in your social circles, as in these areas you forge your identity and find your purpose. Recognition by friends is revitalising, so the way in which creativity is shared and fostered is important. When it is self-centred, the group may serve as the narcissistic mirror rather than the place where creativity is shared. With the Sun in this house the individual seeks friendships where mutual support and admiration enhance the sense of self. Innately this placement suggests the ability to 'father' the group or be the leader, or at least the spokesperson for what needs to be accomplished.

Personal identity is developed through group participation, organizations and community achievements. With the Sun in the 11th the individual identifies with being part of a team; they are not lost in the crowd, but are a vital, integral and necessary link in the creative process of the organism. Satisfaction is found in contributing to the success of the group, and the more one identifies with the goals and aims of the group the greater the sense of self.

The Moon in the 11th House

With the Moon placed in this political sphere, women's issues, the roles of women and all lunar issues are interlinked with social relationships; for instance, family and friends are intermixed. Your friends are your family or family members are your friends. This can suggest longevity in friendship such as holding on to friends from childhood. From an early age it is important to support and protect close relationships outside the family circle. In later years, needing to be embraced by a wider circle and developing attachments outside one's own family is important. The need to participate in the community and be part of a larger system nurtures the soul's need to belong.

Lunar sensitivity is apparent in groups and with friends, contributing to your receptivity to undercurrents and tensions in the group atmosphere, or over-identifying with friends' feelings and emotional states. This instinct to nurture others' needs and attend to their emotional crises may leave you vulnerable and drained. No doubt the Moon in the 11th is nurtured by group participation and supported by friends, but it needs to be cautious of becoming the matriarch for the group or the counsellor/mother for your friends. Home may be found in the wide circle of contacts who share your interests, or equally you may provide the home and shelter to a group of like-minded others.

Mercury in the 11th House

Mercury's urge for communication and interaction finds its natural outlet in the 11th house arena of like-minded peers and colleagues. The mercurial nature can be fulfilled through being a spokesperson for the group, a teacher or facilitator for others. In this communal and often forward-looking place, Mercury is able to speak out on humanitarian issues and voice human concerns, affecting the policies and goals of the system.

As a friend you seek intellectual equality and rapport through a variety and diversity of friendships. The messenger-god Mercury inspires you to be the link in the chain of friends, the instigator of the reunions or the intermediary between others. You sustain relationships through communication and contact. Rediscovering your brothers and sisters through friendships helps you to redress your earlier relationships with siblings and schoolmates. In a group you may find your voice and through friends and associates you may develop your ideas, opinions and intellect. As a friend you appreciate a vibrant exchange of ideas as well as the sounds of silence.

Venus in the 11th House

Friendship and personal affection may become intertwined, and while romance may follow from a friendship, it is important to differentiate between friendship and romance. It is imperative to be aware of how personal dynamics shift when two people in the group become romantically involved with one another. Venus is often susceptible to triangular relationships, but 11th house territory is where you experience belonging to a group, not a dyad. If a subset of a couple develops within the wider group there may be conflict, division and jealousy. Therefore it is important not to confuse the experience of couple dynamics with group dynamics, or mistake friendship for love or confuse a lover with a friend.

The arena of friendship, colleagueship and social contacts plays a pivotal role in the development of self-esteem. Supportive relationships in the community assist you to find the resources that contribute to being valued and appreciated. Friendships and an active social circle are areas of fulfilment that can bring contentment and pleasure. The social circle is a great resource and offers an outlet to express your talent and creativity. Hospitality comes easily and you enjoy creating a space where human interchange can take place. Venus in the social sector suggests the possibility of interesting companionships with creative individuals and being loved and admired in the community of others.

Mars in the 11th House

The presence of the archetype of the warrior in the 11th house suggests that competition and conflict may be ignited in social situations; therefore, any festering sibling rivalries or incomplete anger with current or ex-partners might spill over into friendships. With Mars here, assertive impulses are best focused on leading, not antagonising, the group. Group involvement, whether that is through sports, work, hobbies, political issues or other causes, is where challenges to independence and freedom take place. Sometimes Mars in the 11th house suggests being a target for the group's hostility or the one singled out as the cause of the conflict.

While there may be conflict and arguments with friends, there is also respect and passion. Conflict and difference of opinion are part of every friendship and the challenge with Mars is to manage this so it does not create tension and bitterness. Mars in the 11th house is willing to go into battle for friends and for the group in order to defend their rights and freedom. In all socialization processes the need for independence and autonomy will be activated; therefore, the individual needs to avoid becoming so aligned with the group that they lose their identity, or so independent that they are never part of the group. The challenge is to be part of the group without feeling a loss of identity. Ironically, with Mars in the 11th house it is with our friends and also through group involvement that we will be challenged to forge our identity. Others help to reflect the positive expression of our uniqueness and singularity.

Jupiter in the 11th House

According to traditional astrology Jupiter rejoices in the 11th house where friendships broaden your understanding of and belief in yourself. An eclectic group of friends enriches your life experience and encourages you to grow in understanding and faith. Through your involvement in a community you explore systems of knowledge that help to educate you to become a citizen of the world, and in group participation you find your spiritual path. You share your vision and ideals with others and seek out teachers and mentors in the community. But you also play the role of guide and mentor to others. You have many educational and inspiring experiences with groups, colleagues and friends.

Friendships mark the milestones in an individual's life. Jupiter in the 11th house is a team player, whether part of the hockey team, the debating team or the local council; it needs the group and others to keep its vision and inspiration alive. With this placement your fortune is your ability to have faith in others, trust in the triumph of the human spirit and believe in the integrity and morality of human beings. It also suggests that your positive attitude and optimistic spirit in the world attract generous friends.

Saturn in the 11th House

As the planetary archetype of hierarchy, authority and control, Saturn feels uncomfortable in a place where equality and democracy are valued. Therefore, Saturn may feel defensive and guarded about friendships or feel compelled to lead or control the group. Close association with others reawakens vulnerability, the fear of rejection and the dread of failure. On the other hand, this position also suggests natural leadership abilities and commitment to the group. Not all groups or associations are compatible with your needs; therefore, boundaries between you and the group are important as long as those boundaries are not defence positions. I have often experienced individuals with this placement describe their feelings of isolation, loneliness and/or lack of friends. Perhaps this is the existential feeling of being alone. Or it may be a childhood experience resurfacing in the group – an only child or elder child, lack of playmates in early years, an isolated family atmosphere, much older siblings or strong responsibilities as a child – all may have shaped the feeling of being alone in the group. With Saturn in the 11th house this feeling of aloneness is challenged in adult years.

Friendships are committed and forged over the long term and you have the capacity to be a loyal and supportive ally and companion. As an area of mutuality you do not need to be the dutiful or the responsible one in relationship. Doing the 'right thing' by everyone causes friendships to be a burden and groups to feel restrictive and demanding. Having Saturn in the 11th, you need to recognize the skills of leadership and guidance, as well as the stability and maturity that you bring to a group. When you do, you find support and respect from peers who appreciate your wisdom and guidance in the community.

Chiron in the 11th House

Chiron is marginal; an archetype of the outsider, who finds his tribe outside convention with groups who are interested in the ancient ways. With Chiron in the 11th house an individual may feel excluded from the group. To ensure that these wounds do not become chronic or lifelong, it is imperative to understand that your communal life is not part of an established system. Your colleagues are also marginal and will share the similar wound of feeling left out. Your soul group exists outside the mainstream and your role is to be a mentor and healer to your friends' feelings of disenfranchisement and exclusion. With Chiron in the 11th you can remain on the margins and see clearly what is taking place at the centre of the group. Therefore you can be a spokesperson for radical ideals and groundbreaking social reform. Underlying Chiron in the 11th house is a bigger agenda about healing the tribe!

With Chiron in the 11th you are drawn to friends who are mentors and guides. In return, you offer the healing that is found in the mutuality of companionship. A friend or an experience in a group may wound you by reopening the scar of feeling excluded or left out. But by turning to a thoughtful friend or returning to a sympathetic group, you discover healing through participation with like-minded others.

Uranus in the 11th House

An ability to bring idealism, innovation and illumination to the group is heightened with Uranus in the 11th house. Uranus might be rebellious by nature, but in the 11th house unity comes through diversity by tolerating and accepting other points of view. If a group is too static or stuck in a rut, you become the revolutionary who disrupts the status quo. Therefore this placement suggests an individual who might feel separate from the group, the black sheep who catalyses the group to change by bringing in another point of view or who shocks and awakens leaders from their complacency to propel the group into a new and liberated direction.

You are able to sustain many different friendships from disparate avenues of life. Like lightning, Uranus can strike and then disappear. Friendships, too, can be unpredictable, disengaged or detached. You need a sense of separateness and space or you may unexpectedly separate from the friendship. With Uranus in the 11th house the freedom to be yourself comes through associations with unusual friends in the community.

Neptune in the 11th House

When Neptune is in the 11th house the urge is to merge with friends to find spirituality and creativity through group involvement. However, the tendency to dissolve boundaries between yourself and others could also leave you feeling vulnerable, especially if personal sacrifices have been made. Group energy can be mesmerizing and the enchantment of group participation may lull you into another world or enmesh you in a system that is not supportive.

Neptune's idealism and inclination to sacrifice is at odds with the 11th house environment of equality and affinity. While soulmates and spiritual companions are found through enduring friendships, there may also be a blind spot when it comes to friends, unwilling to see their failings or weaknesses, leaving a trail of disappointment when promises are broken or expectations are unfulfilled. While you bring your creativity and yearning for oneness into your friendships, without mutual engagement you may feel drained and weakened from giving without receiving anything in return. You are a devoted and emphatic friend, ready to give freely and openly of yourself, but you need to differentiate between the hope and the reality of friendships.

Pluto in the 11th House

Pluto in the 11th house suggests that group involvement may stir deep complexes, bringing the passionate need to be desired and loved to the surface for healing. Involvement with groups could be like group therapy, working through darker feelings and earlier issues of acceptability. With Pluto in the social sphere there may be a tendency to be cast as the collective shadow or the dark horse in the field. If there are undercurrents in the group then it is natural for you to feel them. With any group you will probably have a potent impact and be the facilitator for transformational change.

An erotic quality or a desire for intimacy may underpin friendships. Therefore it is important to be clear about the nature of personal involvements with friends so that conflicts do not turn into lovers' quarrels. Pluto in the 11th house suggests being a powerful friend in critical times, and not just being one but having one. Friendships are passionate and intense; hence you have a few intimate friends rather than many acquaintances. To be attached at a deep level is very important; therefore, trust is a priority in your committed friendships. Friendships are enduring, trustworthy and supportive through life's losses and transitions.

– CHAPTER 11 –
THE SPECTRUM OF FRIENDSHIP

I have on my desk a small framed picture of my friend Alex and me. It has been there as long as I can remember. Alex was nine years older than me. His Jupiter–South Node in Aries conjoined my 11th house North Node, while his South Node in Libra met my Neptune, North Node and Mercury. His Moon was on my MC; my Moon was on his Ascendant. We were great friends from the moment our paths crossed. He witnessed major experiences that shaped the way I see the world, and although Alex died over ten years ago our friendship always remains. I remember fondly his acts of kindness, our adventures and mutual support of one another. Our friendship feels eternal.

The spectrum of friendship is wide-ranging; therefore, it is not limited to the domain of the 11th, but can also be housed in the 3rd, 7th or even 8th, depending on the nature of the closeness. Each friendship is an extraordinary blessing. As Anaïs Nin, who we will meet later, once said:

> Each friend represents a world in us, a world possibly not born until they arrive, and it is only by this meeting that a new world is born.[59]

Here are some examples of the unique and special way that our paths cross with those of our friends.

With a Little Help from My Friends
Ella Fitzgerald was one of the most popular female jazz singers of all time, known for her beautiful, melodic, wide-ranging voice. Like many well known singers she had the Sun in Taurus closely conjunct Venus, an astrological symbol reflective of her sublime gift of song. Ella was gifted with a rare talent, but she was also discriminated against due to the dark colour of her skin. Her voice was ageless, but she lived in a racially prejudiced time when laws prohibited equality between blacks and whites.

But friendship does not judge. It celebrates equality, values the other and shares their resources. Friends support you against all odds and through difficult times. Friends break through inauthentic social boundaries and admire you regardless of race, creed, colour, age, religion, sexual preference or political affiliations. And this is how Marilyn Monroe befriended Ella.

Ella described Marilyn Monroe as 'an unusual woman – a little ahead of her time. And she didn't know it.'[60] Ella's Uranus triggered Marilyn's Moon–Jupiter conjunction in Aquarius in the 7th house. Marilyn had Venus on the MC. Always in the spotlight and desired by many, she was christened the 'Goddess of Love' by *Time* magazine. But Marilyn also had Chiron conjunct Venus and she intimately knew the pain of being rejected, unwanted and marginal, a wound she immediately identified in Ella. Perhaps out of her own pain Marilyn befriended Ella. In Ella's words:

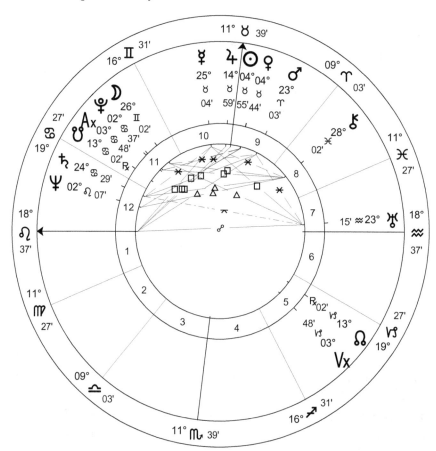

Ella Fitzgerald, 25 April 1917, 12.30 p.m., Newport News, VA, USA

I owe Marilyn Monroe a real debt. It was because of her that I played the Mocambo, a very popular nightclub in the 50s. She personally called the owner of the Mocambo and told him she wanted me booked immediately, and if he would do it, she would take a front table every night. She told him – and it was true, due to Marilyn's superstar status – that the press would go wild. The owner said yes, and Marilyn was there, front table, every night. The press went overboard. After that, I never had to play a small jazz club again.[61]

Ella's time of birth has just been discovered (12.30 pm) revealing the same Ascendant–Descendant axis as Marilyn's. The Ascendant–Descendant axis often features in friendships since it reflects the horizon of the self and the other. In relationship astrology it characterizes two personalities and their approach to relating. Ella

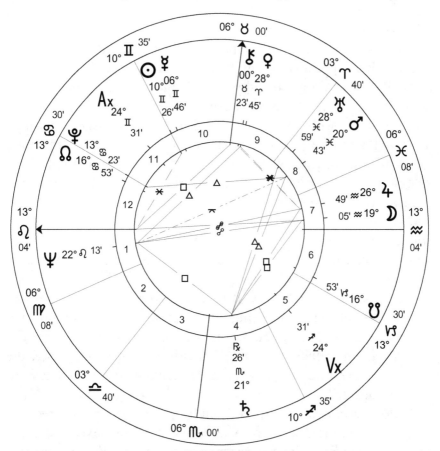

Marilyn Monroe, 1 June 1926, 9.30 a.m., Los Angeles, CA, USA

and Marilyn were born nine years apart, and what is noticeable is that Ella's South Node at 13♋02 is conjunct Marilyn's North Node at 16♋53, drawing their paths together and reflecting the pull of the North Node assisting to turn the tides at the South Node. Ella's Moon at 26♊02 is opposite Marilyn's Vertex: a connective image of paths that cross and leave their impression on the individuals involved. Marilyn's MC also conjoins Ella's Sun–Venus, providing a venue for her talent.

The sign on Marilyn's 11th house cusp is Gemini, ruled by Mercury in the 10th. Marilyn used her contacts and the media to assist Ella. The Sun and Pluto are the gatekeepers of Marilyn's 11th house: the Sun is at its front cusp while Pluto is on the back gate. Strongly identifying with Ella, Marilyn used her power to open up opportunities for her, a friendly act and a snapshot of the fortunes of friendship that turn the tides of our lives.

The Dance of Friendship
In the world of science it seems that friendship with the opposite sex is risky, especially among heterosexuals where there might be a possibility of romance and/or sex.[62] But science is not the final authority on human behaviour, especially love and relationship. In the everyday world of play, study, work and social engagements, men and women must find a way to partner each other beyond romantic or sexual entanglements. A working or professional relationship, a shared creative spirit, collective resources, a mutual passion or a joint mission offers men and women the opportunity to be friends and broaden their understanding of the opposite gender. Cross-sex friendships confront different gender values, sexual attitudes and ways of thinking, but they also assist each partner to befriend their own contra-sexual side.

Cross-sex relationships will be more vulnerable to gossip and scrutiny, sensitive to gender equality and prejudices, and complicated by sexual attraction. Some lovers start out as friends, some ex-lovers remain friends. Perhaps each case is unique; therefore, the horoscope becomes a guide to understanding the uniqueness of each friendship.

Plato's discourse on Eros from the *Symposium* inspired the phase 'platonic relationship' where love was non-sexual, directed towards the divine. Platonic partners often channel Eros into shared creativity: the 11th house. It is the 7th from the 5th house, so the creative impulses of the 5th are partnered in the 11th. Friendship is shared creativity and expression, and when the creative team is male and female, it can be creatively romantic and passionate. Fred Astaire and Ginger Rogers, one of the most famous dancing duos of all time, were masterful at shared creativity. In 1933 Fred and Ginger co-starred together in a film that launched their partnership. Together they made ten films, mostly during the Depression, when their on-screen chemistry and partnership lifted the spirit of the period.

Fred has Jupiter in the 11th house in Scorpio. Ginger, being twelve years younger, shares a Jupiter in Scorpio. Her Jupiter, which rules her 7th and 11th houses, is conjunct the South Node and Vertex, which all conjoin Fred's 11th house Jupiter, highlighting the fated sense of their connection. But what is most apparent is that their

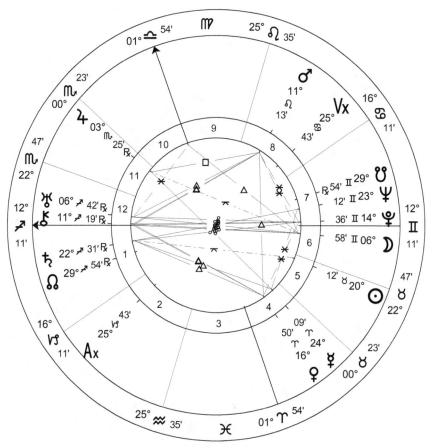

Fred Astaire, 10 May 1899, 9.16 p.m., Omaha, NE, USA

Ascendants are reversed: Fred's Ascendant at 12♐11 is conjunct Ginger's Descendant at 14♐09, while Ginger's Ascendant at 14♊09 is conjunct Fred's Descendant at 12♊11. The modern ruler of Fred's 11th house is Pluto at 14♊36, closely conjunct his Descendant and Ginger's Ascendant. Ginger's Pluto at 28♊03 conjoins Fred's South Node at 29♊54. In 1933, when they made their first film together, Pluto was in Cancer continuing its long passage across Ginger's Sun–Neptune conjunction, which is conjunct Fred's Vertex. The mirroring of each other's Ascendant–Descendant highlights a marriage of personalities. But it is the synchronous contacts between the Vertex and the Nodes that suggest a potentially powerful association.

Fred has the Moon opposite Uranus while Ginger has the Sun opposite Uranus, giving each other enough space to do their own thing. Astrologically this also suggests that the combination may have helped each to be freer and more comfortable being dependent

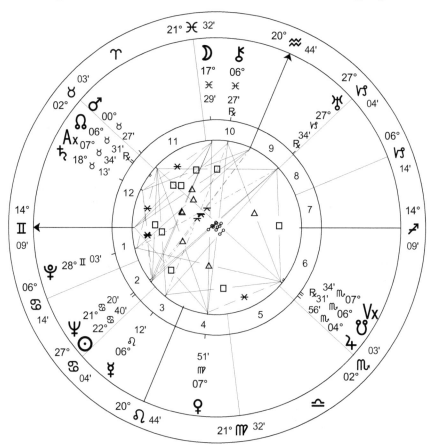

Ginger Rogers, 16 July 1911, 2.18 a.m., Independence, MO, USA

in their partnership. While Jupiter in the 11th house may have blessed Fred with supportive partners, it also suggests his guidance and wisdom were shared with friends. For this his peers honoured him with a special Oscar, presented to him by Ginger. With female dance partners and friends, Fred's Jupiter in the 11th house also epitomizes cross-gender education and equality.

The traditional ruler of Ginger's 11th house is Jupiter, conjunct her South Node in the 6th, aligning work and friendships. Mars is in her 11th house and also rules its intercepted sign. Competition or conflict is placed in the arena of friendships. In her partnership with Fred she experienced the frustration of his top billing and the perception that he was the star. Bob Thaves is quoted as saying that Fred was great at what he did, but 'don't forget Ginger Rogers did everything he did backwards ... and in high heels'.[63] She proved she was equal and masterful at shared creativity, not just individual performance.

Fred and Ginger went on to be highly successful on their own, the consequence of having had such a dynamic yet platonic partnership.

A Case of Collegial Rivalry

Friendships and collegiate support were intensely important to Sigmund Freud, although they often eluded him. In a letter to his colleague, Karl Abraham, Freud expressed the sentiment 'All my life I have been looking for friends who would not exploit and then betray me.'[64]

In so many of his friendships this hope never materialized. During his early years as a psychoanalyst, his intimate friendships with close colleagues like Wilhelm Fleiss and Josef Breuer were damaged by jealousy and rivalry. When Freud was a more mature and prominent figure in the psychoanalytic movement, Alfred Adler became an important colleague; however, this friendship ended unpleasantly. As Freud said:

My emotional life has always insisted that I should have an intimate friend and a hated enemy. I have always been able to provide myself afresh with both, and it has not infrequently happened that the ideal situation of childhood has been so completely reproduced that friend and enemy have come together in a single individual.[65]

Freud's own incomplete and ambivalent feelings about his siblings were likely to resurface with friends and colleagues.[66] Colleagues became his surrogate siblings, his younger associates stirring feelings of rivalry and accentuating his need for control and domination. The developing spirit of community first experienced with siblings, then other children in the school playground, is the foundation stone for friendships and colleagues in the workplace. Social bonds are born out of the renunciation of sibling jealousies and rivalries. Sibling rivalry and the way we manage the associated feelings affect our ability to be within a group, to promote equality and mutual concerns. Astrologically, this is the link between the 3rd and 11th houses. Freud has Mars in the 11th house which trines Chiron in the 3rd house. The ruler of the 3rd house is Saturn in the 8th which squares Mars in the 11th.

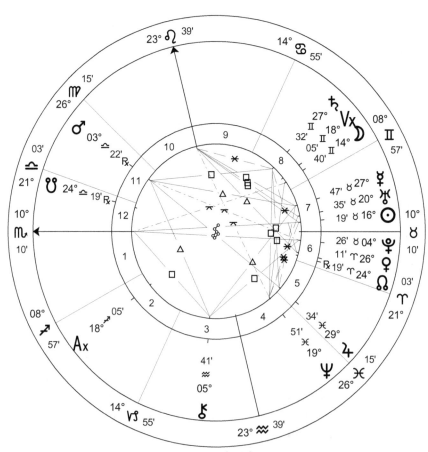

Sigmund Freud, 6 May 1856, 6:30 p.m., Freiberg, Moravia

In Freud's horoscope this theme of rivalry with colleagues is certainly evident through his 11th house retrograde Mars, the ruler of his Ascendant and 6th house. It is in detriment in Libra. As the only planet retrograde and the only one in the eastern hemisphere (not including Chiron), Mars is a planet in high focus. It opposes Jupiter in the last degree of Pisces, squares Saturn and is quincunx Pluto.

Freud's 'crown prince', Carl Jung, once a treasured colleague and his anointed successor, also became estranged and a bitter rival, following the pattern Freud that had so well delineated. In Jung's horoscope, Mars is also in the 11th house but in Sagittarius, and like Freud's it is also quincunx Pluto, similarly inclining Jung towards competition and rivalry with his peers.

Both Freud and Jung had the North Node in Aries, being born nineteen years apart. Mars ruled their North Nodes, perhaps

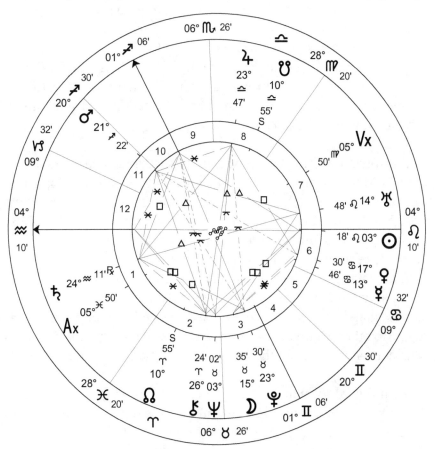

Carl Jung, 26 July 1875, 7.32 p.m., Kesswil, Switzerland

indicating that while each man's destiny was pioneering and individualistic, they faced their nemesis at the South Node in Libra through compromise and cooperation. For each man Venus, the ruler of the South Node, was in the 6th house of detailed work, where their competition was focused. Both having Mars, the ruler of the North Node, in the 11th house reflects the beginning of their passionate friendship through the shared spirit of psychology, but it also illustrates the end of their relationship through rivalry. While Mars may be the god of conflict, we still have the choice of picking our battles. Sharing this natal position means that Mars will repeat itself in the 11th house of their composite chart, identifying this theme as a priority in their relationship.

On 3 January 1913 Freud wrote to Jung:

> I propose that we abandon our personal relations entirely. I shall lose nothing by it, for my only emotional tie with you has long been a thin thread – the lingering effect of past disappointments – and you have everything to gain, in view of the remark you recently made in Munich, to the effect that an intimate relationship with a man inhibited your scientific freedom. I therefore say, take your full freedom and spare me your supposed 'tokens of friendship'.[67]

At this time, transiting Saturn was in its retrograde phase exactly on Freud's Mercury, ruler of the 11th house; the South Node in Libra was transiting the 11th and about to conjoin Mars. Transiting Pluto was exactly conjunct Saturn in the 8th which rules the 3rd house of siblings and seminal relationship patterns. The transits echoed a theme of relationships endings.

An outstanding interaspect occurs between their two horoscopes: Freud's Sun at 16♉19 is closely conjunct Jung's Moon at 15♉35, a classic 'marriage' aspect. Ptolemy, writing in the second century CE, suggested that we first look to the opposite-gender luminaries when considering marriage in the horoscopes of men and women:

> With regard to men, it is to be observed in what manner the Moon may be disposed … But, in the case of women, the Sun must be observed, instead of the Moon.[68]

In a modern context we understand this to mean using the woman's Sun and the man's Moon to delineate some of the characteristics of the inner partner. Contemporary astrology continues to look at the powerful union of the Sun and Moon as an image of the *coniunctio* or *hieros gamos*, the sacred marriage. The traditional astrological statement that Sun–Moon combinations were indicators of marriage inspired Jung to conduct his synchronicity experiment comparing the aspects between the Sun and Moon in couples' horoscopes.[69] Ironically, this aspect reverberated through his friendship with Freud, the 'intimate relationship with a man' that neither was able to sustain.

All friendships impact us, and of course some more than others. Astrology assists us in contemplating the relational impact through the comparison of charts which we will begin to focus on in Part 2. Some of the interchanges between Freud and Jung's horoscopes follow:

Freud	Jung	Comments
Sun 16♉	Moon 15♉	A classic combination of luminaries, yet one may eclipse the other if they cannot manage to exist and be accomplished in the same space?
Chiron 5♒	Asc 4♒; Sun 3♌	Freud's presence stirs feelings of doubt, anxiety and confidence in Jung; however this may also be mutual
N. Node 24♈	Chiron 26♈	Jung's maverick qualities and his interest in the soul's suffering make on impact Freud
Uranus 20♉; Mercury 27♉	Pluto 23♉	Freud's interesting and innovative intellect meets the depth of Jung's. Freud's 7th house Uranus–Mercury would be drawn to bright minds like Jung's.
MC 23♌	Uranus 14♌	Jung's 7th house Uranus unexpectedly influences Freud's direction
S. Node 24♎	Jupiter 23♎	Jung's breadth of insight, relational and therapeutic manner feels familiar to Freud

Mars 3♎	S. Node 10♎	Freud's aggressive instincts touch familiar feelings of rivalry and competition in Jung
Saturn 27♊	Mars 21♐	Freud's Saturn is opposite Jung's Mars. Jung may feel as if Freud is controlling, judging and/or domineering
Mercury 27♉	Saturn 24♒	Freud may feel hindered communicating with Jung, as Freud may feel challenged to be more coherent, structured and prepared

Our friendships confirm we are citizens of a wider community and an integral part of a greater design that offer us hope for the future.

One shares with a friend a unique way of looking at life and experiencing it, and so our friendships perform a kind of astrology of the soul, opening planetary worlds for us, to give our lives culture and articulation.[70]

– CHAPTER 12 –
KARMIC CONNECTIONS
From the Moment We Met

When a relationship compels, captivates and confuses, individuals often seek an astrologer's insight. Astrology is favoured when something numinous, mysterious or fateful seems to be happening since it facilitates reflection on the complexity and confusion of a relationship. Modern astrology uses a variety of lenses to amplify these compelling relationships. But whether the approach is archetypal, evolutionary, psychological or spiritual, it is the astrologer's way of thinking and their personal experience in relationships that influence how the horoscope is approached, interpreted and expressed.

Depending on the astrologer's worldview, powerful attractions might be framed as the result of unconscious projections, familial patterning, karmic patterns, reincarnation, or recognizing a soulmate or twin flame; whatever it is, astrology can reflect on the connection through its symbols. Bonds that evoke memories, fascination, longing, fixation and intense feelings might be referred to as karmic relationships, while the term 'soulmate' could be referring to a relationship that is mutually comforting, supportive and nurturing. A psychic connection may suggest an attachment between the two souls or the unconscious impact of the relationship.

Beyond any expression or concept is the astrological image, which is the key to unlocking the mystery.

Karma
A fundamental doctrine in Hinduism and Buddhism, karma has become a popular concept in western thought.[71] The word means action, work or deed, but it is mostly used when referring to the spiritual principle of cause and effect, where our intentions and actions affect our future. Actions from the past and present accrue to determine our fate. As a law of moral causation, it echoes the early Greek ideas of justice and retribution as well as the Christian

belief of reaping what we sow. But if karma is reduced to a cause and effect hypothesis, it can no longer engage the soul.

The law of karma is not bound by time and space and extends through these dimensions. Being timeless and spaceless, a powerful attraction or repulsion is often referred to as karmic, as it feels as if the two people involved have pre-existed in another time and place. From an eastern spiritual perspective karma is inseparable from reincarnation. In western or psychological thinking it is akin to the psychic principle of heredity. In all systems it has an affinity with fate and destiny; therefore it is an essential thesis for all astrologers to embrace in their own way. According to the astrologer's belief system, karma could be expressed in either terms of past lives, psychic heredity or the eternal return.[72] Whether karma is a living reality or a metaphor, what is most important is to name the underlying astrological archetype/s that are bound up with it, as these are free from cultural and philosophical overtones.

In the context of relationships, karma implies a psychic connection, an intense longing, the recognition of something incomplete or the desire to be completed by the other. A karmic relationship suggests that each individual has been affected by the other's thoughts, emotions and actions. Two life paths intersect to alter the relationship and each other. From a psychological point of view, the couple are pulled towards each other by powerful and mysterious forces emanating from the unconscious. Astrology can help to define the basis of this karmic connection through the examination of the natal chart and its comparison with the other's horoscope.

Certain dimensions of the horoscope lend themselves to considering karmic imprints on our lives. Probably the stand-out astrological image for karmic implications in the birth chart is the nodal axis, which has been used to define past lives since the last half of the twentieth century.[73] Saturn is often referred to as the Lord of Karma, while planets in the 12th house are also frequently interpreted as karmic inheritances from the past. In reality, the whole horoscope is a dynamic fusion of karmic imprints, as the horoscope illustrates the totality of who we are. Many images in the horoscope indicate residual and enduring imprints and patterns from the past. Similarly, in relationship astrology the whole chart needs to be considered in terms of karmic patterning. No single feature of the horoscope will provide a full understanding of the mystery of attraction; however some astrological symbols, more than others, play a critical role when considering karmic relationships.

When focusing on karmic relationships, two axes of the horoscope are very revealing: the Moon's North and South Nodes and also the Vertex–Anti-Vertex axis. Both these axes are points in space created when their orbit or great circle intersects the ecliptic; therefore they are not archetypal like the planetary gods, but represent a direction or course in life. We have already reflected on how another axis, the Ascendant–Descendant, is highly significant in understanding adult relationships. In *The Family Legacy* we considered the importance of the MC–IC axis in terms of familial relationships. All four axes intersect the ecliptic, indicating crossroads in the heavens; in the horoscope they symbolize crossed paths or crossroads. In terms of karmic relationships, the Moon's Nodes and the Vertex locate memorable encounters with others.

Karmic Relationships: The Nodal Axis
The lunar nodes are not planets but points in space where the orbit of the Sun and Moon intersect. Unlike the planets their direction through the zodiac is retrograde. Therefore their nature is not bound by the matrix of time or space in the same way as the planets. Nor are they material or visible in the sky like planets. As an abstract construct in the heavens we can consider them to be metaphysical by nature. Whereas planets are symbolic of human instinct, the lunar nodes signify another dimension of personal experience. They can be likened to a spiritual journey across time and space or through different lifetimes. Speaking about the Moon's nodes, Dane Rudhyar said that 'we are dealing with what might be called the karmic way in which the Moon's function operates in a human being.'[74] The nature of these nodes lends itself to the notion of karma, as they evoke images of timeless experience contained by their southern and northern poles.

Rudhyar suggests that the nodal axis describes an alternative dimension to the natal Moon, representing the embodiment of our emotional processes and attachments. While the Moon symbolizes our emotional and familial connections, the nodal axis adds another layer to understanding these attachments over time and through space. The lunar nodes encourage attachments to be seen through a less personal lens, from the perspective of a spiritual or sacred passage. Similar to a Buddhist perspective, the nodes help us to detach from the emotionality of the Moon, offering metaphysical insights into the pain and suffering experienced through our attachments. The Moon is the soul's vessel that holds the deep feeling life; lunar experiences are acutely felt: the heartbreak of a severed attachment, the pain of an emotional wound or the suffering of neglect and isolation. From a karmic perspective, the nodes situate personal pain in the transpersonal perspective of the soul's journey through time. The Moon is instinctual and her nodal axis is spiritual.

The nodes are cyclical in that they return to their natal position every 18.6 years. And as in all cycles, the successes and failures of the old cycle are carried forward. The North Node is energetic and suggests the possibility of growth in both the present and the future, gleaned from the achievements of the past. The South Node is inert, containing the memory and feeling of former failures, yet it also contains the knowing and experience of past achievements which can be drawn on to move forward. Some interpretations of the nodal axis suggest the necessity to move away from the regressive pull of the South Node towards the North. Since the South and North Node are part of the same system, they are not separate; therefore, we might imagine the movement between the North and South Nodes as a continuing dance through time, not as a task to be completed.

In Chapter 5 of *Vocation*[75] I dealt with the lunar nodes in detail in regard to their placement in the natal chart. Through the lens of vocation we looked at the lunar nodes by sign, house and aspect. Therefore this serves as a resource for understanding the nodal axis in the natal chart. In relationship astrology the lunar nodes have the same meaning, but are now viewed in the context of relationship.

The sign and house polarity of the nodal axis are important as they symbolize crossroads, significant meetings and life paths that intersect. The nodes in synastry help us to begin to address the purpose of the relationship, at least in a spiritual context. The South Node is a point of familiarity, the felt experience or a sense of memory or recognition of the other. The South Node is where we feel connected or secure in knowing the other. The North Node presents the qualities that are in need of development and may be supported through relationships that encourage these attributes. The

North Node represents a link to an important quality in us that seeks its enhancement through interaction and relationship with others.

As an axis of 'destiny' the nodal axis is often reflective of relationships that are significant in helping us to find direction, purpose and fulfilment in our lives. The word 'karmic' is used in the context of the nodal axis to summarize the feelings of familiarity or foreignness, the attraction or repulsion, and the overwhelming sense that the relationship was meant to be. The spiritual quality of the relationship is stirred when the nodes are involved; hence the feelings evoked in the encounter are often described in numinous terms like mystical or magical, something other than here and now.

Returning to Brad Pitt and Angelina Jolie's horoscopes, we see that Angelina's Sagittarian North Node falls in the same sign as Brad's Ascendant in his 12th house. Similarly, Pitt's North Node in Cancer falls in Jolie's 12th house in the same sign as her Ascendant. Each one's North Node direction impacts the other deeply in their imagination, creativity and spirituality. There is a sense that each one's life direction touches something quite sensitive, yet unknown, in the other, triggering intrigue, mysticism and a deeper spiritual connection. It also implies that each may be the catalyst for the other to examine their unexamined life.

Eclipsing the Other
The Moon's nodal axis is intimately tied to the cycle of solar eclipses. When the Sun and Moon are near the nodal axis the Sun, Moon and Earth are aligned; hence, a solar or lunar eclipse can occur at a New Moon or Full Moon. Solar eclipses will always happen at least twice a year. When the lunar nodes are entwined with the Sun or Moon in the horoscope, then the cycle of eclipses may also be of interest in the dynamics of the couple's relationship.

Eclipses played a major role in the turning points in the relationship of the Prince and Princess of Wales. Princess Diana was born with the South Node conjunct the Moon in Aquarius in the 2nd house, while Prince Charles was born with the North Node conjunct the Moon in the 10th. Each having the Moon conjunct a lunar node suggests that inherited dynamics of family, motherhood and the public will be featured in close relationships.

Diana was born when the eclipses were in the polarity of ♌ and ♒: the intercepted polarity of her 2nd and 8th houses. The total solar eclipse before her birth was on 15 February 1961 at 26≈25, within 2° of her natal Moon. She married Prince Charles on 29 July 1981, two days before the solar eclipse of 31 July 1981 occurring at 7♌51, near her Vertex in the 8th house. She was twenty years old.

Diana was the Roman name for the goddess of the Moon. The eclipse of her marriage of 7♌51 fell on Charles's Ascendant. In many ways he was eclipsed by Diana, as she became the celebrity favoured by the people. Camilla Parker-Bowles, the Prince's mistress, whose Ascendant and Saturn are also close by at 3♌06 and 9♌57 respectively, was also eclipsed. Diana, the Moon, had obscured the solar Prince and his lover.

Charles was born when the eclipses were in the polarity of ♉ and ♏. The one before his birth occurred on 1 November 1948 at 8♏44, close to the nodal axis and conjunct Mercury.

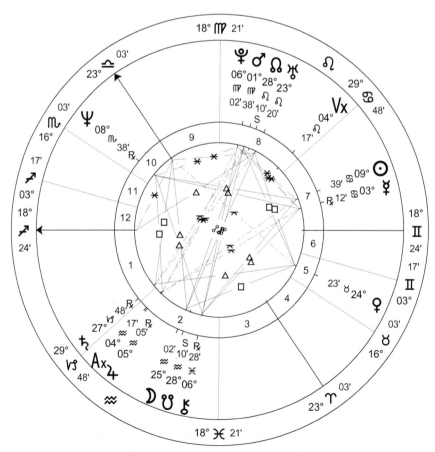

Diana, 1 July 1961, 7.45 p.m., Sandringham, England

During the northern hemisphere summer of 1992 their marriage was in great turmoil. On 30 June 1992, the day before her thirty-first birthday, an eclipse at 8♋57 obscured Diana's 7th house Sun. This eclipse also fell on the Moon–Venus conjunction (9♋56/10♋34) of Camilla Parker-Bowles, the lover of Prince Charles. Later that year, on 9 December, the Prime Minister formally announced the royal couple's separation. It was the day of a lunar eclipse. The degree of the eclipse was 18♊10; the Sun being at 18♐10 and the Moon at 18♊10, exactly on Diana's Descendant, the 7th house cusp of marriage. Unlike the day of her marriage, Diana now was the one obscured by the royal light of the Sun.

Diana died under the eclipse of 1 September 1997 which occurred at 9♍34, close to her natal Pluto in the 8th house. The zodiacal location of the eclipses is close to the transiting nodes which also become significant in the development of a relationship, especially

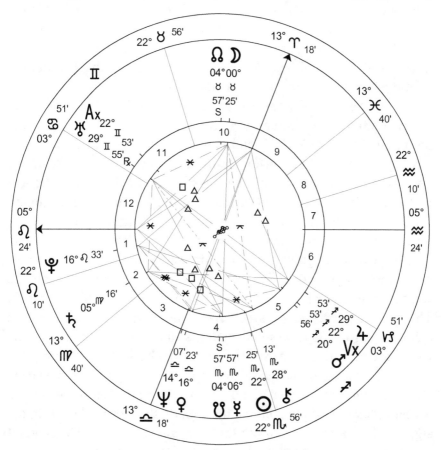

Charles, 14 November 1948, 9.14 p.m., Buckingham Palace, England

if the natal Sun and/or Moon are conjunct one of the lunar nodes. In relationship astrology the natal constellation of the nodes and their interplay between the charts of the partners is highly significant and revealing.

Cosmic Connections: The Vertex

Another angle of the horoscope, the Vertex, belongs to modern astrology because it did not enter astrological tradition until the middle of the twentieth century.[76] It was proposed by L. Edward Johndro, a Canadian astrologer, who began likening its opposite angle, the Anti-Vertex, to an 'Electric Ascendant'.[77] His astrological colleague, Charles Jayne, began experimenting with this point and reported the Vertex to be responsive to solar arc directions. Both agreed that the Vertex was fated and represented issues beyond our control; therefore the Vertex entered astrological thinking strongly imprinted with being a point of compulsion and fate. Falling in the western hemisphere of the horoscope it was naturally aligned with relationship and compromise and having the mystique of something fated or out of control. The Vertex began life symbolizing compelling relationships and strong attachments.

The Vertex–Anti-Vertex is the third angle of the horoscope and in a way it stretches us into a three-dimensional view of the self. It is not vertical like the MC–IC, nor is it horizontal like the Ascendant–Descendant axis. The Vertex is found in the western part of the horoscope and is formed by the intersection of the Prime Vertical with the ecliptic,[78] representing another dimension of self and other. Because it is formed by the junction of fast-moving circles, the Vertex is time-sensitive; therefore it is dependent on an accurate time of birth. Its angularity is not as defined as the traditional angles, being more mysterious, indefinite and less observable. It signifies what is unable to be directly observed on the horizon of experience. The visible Descendant symbolizes the partner's qualities and characteristics. The relational patterns that constellate around the Descendent, which is perceptible, are symbolic of configurations able to reach consciousness, unlike those arranged at the Vertex, which by nature is unseen and unknown. In relationship astrology a revealing exercise is to contrast the sign on the Descendant with the sign on the Vertex, imagining that the qualities of the Descendant sign are more known while those of the Vertex are not.

In moderate latitudes the Vertex will generally be located in the 5th to the 8th houses. In latitudes near the equator the vertex can swing into the 4th or 9th houses. When the Descendant and Vertex are in different signs, there may be a tendency to identify with the Descendant's characteristics in others, but to be blinded to the qualities and patterns represented by the Vertex. However, over time the unconscious agenda of the Vertex surfaces in relationship and can be of great substance and value, albeit often unanticipated and confronting. When the Vertex and Descendant are in the same sign their qualities are intensified and difficult to differentiate. At any latitude, when 0° of the solstice signs, Cancer or Capricorn, are on the MC, then the Ascendant–Descendant and the Vertex–Anti-Vertex are aligned at 0° of the equinox signs, Libra and Aries. When the MC is within orb of 0° Cancer or Capricorn, the Vertex and Descendant will probably be in the same sign.

This angle adds a third dimension to the nature of our interrelationships by offering a different perspective on our significant encounters, the concealed agendas in relationship and compelling rendezvous of our lives. Considering the Vertex–Anti-Vertex axis is similar to putting on 3-D glasses to view the horoscope. All of a sudden something that seemed at arm's length is now right in front of you; what was in the background has come to the foreground. Subtleties are now more obvious. The Vertex has been described as fateful encounters, cosmic appointments and 'run-ins that seem beyond our control'.[79] The Anti-Vertex, located in the eastern side of the chart, complements its polar partner by revealing a layer of self not visible at first glance, a hidden birth mark, an alter ego, an autonomous voice. In tandem with the Vertex, this axis often reveals untapped resources that support and sustain the personality in the tasks of life, especially work and relationship.

The Vertex's earliest associations were with what was 'fated' and beyond conscious control. This refers to the blind spot that the Vertex reveals, the unseen qualities that arise through our relationships and transform who we are. Therefore what might feel beyond our control and unbidden is actually an unconscious agenda coming to light. Ironically, it is these relationships that are the ones that impact on us and often change the course of our lives. My experience has led me to quip that the Vertex represents the relationships you can't get rid of; in other words, they dynamically alter who we are and how we relate. [80]

Modern astrology does not always refer to the Vertex, but my experience of it in the context of relationship astrology is very synchronous with karmic relationships. It symbolizes where there may be a compelling or blind aspect in relationship. The Vertex symbolizes veiled agendas not visible until the relationship has excavated deeper emotional territory, like the image of the alchemical 'left-handed handshake' signifying an unconscious collusion. The agenda of the Vertex is often contrary to the conscious contract of the relationship; therefore the astrological imagery of the Vertex helps to articulate hidden agendas. The Vertex is an image of what we struggle to complete, as well as what keeps us bound to the relationship, or a form of it, until it erupts through the ego defences to be confronted.

The Natal Vertex

Being the third angle of the horoscope, the Vertex–Anti-Vertex plays an important role in character disposition. As already discussed, the Vertex falls in the western part of the chart; therefore it symbolizes relationships where our personal will is compromised, where we feel out of control, compulsive or left with little choice. It can symbolize others who play a significant role in our lives and astrologically this can be seen through contacts to the Vertex.

The Anti-Vertex in the east describes resources that we can use in relationship crises to find a way forward. It is an auxiliary energy that backs up the personality reflected by the Ascendant. Johndro and Jayne's early testing of the two angles favoured the Vertex; hence it has become more widely recognized, leaving the Anti-Vertex languishing on the other side of the chart. But that is its nature: the unrecognized and unseen resources lying in the umbra of the personality. The Anti-Vertex suggests the desires and urges that remain overshadowed by the Ascendant; values and resources that often lie untapped by the self. If they go unappreciated for too long they become a siren's song that may lead us to a fateful encounter.

To interpret the Vertex, first consider its sign, especially in contrast to the sign on the Descendant. Secondly, note the house position of the Vertex. The sign of the Vertex represents unidentified qualities that are seemingly at odds with our conscious intent, yet they are of great value in the scheme of our lives. Therefore, transits to this point awaken these qualities as do a partner's planets when conjoining this axis. And most importantly, consider any planet within a 10° conjunction of this axis as it will play a significant role in the understanding of partnerships and may indicate energies that are often compelling and difficult in terms of relational patterns.

The Vertex gathers images of what is unconscious within relationship. For instance, if the Vertex is in Aries there may be an unconscious rivalry and competitiveness that feels compelling and unable to be satisfied. In Gemini it may reiterate the theme of incompleteness and compulsion around the area of sibling relationships or a haunting need to search for the twin soul. When placed in Scorpio it may heighten the need for sexual and emotional intrigue and drama; complex themes involving love and power or love and possessiveness may colour the landscape of relationship.

Unlike the other angles that are the boundary zones to a new quadrant and house of the horoscope, the Vertex occupies a house. This can be delineated; the house position of the Vertex suggests the area where critical relationships take place. Since the Vertex will generally fall in the 5th to 8th houses (unless the individual is born close to the equator), the house influence should be considered. This environment will often be where encounters with shadows reflected by others occur. The 5th–8th houses, the sector where the Vertex is located in moderate latitudes, are also known as the interpersonal houses of the horoscope, where we are inclined to engage with others.

By house, the Vertex symbolizes the environment or place where we may experience turning points, dynamic meetings or where we might cross paths with others who assist in our transformation. It is an arena of destiny as in this place we encounter something, somewhere or someone that triggers an unconscious memory or deeply felt sense of recognition. For instance if the Vertex is in the 5th house then the relationship with a child, a lover or one's own creativity is enhanced. In the 6th our relationship with work, co-workers, clients, employees, assistants or service providers comes into focus. The Vertex in the 7th stresses the area of equal partnerships and encounters with an intimate friend, a business or marriage partner who may transform your life dynamically. In the

212 From the Moment We Met: The Astrology of Adult Relationships

8th house the Vertex confronts us with the loss of our naivety and the potential death of a special relationship, as well as the themes of trust and betrayal.

Planets on the Vertex are influential forces that steer us towards a profound change through relationship. For instance, for a man, if the Moon is conjunct the Vertex there may be a powerful transference with the women that he encounters throughout his life, first with mother, then sisters, colleagues, wife, sister-in-law and daughters. For a woman, the Moon on the Vertex may suggest that the incomplete relationship with mother or motherly feelings may dominate the quest for an equal relationship.

To summarize:

Images and Symbols of the Vertex	Images and Symbols of the Anti-Vertex
Hidden agendas in relationships, hence what are often seen as karmic or fated connections	Unseen qualities of our personality that are powerful allies when presenting ourselves to the world
Unbreakable bonds and the unconscious contracts in relationships	Creative aspects of our individuality that may be overshadowed
Issues and affairs beyond our control	Anchoring aspects of our character
Deep-seated, compelling and inescapable themes in relationship	Unacknowledged traits and qualities that may not be consciously utilized
Otherworldly; sensitivity to subtle realities	An alternative power or energy source
Relationships and experiences that change our life perspective	A hidden aspect of the self that may change the way we relate to others and the world at large

Relationship
The images and revelations of this angle come alive in relationship astrology. Regularly I see this confirmation of a transformational encounter when working with couples using chart comparisons. When one person's Vertex interconnects with planets or angles in the other's chart this is accompanied by the feeling of a strong

karmic bond; often this is reciprocated by a strong aspect from their partner's Vertex.

Once again, let's consider the charts of Brad and Angelina to demonstrate the Vertex in relationship and how it is often activated in important relationships. In Jolie's chart the Vertex is conjunct Neptune in Sagittarius opposite her Sun. This suggests that her relationship with her father and the archetype of father will significantly impact relationships through the pattern of idealization and disappointment. In the 5th house it also brings the theme of children and creativity prominently into her relationship. Brad's Vertex is in Cancer in the 8th house opposite Venus. The themes of intimacy and familiarity are strong and will be present in his relationships. Strikingly, each partner's Vertex conjoins the other's Ascendant.

Brad has 11♊54 on the Descendant with the Vertex at 27♋22 in the 8th house. Perhaps he is conscious of being drawn to gregarious, witty and intellectual companions, but he may not be so aware of the Vertex in Cancer's agenda to become involved and entangled with family, kinship and parental issues. Angelina has her Capricorn Descendant at 28♑53 with her Vertex at 11♐05. Astrologically we might suggest that she is conscious of her attraction to maturity and self-made success, but what about her awareness of the adventuresome, the mystical and creative needs of her Neptune–Vertex in Sagittarius?

When comparing their horoscopes their angles are intertwined: Brad's Ascendant at 11♐54 is conjunct Angelina's Vertex so maybe he brings some travel adventure and mysticism into their relationship. Angelina's Venus–Ascendant is conjunct Brad's Vertex and she has brought a family of six children into his life. Such a potent enmeshment between the angles was symbolized by the media attention and the couple being dubbed 'Brangelina' by the media.

It is notable that they both have a luminary conjunct the Anti-Vertex. Angelina's Sun in Gemini is on her Anti-Vertex, a potent image for her heroic alter egos portrayed in her films as well as her many accolades for humanitarian work. Underlying the beauty of Venus rising is a charisma, creativity and fatherly factor. Brad's Moon–Venus conjunction in Capricorn on his Anti-Vertex suggests the essence of a receptive and caring authority that underpins the cowboy persona of his Ascendant. Interestingly, in Brad's previous relationships his Vertex and Descendant had been highlighted in different ways. Gwyneth Paltrow was engaged to Brad Pitt. Their relationship lasted three years. Her Moon is at 11♊33, exactly conjunct his Descendant, with her South Node at 23♋05 closely conjunct his Vertex. Both contacts demonstrate a strong and familial bond but one that perhaps is past, not present. He was married to Jennifer Aniston for five years. Her Vertex at 6♊45 aligns with his Descendant while her MC at 27♋19 overlaps his Vertex.

The Vertex plays a major role in chart comparison when studying karmic relationships. The above example shows the mutual interplay between the Vertex–Anti-Vertex axis and the Ascendant–Descendant axis. This is a combination I have seen many times in dynamic relationships. For instance in the royal relationship between the Prince and Princess of Wales this aspect also occurs. Notice that Charles's Vertex at 22♐53 is conjunct Diana's Ascendant at 18♐24 while Diana's Vertex at 4♌17 is conjunct Charles's Ascendant at 5♌24. Each one's Ascendant was the other's Vertex; something invisible and deeply rooted in themselves may have been mirrored effortlessly and automatically by the other, something not always able to be identified or integrated into the partnership. Camilla Parker-Bowles shares Charles's Ascendant and Vertex. Her Ascendant of 3♌06 and Vertex of 20♐04 resonate with Charles's horoscope and replicate the aspects to Diana's chart. By its own nature the Vertex is often highlighted in relationship triangles and affairs.

Strong links to the Vertex between horoscopes highlight the spirit of the relationship. For instance, note in Whitney Houston's horoscope her Vertex at 20♍50 conjoins Bobby's Moon at 19♍57. Bobby's Vertex at 22♌56 is conjunct Whitney's Sun at 16♌41. These contacts fasten the connection, fuel the compulsion and create a powerful link-up. Similar to the Nodes, the Vertex–Anti-Vertex is like a portal for the entrances and exits of significant others. The Vertex often plays a significant role by transit or progression when partners' paths cross or separate. For instance, it is suggested that the relationship between Diana and Charles became serious in the summer of 1980, as Neptune transited Diana's Ascendant and Charles's Vertex. In September 2016, as news broke that Angelina Jolie was filing for divorce from Brad Pitt, Saturn was transiting her Vertex and his Ascendant.

Twenty-five years before Diana and Charles were married, another 'wedding of the century' took place in Monaco between the American actress Grace Kelly and her prince charming, Prince Rainier III of Monaco, a year after they had met. On the day of their first meeting, everything seemed to be going wrong for Grace who wanted to cancel the appointment. However, she was persuaded to go by a friend; yet when she arrived, Rainier was running late.[81] The photo shoot was set for the afternoon of 6 May 1955, just before the Full Moon which would occur later that evening at 15♏36, so the Moon that afternoon was a few degrees shy of this.

Prince Rainier's time of birth is not confirmed, but is sometimes given as 6 a.m.[82] For this time he has Jupiter at 11♏02 conjunct the Vertex at 14♏44 opposite Venus at 11♉32; the Full Moon would conjoin his 'unconfirmed' Vertex axis later that day, but that afternoon the Moon was transiting his Jupiter–Venus opposition. Grace had Mercury at 10♏42 conjunct her South Node at 12♏10 opposite Chiron at 11♉37. Therefore Grace's North Node was conjunct Rainier's Venus while her South Node was conjunct his Jupiter and perhaps his Vertex. In the hours of their meeting the Moon was transiting this interaspect. Although their first meeting was rushed and interrupted by photographers there was something fated about their rendezvous. It was arranged by the French magazine *Paris Match*, we might say matched by *Match*, and while it nearly did not happen, it did. The interweaving of Grace's nodal axis with Rainier's Vertex–Venus and their meeting on the day of the Full Moon which moved across this interaspect also feels destined. The Full Moon heralded the marriage of the Prince and Princess of Monaco.

As already mentioned, many aspects of the horoscope can be amplified when considering karmic imprints on relationships. One way might be to reflect on which archetypes respond to the persuasive amalgam of familiarity and mystery. Two of these archetypes are the fastest and slowest moving of all the planets: the Moon and Pluto respectively.

Familiarity and Mystery
In English our word 'familiarity' suggests a close association or something that has become well known over time. In referring to relationship it is akin to a family footing or intimacy; being close,

dear, even private and trusted. Its root is in the Latin *familialis* which is also the source of 'family'; therefore, feeling familiar with a workmate, partner, colleague or companion suggests a more intimate tie, one that has its origins in the past. Familiarity implies a spirit of connection.

When used as a noun, a familiar referred to a spirit or daimon. Accounts of familiars varied throughout European folklore, witchcraft and shamanism. The familiar spirit often revealed itself in animal form; hence it was intimately connected with the instinctual life as well as the anima or soul. Being closely attached to the individual, the familiar or animal spirit was given a name and recognized as a companion. Imaginary playmates are familiar aspects of childhood. While these experiences may be clinically rationalized and explained or passed off as a childlike fantasy, nonetheless, these experiences are an encounter with familiar spirits that guide us into the later terrain of relationships.

In a way the familiar is like an alter ego, another dimension of the self that is reawakened through the agency of another. There are many ways to reflect on the familiar. One way might be to imagine it as a daimon, a personal spirit that is magnetized by the force of love. When reawakened its force is palpable, both physically and psychologically. Emotions are stirred. What remain after the encounter are the felt experience of familiarity and the recognition of a deep connection. When projected onto an individual, the feeling is as if we have known the other from the past. But from what past?

When an individual experiences a deeply felt response to another it feels eternal, having endured across time and space. In a contemporary context we might suggest this soul-sense of familiarity is the basis of adult attachment. And like all attachments it has an affinity with the past, home and security. Psychologically, an encounter with the beloved, a soulmate or the desired lover can awaken an unremembered past which can become contextualized as something that happened before, from an earlier period. Encountering a soulmate is a kind of recollection, a resonance with something deeply known. Close attachment rekindles the instinct to return home; therefore when there is an intimate bond, emotional closeness, sexual harmony or like-minded friends there is also a sensation of homecoming and safety, like being cradled in the secure arms of another. The lunar archetype resonates with adult attachments that rekindle a karmic sense of familiarity.

Our word 'mystery' implies something that is complex to understand or explain, similar to an enigma, secret or conundrum. There are many similar Greek roots such as *mysterion* which refers to a secret rite or doctrine, *mystes* or one who has been initiated, and *myein* which means to close. These underlying images of the word refer to mystery initiations where initiates would often close their mouths and eyes in order to experience a divine revelation. The most famous mysteries of the ancient world were the Eleusinian Mysteries which personified Persephone's initiatory journey into the underworld after she had been abducted by Pluto. Once initiated in the mysteries, one was no longer fearful of death.

In relationship astrology, Pluto embodies a compelling and transforming encounter, one that is magnetic and engaging. When Pluto enters into the arena of relating, it symbolizes an inevitable journey into a deep and intimate connection. The Pluto archetype of mystery also reflects karmic relationships;[83] therefore both the Moon and Pluto are important to consider in these relationships.

Sentimentality: Lunar Loves

The astrological Moon is sensitive and responsive to the atmosphere of feeling, so any underlying anxiety, tension or sentiment is often registered and remembered. 'Sentiment' suggests what one feels about something; however, in contemporary times, when feeling intelligence is no longer valued, the word has come to suggest exaggerated, nostalgic or self-indulgent feelings of sadness or kindness. The Moon is sentimental and its reactions are meaningful even if they cannot be explained rationally or expressed logically.

The Moon is a vessel for the feeling life. Over time it becomes a strongbox full of all the sensations, feelings, tastes, sights, smells and sounds we have experienced and reacted to but not remembered. As the fastest moving of all the planetary archetypes, the Moon is the most personal. It completes its first revolution of the zodiac in just 27.3 days; in that time we have experienced the Moon in every astrological variant possible, initiating us into our lunar temperament, a deep symbol of what stays habitual and instinctual in us. It is the recorder of our earliest feeling impressions. When extended back through time, the Moon symbolizes past feelings.

The past, whether that is the personal, familial, ancestral or cultural past, is embedded in the Moon.

Memory is a feature of the Moon but it is feeling memory; therefore, memories are awoken through a song on the radio, a smell, a dream or aches and pains. The memories are neither linear nor logical, but powerful impressions of something from before; therefore, the rational mind attempts to find a logical hypothesis to contextualize the familiar feeling in time and space. In relationship astrology the Moon is the comfort and shelter one feels in relationship, but it is also the sense of familiarity and the past. As a result, when the Moon is a strong aspect of a relationship, it can feel karmic.

In relationships that are intimate, familial, tempestuous and filled with feeling, it is common to find the Moon conjunct the partner's angles, or conjunct or opposite the Sun or another inner planet.

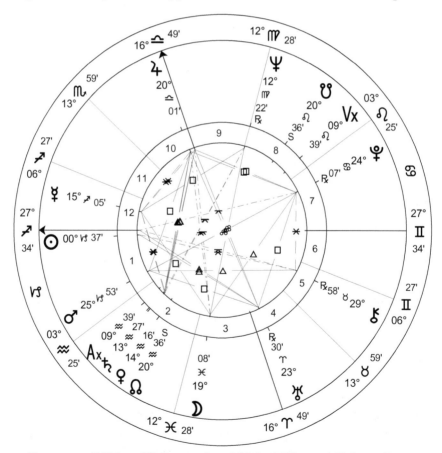

Emperor Akihito, 23 December 1933, 6.39 a.m., Tokyo, Japan

These famous lovers are examples of this: Virginia Woolf's Moon at 25♈19 was conjunct Vita Sackville-West's Venus at 28♈48; Anaïs Nin's Moon at 01♑14 was conjunct Henry Miller's Sun at 4♑41; Rainer Maria Rilke's Moon at 16♒46 was conjunct Lou Andreas-Salomé's Sun at 23♒44; and Elizabeth Taylor's Moon at 15♏26 conjoined Richard Burton's Sun at 17♏42.

The lunar focus of relationship can also be on family and security. Another royal couple, Akihito and Michiko, the Emperor and Empress of Japan, have their Moons conjunct. This image suggests that each individual in the relationship will understand the nuances of feelings, reactions, moods and needs of the other. There is an innate sense of comfort, affection and familiarity. Each individual will also experience the same transits to the Moon within a similar time period. While this allows for empathy and compassion it also suggests that the couple may lack perspective on their feeling life.

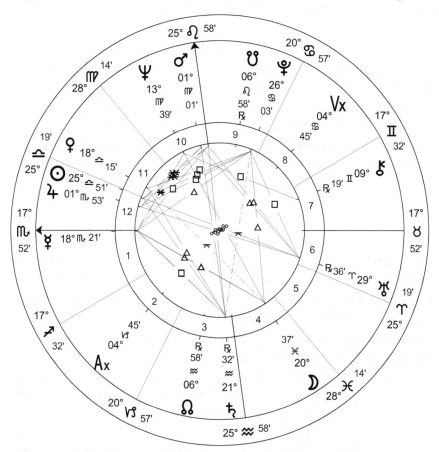

Empress Michiko, 20 October 1934, 7.43 a.m., Tokyo, Japan

Or, being reactive, one partner may take an opposite perspective to try and regain a sense of separateness. With such a powerful bond it is worthwhile noting the potentials and the pitfalls. Since each has the Moon in Pisces it will be carried through to the composite chart, creating a powerful continuity of this image in relationship.

It is also worthwhile noting the nodal and Vertex positions in each horoscope. Born within ten months of each other, their nodal axes will have retrograded about 15° of the zodiac.[84] Akihito's North Node at 20♒36 is conjunct Michiko's Saturn at 21♒32 on the IC. Michiko's North Node is 6♒58, conjunct Akihito's Saturn at 13♒ 27 which is conjunct Venus. Akihito's Vertex at 9♌39 is conjunct Michiko's South Node at 6♌58, while Michiko's Vertex at 4♋45 is opposite Akihito's Sun at 0♑37. With the strong nodal, Vertex and lunar connections there is a sense of a strong karmic imprint.

The Passions of Pluto

Although the presence of Pluto had been suspected for some time, it was not 'officially' discovered until 1930.[85] Named for the god of the underworld, Pluto entered the astrological pantheon between the two World Wars, shortly after the collapse of Wall Street, prohibition and the rise of dictatorships, all synchronous symbols of Pluto breaching the surface. As the god of death his archetype confronts astrologers to find meaning and insight in the depths of his underworld terrain.

In 1970, when Isabel Hickey published her popular text *Astrology, a Cosmic Science* she did not include Pluto as she felt more research was needed. Three years later she released her booklet *Pluto or Minerva: The Choice is Yours* in which she delineated Pluto astrologically as the invisible energy 'which is unknown on the surface but which works ceaselessly in the depths of our being'. Buried beneath the surface, its 'lowest aspect' can erupt in violence. But she also described the 'highest aspect' of Pluto which transforms the person from within. They are purged and regenerated and 'never again in the same state of consciousness'.[86]

Isabel's spiritual perceptions and belief in reincarnation enabled her to view Pluto from an evolutionary perspective. A choice was available in how we dealt with our beasts of desire, passion, temptation or ambition, whether they were used as a force for light or dark. In the 1990s Jeffrey Wolf Green developed an approach called

Evolutionary Astrology, which focuses on the soul's growth through its various incarnations. One of the focal points of this work is Pluto and its correlation to the soul as well as its karmic implications in relationship.[87] As a planetary archetype, Pluto constellates intrigue, power, challenges and catharsis. It is astrologically aligned with both the soul and karma in the sense of its mystery initiations and purification processes. In relationship astrology it serves as a symbol of passion, desire and the confrontation with the taboos and trials of a soulful relationship.

One of the hallmarks of Pluto is its intensity of feeling. It loves and hates deeply. Characteristic of all or nothing, there is an attraction/ repulsion dynamic that operates when feeling threatened or jealous. Its position and aspects in the natal chart help to identify what will be brought into the sphere of relationship. When highlighted in the relationship sectors or in aspect to inner planets, we are alert for the passionate personality to emerge through relating.

Bobby Brown's horoscope has Pluto in the 8th house conjunct the Moon, while in Whitney's chart Pluto is in the 7th conjunct Mercury. Both having Pluto in a house connected with intimacy suggests the passion and intensity of their interaction. Whether we would place this in the context of past lives depends on the astrologer's worldview; however, in terms of a planetary archetype, Pluto brings the past and what lies unacknowledged to the surface in personal relationships.

Being close in age, Akihito and Michiko have their Plutos in close proximity. Both are in Cancer, ruled by the Moon, and each is trine to the Moon in Pisces. Akihito's Pluto is in the 7th house opposite Mars, and both are involved in a Grand Cross with Jupiter opposite Uranus. Michiko has Scorpio rising; therefore the modern ruler of her horoscope is Pluto, which is square to Venus and her Sun, defining her as strongly Plutonic and attractive to Akihito's 7th house Pluto. Having Michiko's Pluto close by suggests that her Pluto will intensify Akihito's Grand Cross. While they share the familiarity of the Moon, both Akihito and Michiko also share in the intense archetypal field ruled by Pluto.

– CHAPTER 13 –
TEMPERAMENT AND RELATIONSHIP
Elemental Compatibility

Beginning the analysis of a horoscope by assessing temperament can be particularly informative in establishing possible relationship strengths and vulnerabilities. Susceptibility to our temperamental strengths and limitations is encountered and partnered in our close relationships; therefore, an awareness of temperament helps to bring order into the chaos of a relationship. It also increases tolerance and an appreciation of the differences between partners. While temperamental differences may not be clearly evident at first, they often begin to emerge in committed relationships after the first anniversary of living together when dissimilarities in energy, values, moods and communication might appear.

Each horoscope reflects an individual's natural temperament and how this may function in relating. But first let's consider an astrological perspective on temperament.

Temperament
Liz Greene first published her book *Relating, an Astrological Guide to Living with Others* in 1977. In this book she introduced many of Carl Jung's ideas, amplifying them to enrich the understanding of astrological symbols. Nearly ten years after its first publication Liz Greene rewrote the foreword to her book, acknowledging the developments and advances that had taken place in the field of astrology in that past decade. Of note, she writes 'I feel now, even more strongly than I did then, that the four elements of astrology are the essential building-blocks of the horoscope', emphasizing that:

> if one begins an assessment of the horoscope with the particular individual balance of elements then the essential spinal column of the chart is depicted and the overall story of the individual's development pattern is displayed.[88]

This compelling validation for the necessity of elemental analysis in each horoscope recognizes the age-old tradition of temperament. To temper suggests to moderate, to regulate and to balance. The Latin root refers to a proper mixture, a continuance of the Greek medical conviction that health could be achieved through the proportioned mixture of constitutional elements. Physical matter is composed of the four elements of Fire, Earth, Air and Water, while nature was seen to be the dynamic interplay between the four qualities of hot, cold, dry and wet. Metabolically, the four humours of yellow bile, black bile, blood and phlegm were symbols of the four elements in the body which lent their names to the four temperaments: choleric, melancholic, sanguine and phlegmatic respectively. Temperament has a rich history and its theories have evolved since the early Greek medical notions of health. These ideas underpin the development of our astrological thoughts on the four elements and the three qualities which are fundamental to introducing the individual to their astrological temperament.

Other practices were also influenced by the symbolism of the elements. Tarot tradition developed four suits of Wands, Cups, Swords and Pentacles. These Minor Arcana cards express the nature of daily life.[89] Alchemy also suggested calcinatio, coagulatio, sublimatio and solutio as four stages or categories in transformational development.

Alchemists believed the basis of the material world lay in the *prima materia* or principal chaotic matter. It was through the facilities of the four elements that form could be shaped out of the chaos.[90] In the alchemy of a relationship elements are also mixed together. Out of the original chaos of the relationship a more conscious approach to relating can emerge through the awareness of temperamental differences. Mixing elements together in different ratios and combinations leads to infinite possibilities. As astrologers we have a rich tradition and imagination to reflect on the temperamental mixture of elements in each horoscope. Therefore in the context of relationship analysis, temperament is a perfect place to begin as it orientates us to the notion of compatibility and balance. It leads us to question our imbalances and how we respond to these in the world outside our self. Temperament is inborn; therefore it is resonant with the horoscope which is a natural exposition of inherent qualities. Being innate, it is also psychodynamic. It indicates an inner style of relationship and the soul's natural orientation to the outer world. Relationships confront us with temperamental differences, and more often than not, our natural disposition is at odds with those we love and partner.

Carl Jung presented his four psychological types of intuition, sensation, thinking and feeling in his treatise on psychological types first published in German in 1921. Influenced by alchemical principles and astrological doctrines, Carl Jung formulated his theory by acknowledging astrology's pioneering contribution: 'What was first represented by the signs of the zodiac was later expressed in the physiological language of Greek medicine.'[91] Jung also acknowledged astrology's seminal role in typology:

> From earliest times attempts have been made to classify individuals according to types, and so to bring order into the chaos. The oldest attempts known to us were made by oriental astrologers who devised the so-called trigons of the four elements – Air, Water, Earth and Fire.[92]

Jung's four functions describe how individuals might orient themselves to the archetypal world. These psychological types can be equated with the four elements. Like all systems of thought they do not completely match up; however, they can be used to amplify and reflect upon the astrological elements. For me, the value of Jung's explanation is in how the four types (intuition, sensation, thinking and feeling) relate to each other, which can inspire our understanding of the elemental interaction between two individuals. Astrological tradition has developed a variety of ways for assessing temperament from the horoscope and all can serve as a starting point for the consideration of temperament astrologically.[93]

Temperamental Imbalances and Relationships
Jung's typology differentiated the functions of sensation and intuition as perceiving, while thinking and feeling were judging functions. Each function was also modified by either an attitude of extroversion or introversion. Extraversion suggests that psychic energy is directed outward onto the world of external objects, events and relationship while introversion directs the channel of psychic energy internally. An introvert derives meaning from

subjective responses, unlike the extravert who finds meaning in external reactions. While extraverts enjoy the social world, an introvert withdraws from the crowd. Since opposites are curious and fascinating, this natural polarity is regularly encountered in relating. The astrological model has numerous ways of thinking about this polarity through masculine and feminine signs and planets, the upper and lower hemispheres, and also aspect combinations. As Jung suggested we have both extraversion and introversion; therefore each astrological element and sign can be expressed either way.

Astrologically, Fire and Air signs tend to be concerned with changing the situation while Earth and Water signs prefer to sustain the status quo. While this categorization is similar to extraversion/introversion, in essence the temperament of each sign could be expressed either way. Fire and Air signs need activity, action and movement, but the flow of this energy may be directed outwardly (extravert) or inwardly (introvert). Water and Earth signs are more naturally inclined to be reflective, careful and inclined to wait. This tendency could be projected onto the world (extravert) or remain internalized (introvert).

The function of judging orders the external world. These temperaments are inclined to regulate and control their environment, being systematic and organized, similar to fixed signs. Perceiving tends to be more spontaneous and adaptable in its approach to life and is similar to mutable signs. The function of perception takes in information, keeping its options open. Temperamental differences are met in relationship in the simplest ways, most often in the everyday rituals of life; for instance, one partner may prefer to be spontaneous while the other favours planning; one sees the detail, the other the larger picture.

The three qualities of cardinal, fixed and mutable play a role in temperament. These modalities influence the natural expression of energy. While each element may represent a season, each modality represents one seasonal trimester. Cardinal represents the beginning of the season and by temperament it is initiatory and restless. Fixed represents stability and is the second trimester of the season. Temperamentally, fixed signs are inclined to constancy and permanence, often resistant to change. Finally, the season ends and its changeability is symbolized by the mutable modality. As a temperament, this implies flexibility, often instability. The three qualities can also be seen as a complete process of which cardinal is the beginning, the seminal idea and initiatory action. Fixed is the middle of the process where construction and creation of the seed idea bring it into form. Mutable ends the process with the distribution and dissemination of the final product.

Astrologically there are many comparisons between Jungian and astrological types, such as:

Jungian Typology	Astrological Imagery
Intuition	Fire
Sensation	Earth
Thinking	Air
Feeling	Water
Extraversion	Above the horizon (Ascendant–Descendant axis)
Introversion	Below the horizon (Ascendant–Descendant axis)
Perceiving	Mutable; cardinal polarity of Aries–Libra
Judging	Fixed; cardinal polarity of Cancer–Capricorn

The Jungian model enhances an astrologer's psychological understanding of the four elements and the ways they operate within the human psyche. Like his ancient mentors, Jung suggested that one of the four types was more accessible to consciousness and possibly overshadowed the others. The ego identifies with this type more easily. Jung called this function the *superior function*, suggesting it had a psychological opposite or unconscious complement, which he labelled the *inferior function*. The inferior function would be the least accessible to consciousness.

If one type is consciously dominant, its psychological opposite is relegated to the unconscious. It is this unconscious element that we are introduced to through the agency of relationship. Jung paired the types in the superior–inferior opposition model as thinking–feeling and intuition–sensation, and vice versa. For example, if thinking is the individual's dominant type, then feeling automatically becomes the inferior function. In a lived experience this suggests that we cannot think and feel at the same time; therefore one part of the polarity is put to sleep. In terms of temperament, if we are a thinking type, feeling would be our nemesis and we would continue to meet her in all our relationships.

The inferior function makes its impact on consciousness in a myriad of ways, most commonly via projection onto others, events, slips of the tongue or objects in the environment. It could also erupt into consciousness through an illness or an obsession, something that demands the ego's attention. Equally the ego is energized and inspired by the inferior element. The inferior function is akin to the fairy tale theme of the youngest brother, who appears to be slow and dim-witted yet in his own way resolves the crisis in the kingdom. It is this inferior element in ourselves that is our hero, yet becomes projected onto others, especially those we partner.

In Jung's typology of psychological opposition, *thinking* (Air) is psychologically opposed to *feeling* (Water) and *intuition* (Fire) is opposed to *sensation* (Earth). In astrological language this translates to Air being psychologically opposed to Water and Fire being psychologically opposed to Earth. Jung suggested there is an *auxiliary* function that is secondary or supportive to the superior function. For thinking this would be intuition. For sensation, this auxiliary function would be feeling.

THINKING (AIR) _____ **FEELING (WATER)**

Semi-sextile
Square
Quincunx

SENSATION (EARTH) _____ **INTUITION (FIRE)**

In the zodiac, Air signs are one, three and five signs away from Water signs. Similarly, Fire signs have the same angular separation from Earth signs, constituting a traditionally difficult angular relationship or aspect. These relationships yield inconjuncts (the semi-sextile and the quincunx) and squares, which are traditionally complex aspects. These challenging aspects combine psychologically opposed elements. When these elemental pairs are emphasized in comparing two horoscopes, they constellate a temperamental polarity. When planets are in these opposed elements, the tendency is to consciously support one, yet deny the other. The planet expressing through the inferior function or element may be more easily projected, denied or repressed.

Through relationship we are introduced to our inferior type or weak or missing element. For instance, Fire's enthusiasm can find Earth's stability very calming, while Earth's caution finds Fire's spontaneity exhilarating. Initially the pair seems well suited but over time the temperamental differences become harder to manage without awareness and compromise. Fire may become impatient with Earth's slower pace, while Earth is disturbed by Fire's activity. At the outset Air is drawn to Water's care and concern, while Air's stimulation and insight appeal to Water. Without alertness to this dynamic the fascination may fade, with Air feeling smothered by Water's attention and Water feeling abandoned by Air's lack of awareness of feeling.

The Four Elements as Temperament

As suggested, temperament is innate; hence, it is compatible with astrological ways of thinking. This can be illustrated through the elements of Fire, Earth, Air and Water. The three signs of each element form the sacred triangle, a geometric structure representing harmony and balance. Let's review each temperament individually.

Fire: Aries, Leo and Sagittarius

Future-orientated Fire is inclined to be high-spirited, enthusiastic and optimistic, capable of being motivated and inspired by innovative concepts and ideas. Fire appears self-confident and adventurous, taking risks and defying the odds. Earth, its psychological opposite, underscores this buoyancy and is often felt as threatening and restrictive; therefore Fire has difficulties in manifesting or accepting the reality of a situation, feeling limited by structures and rules. Not wanting to be bothered with details, Fire's impulse is to promote the wider picture; therefore the exuberance of Fire's faith and vision can be fraught with impracticality.

Aflame with desire and passion, Fire can become out of touch with its melancholic side, which can easily be cast over their partners like a dark and dreary cloak. Fire's difficulty with negative feelings rejects their partner's depressive elements rather than recognizing them as a symptom of something deeper that is demanding attention. This could lead to overcompensating for inferior feelings by constantly proving oneself or taking inappropriate risks or action. Insecurities can be well hidden behind an over-confident persona.

A fiery temperament is restless and continuously searches for stimulation, being drawn to what is novel, exciting and promising. It is an element of questing, searching for the answer, the idea or concept to fulfil a deep yearning. Truth, reason and morality motivate their quest; however, without a realistic attitude, this journey often leaves its search for enlightenment extinguished by false gurus and prophets. This need for purity of vision is often paired with naivety.

Astrological Fire corresponds to the intuitive type. Intuitives have an attitude of expectancy, arriving at an answer without necessarily being conscious of the process, convinced that they are correct. An air of conviction and expectancy usually accompanies their certainty. The intuitive is more prone to questioning the meaning of things rather than accepting commonly held beliefs or accepting things at face value. Energetically, an intuitive type can be spasmodic: initially expressing great energy and enthusiasm, followed by exhaustion and collapse. Their nature is to over-reach and overcommit. Working with hunches, the intuitive is able to come to conclusions through linking dissimilar ideas together. Their ability to see the overall pattern endows them with a creative imagination and vision.

Therefore when Fire is extraverted it wants to leap ahead and get things done, often quicker than is possible. Being highly intuitive, they are able to be inspired and ignited quickly, perceiving the larger picture before any facts or models have been established. Hence on the one hand they might be constantly chasing the ideal, yet on the other they are great motivators, innovators and salespeople. Extraverted Fire is a motivational energy, a coach or a teacher who helps others to believe in their potentials, whether real or imagined. With cunning perception they can see through and beyond the literal world, but the extraverted Fire's Achilles heel is lack of patience and reflection.

Introverted Fire is a visionary and a weaver of dreams. When Fire turns inward, intuition is directed towards the inner life and the imagination. This combines to create the artist, the mystic, the poet, the prophet, yet may also result in the misguided, the misunderstood and the invisible one. An enigma to their friends, they often feel unable to express outwardly the multi-dimensional sense of their inner world.

Earth: Taurus, Virgo and Capricorn

This element is realistic and productive, striving to create something concrete that can be literally assessed. While the earthy element excels at accumulating facts, it often misses the significance or meaning of the connection between them. Its function is to determine that something exists and it utilizes the five senses as a measure of reality. Anything beyond the five physical senses is suspicious and not real. Unlike Fire, which is more inclined to use intuition, Earth employs the physical certainty of the senses. Jung called this sense perception 'perception mediated by the sense organs and "body senses".'[94] Earth is the element of the physical world and it is to this world that these types habitually turn.

As the element of incarnation and materiality, resources and assets are important to Earth. Money and possessions, which are contemporary symbols of value and worth, are their icons. Having an affinity with the tangible world, Earth forms a relationship with both nature and inanimate objects and possessions. While there needs to be a cautionary note about becoming too identified with materialism, Earth's gifts are resource management, material security and its instinctive ability to get the job finished. Psychologically, Earth is about one's values, one's self-worth.

Earth needs to define boundaries within their relationships without cutting off the life force, having a stable relationship without it becoming too fixed and bound to routines. Unlike Fire, the natural inclination is to move slowly and cautiously into relationships. Needing stability and security, Earth requires life to provide them with continuity and structure. While Earth can appear passive, it is far from submissive when its security is threatened or when something of value might be taken away. Earth is serious about relationships because they require an investment of emotional, psychological and economic resources, including the commitment of time. When Earth types feel insecure they can become possessive and controlling, inhibiting the other's freedom and privacy. Control, possession and the equal sharing of resources become important issues in relationships.

Change is not Earth's forte. Because it is attracted to constancy, it can often misread immobility and idleness in others as dependability, becoming disappointed when others do not share their own level of commitment, responsibility or reliability. In a rapidly evolving world it is the Earth element that we often disregard. When Earth is ignored, the ability to relax, be in the moment, take our time and move slowly becomes compromised.

Like Earth, sensate types rely on their physical senses for determining things of value. Sensate does not judge a particular situation intellectually or conceptually but weighs and values it according to the pleasure or sensation that is experienced. Common expressions like 'salt of the earth', 'matter of fact', 'feet on the ground' and 'down to earth' apply to sensate types. They are observant of the facts, practical and comfortable when following methods that have proven successful. At home with specifics, details and instructions, they can be suspicious of symbols, signs and metaphors. Sensates learn best when shown through demonstration or when they have an instruction book to guide them. Unlike intuitive types they are inclined to read the whole manual from beginning to end. They are comfortable with a step-by-step approach, but having mastered the technique they are more relaxed about exploring other options. Energetically, they tend to be able to pace themselves and set appropriate boundaries, being more aligned with their physical bodies.

One of the dangers of extraversion is to become attached to objects and, in extreme cases, possessed by them. Perhaps this is more difficult for the extraverted sensate type since they naturally gravitate towards the physical world and tangible objects. This type seeks out objects, people and situations that arouse strong sensations. Being practical, realistic and matter-of-fact they are adept at handling, fixing and crafting. However, it is this industriousness and competence that they may use as a defence mechanism when feeling uncomfortable. Doing things avoids feeling and being present in the relationship.

Introverted Earth is not as attached to the outer world of sensations and objects, but is directed internally to find pleasure and stimulation. They often develop a high degree of physical sensitivity, aware of details, textures, sounds and vocal changes. Because they are so grounded in the present they may have difficulty perceiving the future, becoming attached to what they are currently engaged in without any sense of where it leads.

Air: Gemini, Libra and Aquarius

Air seeks a multiplicity of experiences and shares its ideas and experiences through many differing relationships, sometimes being indiscriminate about privacy and containment. Relationships are an arena of curiosity and often Air's inquiring and interactive manner is mistaken for a deeper emotional or more intimate interest. Air uses objectivity and separateness as a barrier against relationship, mobilizing their intellect to criticize the irrationality of emotional encounters. Their analysis of relationship and need for space and distance is often defensive, protecting them from the uncertainty and lack of control that the actual experience of relating brings.

Air is concerned with communication, the fostering of ideas and the development of language, links to others and the process of relating. Air learns quickly and is able to think abstractly. It is rational in its approach to life and often fears the irrationality and mystery of the unconscious. To understand itself and its motivations it needs to talk openly and share its feelings. It is discussing the complexity and confusion of feelings that allows Air types to emote. Air is the element of perspective and distance; therefore its ability to detach can often be very useful, but it also serves to protect feelings and the interior life. While Air needs to be fair and just, it may vacillate on important decisions, so it avoids identifying contentious issues.

Like all elements, Air needs relationship. It is comfortable with the issues of equality, sharing and the theory of relatedness but has difficulty in the sphere of intimacy and emotional constancy. With Air it is natural to experiment with a range of relationship possibilities, satisfying its curiosity and enquiring mind. Air types need a great amount of space, emotionally, physically and psychologically, before they are comfortable enough to 'settle down'. The ability to change is natural, and without enough space Air feels stifled and unable to breathe, increasing its levels of anxiety. Communication on all levels within relationship is important, and while Air attempts to be clear and articulate, it is often emotionally very unclear and inarticulate, acting covertly rather than in an emotionally honest way.

Individuals with a highly developed thinking function orient themselves to the world in a well-organized, systematic way. Their decisions are measured, weighed and judged objectively, trying as much as possible to detach from the affect of feeling. They possess the facility to link together ideas and thoughts into an ordered and linear theory or concept and are inclined to be more independent and self-reliant. However, their emphasis on logic and rationale may lead to an unintentional wounding of others.

An extravert's life philosophy and ethics have a strong sense of altruism and are often dependent upon public opinion influenced by the majority consensus. Therefore when Air is extraverted, their thoughts, ideas and communication are organized around what is socially viable or current. Whether it is agreeable or not, it needs to be socially topical. Extraverted Air has a great capacity for thinking, organizing facts, reasoning and analysing; however, this obsession may also leave them disengaged from the very social circle they crave to be part of. When Air is extraverted the urge to relate may become so idealized that they find themselves perceived as out of touch or aloof from their feelings. Justice and truth are important, yet these may also contribute to their losing touch with familial and personal feelings and values.

When Air is introverted in an individual their acute reasoning and critical faculties are focused inwardly, helping them to clarify ideas and make sense of complexities: more depth than breadth of thinking. When focused, introverted Air can be astute at finding the errors in the formula, the illogical statements and the incorrect punctuation; however, this critical thinking can also be turned inward so they become their own worst critic. They may be more engaged with ideals and principles rather than feeling and relating. Through the complexity of relationship, feelings that were previously analysed, rationalized and managed begin to be awakened and felt deeply.

Water: Cancer, Scorpio and Pisces

Akin to the element in nature, Water meanders and changes course, ebbs and flows underneath the visible surface. Watery types are attracted to and repelled by the 'vibrations' of others, often unable to articulate the invisible threads that pull them into relationship nor the impulse that drives them away. Being emotionally idealistic, Water can become enmeshed in unrealistic and dysfunctional relationships, led by their feelings and aroused by empathy and compassion for another.

Quite instinctively, Water is able to sense and grasp another's pain and despair. Being astute at sensing what others need, they habitually and spontaneously serve the needs of others in unspoken ways. Without invitation from the other, the watery type often tries to soothe the pain, attend to the discomfort and nurture the broken-hearted. When these feelings are not reciprocated they feel unsupported emotionally. For the watery person, this sense of abandonment and emotional inequality is enormously painful, yet ultimately necessary in learning the difficult task of separateness. Water confuses the boundaries between self and other.

Watery energies are often expressed without appropriate boundaries. The urge to merge is heightened and the unconscious desire to annihilate differences and boundaries can leave Water exposed, unprotected and vulnerable. The Water element embraces the feeling life, not just in itself, but also in intimate others. Familial and ancestral patterns are carried through the element of Water, whose origins reach deep into the collective. Easily possessed or entranced, Water longs for escape by surrendering to the complexity of the feelings or by transcending them through the vehicle of mind-altering devices, either natural or chemical. Water is an element that longs to be released from the mundane world.

Water is the psychic element as we have seen, merging with what is around it. However, Water is also the element that is able to part the veil between the two worlds of the visible and the invisible. It has a natural affinity for symbols and signs; its natural inclination is to see the source not the symptom, able to read what is below the surface of situations. Water in essence has no form and needs to be contained. Without containment its potential to invade or erode is relentless. By nature it is an element that will absorb and assimilate what is in the environment. Psychologically it is difficult for Water to let go of the effect of feelings, becoming a collector of memories and mementos of its feeling life. It is an element of nostalgia and sentimentality, as well as the depth of intimacy and union.

Feeling types form decisions around values they consider important and meaningful. Jung suggested that feeling was a subjective process which influences the way judgements are made.[95] Generally there is a strong need for harmony in relationships and the feeling type tends to be agreeable, even compliant, in order to accomplish this.

For the extraverted watery type, feelings are intense and often overwhelming, ranging from strong emotive responses of anger to love, or from moodiness to warmth. They are able to form attachments quickly and thrive best in atmospheres where there is cooperation and harmony, often over-sensitive to negative feelings and criticism. Extraverted feeling is exhibited, or as the expression suggests they 'wear their heart on their sleeve'.

To describe the introverted feeling type Jung used the phrase 'still waters run deep'.[96] Difficult to read, they are often misunderstood as being indifferent or unfeeling, as their silence is often mistaken as disinterest. Therefore they seem mysterious, even alluring or charismatic, yet inwardly they are inhibited. Since they have difficulty measuring themselves against their ideal standards they often suffer from self-doubt and inferiority. While introverted Water can often feel melancholic, their rich internal feeling life gives soul and eros to their life experience.

The Inferior Element

The inferior element is the one least developed in the horoscope. Perhaps a more descriptive word might be 'interior' element since it has the least accessibility to consciousness and the outside world. This might be an element containing no planets or one psychologically opposed to the dominant element. This element is silently strong yet lacks a clear access to conscious life. Therefore some individuals may explore this element of their personality passionately, as if it were a calling, a fascination or an obsession. A missing element forms a void; the force of the lack fills the psychic vacuum, fertilizing the space, inviting the individual to develop that energy. Joan of Arc heard voices, followed her visions, inspired the armies of France and died tragically a heroine at the hands of Fire, the very element lacking in her horoscope. Virginia Woolf drowned in her lacking element. Even though she had no Water in her chart, her writing was poignant and evocative; words that constellated feeling and had an emotive impact. Helen Keller developed a language that facilitated communication between handicapped individuals previously unable to relate. Lacking Air in her elemental make-up, she reached beyond this lack to explore ways to help individuals communicate with one another. And the only planet in Earth in Michelangelo's horoscope was Pluto, not yet discovered in his lifetime. With no Earth in his horoscope, he still was able to draw the beauty out of the cold and lifeless marble.

Astrologically, the missing element holds enormous power, a power fuelled by its desire to be known. The 'inferior' element can be projected onto another, endowing them with the qualities that we feel are missing in us. In a way the lacking or 'inferior' element is fated in that we are obliged to relate to it, if not in ourselves, then through others. This missing function often appears in the guise of our partners, our bosses, our parents and our children. But it is through our significant relationships in adulthood that we become more consciously aware of our own temperament through the recognition of differences in our partners. And since the inferior function wants to be known, it often makes its presence felt in relationships.

Astrology also has a system of oppositions, which occurs in the natural zodiac. Fire is always opposite Air, and Earth is always opposite Water. Astrology's oppositions are relatively compatible functions. We might think of each set of oppositions as a polarity, rather than an opposition. While visibly opposite one another, the signs in an astrological opposition are partners in a similar polarity. Astrological oppositions invite compromise and awareness of difference; however, if the astrological opposition is stretched to an extreme, the polarization may become so unbalanced that the opposite energy is forced into the unconscious.

Astrological Oppositions as a Polarity	Jungian Oppositions as a Dynamic
Fire–Air	Fire–Earth
Earth–Water	Air–Water
These signs are part of a natural polarity	*These signs have psychologically opposed viewpoints*
Aries–Libra	Fire: Aries–Leo–Sagittarius Earth: Taurus–Virgo–Capricorn
Taurus–Scorpio	
Gemini–Sagittarius	
Cancer–Capricorn	Air: Gemini–Libra–Aquarius Water: Cancer–Scorpio–Pisces
Leo–Aquarius	
Virgo–Pisces	

Combining Elements

The elements in nature are an apt metaphor for human temperament. How they combine in the natural world is also metaphoric of how they might combine psychologically. Relationship gives us both the venue and the opportunity to work with elements that are difficult to blend in our selves. Through the intermixing of elemental differences in our relationships we become more tolerant of our temperamental struggles.

Elemental combinations produce specific aspects; therefore in relationship analysis this also highlights planetary aspects. When two or more planets are in the elemental combination of *Fire and Earth* or *Air and Water*, they form the aspects of semi-sextile, square and quincunx. Similarly, the combinations of *Fire and Water* and *Air and Earth* are also complex and they too produce the more traditionally difficult aspects of semi-sextile, square and quincunx. When two planets occupy either masculine or feminine signs they form sextiles or oppositions, while planets in the same element forge conjunctions or trines. Understanding elemental combinations will also help us to understand the nature of aspects. The following table summarizes these combinations which are based on the natural wheel of the zodiac. Planets near the cusps of signs may combine different elements, which has a subtle influence on the aspect. For instance a planet at 2° Aries squares a planet at 28° Gemini. Although still a square aspect, the elements are in the same masculine mode, thereby easing the embedded tension in the aspect.

Aspect	Elemental Combination
Conjunction 0°	Fire–Fire; Earth–Earth; Air–Air; Water–Water
Semi-Sextile 30°	Fire–Earth; Fire–Water; Air–Water; Air–Earth
Sextile 60°	Fire–Air; Earth–Water
Square 90°	Fire–Earth; Fire–Water; Air–Water; Air–Earth
Trine 120°	Fire–Fire; Earth–Earth; Air–Air; Water–Water
Quincunx 150°	Fire–Earth; Fire–Water; Air–Water; Air–Earth
Opposition 180°	Fire–Air; Earth–Water

The aspects between two individual's charts are really combinations of elements unless the aspects are out-of-sign. When looking at two charts consider first how the elements might blend or separate.

This exercise allows you to sense how two types operate together; however, it also allows you to reflect on aspects. Let's look at some of the more difficult combinations.

Fire and Earth are psychologically incompatible, as Earth strives to be realistic and practical in its approach to life. In nature Fire can be extinguished by Earth, yet Fire can also decimate Earth. To be able to work together in a relationship, an awareness of these temperamental differences needs to become conscious. Being idealistic and intuitive, Fire is future-orientated, alive with the possibilities of what can be, while Earth is located in the present, contained within the realism of what is. Earth does not want to be rushed, while Fire does not want to stand still for too long. When a team works with the tension of this combination there can be much achieved and accomplished through the amalgam of both vision and pragmatism. However, the tension needs to be managed so that one way of being does not override the other in the relationship. In working together the couple needs to find the right mix of idealism and practical application.

Fire and Water are also unsuited; in nature Water can put out Fire. What might these elements have in common? First, both elements are highly passionate. As in nature, this can produce steam. Secondly, both elements are idealistic in their life view, and creative and engaged when channelled. Thirdly, both are warm and engaging elements. Therefore, as a couple working with these temperamental differences, it is helpful to recognize that there are similarities, yet differences, in the way they are expressed. Both need fulfilment in what they do, to be passionately involved and be free enough to express the creative elements of their being. But Fire looks to the future while Water turns to the past; Fire emotes whereas Water tends to hang on. Fire can feel held back by Water's sensitivity while Water can feel bruised by Fire's brashness. It is important for the couple to recognize that their essential orientation to life is very different and to create enough time and space to let these differences find a path of reconciliation.

Air and Water also have a difficult time co-existing or inhabiting the same space. Air is inclined to be objective; Water tends to be subjective. In terms of relating, Air is separate, Water is engaged; Air needs space and distance, Water needs intimacy and support. This is a tricky dance; one element approaches, the other avoids.

Therefore, in relationship this can be a difficult combination as Air can feel dampened by Water's need for contact and emotional connection, while Water can feel wounded by Air's remoteness and inaccessibility. But when the balance is struck the couple works well together to create boundaries between their social and private lives. While Air needs freedom and Water needs closeness, both can be managed in context of the home and relationship through awareness and tolerance of difference. Constant communication, feeling heard and being able to express feelings freely is the key.

Air and Earth need a conscious effort for their natures to be coordinated. Naturally, we know that Air scatters the Earth. Similarly, the tendency for Air to be changeable can weaken the resolve of Earth. While Earth is comfortable being contained and stable, Air needs distance, space and mobility. This is a dilemma for these two elements when they are focused on different courses and are on different time schedules. Therefore, consultation and scheduling are essential. It is also important that the couple manage their time efficiently, with enough communication about what needs to be finished and when. Both need an agenda: for Air this may be conceptual but for Earth it is practical. As a team this needs to be discussed, put in a time frame and managed. Striking the right chord between doing one's own thing and being responsible to the other is a priority. The mix of these elements can also produce aridity and dryness; therefore, the couple needs to find ways to promote feeling connected and engaged.

A Methodology of Temperament
Establishing temperament based upon astrological balances in a horoscope is not as straightforward as we might hope. Medieval astrologers used the Ascendant and Moon sign, their rulers, the phase of the Moon and the season of birth to assess temperament. Astrological software can compute a score for essential dignities, planets in elements, etc., but these are techniques, not temperamental truths. What is important is that the horoscope is used to validate an individual's temperamental balance so they can become more self-governing and aware of their natural tendencies. Elemental energies are also inherent in all facets of the horoscope, such as aspects, houses and the nature of the planets themselves.

We cannot assume if a horoscope has a predominance of one element that this element can be recognized by the individual as the superior function because environmental factors, ancestral influences, the familial atmosphere, birth order, education and so on may have emphasized elemental themes which are not inherent in the individual's horoscope. An individual with many planets in Air could have been raised in an atmosphere where the parents and the siblings were predominantly Water. This exerts its influence on the individual who may abandon his natal propensity and develop watery qualities to fit into family life. While Air may be the horoscope's outstanding element, Water may have dominated the family atmosphere; hence it becomes more familiar to the individual, even though it is not his or her superior element. While Jung suggested that the astrological criterion for element strength was 'simple and objective: it was given by the constellations at birth',[97] the human psyche is not so literal. As individuals we move in and out of balance and through time, which brings different elements to the fore.

When the 'natural' function is replaced in consciousness by another function, Jung called this the *inverted* function. A popular term for this is the *turn type*. June Singer defines the turn type as 'someone who by force of circumstances was attempting to function in a type that was not his natural superior function, but rather the inferior function.'[98] This type may be convinced that they are opposite to their innate temperament. While we may be able to determine every horoscope's elemental balance this is no guarantee that the individual has developed this temperament.

In focusing on the elements there are different procedures we can follow to try to determine the 'elemental weight' of a particular horoscope. My first criterion is to establish what significance would be given to each planet, as each planet will be functioning through a particular sign that is part of an elemental trinity. The inner planets, including the luminaries, and the Ascendant are individualistic energies which exert a great influence on individual temperament; therefore, I acknowledge their placement in elements with a greater weighting. The trinity of the Sun, Moon and Ascendant have the greatest impact on temperament and this is also shown in their higher weighting. Since the Ascendant is an angle, not a planet, I have weighted the Ascendant and its ruler equally. Outer planets in elements represent generational energies and are not as individual; therefore, I give them less weight than the inner planets.

Temperament Worksheet

NAME _____

Planet or Angle	Sign	Points	ELEMENT				QUALITY		
			Fire Yang	Earth Yin	Air Yang	Water Yin	Cardinal	Fixed	Mutable
Ascendant		4							
Ruler of Ascendant		4							
Moon		8							
Dispositor of Moon		2							
Sun		8							
Mercury		5							
Venus		5							
Mars		5							
Jupiter		3							
Saturn		3							
Uranus		1							
Neptune		1							
Pluto		1							
		50							

TOTAL: Fire + Earth + Air + Water + Cardinal + Fixed + Mutable = 100

There are many variations that could be argued, but for exploration purposes I have weighted the planets or points, not to determine their strength but their temperament. I find that focusing on the elemental and qualitative make-up of the planet helps me to consider their temperament in relationship. The Temperament Worksheet opposite and in Appendix 3 is the guide that I use. In Appendix 4, there are complete examples showing how the following temperament grids were tabulated.

Filling the Void

When introducing Angelina Jolie's horoscope in Chapter 4 it was apparent that she has no planets in Earth and the only angle in Earth is her Descendant. Brad Pitt's horoscope has an abundance of Earth. However, he lacks Water, as shown below.

Fire	Earth	Air	Water
19	25	5	1

Angelina has Water rising with Venus in Cancer on the Ascendant. The close conjunction of Venus on the Ascendant conjoins Brad's Vertex and opposes his Moon–Venus conjunction in Capricorn. This suggests a strong affinity, but also draws attention to Angelina's lack of Earth and Brad's void of Water being filled by the other. They share an abundance of Fire; therefore, they may share passions and ideals, but may encounter differences in feelings and practical concerns. They may also rush into situations before reflecting on the emotional and realistic consequences of their actions.

Let's meet another couple: Virginia Woolf and Vita Sackville-West. As mentioned previously, the horoscope of Virginia Woolf lacks the Water element, which contributes to its psychological opposite of Air being the dominant element. In tabulating the elemental balance in her horoscope, Air, the psychological opposite to Water, is the function most represented.

Virginia Woolf	Fire	Earth	Air	Water	Cardinal	Fixed	Mutable
	8	14	**28**	0	13	**25**	12

The dominant element is Air while Water is lacking. The superior quality is fixed and the least represented qualities are cardinal and mutable. When combining these into a sign or a signature the dominant signature is fixed Air or the sign of Aquarius. The inferior signature would be cardinal Water or mutable Water, the signs of Cancer or Pisces respectively.

One of the ways that a lacking element will seek expression is through relating. Vita Sackville-West was one of Virginia Woolf's intimate partners, not only sexually but creatively and through an enduring friendship. Vita had the Sun in Pisces and the Moon in Cancer, Woolf's inferior signature, which is an example of temperamental attraction.

Vita Sackville-West's elemental balance is:

Vita Sackville-West	Fire	Earth	**Air**	Water	Cardinal	**Fixed**	Mutable
	10	11	**2**	27	19	**1**	30

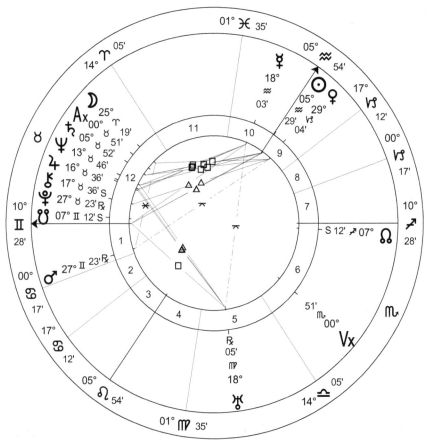

Virginia Woolf, 25 January 1882, 12.15 p.m., London, England

Her dominant element is Water with Air least represented. The superior qualities are cardinal and mutable and the least represented quality is fixed. When combining these into a signature, cardinal or mutable Water, the signs of Cancer and Pisces, dominate. The inferior signature would be fixed Air, the sign of Aquarius, Virginia Woolf's Sun sign. In their relationship, each partner's lacking element is well supplied by the other.

	Fire	Earth	**Air**	Water	Cardinal	**Fixed**	Mutable
Virginia	8	14	**28**	0	13	**25**	12
Vita	10	11	**2**	27	19	**1**	30

Once familiar with individual temperament, we can begin to explore how this impacts on relationship. Relationship astrology offers us a lens to see through temperamental differences which when made conscious can lead to tolerance and acceptance of the other.

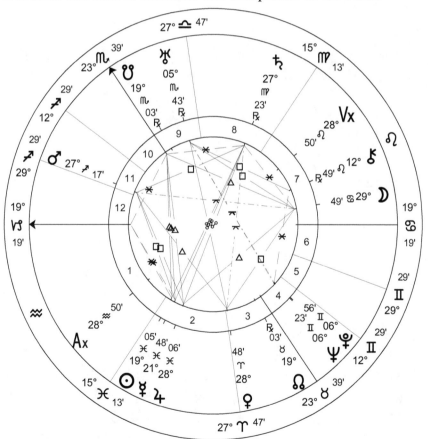

Vita Sackville-West, 9 March 1892, 4.15 a.m., Knole, England

– CHAPTER 14 –
THE PRESENCE OF ABSENCE
Voids in the Horoscope

In essence a horoscope does not lack anything, as each chart contains the primary factors that constitute the full spectrum of astrological energies. Each horoscope is individualized; a unique arrangement with some energies being more emphasized than others. Therefore, voids are created where astrological components are not well represented. When something is not well developed or is 'lacking' in a horoscope, an individual may be unaware of this, vulnerable to denying, overcompensating or disowning this energy, which is at risk of becoming projected onto close friends and intimate others.

Psychologically, an astrological lack symbolizes an exposed area in relationship, as what is missing or unconscious is like an empty space, an energetic complex looking for a home. Psychologically, this energy might pour itslf into a container that can hold it in a complementary way. But since the energy is not acknowledged as part of the individual, it becomes recognizable via projection onto others, whose visible qualities fulfil what is sensed as lacking.

In a similar way we may be repelled by facets of others that are denied in us. On a positive note this encourages us to become familiar with this absence and more comfortable with that energy in ourselves. On a negative note it could mean that we assign this energy to the partner, leaving it as a potentially unexamined part of our self. It is these unexamined or unlived aspects that encourage patterns to be played out over and over again in relationship. In this way, voids in the horoscope are mesmerizing; however, they can also reveal behaviours that can eventually bring consciousness to bear on repetitive relational patterns.

A void is often equated with an abyss or an empty space; it evokes the impression of emptiness, hollowness or nothingness. From another perspective a void could be seen as no-thing-ness, something not yet identified or manifest. In a way it is similar to the early Greek understanding of Chaos, the 'yawning void' where all possibilities existed and it was through Chaos that creation, including Eros, emerged.

It is through the agency of relationship that our personal voids become more obvious.

Voids and Relationship

Astrological tradition has always endeavoured to ascertain the strength or weakness of each planet before making judgements or predictions. In assessing relationship attitudes and patterning it is useful to consider strengths and vulnerabilities in each horoscope. From my experience of intimate couples, a lack in one horoscope is often compensated for by an asset in the other's. What feels lacking in us, yet embodied in another, is attractive, magnetic and potentially seductive. However, it becomes an energetic complex where power differentials can fester and insecure feelings are constellated. What once was engaging can become a source of conflict.

Psychologically, what we sense as lacking in ourselves can be experienced as numinous, alluring, even soulful when met in someone else. Even though our 'voids' may be veiled, unknown or in shadow, ironically they are close to the soul. When we encounter our voids being revealed by another, the soul stirs. Something unfulfilled in us feels completed by the other. Paradoxically, we are often ensouling the other through the exaltation of the quality we feel lacking in us. Without being familiar with the other, it is natural to assign our soulful reaction to them, crediting their inspirational presence with the quality, rather than the inner connection to our self.

From the other's point of view the positive projection is warming and gratifying. However, the projection cannot be sustained and it eventually darkens as intimacy develops. When the shadow appears, the task of deepening the relationship begins. Inherent in these lacking energies is the notion that opposites attract. However, it is not actually an opposite that someone is attracted to, but a polarity, a compensatory energy at the other end of the continuum. This is where astrological images can be very perceptive in recognizing the spectrum of imbalances between two individuals and how that might be acknowledged in relationship. Close bonds and intimate relationships arouse these lacks, and while they are strong attractors they also act as repellents when they remain unconscious. When what is missing is acknowledged authentically by each partner, the wisdom of the void can reveal itself and, through an acceptance of differences, the relationship matures.

Therefore, let's examine what could be considered as voids in a horoscope and how these qualities might be projected onto someone else in order for us to feel complete. Through relating to this individual we are also relating to the missing quality in our self. The journey with a supportive friend, partner or intimate other helps us to become aware of these qualities in ourselves and allows more space emotionally and psychologically in which the relationship can grow.

Voids in the Horoscope

There are many ways to think about energies that might be lacking, missing, underdeveloped or out of balance in the horoscope. I refer to these as voids; however, from the viewpoint of the soul, these are not deficiencies, only untapped resources. And it is often through the alchemy of a relationship that these voids can be reinstated consciously so an individual becomes more aware of the quality that once felt inaccessible.

To begin let's consider the following voids. Again, this is only one way of thinking about vulnerabilities that may be exacerbated in a horoscope. Each analysis, like each relationship, will be unique; therefore there will be different combinations and patterns that become apparent. Without being rigid or formulaic it is important to make a note of any voids or accents that are obvious. The following scenarios are not equal in priority. In relationship analysis, what is often most evident is the lack of an element or quality, but other voids are also of interest. It is also important to consider an overemphasis of any astrological energy.

- *A missing or weak element.* This suggests that one of the four elements is not tenanted by a planet, or if it is, then it is one of the outer planets.

- *A missing or weak quality.* This implies that one of the three modalities is not tenanted by a planet, or if it is, then it is one of the outer planets.

- *A vulnerable planet; one that is poorly aspected or unsupported in the horoscope.* This is open to the astrologer's discretion, but generally will be recognized as a planet that has few channels of expression. In traditional astrology this might be expressed as a besieged planet[99] or one in the 'Via Combusta'.[100] In modern and psychological astrology we might see this as a planet that is unaspected or having difficult aspects. The planetary energy is compromised in many ways, whether by detriment, fall, aspect or placement.

- *An unaspected planet.* This is a planet that does not make any Ptolemaic aspects with another planet, given agreed upon orbs. The planet is seen to stand apart and has difficulty in connecting to other planets. It can be restless and highly creative but seeks conscious expression. One way is through relationships where this energy may be encountered through the partner's horoscope.

- *A lack of planets in masculine or feminine signs.* This refers to a horoscope that has all planets in the feminine signs of Water and Earth and none in the masculine signs of Fire or Air, or vice versa.

- *A lack of an aspect.* This refers to a horoscope in which one of the following aspects is missing: a conjunction, opposition, trine, square or sextile.

- *A hemispheric lack in the horoscope.* In the horoscope this proposes one of four possibilities: that there are no planets above or below the horizon or no planets east or west of the meridian. It is also of interest when one of the four quadrants does not have any planets.

- *Lack of retrogrades.* When a horoscope has no retrograde planets, the chart shape is generally a bundle or a bowl or a bucket with the Moon as a handle. Having one planet retrograde stands out as well, and may be significant in the relationship analysis.

• *Intercepted signs.* In the earliest astrology of the Greeks, house division was based on the whole sign; therefore intercepted and duplicated signs were not part of classical astrology. However, when using a quadrant-based (unequal house) system such as Placidus or Koch the occurrence of intercepted signs becomes an issue to consider. An intercepted sign polarity is unique as it stresses a particular house axis and renders the signs vulnerable due to their inaccessibility.

• *Empty houses.*

Voids will also have their counterbalance. This occurs when the void is compensated for in another's horoscope. When this happens there is a strong possibility of projection, idealization or enmeshment. A relationship complex could develop around this theme.

• *The superior element.* This refers to the element that is most highlighted as it contains the Sun, Moon, the Moon's dispositor, personal planets, Ascendant and/or Ascendant ruler.

• *The superior quality.* This refers to the modality that is most highlighted as it contains the Sun, Moon, the Moon's dispositor, personal planets, Ascendant and/or Ascendant ruler.

• *A planet in high focus or angular planets.* This suggests a strong planet, on an angle, well aspected, in aspect to a luminary or in good condition in the horoscope.

• *An emphasis of planets in masculine or feminine signs.* This counterbalances the chart that has no planets in the feminine signs of Water and Earth or none in the masculine signs of Fire or Air by being strong in the area that the other chart lacks.

• *An emphasis of an aspect.* This refers to a horoscope that stresses one of the major aspects: conjunction, opposition, trine, square or sextile.

- *A hemisphere highlighted.* One of the two hemispheres or one of the four quadrants has an abundance of planets.

- *More than five retrograde planets.* Five or more retrograde planets are rare. When the superior planets are retrograde they are on the opposite sector to the Sun, so with five or more retrograde planets there may be an emphasis on a hemisphere or the possibility of a see-saw chart.[101]

- *Duplicated signs.* When using a quadrant-based or unequal house system there is a possibility that a sign polarity will be duplicated on house cusps, compensating for the intercepted polarity.

- *Three or more planets in a house.* When there is an emphasis on a particular house this environment may play a major role in the individual's life experience.

Let's recap some of these voids and what might compensate for this lack. These dynamics will be at play in a natal chart and will become accentuated in a relationship analysis

Void	Compensation	Chart Example
A missing or weak element	The superior element	Virginia Woolf had no Water; Vita Sackville West's superior element was Water
A missing or weak quality	The superior quality	Virginia's superior quality was fixed which was Vita's inferior element
A vulnerable planet; unaspected, poorly aspected or unsupported	A planet in high focus or an angular planet	Mars in Whitney's horoscope is in detriment in the 7th house, whereas Bobby's is dignified in the 10th
A lack of planets in masculine or feminine signs	An emphasis of planets in masculine or feminine signs	Musician Kurt Cobain had all his planets in feminine signs. His wife Courtney Love had retrograde Venus in the masculine sign of Gemini conjunct his MC

A lack of an aspect	An emphasis of an aspect	Virginia has no oppositions in her chart whereas Vita has Venus opposite Uranus and Saturn opposite her stellium in Pisces
An empty hemisphere or quadrant	A hemisphere or quadrant highlighted	Bobby Brown has no planets in the 2nd quadrant or the 7th house. Whitney has three planets, including her Sun, in the 2nd quadrant and three planets in the 7th house.
Lack of retrogrades or one planet retrograde	More than four retrograde planets	Charles has only one planet retrograde, which is Uranus at 29♊55. Diana had five planets retrograde, including Chiron
Intercepted signs	Duplicated signs	Diana had Leo–Aquarius intercepted and Sagittarius–Gemini duplicated; Charles had Leo–Aquarius duplicated and Sagittarius–Gemini intercepted
Empty houses	Three or more planets in a house	Angelina has no planets in the 2nd house; Brad has four in the 2nd house

Split in Two

Each chart has what I refer to as a *split*. By 'split', I suggest that a potential fault line runs through each horoscope where two strong energetic complexes are in conflict and struggle with one another. By nature each side of the conflict is hard to reconcile with its opposite and one may become more dominant. The split becomes vulnerable in relationship as the partner may embody or favour one side of the complex at the expense of the other. On the other hand, relationship is how the warring factions of our self become identified and engaged.

The lack of Water in Virginia Woolf's horoscope is very apparent. But what is also apparent is her packed 12th house. The 12th house environment of desolation and loss became difficult for her to manage throughout her life. A spilt in her horoscope is noticeable: no Water and the strong presence of the 12th house are countered by the Sun in Aquarius on the MC and 10th house Mercury in Aquarius, suggesting a vibrant intellect and worldly presence. In her horoscope, a split between the outer intellectual world and the inner emotional one is clear. This was echoed in her personal life by the divide between her intellectual and social circles with her personal despair and depression.

Vita Sackville-West's five watery planets, including the Sun and Moon, may have provided an emotional anchor; however, it was Vita's aristocratic background, social skills and life-affirming qualities that seemed to capture Virginia in the outer world. Vita's Piscean stellium is caught up in a T-square involving Mars and Saturn. A split occurs between the idealism, creativity and mutability of the Piscean planets and the reality, discipline and caution of the Mars–Saturn, a combination perhaps she saw in Virginia. Often each partner's splits are mutually engaged through relationship.

A Missing or Weak Element

Richard Idemon notes that a missing function is 'one of the first things I would look for in a chart to glean a sense of what relationships would be for that person'. By 'function' Idemon is referring to the lack of planets in an element, modality, masculine or feminine signs or personal (Aries, Taurus, Gemini, Cancer), interpersonal (Leo, Virgo, Libra, Scorpio) or transpersonal (Sagittarius, Capricorn, Aquarius, Pisces) signs. He confirms that a missing function is 'likely to be projected into another person'.[102]

What is lacking or undeveloped in us is often appealing when held by someone else. Any lacking element may be drawn instinctually to the very energy it lacks. However, if the element or function remains projected, a pattern or issue may develop around the theme of this lacking quality. For instance, the abundant enthusiasm and spontaneity of one partner may warm a lack of Fire in the other, yet while the individual may be initially inspired, they become frustrated with their partner's lack of commitment or routine. When Earth is lacking the individual may be enthused by the other's discipline, effort and dedication, but tire of their attention to detail and single-mindedness. Lacking Air, an individual may feel drawn to social types who are witty conversationalists, but become nervous and anxious in their presence. A lack of Water may be drawn to others who display warmth and express their feelings, but soon may feel overwhelmed by their partner's moods and emotional demands. Note any missing or weak element, as without an awareness of temperamental differences, each partner may continue blaming the other for their lacks.

Having ascertained the elemental weighting it might be also worth considering:

- If an individual lacks Fire, they may be prone to perceiving the spirit of Fire in others through an abundance of planets in Fire signs or through the fiery planets Sun, Mars and Jupiter. Planets in the houses of life (1, 5 and 9) and their rulers might play a prominent role by aspect or be angular in the other's horoscope.

- If an individual lacks Earth, they are prone to sensing Earth in others through an abundance of planets in Earth signs or perhaps planets in the houses of substance (2, 6 and 10). The earthy planets Mercury, Venus and Saturn might play a prominent role by aspect or by being angular in the other's horoscope.

- If an individual lacks Air they recognize the spirit of Air in others through an abundance of planets in Air signs or perhaps planets in the houses of relationship (3, 7 and 11). The airy planets Mercury, Venus and Uranus may be strongly aspected or angular.

- If an individual lacks Water they are susceptible to feeling Water flowing in the charts of others who have an abundance of planets in Water signs or in the houses of endings (4, 8 and 12). The watery planets the Moon, Neptune and Pluto might be prominent by aspect or angular in the other's horoscope.

For example, in the horoscope of Brad Pitt, the element of Earth is well represented. The Moon is in Capricorn conjunct Venus and Mercury in the 2nd house. Mars is also conjunct the South Node, completing the stellium of planets in Capricorn. The MC is Virgo, and being born in 1963 he has both Uranus and Pluto in Virgo. Earth stands out as his dominant element. Mercury and Venus, the planets that rule the Earth signs, are in Capricorn in the 2nd house. Their dispositor Saturn is in its own sign in the 2nd as well.

In the horoscope of Angelina Jolie, the element of Earth is definitely lacking. There are no Earth planets and the only angle in this element is the Descendant, an astrological 'hot spot' when it comes to projection in relationship. Brad's first highly publicized marriage was to Jennifer Aniston. Her horoscope also lacks Earth. The only planet in Earth in Aniston's chart is the generational giant Pluto. The only Earth angle is the IC at 27ß19, ironically only 1° of separation from Angelina's Descendant at 28ß58, both conjoining Brad's Moon–Venus.

	Fire	Earth	Air	Water	Cardinal	Fixed	Mutable
Brad	19	25	5	1	30	6	14
Angelina	23		15	12	36		14
Jennifer	20	1	23	6	22	19	9

Pitt has the Sun in Sagittarius with Sagittarius rising, a gregarious, approachable and adventuresome combination. Earth is the element in abundance that underpins his horoscope and is the measure of attraction in these relationships. However, it is also the void in his partner's chart, which may become a problematic theme. Therefore, I would note this motif and how it might play out in the relationship.

While there is an innate attraction to a missing element, there is also the propensity for difficulty. An abundance of Earth is stable, so Pitt will be attracted to the spontaneity of Fire. Both Jennifer and Angelina have their Moons in Fire. But can Fire and Earth relate? In the Pitt–Jolie relationship, Jolie's Fire would be enormously attractive, just as Pitt's Earth would be magnetic for her. But in the cauldron of relationship, can this be tempered and worked through? A conscious effort on the part of both is needed to understand the diverse and often opposing desires of each element. In consciously working together the relationship can become an alchemical vessel that transforms what feels missing into a grounding element in the partnership.

A Missing or Weak Quality
Similarly, if one of the modalities of cardinal, fixed or mutable is weak or missing in a horoscope it may be vulnerable in relationship, attracted to what is cultivated by the partner, yet still underdeveloped in the self. When partners share the same lack in their horoscopes, this is also significant to note. If both partners lack the same ingredient then it is important to recognize how the relationship

responds when this aspect needs to be expressed, acted out or dealt with. Sometimes the lack may cause the pair to polarize; one of the partners may continually take responsibility for attending to what is missing or lacking, which stresses and separates the couple. In a dynamic relationship hopefully the responsibility for what is lacking or missing is shared. When it consistently falls on only one partner's shoulders, then it is a burden for the relationship.

In Brad Pitt's chart the modality of fixed signs is less represented than the other modalities. The only fixed signs are the square between Saturn in Aquarius and Neptune in Scorpio. In Angelina Jolie's chart, fixed signs are also lacking. A question for their chart comparison might be how the relationship stays focused, consistent, follows through and works to resolve their difficulties. Both have the modality of cardinal signs highly developed; therefore they both might act before considering the consequences, instigating change and starting projects, rather than staying with a difficult process until completion.

A Vulnerable Planet

What is often apparent in synastry is that there is an attractive quality about a certain planet and/or planets that is undeveloped or vulnerable in one's own chart. Mystery is attractive. A planet that is unaspected or even heavily aspected, in detriment or in fall, repressed or 'hidden' in the 8th or 12th house, a singleton by element or the only planet retrograde, etc., would qualify as vulnerable. This planet may symbolize issues and themes that may be sensitive or exposed in relationship. A planet that is unintegrated has greater potential to remain unconscious of its own patterns. A supportive relationship has the potential to assist in integrating this energy into the life more effectively. Therefore, if you consider a planet to be vulnerable it is important to consider how this archetype is being expressed through your relationships.

For instance, consider Mars in Whitney Houston's chart. It is in Libra, in detriment as well as in the 7th house. Its only aspects are a sextile to Venus and a wide opposition to the Moon. Mars is not strongly supported, leaning towards relationship rather than individualism. Her partner, Bobby Brown, has Mars culminating in its own sign of Scorpio. It rules the MC and is conjunct it in the 10th house. Being angular and strongly aspected it appears to be focused on personal ambition. With this discrepancy in the strength of Mars in each horoscope, I would be alert to how this archetype found expression in their relationship.

A Planet in High Focus

If a planet is a stand-out in the horoscope, it may be both magnetic and attractive; on the other hand it might also be susceptible or overwhelming to the other. A planet that is in high focus would be an angular planet, the only planet in a hemisphere, perhaps the handle to a bucket chart or the only planet in an element or modality. If the planet is the only planet retrograde or unaspected it might be more susceptible and inhibited in some areas of relating.

A Lack or Emphasis of an Aspect

If a particular aspect is lacking, this way of considering the environment may be unknown and therefore of interest and attraction. For instance, both Pitt and Jolie have strong stelliums; therefore they are probably used to being highly motivated, subjective and focused. Jolie has stronger oppositions in her horoscope, especially to the Sun and Moon, and, of the two, may be more inclined to be objective. This might contribute to a pattern of Pitt being more instinctual and subjective in his decisions while Jolie might have to play the part of being more detached or unbiased.

Virginia Woolf has no oppositions between planets in her horoscope. With five planets plus Chiron in the 12th she may be more subjective in her approach. Vita has Saturn opposite her three planets in Pisces, which perhaps brings a more objective outlook to the Piscean sphere.

The Hemispheric Emphasis in a Chart

If a person has all their planets in the eastern hemisphere of the horoscope they may be prone to feeling complemented by others who have the majority of their planets in the western part of their chart. The eastern hemisphere suggests that the individual may be more self-motivated and focused, whereas the individual whose planets are mostly in the west will be other-orientated and used to compromise and considering others. Individuals with planets mainly below the horizon may naturally feel complemented by individuals with planets above the horizon, as the subjectivity of the planets below the horizon may feel met by the objectivity of those with planets above.

Lack of Retrogrades

Retrogrades suggest a different process and orientation than that of a direct planet. An individual who lacks any retrograde planets may be drawn to someone who has many retrograde planets. While this may be a natural attraction it also suggests that there may be a polarization in the relationship between the partner who wants to move forward and assert themselves and the partner who pulls back to reflect and reconsider. While this can work in a very positive way to solve problems and consider both sides of a situation, the relationship could become static and stuck because of being unable to settle or move forward.

One retrograde planet is a singleton in the horoscope and is prone to needing to be met and understood through relating. Notice that in Angelina Jolie's horoscope the one personal planet that is retrograde is Mercury and this is in Brad Pitt's 7th house exactly opposite his Sun. He has no personal planets retrograde but, like Jolie, has Uranus and Pluto both retrograde.

Another example is Bill Clinton who has no planets retrograde in his natal horoscope. His wife Hillary has two planets retrograde, one of which is Mercury at 21♏ opposite Bill's Moon at 20♉ and square his Sun at 26♌. His nemesis Monica Lewinsky has three planets retrograde, one of which is Jupiter at 8♒ opposite Bill's stellium of Saturn, Mercury and Pluto in Leo. Having no retrograde planets natally, he may have been more susceptible to these retrograde planets aspecting important parts of his horoscope.

Interceptions and Duplications

Intercepted signs suggest energies that may be difficult to consciously access and therefore fairly vulnerable to being expressed by others in relationship. When there are intercepted signs, naturally there are duplicated signs on other house cusps. Therefore the double-housed polarity might be more developed than the signs that are not on any house cusp and intercepted. An example of this is in the relationship between Charles and Diana.

An example of this is in the relationship between Charles and Diana, as previously demonstrated. The interception in one horoscope shows up duplicated in the other's. Of interest is that each one's interception is the other's Ascendant–Descendant: the axis most apparent in relationship.

What follows is a worksheet using Brad and Angelina's horoscopes to note astrological lacks and resources. A blank version of this worksheet appears in the appendix and may be useful when comparing natal horoscopes.

Synastry Worksheet: Assessing the Natal Horoscope – Astrological Lacks and Resources

Chart A: Angelina Jolie   Chart B: Brad Pitt

Horoscope Lack/Emphasis	Chart A Angelina	Chart B Brad	Comments
Elements: Fire	☽ ♂ ♃ ⚷ ♇ MC	☉ ♃ ASC	Brad's Sun would identify with Angelina's abundance of Fire
Elements: Earth	Lack of Earth	☽ ☿ ♀ ♂ ♅ ♇ MC	Angelina's lack of Earth is compensated for by the abundant Earth in Brad's horoscope
Elements: Air	☉ ☿ ♅ ♇	♄	Brad's lack of Air is fulfilled by Angelina's Air planets
Elements: Water	♀ ♄ ASC	⚷ ♇	Brad's Vertex in Cancer is conjunct Angelina's Ascendant

Modes: Cardinal	☽ ♀ ♂ ♃ ♄ ⚷ ♅ ♇ ASC MC	☽ ☿ ♀ ♂ ♃	Each has an abundance of cardinal planets in their horoscope which adds enthusiasm and passion; however, there is little fixity to secure and anchor this energy
Modes: Fixed	Lack of Fixed	♄ ♇	
Modes: Mutable	☉ ☿ ♇	☉ ⚷ ♅ ♇ ASC MC	Angelina's Sun is square Brad's Uranus–Pluto conjunction
Vulnerable Planet/s			
Angular Planets	♀ rising; ♃ ☽ ♂ culminating		Angelina has potent angular planets which aspect Brad's planets dynamically
Aspect Patterns	☽ ♂ ♃ stellium in ♈ conjunct the MC; ♀ ⚷ ♅ cardinal T-square	♂ ☿ ☽ ♀ stellium in ♑	Both cardinal stelliums contain the Moon and Mars; Angelina's Mars is exactly square Brad's, which suggests going in different directions
House Emphasis	No planets in the 1st, 2nd, 6th, 7th or 8th houses; 9th house stellium	Sun and Mars in 1st with stellium in the 2nd	Brad has an emphasis on the 2nd house while Angelina has no planets here
Hemisphere Emphasis	Emphasis above horizon in 3rd and 4th quadrants	Emphasis below horizon in 1st quadrant	Different emphasis: 1st quadrant of self highly emphasized in Brad's chart, but not in Angelina's

Retrograde Planets	☿ ♅ ♆ ♇	♅ ♇	Angelina has the only personal planet retrograde
Lunation Cycle	Last Quarter	New Moon	Reflection vs. projection
Interceptions Duplications	None	None	
Other Considerations	All Angelina's personal planets are above the horizon – only the three outer planets are below	All Brad's personal planets are below the horizon – only the three outer planets are above	This is an interesting symmetry as each partner complements the other; however, it would be important to consider that Angelina may be more aware of the outer 'day' world than Brad

PART 2

SYNASTRY

The Art of Chart Comparisons and Combinations

The meeting of two personalities is like the contact of two chemical substances: if there is any reaction, both are transformed.[103]

C.G. Jung

– CHAPTER 15 –
SYNERGY AND SYNASTRY
The Power of Two

What brings two people together? Because it is so mystifying we have divergent hypotheses ranging from karma to the unconscious; for those who are more pragmatic, it is happenstance, just the way it is. From a soul perspective there are no accidents, so whatever premise we use they are all encompassed by fate, an intelligent force beyond our control and understanding. For questions and reflections beyond the limits of science, the tradition of astrology is insightful in revealing meaning and inspiring understanding. For questions on relationship patterns and purposes we turn to synastry, the sphere of astrology dedicated to considering two or more horoscopes in the context of their affiliation. As Thomas Moore suggests, we need to 'respect whatever arrangement of stars brought us into this story.'[104]

What do we need and seek in relationship? Richard Idemon suggested that 'the most fundamental need in relationship is the revalidation of our basic myths'.[105] Or, perhaps as Plato alluded to, relationship is a link to our spiritual heritage, the partner being a window into the divine. Relationship is an archetypal element of the human experience and of enormous significance and concern for all. Astrology excels at helping us to consider our basic myths and relationship patterns. In the first section we examined relationship through the lens of the natal chart; now we will begin to focus on the astrological interaction between two charts and the formation of a bond between two individuals. This is known as synastry.

The etymology of the word 'synastry' combines the prefix *syn* with *astre*. *Syn* is Greek in origin and used in many technical terms. Its various meanings suggest being together: 'with', 'together', 'jointly', 'at the same time', 'alike'. *Astre* refers to a star or celestial body and is ultimately borrowed from the Greek *astron* or star. Therefore, synastry implies being together with the stars and is the area of astrological study that analyses two or more charts in relationship with each other. Its aim is to reveal the patterns, purpose and nature of the relationship, explore areas of potential conflict and compatibility, and delineate core issues within the relationship. Synastry is a valuable guide in helping us to understand relationships in general as well as the specifics of a given relationship.

Comparing two nativities or natal charts is mentioned by Ptolemy in *Tetrabiblos*; however, no methodology or ancient manuscripts have come to light to reveal how this could have been applied by early astrologers. Delineating compatibility and conflict between two individuals found favour in the twentieth century as modern astrology developed.[106] Yet astrological tradition has always judged compatibility between signs, planets and other astrological symbols. For instance, the element of Fire is more compatible with Air than it is with Water or Earth; and the Moon is well placed in the signs of Taurus and Cancer, but not as secure in Scorpio or Capricorn. Signs may be compatible, but this does not always convert to individuals with these signs being well matched. Temperamentally, astrology can propose whether individuals are compatible, but whether the couple is companionable or not is up to them.

What astrology reveals are the possibilities and probabilities of ease and conflict in relating, as well as the identification of patterns and processes between the two horoscopes. How individuals form a relationship when they have temperamental incompatibilities is the work of human relationship. This is where synergy or working together makes all the difference. Synergy is the dynamic force between two or more individuals working in tandem to achieve something greater than they might do on their own. A combined power is greater than the sum of its separate forces.

Since synastry examines more than one horoscope, the amount of detail and data that is generated increases substantially so it is helpful to follow some steps and guidelines when analysing the astrological data. There are stages to the process of synastry which can assist in studying two horoscopes at the same time. I have also found that compiling tables and keeping separate folders of synastry charts is very helpful. Astrological software is a great boon to generating the data, but ultimately it is our analysis and astrological vision that enable us to read the underlying meaning and significance of the data.

Synastry is a natural feature of all astrological work. Inevitably, clients ask a question about their partner or concerned parents seek insight through their child's horoscope. Yet, even before we encounter this inevitable question about the other, synastry is quietly in play in the relationship between us as astrologers and our client or friend – it is present every time we read another person's horoscope. Synastry, this cosmic guidebook to interrelationships, is ever present in each relationship, no matter how momentary or long-lasting the interaction. It is not consciously available if we do not have access to another's horoscope; however, the archetypal and temperamental interactions still take place. Implicit in synastry is how we engage in and experience relationship. Although we might not consider this, we are in a type of relationship with the person whose horoscope we are reading or the student we are teaching. Hence, synastry is not just the compilation of astrological techniques for analysing relationship, but an art – and one that highlights our participation both as an astrologer and as a personality.

We could reflect on two distinct levels of synastry: one is the correlation between the symbols of the two horoscopes, and the other is the relational bond formed between the astrologer – as the reader of the chart – and the person we are reading for. In other words, there is a relationship between the two charts and also the two people. We can read any horoscope and interpret its symbols, but when we are participating with the person for whom we are reading, a broader, deeper understanding is evoked through the interaction. When we read a horoscope without any relationship with the person who owns the chart, our astrological signatures are still contrasted with theirs, whether we are aware of this or not. This reading is most likely more information-based and less personal. However, when a trusting and interactive relationship develops between astrologer and client, the symbols of the horoscope become more animated and revealing.

Synastry appreciates the archetypal nature and patterning of relationships, and acknowledges the synergetic force that exists between humans, which is an enormously satisfying area of astrological practice when we find our *right* approach. By 'right' approach, I mean setting appropriate boundaries, taking ethics into consideration, cultivating a reflective style and recognizing the value of learning on the job, because it is in the practical application of astrology that we are confronted with the ethical undertones of what we perceive in the horoscope.

To begin I have outlined five distinct stages in the process of synastry, summarizing the steps to take before we explore fully the interactive dimension between two horoscopes. Bearing in mind the uniqueness of each relationship, it is helpful to develop an approach and method for working with chart comparisons.

Synastry Steps

1. Relationship Themes in the Natal Charts
Synastry is utilized to enhance the understanding of a relationship, so it is important to recognize the type of relationship you are analysing. Since each relationship is inherently unique, different aspects of the horoscope will be emphasized and studied given the nature of the interaction. Synastry can be effective in all forms of relationships, such as parent–child, siblings, lovers, co-workers, friends, colleagues and marriage or business partners; therefore, delineation can be tailored for the particular relationship. There are different customs, conventions, codes of conduct, power structures and familiarities in every relationship. Although the focus on astrological symbols and the way the information is presented may change, the techniques do not. Even though we are concentrating on the synastry of adult partnerships, the procedures and techniques can apply to a myriad of other relationships.

The Natal Charts
'Before I would assess any chart comparison, I would always look at the individual chart before anything else. The reason for this is that you can't put anything into a relationship except yourself.'[107] Liz Greene's advice when beginning a synastry analysis honours the individual first, as it is their temperament, intention and awareness that are the raw materials for forming a partnership. Therefore the first step in synastry is to study the natal charts of each individual, concentrating on relationship patterns and possibilities.

This would include the horoscope's images of primary relationships, including the parents, the parental marriage and their intimate partnership, the family atmosphere and the sibling system. When examining an adult relationship, we are trying to ascertain what the individual is seeking through their relationships, what aspects of themselves will be engaged in interacting with others and what patterns might be activated in the exchange. We are looking for themes and patterns that may be triggered but of which the individual may not be fully aware. The horoscope is a vivid indicator of what the individual may unwittingly attract to themselves. I feel my role as an astrologer is to facilitate the individual to feel more authentically themselves in the relationship, as well as to identify avenues that encourage conscious interaction and relating.

2. Chart Comparison

When we are comfortable with the relationship motifs of the two natal horoscopes, these can now be contrasted and compared. Chart comparison attempts to see how one individual's horoscope impacts their partner's horoscope and what this might suggest about their interaction.

This can be done in a variety of ways. One way to begin this process is to ascertain what is lacking in each horoscope and whether the other is fulfilling this lack. What has the individual imported into this relationship experience? From a relationship point of view we are asking 'What is this individual compensating for?' or 'What might the partner be unaware of?' in this pairing. These areas of lack in the horoscope are more prone to projection, transference or distortion by one partner. We have begun this process in the preceding chapter. The relational areas of the natal charts will now be compared to determine where the links and disconnections occur.

Another technique highlighted by Stephen Arroyo in his book *Relationships and Life Cycles* is to place the partner's planets and angles in the other's horoscope, and vice versa.[108] Two bi-wheels can be created, with one partner's planets on the outside of the other's chart. This gives a visual image of the influence that one partner is making on the energy field and environment of the other. This is a primary overview of the relationship. Although it may not pinpoint the dynamics of the relationship in the same way as the interaspects and composite chart might, it does offer a snapshot of the areas of each partner's life that are affected by the other.

3. The Aspect Grid

One of the most dynamic techniques in chart comparison is analysing the interaspects between each chart. Here it is necessary to understand the nature of each planet and how it influences other planets when there is a major aspect.

The aspect grid or synastry grid illustrates the planetary interchange and dynamics between two individuals. Each planet in one chart is compared to each planet in the other in order to ascertain the most dominant and powerful aspects between the two charts. But before you create the synastry grid it is important to define your parameters; in other words, which planets, angles, asteroids or other astrological points will you be using in your comparison? Which aspects and orbs will you choose? An aspect grid for two individuals can be produced using astrological software.

When the parameters have been set the aspect grid is generated and studied for specific interchanges between planets, as well as any shared interchanges when two planets mutually aspect each other. Mutual interaspects highlight a dynamic interchange between two planetary archetypes which often is reiterated in the composite chart.

4. The Combined Chart
After the two charts have been thoroughly compared and analysed, two other charts can be created from the combination of the two. This are known as the composite chart and the relationship chart, and both attempt to delineate the energies of the relationship itself when two individuals merge as one entity and act out of this shared space. Unlike the relationship chart, which has a birth time and place, the composite chart is forged out of the midpoints of mutual planets. Therefore there are variances within the composite chart which make it unique in the study of synastry. This dynamic chart offers the astrologer another view of the alchemy and uniqueness of the relationship they are examining.

Meeting and Marriage Charts
Other charts which can also be important are marriage and/or meeting charts. Transits and progressions are important at the time of meeting because these are the founding energies of the relationship which are carried through the chart comparison and into the combined chart. Using the meeting chart or the chart of the first intimate exchange provides astrological continuity in the progression of the relationship.

5. Synthesizing the Astrological Data

Mastering synthesis in synastry is a matter of practice. Since so much information is available from the many charts analysed, it is important to keep in mind the significance of recurring patterns that were identified in the natal charts, then repeated in the chart comparison and again noted in the composite chart. The data needs to be prioritized; for instance, this might be done in terms of recurring patterns, angular planets, major aspects, etc.

Before you begin the process of synastry, it is helpful to make a checklist of what needs to be covered in order to ensure your preliminary astrological work has been carried out. A checklist is included in Chapter 22 that you can use or modify for your own purposes. Once familiar with the details of synastry, you will develop your own style and approach.

Timing Techniques

Transits to the individuals' charts and their composite chart are also important to consider because these can help to illuminate the development and evolution of the relationship. Each natal chart can be progressed to the same date and compared. What is interesting to note is how natal themes in the relationships have been altered through the progressions. A composite progressed chart can also be generated from the midpoints of each partner's progressions.

Personal Biases

While we consciously endeavour to be as objective, neutral and nonjudgemental as possible, there will be relationship dynamics and issues that will disturb and delight us and some that we are not prepared to entertain. Therefore, it is wise to reflect on your personal biases, beliefs and judgements about relationships and how these may colour the way you read the horoscope.

Ethics and Referrals

It is important to reflect on an ethical way of approaching relationship astrology; for instance, what can you tell a client about their relationship and how do we respect a partner when they are not present, even though the client may be speaking about them? What are your principles about discussing someone else's horoscope when they are not there? If you do see astrological clients in a relationship context it is also helpful to have referrals to other professionals.

Using Astrological Software for Synastry

My preferred astrological software is Solar Fire, which is helpful for preparing the astrological charts that are needed for the analysis. First, the two natal charts along with their transits and progressions are generated. Two bi-wheels are created; each one has one partner on the inner wheel and the other on the outer. The synastry grid is then produced, detailing the aspects between the two partners. And finally the composite chart is created. Please consult the Appendix for instructions on how to create these charts using Solar Fire.[109] I prefer to print out the charts and the aspect grid, and then to highlight areas, making notes and formulating questions.

Astrological software provides numerous techniques and options; so many, in fact, that I find it impossible to know what they all mean. I encourage you to use only the techniques that you are comfortable with, whose convention you understand or which have a meaning that you can grasp. At the beginning, the amount of information can feel overwhelming. So let's set out the groundwork a step at a time.

One Relationship; Two Charts

Before you begin the process of synastry you should be familiar with the relationship themes and patterns in each of the partners' charts that you are about to place side by side. In Part I we began this process and now we will review some of these areas. While you may have already formed impressions about each individual and their propensity towards relating, try to keep these impressions in the context of the horoscope symbols.

If the relationship is between a child and their parent then we also have to recognize that the child's chart represents the transits to the parents' horoscopes at the moment the child was born. If it is two business partners then be aware of the contracts, agreements and expectations they have with each other and how the impact of each chart might clarify or confuse these issues. With partners we are aware of how receptive one partner might be to certain parts of the other's horoscope, unconsciously creating and colluding in patterns. At this seminal point in synastry we are assessing the horoscopes in certain ways to glean insights into the patterns and potentialities of their relationship. Our focus will be mainly on adult relationships but this can always be modified for other types of relationships.

A Telescopic View

Our first impression of a horoscope reveals a great deal. Because it is a map of symbols we are intuitively receiving impressions of many images and associations, whether we are consciously aware of these or not. These imprints are unique to our self and inform the way we see the horoscope. However, like all intuitive responses they need to be earthed and explored in context for them to be meaningful. Our anchor for our felt responses is our knowledge of astrological symbols. It is wise to acknowledge your first impressions of the chart and to confirm objectively whether these are mirrored in the horoscope or not.

Put both charts that you are examining side by side and reflect on them. Before you apply any delineation techniques it is informative just to note what stands out for you, what you see first, how the charts are shaped or what images come to mind. I begin to write notes on the charts for myself. Now we are ready to begin to analyse what it is we might have seen or felt intuitively.

Temperament

In Chapter 13 we looked at temperament and developed a worksheet to analyse this disposition in each chart and how that might play out in the dynamics of the relationship. Reflect on the temperaments in each chart, noting the dominant and lacking elements and qualities and how these may invite and obstruct authenticity in the relationship.

Voids

In Chapter 14 we expanded our examination into considering other voids in the horoscope which could also attract transference or projection in the relationship. We may be attracted to developed qualities in our partner that we lack ourselves, but this may also inhibit areas of our personal development. Roles may develop around the void, which can contribute to a setback in each partner feeling equal in the development of their relationship.

Archetypal Needs: Pairing the Planets
Each planet in both charts has its own unique urges and desires. In relationship these archetypes need to be expressed authentically, yet the nature of partnership also requires compromise in order to accommodate the other's needs or wishes. A horoscope illustrates an individual's unique orientation to each planetary archetype; synastry symbolizes the interaction between the archetypes. The interaspects between the charts are erotic because they bring archetypes into contact, mingling the gods together in the relationship. The synastry grid will be helpful in compiling all these aspects.

But to begin we can familiarize ourselves with the planets in each chart in context of relationship as we did in Chapter 1. The Sun, Moon, Venus and Mars, as the archetypal quaternary, are paramount to assess in terms of an adult intimate relationship. These are the formative masculine and feminine inner figures that are met in the external world through relating.

Animus: The Sun and Mars
Being masculine archetypes, the Sun and Mars are more outer-orientated, representing spirit and drive, the self and individuality; therefore these archetypes seek to be complemented through receptivity. In contemporary astrology it has been suggested that the Sun and Mars are representative of the animus or inner qualities and complexes in the woman that shape her outer image of the man she may be attracted to. The personal father (Sun) and the brother, uncle or other male figures (Mars) are the first outer images that personify and profile the figure that she seeks in relationship. This is a way of thinking about how masculine archetypes are formed and expressed by men and women, not a gender classification or image of sexual preference.

Anima: Moon and Venus
Similarly, the Moon and Venus represent the anima or inner qualities and complexes in the man that shape his outer image of the woman he may be attracted to. The personal mother (Moon) and the sister or childhood friends (Venus) are the first embodied images that profile the outer figures he seeks in relationship.[110] Being feminine archetypes, the Moon and Venus are inner-orientated, representing

soul and love, caring and sensuality; therefore, these archetypes seek to be complemented by being engaged and met.

The sign qualities and aspects to these planets help to characterize a partner that the individual may find attractive. While this is a valid model it is important not to think of the anima or animus as fixed or an actual aspect of the individual, but rather as an inner image or symbol that evokes and illustrates qualities of others that are attractive and complementary. When working on the anima and animus it is important to see them as archetypal, not gender-specific or gender-biased.

Lines of Communication: Mercury
A vital part of every relationship is communication, conversation, sharing ideas and opinions. Mercury is both communicator and connector, and its placement in each chart shows the natural mode of expression. When these are compared it reveals whether the lines of communication are easily opened or not. For instance, Brad has Mercury at 16♑ in the 2nd house, suggesting that he might communicate and listen in a pragmatic and structured way, thinking things through, being careful in his explanations and cautious when expressing himself. Angelina has Mercury retrograde in the 11th house at 22♊. Her mode of communicating is very different, perhaps speaking out before the idea is fully formed, jumping ahead in the conversation or having many things happening at once. At a glance it is clear that astrologically the function of Mercury is expressed very differently. The articulation of this pattern would encourage each partner to become more conscious of the potential patterns discharged through their language, ideas and modes of communicating.

Beliefs and Culture: Jupiter
Jupiter brings cultural motifs into focus when highlighted in synastry, such as religious beliefs, educational backgrounds, social circles, and racial or language differences. Brad and Angelina both have Jupiter in Aries due to the fact that they were born twelve years apart. Even though the quality of Jupiter is similar, the age difference suggests a cultural and generational gulf in understanding the nature of the world.

Goals and Challenges: Saturn

Interactively, Saturn can be the fastening agent in relationship. Its aspects to the partner's planets can help to mature and contain the archetypal energy; however, it can also be heard as a critical or parental voice. It is through time and acceptance that the disapproving and authoritative voice we hear in our partner becomes the familiar internal voice of our own feeling of inadequacy. Angelina has Saturn in ♋ opposite Brad's stellium in ♑ which includes the Moon and Venus, illustrating that her power and presence makes a strong impression on Brad, who may feel criticized.

Generation Gaps: The Outer Planets

Chiron and the outer planets play their role in synastry through their aspects and interchange with the inner planets. The outer planets will be near each other in charts of those born close together; therefore, the outer planets echo aspects that are already in their partner's chart. But when there is an age difference the outer planets may be in different signs, signalling a generational difference; therefore, the familiarity of what we have grown up with may not be as easily shared.

Me and You: The Ascendant–Descendant Axis

As the axis of self and other, the Ascendant–Descendant is a focal point in synastry for connectedness between two individuals in an intimate partnership, equal partners, close friendships or business collaborations. The Descendant and the 7th house are the place of the partner and are of primary interest in the synastry of couples who are emotionally, economically, sexually and psychologically close. This is the sphere of me and you, and where our personalities blend together in the dance of individuality and togetherness.

As discussed in Chapters 6 and 7, the sign on the Descendant is indicative of qualities that attract us to others. Its ruler also plays a role; for instance, if it is well aspected or supported, then relationships may feel accessible or welcoming. If the ruler of the 7th house is not well supported, then consider that there may be difficulty in committing, being interdependent or feeling equal in relationships.

The 7th House

Seventh house stelliums are complex by nature because the psychic activity stirred by the partner may feel overwhelming. One way to handle the complexity is to polarize the energy into the 1st house, mobilizing a strong sense of self that might collude in warding off relating and intimacy. Another is to work through the complex, slowly unravelling one planetary pattern at a time. Often different relationships embody the differing themes of the 7th house.

If there are no planets in the 7th house but there are planets in the 8th, what may happen is that the process of establishing relationship is sacrificed for the intensity of relationship that the 8th house offers. The dating and preliminary phases of building a relationship are relinquished for the impact of intense emotional bonding. The relationship may not have anything to fall back on in times of crisis and deconstructs as quickly as it was constructed. In this instance it is wise to allow time for relationship to develop, as the tendency to rush into intimacy without establishing a solid foundation is complicated with projections and idealization.

Projecting 7th house planets exclude them from the rest of our life. They have no animation as they are being lived out through the partner. An interception in the 7th house adds another layer to the relationship because the intercepted sign symbolizes other qualities that emerge in the process of relating.

Mine and Ours: The 2nd–8th House

The 2nd and 8th house cusps are the borderland where personal and shared values become apparent. These houses locate the attachment to what is mine and how I share that with another. The 2nd house is where value is placed on what I have; the 8th house is sharing with intimate others. We can only offer what we own; therefore, the 8th house is where the private self is exposed and vulnerable to the other. The 8th is the underworld of the relationship, where intimacy is located and felt.

The 8th House

The sign on the cusp of the 8th and its ruler can be thought of as an extension of the 7th house relationship. But the cusp separates equality from intimacy in the relationship. When the same sign is on the cusp of both the 7th and 8th houses, it is difficult to make a distinction between these two life arenas. The individual is at risk of opening up too quickly or rushing into an intimate encounter without adequate preparation. The urge to give oneself over to the other is strong, because adequate boundaries or discrimination may not be in place to protect the immersion of the self into the other.

Familiarity with the 8th house in each chart allows us to be more aware of patterns of sharing resources, trust and intimacy. For instance, in Angelina's chart the cusp of the 8th house is 20♒ and this is close to Brad's Saturn at 19♒. Brad's 8th house cusp is 14♋ very close to Angelina's Saturn at 17♋. Here is a mutual interaspect, which will recur as Saturn is conjunct the 8th house cusp of their composite chart. The cautionary themes of Saturn and the 8th house are brought into the relationship and shared. They also flag potential intimacy difficulties in sharing the private and secret self.

Relationship Houses

In analysing relationship, all the houses play a key role, especially those houses that describe others or are tenanted with stelliums. When analysing the emotional needs and experiences of relationship, family influences, patterns and the traditions that affect relationship, then the 4th and 12th houses are considered. These houses assess the weight that family history and patterns exert on the present relationship. The 12th addresses qualities projected onto others since they are often deeply unconscious. Longings, dreams, fears, phobias, chronic patterns and unexpressed creativity are contained in the vessel of the 12th house and are important considerations in any relationship analysis. The 4th house addresses the experience of attachment and safety in relationships and the familial patterns transferred into adult relationships. All houses are important considerations, and your skill in navigating their depth and complexity will inform how you understand their influence on adult relationships.[111]

The houses of relationship also include the 3rd house of siblings and the 11th house of friends and colleagues. These areas are important in assessing other equal relationships such as those with siblings, peers, close friends, colleagues, etc. Be aware of planets in the interpersonal sector from the 5th to the 8th houses. The cusp of the 5th house symbolizes a threshold between primary attachments and emotional relationships in adulthood. The 5th house considers our creative potential and need for self-expression in relationship. It is the house of love affairs, children, play and recreation. In synastry, the 5th house is important in assessing the roles children might play in the relationship as well as the role of the creative inner child. Here in the safety of relationship, a different and beneficial experience of the inner child could occur. The 5th house as the relational landscape of play, sex and expression is important in terms of addressing these needs in relationship.

While the 6th house is often referred to as representing 'unequal' relationships, it is here where a more conscious process of self-reflection occurs. This sphere symbolizes the preparation of psychological processes in equal relationship. As the house of the everyday, it is important in relationships where daily life, working together and cooperating in routines, habits and daily housekeeping rituals take place.

Karmic Relationships: The Nodal Axis and the Vertex
As explored in Chapter 12, the nodal axis and the Vertex–Anti-Vertex angle often feature significantly in relationships that feel immediately familiar or destined, as if crossing paths was inevitable. When highlighted in synastry there is a purposeful feeling to the relationship, a spiritual sense of meaningfulness as well as a mutual sense of learning from each other. It is often a feeling that is difficult to articulate but resonant with images of soulfulness and significance.

Synergy
Focusing on these areas of each chart will have already flagged up many areas of potential ease or difficulty that will be helpful to take into account in the relationship. Again, creating a worksheet to summarize the data will be helpful. The following worksheet, which is in the Appendix, is one I use to jot down notes that I feel may be significant when synthesizing the chart comparison. Below is an example using Angelina and Brad's horoscopes.

Synastry Worksheet: Assessing the Natal Horoscope – Relationship Themes

Chart A: Angelina Jolie   Chart B: Brad Pitt

Feature	Chart A Angelina	Chart B Brad	Comments
7th House: Sign Ruler & Planets	♑, ruler ♄ in 12th □ ☽, no planets	♊, ruler ☿ in 2nd ☌ ☽, ♌, no planets	Both rulers aspect ☽ highlighting issues of family and security. Brad's ☽/ ♀ rests close to Angelina's Descendant. Angelina's ☉ falls on Brad's Descendant
8th House: Sign, Ruler & Planets	♒, ruler ♅ in 4th □ ♀, no planets	♋, ruler ☽ in 2nd conjunct ♀	Both rulers are aspecting ♀. Angelina's ♄ falls on Brad's 8th cusp; Brad's Saturn falls on Angelina's 8th house cusp, highlighting their different orientations to intimacy
Relationship Houses	Angelina has Earth cusps	Brad has Air cusps	Angelina has ♀ in the 3rd and ☉, ☿ in the 11th while Brad has ⚷ in the 3rd and ♆ in the 11th
Nodal Axis	☊ in ♐ in the 5th, ☋ in ♊ in the 11th	☊ in ♋ in the 7th, ☋ in ♑ in the 1st ☌ ♂	Angelina's nodes fall across Brad's 6th–12th houses; similarly Brad's nodes fall across Angelina's 12th–6th houses

The Vertex	11♐05 ☌ ♆ in the 5th	27♋22 in the 8th	Brad's Ascendant at 11♐54 is conjunct Angelina's Vertex: Angelina's Ascendant–Venus conjunction is conjunct Brad's Vertex
Animus: The Sun	13♊25 in the 11th ☍ ♆	25♐52 in the 1st	Angelina's Sun is conjunct Brad's Descendant, with her Neptune on his Ascendant accentuating the spell of projection
Anima: The Moon	13♈05 in the 9th ☌ ♃ ☌ squaring ♄ ☍ ♇	22♑50 in the 2nd ☌ ☿ ♀	Brad's Moon is conjunct Angelina's Descendant and opposite her Venus, hooking his inner image of both the nurturing and sexual feminine
Anima: Venus	28♋09 ☌ ASC squaring ⚷ and ♅	23♑28 in the 2nd ☌ ☿ ☽	Brad's Venus falls on her Descendant and opposite her Venus. Angelina's Venus falls on Brad's Vertex in the 8th, which could feel fated or a compelling or complex attraction
Animus: Mars	10♈42 in the 9th ☌ ♃ ☽ squaring ♄ ☍ ♇	10♑02 in the 1st ☌ ☋ ☿	Each one's Mars squares the other's, making for a passionate joust; being on Brad's South Node it might feel familiar, while with Angelina it might feel like a great challenge

Communion: Mercury	22♊20 in the 11th retrograde	16♑07 in the 2nd ♂ ☋ ♂ ♃ ♀	Communication needs are strong – Angelina's retrograde Mercury is opposite Brad's Sun. His Mercury conjoins the South Node and the Moon
Ethics & Morals: Jupiter	17♈25 in the 9th ♂ ♃ ☽ ♂ squaring ♄	9♈50 in the 5th squaring ♂ ☋	Both share Jupiter in Aries's vision, but are 12 years apart; Brad's ♃ is square his ♂ and conjunct Angelina's ♂; his beliefs may be at 'right angles' with his desire and ambitions
Commitment: Saturn	17♋23 in the 12th squaring ♂ ☽	19♒09 on the 3rd cusp square ♇	Saturn is quincunx Saturn. Each one's Saturn falls on the other's 8th house cusp; therefore strong assurances about love and loyalty are necessary
Generational Influences: The Outer Planets	♅ in ♎ ♆ in ♐ ♇ in ♎	♅ in ♍ ♆ in ♏ ♇ in ♍	All being in different signs suggests there will be generational differences in values and attitudes.

Hooks in the Horoscope

When analysing the individual horoscopes you would have already become aware of certain areas of the horoscope where there is a tendency for projection to take place or where one individual is vulnerable to letting the other fill the gap: a lack or excess of an element, the 7th house cusp, etc. While this is alluring and attractive, it is also a void which may become filled with feelings of hopelessness, resentment or confusion. These areas need the conscious attention of the partners.

Make a list of some of the potential areas where this might occur and consider ways to recognize the pattern and recommend strategies to deal with the situation. It might be helpful to make a table as below. A represents Angelina Jolie's horoscope while B represents Brad Pitt's horoscope.

Chart A Angelina Jolie	Chart B Brad Pitt	Possible Patterns	Strategies
Lack of Earth	Strong Earth	Structure, responsibility, authority may be projected onto B; therefore, he is first experienced as worldly and accomplished, but could later be felt to be controlling, cold, paternal and patronizing	Being aware of structuring their time effectively, planning and budgeting together, sharing responsibilities and agreeing on what is valuable; maintaining routines and continuity; making time to get things finished
No fixed signs	Saturn square Neptune in fixed signs	Both partners lack fixed signs; therefore they may be unable to see things through to the end. One may become manoeuvred into finishing off what the other has started	The need for structure, containers and follow-through; reflection and discussion on commitments beforehand; completing projects and following up on them

284   *From the Moment We Met: The Astrology of Adult Relationships*

Descendant is 28 ♑	Moon–Venus conjunct at 22/23♑	Tendency for B to be feel split between being a carer and a lover, being kind and responsible, yet not feeling valued or reciprocated for the roles and tasks he manages	A needs to become aware of her responsibilities and duties in the relationship without expecting B to instinctively do these for her; awareness and differentiation of B's roles in relating
Sun is 13♊	Descendant is 11♊	Tendency for B to see his partner as getting more limelight, attention and creative breaks than himself. Perhaps B imagines his partner to be more socially skilful, communicative and adaptable	B needs to find the avenue for expressing his own creative ideas and needs in the relationship; A needs to shine in her own way in social situations and with friends

Starting to compile and analyse these potential danger zones assists a couple in being more aware of the patterns that may be unconsciously repeated on the stage of their relationship.

– CHAPTER 16 –
CHART COMPARISON
Swapping Houses

A merger of systems occurs when two individuals form a relationship. Not only do we bring our ancestral, cultural, familial and relational past into the mix, but a host of sub-personalities tag along, some being more demanding than others. Nonetheless a congregation of needs and desires seek to find a place to belong. Our pride, feelings, opinions, tastes, annoyances, beliefs, criticism, wounds, eccentricities, idealism and cynicism all vie for recognition and acknowledgment. These ways of being are our planetary archetypes each of which needs to find their place in the relationship. There are two ways we can begin to evaluate the planets and their ease or difficulty of expression:

First, we can place our planets in our partner's chart examining in which houses they fall. Any house that our planets occupy will represent the sphere of life and the environment where this energy impacts our partner. To study how one partner's archetypal characteristics might impact the other's natural world astrologically, a bi-wheel using the two horoscopes can be prepared.[112] This creates a dynamic snapshot showing how one partner's planets fall in the other's houses. Two bi-wheels are created, one for each partner; however this can only be done when there is a known birth time. This is not definitive of the relationship, but indicates settings where one might be open, vulnerable or reactive to the other. Imagine the houses of your horoscope like your ecosystem, your personal atmosphere or your force field. As your partner's planets fall in particular areas, it suggests an impression, sensation or felt experience synonymous with that planetary archetype. This is often much more noticeable at the beginning of a relationship before becoming familiar with the partner's responses, routines and patterns.[113]

Secondly, we can look at the aspects our planets make to our partner's and vice versa as a gauge of how the archetypes interconnect through relating. This is visible in the bi-wheel, especially when there are strong conjunctions and oppositions but the extent of the interaction becomes evident in the aspect grid which we will examine in the next chapter. Aspects between charts are identified as interaspects

Accommodating the Partner's Planets
To begin, let's summarize what each planet represents in relationship, then reflect on how each planet affects the other's environment when it falls in one of their partner's houses as well as how each planet influences another by aspect. Here are some ideas to begin the process.

The Sun
A symbol of energy, strength and identity, the Sun vitalizes the house it occupies in the partner's chart, shining its light on this area of their life. By aspect it stimulates and energizes the partner to find more of their identity through self-expression and creativity. It represents the forging of selfhood. A planet aspecting the Sun in synastry shapes and influences the emergent sense of self.

The Moon
Wherever the Moon resides in the partner's chart is an environment invested with feeling, influencing emotional stability and the cultivation of security. It is also where the partner's emotional temperament affects the atmosphere of this situation. It brings its urge for nesting, nurturing, comfort and protection to this setting, impacting the partner's needs, habits, living style and emotional safety. The Moon is a barometer of how the couple might share their living space and how familial habits, instinctual responses and daily behaviours are responded to by the partner.

Mercury
A common complaint in relationship is a lack of communication, of feeling unheard or misunderstood. This is Mercury's domain and where he falls in the partner's chart is the area where communication, ideas and interchange are highlighted. Aspects to Mercury stimulate and influence the lines of communication and reveal challenges to effective communication and listening. Whatever planet aspects Mercury is the force that needs to converse and be heard.

Venus

Likes, dislikes and an appreciation of beauty are Venus's domain, so the house she occupies is where she influences the partner's environment with her tastes and values. Aspects to Venus weigh up the impact on the partner's senses and what is considered valuable, beautiful or worthwhile. Psychologically, each partner's self-esteem is challenged, which might manifest through resources such as assets, property and money as well as the ability to love and be loved.

Mars

Mars is a vital masculine archetype which brings its conflict and rivalry to the house it occupies in the partner's chart. This area is where the partner may be challenged and pushed but also championed; it is the sphere where the partner's competitive streak may be most overt. Aspects to Mars will illustrate how the partner may stimulate or provoke, or where the individual is confronted to be more spirited and emotive. Mars personifies anger, and aspects to Mars may reveal how aggression, competition and irritation are triggered in the relationship.

Jupiter

Cross-cultural and other experiences beyond social and familial boundaries evoke Jupiter; therefore, the house that your partner's Jupiter occupies in your chart suggests where you may be open to new beliefs, adventures and spiritual ways of being. This could be a place in yourself that expands and develops because of your partner's influence. Through interaspects, Jupiter encourages growth, education, travel, new philosophies and beliefs. However, Jupiter could also signify the clash of cultures, morals and beliefs which are ignited through its contact with the partner's planetary archetypes.

Saturn

While Saturn represents where obstacles or control may be focused, it is also the glue of a relationship. Saturn brings its high standards into relationship; hence the house that Saturn inhabits in the partner's chart may feel limited or more self-conscious. It is also the area in which one partner, through intent and hard work, assists the other to mature and take responsibility for their ambitions and goals. By aspect, Saturn's influence on the partner's planets might feel paternal or patronizing, even negative and controlling. On the other hand, Saturn's skill is in building authority and boundary, which is a constructive influence to be more responsible, authoritative, serious and accomplished.

Chiron

Essentially, one of Chiron's main features is that it is unbranded or unable to be systematized. In chart comparison Chiron may unintentionally open a wound in the house it occupies in the partner's chart. It may be an area which is vulnerable and painful, yet ultimately healing, as both live side by side. By aspect it could suggest which wounds become re-opened through the relationship, yet also where healing may take place. Chiron points to areas of the self that are marginalized. Through the support of their partner, an individual feels able to accept this part of themselves.

The aspects from the outer planets, especially to the other partner's inner planets, suggest that strong instincts, thoughts, feelings, reactions and emotions may be experienced that are not consciously intended by the other. When there is an age gap of more than seven years the outer planets also reveal generational differences and experiences.

Uranus

As the archetype of the unexpected, Uranus is the herald of change, upheaval and a radical departure from what is known. It brings excitement into relationship, but also a high level of anxiety as it stirs what is unknown and uncertain, asking the partner to risk their security and stability. The house it inhabits is where separation from what the partner has been used to, or what the partner expects, might occur. Change and upheaval take place in this environment, which at first might feel chaotic, yet it also brings freedom and liberation, something new and transforming. By aspect Uranus awakens what it touches, electrifying this part of the partner. While experienced as a shock or sudden disruption, something probably does need to change. The partner might feel as if they are risking a part of themselves for the possibility for future growth.

Neptune

Neptune's influence on another's horoscope ranges from magical to disappointing. Neptune's spell diffuses and dissolves, enchants and deceives; it is like a hallucinogen that alters the perception and understanding of the self. A veil is placed over the area that Neptune influences and whichever house Neptune touches may be affected by creativity and spirituality. A more profound resonance with this part of the self may happen. Remember that people born in the same generation will most likely experience their partner's Neptune in the same house as their own. By aspect, Neptune can either inspire or confuse; however, either of these experiences will shift the awareness of the partner, challenging them with something mystical and more profound, as well as confronting them with the uncertainty and mystery of life.

Pluto

For individuals born close to one another, a partner's Pluto will be in close proximity to their own. Most likely, Pluto will then be in the same house and repeat the partner's natal aspects. The partner stresses the need to strengthen and transform this aspect of the partner. Wherever Pluto influences, it brings with it the process of confronting the truth, revealing the denials and unearthing the secrets and taboos. This process is not to invoke shame or negativity but to let go of what no longer promotes life. By aspect it reshapes and transforms the partner's experience into a more authentic and honest expression. Pluto challenges the individual to trust themselves in this area and to confront their authenticity.

House Sitting: The Environmental Impact

Before we outline how planets might impact the partner's house system, let's create a bi-wheel using Brad and Angelina's horoscopes. The first bi-wheel is from Brad's perspective, with Angelina's planets placed in the outer wheel. Since she is younger, these would also represent the transits to his horoscope when she was born. He was 11½ years old, having just experienced his first Jupiter return.

Immediately visible is her Aries stellium falling in his 4th house, affecting him at the deepest layer of being, stimulating his beliefs about home and family. The 8th and 12th houses are also tenanted, indicating that she impresses the deeper feeling and soulful levels of his being. Her Vertex on his Ascendant is also immediately visible, as is her Sun on his Descendant.

To reflect on the nature of the planetary impact I use a worksheet (see Appendix) to compile notes. Below the bi-wheel is my worksheet based on Angelina's planets in Brad's houses.

The retrograde planets are not shown, so take note of these from the natal chart. I have not included the aspect lines so we can focus more on the impact of Angelina's planets on Brad's houses.

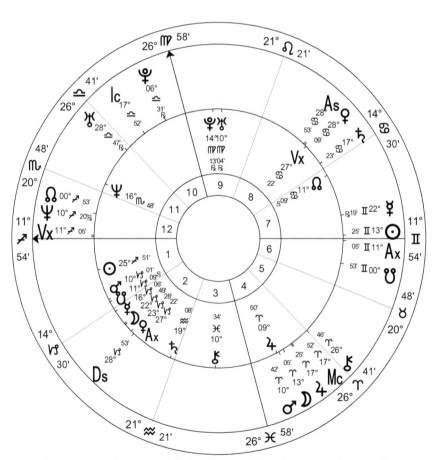

Inner Wheel is Brad Pitt; Outer Wheel is Angelina Jolie

Synastry Worksheet: House Sitting
– My Planets in Your Houses

Angelina (A) Planet/ Point	Falls in Brad's (B) House	Notes
Sun	7th; conjunct Descendant	Strong attraction; creative qualities, confidence and charisma are first noticed. A tendency to fall under a spell or shadow, creative competition
Moon	4th; conjunct Jupiter	A's dynamic nurturing style affects B's security but also cultivates and encourages his beliefs about himself, family and belonging
Mercury	7th opposite B's Sun	A's communicative style may need to be aware of not misunderstanding or assuming what is said
Venus	8th; conjunct Vertex	A's values of home and security, appreciation of beauty are deeply tied into B feeling close, connected and intimate
Mars	4th; conjunct Jupiter	A's courage and dynamism challenge B to be more optimistic and speculative when it comes to home, family and the place to belong
Jupiter	4th; conjunct Jupiter	A was born twelve years after B and her beliefs and ethics deeply affect B's outlook on life
Saturn	8th; widely conjunct Vertex	A's strong sense of what is right for family, how to nurture and care for others, affects the level of intimacy and feelings of deep connection
Chiron	5th; conjunct cusp of 5th	A's sense of her own isolation and marginalization influences B's attitudes towards children and creativity
Uranus	11th	A brings her individuality and generational attitudes of freedom, friendship, technology and community to B's social circle
Neptune	12th; conjunct Ascendant	A's intrigue and enchantment is like a siren to B, who senses her otherworldly nature and creative ways of being

Pluto	10th	A strongly impacts B's vocation, his career designs and his role in the world. She strongly influences his plans and brings persuasion and power to bear on his choices and direction
North Node	12th	A's life direction awakens a deeper spiritual longing for B
MC	4th; conjunct Jupiter	A's vocation and higher purpose affect B's beliefs about family and home
Ascendant	8th; conjunct Vertex	A powerful alignment takes place between A's personality and life force and B's deep sense of self. This suggests that A's personality is highly compelling and gripping. Therapeutic by nature, she stimulates B to become more aware of his own deeper complexes
Vertex	12th; conjunct Ascendant	A's mysterious needs and compulsions are brought into the open through B's personality and the way he approaches life

What follows is a consideration of the impact on the house that the partner's planets might make when falling in that sphere:

One Partner's Planets Falling in the Other's 1st House
When a partner's planet falls in an individual's 1st house, it immediately makes an impression on their energy field or aura, either stimulating or confronting the person. The personality is engaged. For instance, the person may feel the other's Sun as an attractive and vital energy. There may be an immediate recognition and warmth. On the other hand, Saturn could feel cold or judgemental, provoking anxiety or self-consciousness. Another person's planet contacting the 1st house is experienced immediately, on first meeting, impacting the vitality and personal sense of self. If the planet conjuncts the Ascendant these reactions are intensified.

One Partner's Planets Falling in the Other's 2nd House
When planets fall in another's 2nd house they influence their value system, tastes, likes and dislikes as well as their attitudes towards possessions and resources. On the one hand, depending on the nature of the planet/s and the partner's attitude towards financial

matters, the 2nd house could receive a boost or assistance in the areas of finance, money and assets. However, if the planet is not well integrated, the partner may seem to withhold or be critical of their values and attitudes towards wealth.

One Partner's Planets Falling in the Other's 3rd House
Communication, exchange of ideas, language and sibling dynamics may be involved when a partner's planets fall in the other's 3rd house. Depending on the planet, there may be a rapport with the energy which stimulates new ideas, thoughts and conversation. The 3rd house individual feels energized by the other's power and presence in this area. The partner may also feel the other is confronting them with new ideas and ways of thinking and connecting. Old patterns of communication and learning may be challenged in this relationship.

One Partner's Planets Falling in the Other's 4th House
When one's planets are positioned in the partner's 4th house, their foundation stones, innermost feelings and emotional security are impacted. On the one hand they may feel more secure and supported, but on the other they might feel unprotected and unsafe. Planets in the 4th challenge the individual's sense of security and deeper knowledge of themselves. They facilitate the need to feel secure and to create structures that support them in the world. The patterns from their family of origin are emphasized and challenged by the planetary archetype that now occupies the 4th house.

One Partner's Planets Falling in the Other's 5th House
Planets influencing the other's 5th house can energize the partner's creative side. Whether that is a question of children, artistry, creativeness, originality or self-expression depends on the partner's planetary influence; nevertheless, the focus on the individual's playful and expressive aspects are highlighted. The relationship influences the partner to be more aware of their creative and dynamic potential. The awareness of play and happiness, the freedom of self-expression, and originality without fear of disapproval are emphasized. An opportunity for nurturing and healing the inner child and imagining new creative possibilities is likely.

One Partner's Planets Falling in the Other's 6th House
When the 6th house area is influenced then the individual's routines and daily rituals are affected by the other. New daily ways of being are encouraged by the partner. The 6th house individual may be more inclined to be in the moment and share in the daily routines with their partner. Stimulating new work routines or patterns may develop. Perhaps they have met at work or are working alongside each other. The need to communicate and share in the day-to-day dilemmas with the partner is important for relationship continuity and to deepen the experience of one another.

One Partner's Planets Falling in the Other's 7th House
When the 7th house is tenanted by another's planets, cooperation and compromise are brought to light and projections are more visible. Planets that fall in the 7th stimulate self-awareness. The 'other half' may be a catalyst to acknowledge qualities and characteristics not easily recognized by the 7th house partner. The significant other is challenged to be a partner, to cooperate, negotiate and compromise.

One Partner's Planets Falling in the Other's 8th House
When the partner's planet/s falls in the 8th house they act as a lever to lift the lid of the psychic vessel that contains the most intimate and private feelings and memories. Vulnerability and sensitivity to feelings are heightened. Intense feelings and controlled desires are more easily stirred; the partner feels uncovered and confronted to be honest and open. While the 8th house person is challenged by the other, they may not be ready to be as open and honest as their partner desires. This may take time. Issues of sharing resources, especially money and sex, and the disclosure of secrets may be part of the relational terrain.

One Partner's Planets Falling in the Other's 9th House
The partner whose planets fall in your 9th house can either inspire you with visions for the future or provoke you into being more genuine about your beliefs and ethics. This partner may be a helpmate in exploring new ideologies or a mentor and guide into higher realms, an educator or adventurer when it comes to understanding life. When planets fall in your 9th, these energies can promote a broader horizon of the world or a greater thoughtfulness of what

you are seeking. Your beliefs, ideals, philosophies, education and aspirations are being experienced in a new light.

One Partner's Planets Falling in the Other's 10th House
Since your 10th house is where you forge your identity and status in the world, another's planets inhabiting this house affect your professional and worldly affairs, contributing or inhibiting your sense of comfort in the world at large. This might suggest a business or professional relationship, a shared vocation or profession, or even a parental or mentoring influence. The 10th house individual is affected by the attitudes and ambitions of his or her partner. The relationship can help to forge a more conscious intention of one's role in the world and what is ultimately important to contribute.

One Partner's Planets Falling in the Other's 11th House
Friendship, equality and social concerns are brought out into the open when one partner's planets fall in the other's 11th house. The 11th house partner might be stimulated to join new associations, relate to new friends and find new possibilities of community participation. Planets in the 11th are metaphors for the avenues that are opening up socially because of the relationship. Issues of equality, social concerns, community participation and the commonality of friends become more apparent for the relationship's agenda.

One Partner's Planets Falling in the Other's 12th House
You may be inspired to delve into the unknown if your partner's planet/s falls in your 12th house. On one level this can bring new understanding, insights and creative impulses to the forefront; yet on the other it may also bring deeply buried fears or complexes to the surface. Either way, the partner acts as a catalyst for insight and revelation. Ultimately, the 12th house partner stimulates a more authentic spirituality and personal creativity. Ancestral ghosts may be awakened that help to address missing pieces of the family puzzle.

Having reflected on the planets affecting the partner's horoscope, let's now look at the second bi-wheel, which is generated by placing Brad Pitt's planets on the outside of Angelina's horoscope.

What is first visible is his ♑ stellium impacting her 6th house of work. Their first relationship was a working one, meeting on the set of a movie where they played the role of a married couple. His Uranus–Pluto conjunction falls in her 2nd house, influencing her security and grounding. While she influences the emotional landscape of his life, hers is being impacted in the work and material areas of life. B's Ascendant at 11♐ falls in A's 5th house on her Neptune–Vertex conjunction, suggesting that his approach to children, and her idealism about them, are featured.

His Vertex falls on her Ascendant; being in Cancer, it addresses his deep issues about family and home and these are brought out

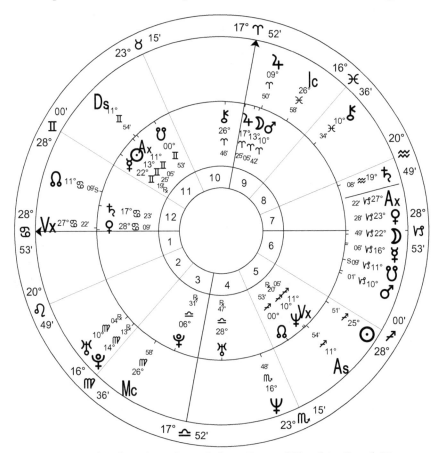

Inner Wheel is Angelina Jolie; Outer Wheel is Brad Pitt

into the open by A. Venus conjoins her Ascendant; therefore the strong values and integrity she brings to family and caring confront B's unlived responses to family, home and feeling safe. While these images are visually apparent it is worthwhile summarizing the impact Brad has on Angelina's energy field. As we make notes on each of these astrological images, repetitive patterns emerge.

Synastry Worksheet: House Sitting – My Planets in Your Houses

Brad (B) Planet/ Point	Falls in Angelina's (A) House	Notes
Sun	5th	B shines light on A's creativity and self-expression
Moon	6th; conjunct Descendant	There is an immediate sense of comfort and ease with B's Moon on A's horizon. It falls on the 6th house side, suggesting that B's moods and feelings impact A's everyday life
Mercury	6th	B stimulates the need to converse and debrief on work and everyday routines
Venus	6th; conjunct Descendant	An immediate attraction and appreciation of the other is apparent with B's Venus on A's horizon. B may help A to feel more valued and appreciated in her everyday world
Mars	6th	B's Mars stimulates and encourages A to be more focused on her routines of work and well-being
Jupiter	9th	A has Jupiter in the 9th, so B reinforces her ideals and outlook. As it conjoins A's Mars–Moon in Aries, B's Jupiter may bring more adventure, travel and international contacts and residences into her life
Saturn	7th; on 8th house cusp	While Saturn is known as being critical, in the 7th it might also suggest an intention to work on the relationship. B may challenge A to be more present and cooperative in relating
Chiron	8th	B may constellate some intimate wounds and painful memories in A

Uranus	2nd	B was born in the seminal phase of the Uranus–Pluto conjunction and he brings his generational values into the relationship. B may alter A's views on her sense of self, values and resources
Neptune	4th	B may inspire a new way to imagine family closeness, offering a more inspirited window of faith to see into her fractured feelings of family life (Uranus in the 4th). However, this could also suggest a family disappointment
Pluto	2nd	Along with Uranus, Pluto is stressing a more authentic view of A's self-worth and ability to share her creative resources
North Node	12th	A may inspire a sense of destiny and of being on the right path for B; and B arouses a greater sense of comfort with the inner world in A
MC	3rd	B's direction in life is familiar to A's; she might be a sister to his goals or he can be a brother to hers
Ascendant	5th; conjunct Vertex	B's enthusiasm and vision are a boon to A's creativity. B's Ascendant also conjuncts A's Neptune–Vertex so her idealism and sense of mission about children and creativity are brought to light by B's personality
Vertex	12th; conjunct Ascendant	B's Vertex in Cancer conjunct A's Ascendant suggests that the road less travelled of family and closeness is brought into consciousness through his relationship with A

The ruler of Brad's Sagittarius Ascendant is Jupiter in the 4th house at 9♈50. The ruler of Angelina's Cancer Ascendant is the Moon in the 9th at 13♈05. Both conjoin in Aries, bringing their two rulers together. In Angelina's chart these conjoin in the 9th, while in Brad's chart they are in the 4th. This alignment continues the recurring theme of re-visioning family and security issues in the light of international and cross-cultural family values. Faith and hope are nurtured in the creative and meaningful areas of life.

Angelina's natal Moon is conjunct Brad's Jupiter, but Brad's Moon at 22♑49 is square Angelina's Jupiter at 17♈25. Since this interaspect goes both ways it is mutual and brings the archetypes of the Moon and Jupiter into high focus, one we have already noted in the chart comparison. The details of interaspects will become more apparent as we now move to the next step of creating a synastry grid of aspects.

CHAPTER 17

JUST BETWEEN US
The Aspect Grid

Aspects are the life lines of the relationship as they join particular forces together in compatible or conflicting ways. Like Eros, aspects mingle the gods together. Because aspects are based on divisions of the circle they link elements together, reminding us that temperament is an essential component of an aspect. Aspects bring elements into focus, so to begin I will review aspects by combining the elements. If we can imagine how planets in elements might combine we begin to understand aspects in synastry.

No doubt you will have already experienced that aspects by whole sign in chart comparison reveal meaningful patterns. For instance, if one partner has the Moon in Pisces and the other has the Moon in Gemini, then this tension is felt in the relationship regardless of the orb of the aspect. The qualities of the signs Pisces and Gemini suggest very different orientations and experiences. Simply speaking, the needs and habits of each are quite dissimilar; therefore in relationship these differences would need to be consciously understood and addressed.

Planetary Appearances in Relationship

The traditional view of the aspects remains the same in synastry, but rather than an internal dialogue between two archetypes, there is a dialogue between these archetypes in the two individuals. The aspects come to life as they are lived out by people in relationship. The partner exists outwardly and the interaction between the two planetary archetypes is brought to life in the external world. Here are the six aspects that I will use in the synastry grid:

Conjunctions and Trines

These aspects combine the same element; therefore they are often seen as harmonious or, in the case of the conjunction, sometimes ambivalent. Although the same element focuses the couple in a similar direction, some balance and difference needs to be applied.

Fire–Fire

This is a volatile combination that suggests a quick, enthusiastic, spirited beginning but little to sustain the passion once it wanes. Passionate fires may burn quickly or burn each other; therefore when two fiery people meet there may be fireworks, loads of action and plenty of passion, but the craze may wane when it becomes routine or too familiar. By aspect, two planets in Fire share an elemental nature but may be inclined to excite and stir each other up.

Air–Air

While this is a socially stimulating combination it suggests that being personally involved and engaged may be difficult. There is no lack of ideas or ability to explore these ideas; however, the implementation of plans and schemes may be difficult. Two airy people might share common thoughts and experience a meeting of minds, but the atmosphere may become too dry for any connection to take root. By aspect, two Air planets may be very stimulating but may also become ungrounded and carried away.

Water–Water

Water is adept at being sensitive to the environment and the other, especially the other's interior world; therefore this combination suggests a hypersensitivity to another's moods. When there are two watery people in relationship, each may try to 'read' the other and feel rejected or isolated when the other does not respond to their unspoken needs. There is an abundance of feeling and sensitivity but not enough objectivity or spark to ignite the relationship. By aspect, two Water planets can inspire one another but they might also drown each other.

Earth–Earth

This combination could promote a sense of being overly cautious or safe. There is an enduring ability to work things through; however, there is also the ability to get stuck. When two earthy people combine there is the potential to build up resources and be successful in the world, yet the relationship may lack fervour and excitement. By aspect, two Earth planets may support and contain one another but could also block the other or become inert.

Sextiles and Oppositions
These aspects combine either masculine or feminine signs. The opposition in synastry can be considered a pairing and exchanging of energies.

Masculine Signs: Fire–Air
This is a natural polarity which suggests good potential for communication and partnering. Fire does not remain detached and Air cannot sustain the heat, which could lead to a breakdown in communication and understanding. In a personal relationship each can support the other, yet the Air individual's ideas could become overheated and ungrounded while Fire's vision may become inflated and excessive. By aspect, they tend to stimulate each other but need tempering.

Feminine Signs: Earth–Water
This other natural polarity is sympathetic to one another. However, Earth grapples to understand the depth of the feeling life and its changeable moods, while Water may struggle with the discipline and structure that Earth needs. Two individuals can learn to support each other and work together when the feelings and moods are acknowledged and there is enough routine and security. By aspect, they support one another but may be inclined to either become stuck or to sink.

Squares and Quincunxes
These aspects combine elements that are psychologically opposed to each other; therefore, they are not at ease with each other if they are in the same space or exist at the same time. In synastry, they can represent the more difficult dialogues between the planets.

Fire–Earth
Fire represents vision, spirit and flight, while Earth suggests incarnation, consistency and continuity. Fire can often feel imprisoned by the rigidity and structures of Earth while Earth feels frustrated and devalued by Fire's restless chaos. Working together, this is a dynamic force. There is often a secret affinity and attraction between the two elements which is not visible at

the beginning. In relationship, these two elements are antithetical yet are often fated to be together.

Fire–Water
Both are highly emotive elements. Fire expresses its feelings but Water often contains or withholds its feelings. They often have a difficult time accepting each other's viewpoint since Fire conceptualizes feelings whereas Water has difficulty in articulating them. This is a passionate combination, sometimes quick-tempered, at other times hot-blooded. By aspect, it is important to note the compulsive theme to this combination; however it is also important to recognize the intensity and passion that can be creative and fertile.

Water–Air
Water is frustrated by Air's lack of feeling response and inability to pick up on their moods and needs. Air is perplexed by the complexity of Water's feeling life, being uneducated in the world of feelings and moods. Therefore there is often a feeling of missing each other. Although these two elements are often unconsciously drawn to one another, their elemental fate is to swing between being engaged and then disengaged. They strive to find the suitable balance between separateness and closeness, space and togetherness. With two individuals there is often a lot of frustration and misunderstanding; with planets in Water and Air, it is important to recognize the need to articulate feelings as well as trying to be objective without compromising the feelings.

Earth–Air
The mythological marriage of Heaven and Earth symbolizes the ongoing tension between the sky gods and understanding the rhythms and cycles of the earth. From Earth's point of view, Air is disinterested and restless; from Air's vantage point Earth is too routine and pragmatic. In relationship, this can lead to conflict about how to do things, getting caught up in details or arguing over what is not important. The focus of these two elements is quite different; therefore they consciously require encouragement to work together, finding appropriate ways to bring their separate energy into the relationship.

Now let's consider the aspect by itself and how this might function between two individuals.

The Conjunction

In natal astrology we use keywords such as emphasis, focus, concentrated, intense, merging, unifying and joining for the conjunction. When two planets are fused together in the same zodiacal space their energies need to learn to share the same space and outlook. Being so closely aligned means there is little distance to maintain objectivity; therefore, the conjunction is considered to be highly subjective. In synastry, when one partner's planet is conjoined with another's it is critical that their archetypal natures cooperate and work together towards unified and common goals. Depending on the nature of the planets, one could dominate the other or be submissive, even subversive. Therefore both partners need to be aware of the power differentials when planets conjoin. If both planets try to act at the same time or in the same space there may be conflict. The conjunction is the harmonic of one so it may be inclined to be singular. An image of the two planets combining in relationship is a useful metaphor to examine ways they could function together.

The Opposition

This is the second harmonic and a natural aspect for synastry; like relationship, this aspect addresses the nature of polarity. The opposition points to an energetic combination that needs to be shared and issues that might need compromise, debate and agreement. It could refer to areas where each partner holds their ground. In natal astrology we use the keywords awareness, contradiction, projection, equality, pulling apart, at odds with one another, counter-balance and creating symmetry: images that are important when two individuals have planets that oppose one another. When considering the two planets involved, assess whether the archetypal inclination is to work together or pull in opposite directions.

The Square

Two planets, which may or may not be comfortable together, are arranged in a challenging situation. In synastry, the square places each partner's planet in a stressful relationship, suggesting these archetypes may be at cross-purposes with one other. This aspect highlights the need for each partner to be aware of the friction, so neither one works against the other when the tension of the aspect arises. The natal themes of challenge, tension, crisis, conflict, dynamic resistance, motivation and discord are now embedded in the relationship between the partners' positions personified by the planets. The square in synastry is dynamic by nature and potentially fastens the relationship together; however, when left unacknowledged it can wear down intimacy. The square is the most difficult combination, yet full of life, bringing opposing natures into consciousness and offering the possibility to create something out of the tension and conflict.

The Trine
This brings the flow of elements together. While the orientation and direction of the planets may be similar, stimulus and incentives for growth could be compromised. The natal themes of blending, flowing, affiliation, combining talents and skills and an easy association are helpful for creating security and stability, but could also be taken for granted. Trines in synastry suggest energies that can stabilize and develop the relationship; however, they need to be activated and directed.

The Sextile
The natal keywords like opportunity, affable, combining, reinforcing, facilitating and assisting reflect the potential positivism of the planets involved in a sextile, which can combine in a partnership to quicken a process, create an opportunity or turn a corner. Both planets can focus on establishing supportive platforms and creating opportunities for the relationship.

The Quincunx
Like the square, the quincunx challenges the planets to maximize their potential by combining different points of view. Adjustment, strain, making choices, going off track, separating, interrupting, branching out and redirection are some natal themes that can be applied in synastry to planets in quincunx. Like the square, an incompatibility in the elements occurs, suggesting there needs to be an application of conscious intent to combine the energies

effectively. This is a dynamic aspect in synastry, potentially demanding and testing, yet ultimately rewarding, as it challenges couples to find another way to cooperate.

Generating the Synastry Grid

We are ready to generate the synastry grid which outlines the network of aspects between the two charts. This can be done on Solar Fire and instructions can be found in the Appendix. Before the grid is created, it is important to define the parameters that will be used: which planets, points and any other astrological considerations, as well as which aspects and orbs, will be used. This will help you to be consistent when collating data, as well as to control the information generated. Without defined limits, too much excess and irrelevant information could be produced. I find it helpful to have a working structure so the aspect grid can be analysed not only for the aspects between the two charts, but also for the number and types of aspects as well. Of course, once you become more familiar with using your aspect grid you will be able to add more points or asteroids, etc. But to begin the process of analysing the synastry grid, I suggest that at this point less is more.

Setting the Parameters

To begin I suggest using the planets you are familiar with. For the synastry grid I am using the ten planets (Sun–Pluto) and Chiron. I will also include the three angles of the Ascendant, Midheaven and Vertex as well as the North Node. I have chosen one angle of each axis and one node, as the other angles and node are naturally embedded in the aspect.

Next, choose which aspects you will use and what orbs you will assign for each aspect. There are no hard and fast rules here, as some astrologers suggest using wider orbs for synastry, while others suggest tighter ones. In setting parameters you will be consistent in your study of aspect grids and gain the experience of recognizing whether a relationship has several or few aspects, because the more aspects between the partners' planets, the more dynamic or complex the relationship may be. Orbs are arbitrary lines of demarcation and need to be used fluidly, not as a rigid boundary. The orbs I have used for the synastry grid are those also used in Chapter 4:

Aspect	Exact	Orb
Conjunction	0°	+/– 10°
Opposition	180°	+/– 10°
Trine	120°	+/– 8°
Square	90°	+/– 8°
Sextile	60°	+/– 6°
Quincunx	150°	+/– 5°

When the aspect between the charts is tight, the shared experience between the couple is heightened. The closer the orb of aspect, the greater the tension or ease between the planets. This becomes magnified during certain transits. Be aware of aspects by sign alone, applying the orbs to define and pinpoint areas of ease and tension more readily. When you have examined each chart individually you will have recognized certain signs that are prominent in each chart. For instance, in Brad's chart Capricorn stands out; hence Angelina's planets in Aries are squaring by sign and her planets in Cancer are opposite by sign.

Following is the synastry grid for Brad and Angelina. Brad's planets are the horizontal line across the top, while Angelina's are the vertical ones down the left-hand side of the grid. Notice that there are fifteen boxes across and fifteen down, representing the ten planets, Chiron, the North Node and the three angles of the Ascendant, MC and Vertex. As already mentioned, the South Node, the Descendant, IC and Anti-Vertex will make a complementary aspect and their opposite polarity already reflects the aspect. Therefore on the grid there are 225 boxes. To begin your analysis of the synastry grid, it is interesting to note the number of aspects made to each of the planets, remembering we have only used the Ptolemaic aspects plus the quincunx.

	☉	☽	☿	♀	♂	♃	♄	♅	♆	♇	⚷	☊	As	Mc	Vx
☉			⊼ 2A41		⊼ 3S23	✶ 3S35	△ 5A43	□ 3S21	⊼ 3A22	□ 0A48	□ 2S50		☍ 1S30		
☽			□ 3A01		□ 3S03	☌ 3S15		⊼ 3S00	⊼ 3A43	⊼ 1A08			□ 1S55	△ 1S10	
☿	☍ 3S32	⊼ 0S30		⊼ 1S08		△ 3A11								□ 4S39	
♀	⊼ 2S17	☍ 5S19	☍ 4S41										✶ 1S10	☌ 0S47	
♂		□ 5A24		□ 0S40	☌ 0S52			⊼ 0S38		⊼ 3A31			□ 0A27	△ 1A12	
♃	□ 5A24	□ 1S18	□ 6A02	□ 7S23	☌ 7S35	✶ 1A43			⊼ 0S37	⊼ 3S11			□ 6S15	△ 5S30	
♄	☍ 5A26	☍ 1S16	☍ 6A04	☍ 7S21	□ 7S33	⊼ 1A45			△ 0S35	✶ 3S09	△ 6S48	☌ 6S13			☌ 9A58
♅	✶ 2A56	□ 5A58	□ 5A19												□ 1A25
♆				△ 0A30				□ 0A16		□ 3S53	□ 0S14	⊼ 0S49	☌ 1S34		
♇				□ 3S30	☍ 3S18						⊼ 4S03	□ 4S38	✶ 5S23	☌ 9A32	
⚷	△ 0S54	□ 3S56	□ 3S17										⊼ 0A12	□ 0A35	
☊													✶ 3S54	△ 3S31	
As	⊼ 3S01	☍ 6S03	☍ 5S25										✶ 1S54	☌ 1S31	
Mc	△ 7A59	□ 4A57	□ 1S45	□ 5A35	□ 7S50	☌ 8S02	✶ 1A16		⊼ 1S04	⊼ 3S38			□ 6S42	△ 5S57	
Vx				△ 1S15					□ 1S01	□ 3A07	⊼ 0S31	⊼ 0A03	☌ 0A48		

The Aspect Grid: Brad Pitt and Angelina Jolie

Analysing the Synastry Grid

To begin, we will tabulate the number of aspects made to each of the planets in the synastry grid. This will give an overview of the number of aspects and dynamically aspected planets. This exercise is a way to begin an analysis of the relationship dynamics. The number of aspects suggests the intensity of interactive planetary dialogues; however, the grid needs to be studied in detail to differentiate and prioritize the aspects. Below is a grid which summarises the hundred aspects that occur between the two charts.

Given the parameters used, my experience would be that when the total number of aspects exceeds 40%, the synastry grid is dynamic, perhaps suggesting the interactive nature of the couple. It does not make a statement about the quality or compatibility of the relationship, but more an overall view of the connective links, or what I like to refer to as the 'ley lines'[114] that underpin the relationship.

	Number of aspects made to Angelina's planets	Number of aspects made to Brad's planets	Notes
Sun	9	6	Angelina has Saturn square the MC; many synastry aspects are made to Saturn and the MC. Brad's stellium in Capricorn opposes Saturn and squares the MC, which increases the amount of aspects and highlights this theme. A has Capricorn on her Descendant; the Saturn/Capricorn theme is highlighted in relationship.
Moon	8	8	
Mercury	5	6	
Venus	5	8	
Mars	7	7	
Jupiter	10	9	
Saturn	11	5	
Uranus	4	5	
Neptune	6	5	
Pluto	6	8	
Chiron	5	5	
North Node	2	8	B's planets are more evenly aspected but Jupiter receives the most due to A's stellium in Aries
Ascendant	5	8	
Midheaven	11	6	
Vertex	6	6	
Total Aspects	**100 44% of total grid**	**100 44% of total grid**	

In this case the aspects to the stelliums increase the number of aspects. Note that Angelina's Saturn and Midheaven have the most aspects, suggesting that the relationship strongly influences these archetypes. Her direction, purpose and public contributions may become more focused due to this relationship. In Brad's chart, Jupiter has the most aspects, suggesting that Angelina influences Brad's perceptions and beliefs about the world he inhabits. On the other hand, the excesses of Jupiter may be called into line by the firmness of Saturn. Both social planets are strongly aspected, bringing the social archetypes to the forefront of their interaction.

Consider which aspect occurs most in the synastry grid. Before analysing the number of aspects, it is important to remember that the conjunction and opposition only occur once in the cycle of aspects whereas the others can be both waxing and waning; therefore it would be reasonable to expect fewer of these aspects. The sextile and quincunx do not have as much orb allowance as the trine or square, which do not have as much orb allowance as the conjunction and opposition. However, given these considerations it is apparent that the square and the quincunx are very strong. The cardinal squares are highlighted. The easier aspects of the trine and sextile are few. We could suggest that this relationship has its share of challenges but the dynamic tension that brings the partners into relationship can be erotic and productive.

Conjunction	11 aspects	
Opposition	11 aspects	
Trine	13 aspects	
Square	35 aspects	
Sextile	9 aspects	
Quincunx	21 aspects	Total 100 Aspects

Total Number of Aspects in the Pitt/Jolie Aspect Grid

I have used the same parameters with the other couples whose charts have been presented. The highly aspected planets or points are of interest, as these underline the highly accentuated archetypes in the relationship.

- Diana and Charles have 99 aspects representing 44% of the number of possible aspects. Charles has most contact to his Moon and Nodes, while Diana has the most contacts to her Nodes and both luminaries.

- Akihito and Michiko have 96 contacts or 43%. Akihito's Venus receives more contacts while for Michiko most planets are fairly equal with Pluto receiving more aspects.

- Anaïs Nin and Henry Miller also have 96 aspects represented in their synastry grid. Both have the highest number of aspects to their Vertex, while Anaïs receives more aspects to her Saturn with Henry receiving most aspects to his MC.

- Virginia Woolf and Vita Sackville-West have 92 contacts or 41%. For Virginia, Chiron and the MC receive more aspects while for Vita, Venus and Pluto have many more aspects than her other planets and points.

- And finally Bobby and Whitney have 78 or 35% contacts. Bobby's Mars is more highly aspected, while for Whitney her Ascendant receives the most aspects.

Planetary Dialogues among Related Archetypes
To begin analysing the aspects within the grid we can start with aspects between the similar planets, especially the inner ones as these will be most personal and individualized. For instance, Bobby Brown's Sun at 16♒27 is exactly opposite Whitney's Sun at 16♌41, highlighting their different characters, yet also the opportunity to see a side of their character reflected by the other. Akihito and Michiko both have their Moons in Pisces which suggests an emotional union because each one can understand their partner's feeling life through their own experience. Since their emotional and deeply personal life is tied together they will also move through similar transitions and feelings at the same time. Brad and Angelina have Venus opposite each other while their Mars are square each other. This suggests that their values and what they like and appreciate may be quite opposite; how they motivate and assert themselves could also be at odds. Once conscious of these differences they can be acknowledged and integrated into the relationship. From an erotic point of view this combination is intense and passionate as the god Eros is fond of bringing opposites together.

The grid offers us an outlook on an overview of each planet. Therefore if the agenda of the couple is about communication and sharing ideas, Mercury and its aspects become significant; if it is values, money, resources and self-esteem we would be inclined to focus on Venus; while if anger, desire, motivation and conflict are the issue Mars would be the focal point. When there are aspects between similar planets the nature of the aspect informs us as to how this archetypal energy may be expressed between the couple.

Mutual Interaspects

A mutual interaspect occurs when the same planet in each partner's horoscope makes an aspect to the identical planet in the other's horoscope. For instance, Angelina's Jupiter is square Brad's Moon while Brad's Jupiter is conjunct Angelina's Moon. Each partner's planet makes an aspect to that same planet in the partner's chart. When there are mutual interaspects, the dynamic of the planetary combination is highlighted in the relationship, suggesting that each influences the other in a similar way. On one hand this could be an area where the couple become stuck by not allowing the necessary compromise to occur, yet on the other it suggests the combination of two energies that can create a powerful ally in forging a deeper understanding for each individual and offering a creative synthesis when together.

Mutual interaspects aspects to the Moon in the Pitt–Jolie synastry grid stress the need for emotional space and independence in the relationship. The interaspects also point to the possibility of travel, change of residence and an expansion of the family in unusual ways. These mutual interaspects occur in the following combinations:

- A's Mercury is quincunx B's Moon; B's Mercury is square A's Moon. This highlights the challenge in comprehension, understanding and communication between the couple. They may not be aware of each other's needs or moods or may have difficulty understanding what the other is expressing. Some of the communication patterns may also be a relic of their familial dialogues. When harnessed, this dynamic interchange suggests that each one can support the other to express and accept difficult feelings. Each one can also see another side to the situation which opens up possibilities and choices to make the situation clearer and easier to deal with. The aspect implies being aware of the inherent difficulty in communicating and listening before the pattern can be changed. Misunderstanding is highlighted; therefore there is a strong need to articulate feelings and emotions in a more neutral fashion.

- A's Jupiter is square B's Moon; B's Jupiter is conjunct A's Moon. This interaspect suggests contrary needs for safety and freedom, as well as the diametrically opposed urges to nest and travel. Each one seems to challenge the other to move out of their safety zone. When one partner wants to take a giant leap, the other might withdraw into a routine or feel insecure and unsure. However, the dynamic possibility of this interaspect is that each one brings new life, opportunities for growth and inspires wider vision and possibilities in their relationship. Therefore when each one feels safe in the relationship, the possibilities for movement, travel, living abroad, international associations and growth are magnified. However, it is wise for the couple to understand that the unconscious dynamic might be that as one moves forward, the other may stall.

- A's Uranus is square B's Moon; B's Uranus is quincunx A's Moon. Similar to the previous interaspect, the desire for both freedom and closeness is highlighted. Each partner's comfort levels, habits and needs are being stirred up through this mutual interaspect. There is a great possibility that each partner may feel that the other disconnects or separates just when they need them, or is too involved with other interests to be there for them. Each one is being challenged to become more emotionally secure, to risk new attachments and ways of being.

- A's Moon is Trine B's Ascendant; B's Moon is opposite A's Ascendant. With the interconnection between the Moon and the other's Ascendant, comfort and safety in the relationship needs to be identified. This suggests that emotional bonds, mutual care, protection, comfort and a sense of familiarity and ease are on the horizon of the relationship.

There are also four interaspects to the Sun: Sun–Mercury; Sun–Uranus; Sun–Chiron and Sun–Ascendant. The Sun's aspects to the horizon suggest an immediate sense of attraction and recognition. Brad's Sagittarius Sun quincunxes Angelina's Cancer Ascendant, suggesting there may have to be an adjustment or path cleared; nonetheless there is a magnetic contact. The Sun–

Mercury is reiterating the theme of communication and exchange of ideas while the Sun–Uranus emphasizes the motif of identifying freedom and individuality within the relationship. The Sun–Chiron interaspect suggests identifying with the wounded aspects of one another; however, it also implies that healing and attending to the disenfranchised parts of the self is vital.

Due to the many connections between the couple, there will be more interaspects which are important to address in the context of their archetypal interaction. The interaspects involving the inner planets are a priority as these suggest that the relationship challenges the identity of each partner and how each individual has come to understand themselves to date.

Subsections of the Grid
The grid can also be divided into subsections which highlight planetary interchanges and archetypal dialogues as follows.

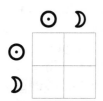

1. The Sun–Moon Sub-grid
There are four boxes that contain the interaspects between the Sun and the Moon. Aspects between the Sun and Moon are the first priority to analyse. These are core energies symbolizing primary characteristics of the personality. Aspects between the Suns suggest how each one's identity is influenced by the other. Aspects between the Moons reveal how the two individuals emotionally interact and become familiar with each other's moods, feelings and needs. These aspects constellate family dynamics and parental issues, as well as issues about how the couple identifies and supports each partner's creative uniqueness and inner life.

When comparing horoscopes of partners or potential partners, astrological tradition suggests that interaspects between the Sun and the Moon are of priority. The classical significator was first suggested by Ptolemy, writing in the second century CE. He suggested that we first look to the opposite gender luminaries when considering marriage in the horoscopes of men and women.[115] This is also echoed by modern astrology:

The Sun as the masculine 'dominant' principle is naturally complemented by the feminine receptivity of the Moon. In fact, the classical significator of harmony between couples is when the Moon of the female partner is conjunct the male's Sun. This is also true in reverse when the male's Moon is conjunct the female's Sun.[116]

Sun–Moon links in adult relationships may also suggest the amount of companionship and levels of comfort between two partners. In the Pitt–Jolie aspect grid there are no such aspects. Between the Prince and Princess of Wales there are two aspects or 50%, while for the Emperor and Empress of Japan there are also two boxes showing aspects. Although the Sun and Moon are the archetypal image of the marriage of masculine and feminine they represent the traditional process of union, not literal marriage. Each relationship is both unique and sacred in its own right and needs to be observed from this perspective.

2. The Venus–Mars Sub-grid

	♀	♂
♀	♂ 4S41	
♂		□ 0S40

In a creative and/or romantic relationship Venus–Mars aspects reveal the level of passion and intensity. Aspects between each person's Venus describe how the values either clash or interact, while aspects between each person's Mars suggest how the energy levels and aggressive instincts are experienced. Venus aspecting Mars is an erotic interchange which could also suggest the potency of sexual exchange and compatibility. In an adult relationship these aspects are the barometer of passion, intensity and attraction. In the Pitt–Jolie aspect grid there are two aspects in the Venus/Mars sub-grid –Venus is opposite herself while each one's Mars is square the other.

3. The Nodes and Angles Sub-grid

	☊	As	Mc	Vx
☊			✱ 3S54	△ 3S31
As			✱ 1S54	☌ 1S31
Mc	□ 6S42	△ 5S57		
Vx	⊼ 0A03	☌ 0A48		

This sub-grid highlights the axes of the two horoscopes. The angles of each horoscope are the framework upon which the horoscope is constructed. Interactions between these lines are crossroads where the couple meet and construct new frameworks and structures. These are the roads we travel, and with aspects between these nodal points life paths intersect in a purposeful way. This sub-grid includes the four axes: the nodal axis, the Ascendant–Descendant, the MC–IC and the Vertex – Anti-Vertex.

Each axis has its own orientation: for instance, the Ascendant–Descendant is the crossroads where personalities meet and each other's individuality and personal development is highlighted; the MC–IC is the intersection of domestic and worldly roles; the Vertex axis is where unconscious agendas meet and are met; while the junction of the nodal axis is where the process of individuation is encouraged. This box assists in answering questions about the direction, purpose and agendas of the relationship. In Brad and Angelina's relationship, there are several aspects in the Nodal sub-grid which reveal the many interconnected pathways in their lives.

Generational Interaspects
When the slower-moving planets aspect each other, generational issues and age come into focus. For instance, if one partner's Saturn squares the other's then there are either seven or twenty-two years difference in age. If the Jupiters are opposed then there is a six- or eighteen-year difference. If the Nodes are opposite then there is a nine or twenty-seven year difference. In the Pitt–Jolie aspect grid their Jupiters are conjunct, which is reflective of their twelve-year age gap. Their Saturns are quincunx each other, representing the twelve years as well. Perhaps they might be able to share ideologies, but may experience their attitude to rules, structures and systems quite differently.

If the partners are born in different generations and the outer planets do aspect each other, then generational biases and influences impact the relationship. For instance, if one partner's Saturn is square the other's Neptune then generational rules and regulations may conflict with the ideals, dreams and spirituality shaped by their partner's generation. In the Pitt–Jolie aspect grid, Brad's Uranus and Pluto square Angelina's Neptune, which might suggest that the imprint of his generation's radical and transformational intentions are at odds with her generation's ideals. Although not personal, it may arise when involved in more collective or communal endeavours.

Akihito and Michiko were born within a year of each other; therefore in their grid Saturn, Uranus, Neptune, Pluto and Chiron are all conjunct. This means that any aspect the individual has to these planets will also be aspected by their partner's outer planet. For instance, Michiko has a Sun–Pluto square, so Akihito's Pluto will also square her Sun, suggesting that the relationship accentuates her natal aspect.

Other Considerations
Here are some more reflections on how the aspect grid can be useful.

Outer Planets Aspecting Inner Planets
When an outer planet aspects an inner planet, the partner with the inner planet may feel overwhelmed, confused and uncertain when impacted by this particular energy. The generational imprint is felt, but there is also a sense that the partner awakens with new energies and experiences. If the partners are from the same generation and born close to one another, then the outer planet aspect to the inner planet will be magnified, as mentioned with Akihito and Michiko.

Aspects to Angles
Planets in one horoscope conjoining a partner's angle make a strong impact on this individual. If a planet falls on the Ascendant, the partner immediately feels a connection to this attribute in the other, since it is immediately seen and felt. If a planet falls on the Descendant then this energy triggers a response in the other, as the Descendant partner feels something familiar which can be either appealing or repellent. If a planet falls on the MC then the individual mirrors back goals, aspirations and challenges in the world. The person's planet personifies how they can help and guide the other in the world, especially on their vocational path. If a planet falls on the IC, then there is something familial, remembered or deeply resonant about the partner. The planet on the partner's IC might stir an early memory or image from childhood. The sense might be a feeling of either safety or insecurity, but something is deeply felt by their presence.

Assessing Other Aspects
Since there are many aspects in the grid, you can assess and prioritize these in different ways. Firstly look at the orbs: the closer the orb the more dramatic the aspect will be. Secondly, prioritize

according to the aspect: the conjunction has the highest priority, then the opposition, square, quincunx, trine and sextile. The tension-creating aspects are the priority in chart comparison. Thirdly, assess the planets according to the relationship. For instance, with couples who are living together, the Moon plays an important role; however, for business partners the Moon may not be as important, as their attachment may not be emotional or familial. As a rule, the Moon, Sun, Ascendant and MC are high priority in all relationships, but with adult relationships precedence is also focused on Venus and Mars. Analyse the other planets according to the archetypal themes, i.e. Mercury for communication, Jupiter for religious beliefs and morals, etc.

For example, in the Pitt–Jolie aspect grid there are many important aspects to the Sun and Moon which are less than 4° of orb. Another high priority aspect is A's Mars conjunct B's Jupiter with an orb of less than 1°, as we have discussed before. This might suggest that the way Jolie goes after what she wants and how she expresses her desires and anger challenges Pitt's deep attitudes about himself, resulting in a clash over beliefs, a fight for principles or a competition over who is most convincing. However, this might also signify a challenge to move farther afield, to become involved in cross-cultural concerns, education and cultural reform. When combined it becomes a dramatic image of accomplishing a great deal, taking gambles, challenges and trials with courage and gusto.

CHAPTER 18

COMBINED CHARTS
Two Individuals, One Relationship

A well known maxim, often ascribed to Aristotle, suggests that the whole is greater than the sum of its parts. In essence this is the nature of the combined chart. A union of two individuals creates the possibility of something greater. But the prerequisite requires that the two partners work together to create this possibility. A combined chart offers images of the intention and fulfilment of the relationship when individuals become jointly involved. The underlying premise is that combining two horoscopes generates cosmic alignments more powerful than for a singular individual. This is synergy, the dynamic force that results from working together to achieve something greater.

A combined chart can be created between our self and anyone we choose, but experience has taught me that while the combined chart is enormously valuable, it is only animated and brought to life when two individuals are committed to their bond. It is a map of a merger and shows possibilities and patterns. When the connection is mutual, then the composite energies become opportunities and options. In many cases the promise shown in the combined chart may never manifest because the individuals involved do not work together to ignite the potential of their relationship.

When Horoscopes Coalesce

The combined chart has been likened to an alchemical procedure. The alchemical union of the Red King and White Queen is an allegorical representation of the process of uniting opposites to create a greater outcome. Alchemy is an apt metaphor for the combined chart because when two energies are mixed in a vessel the amalgam creates a new substance. The combined chart symbolizes the soul of the relationship forged from blending two similar planets, points or angles. Imagine putting the Sun in Aries and the Sun in Gemini in an alchemical vessel to form the Sun in Taurus. Astrologically, the nature of Fire and Air combine to produce Earth, while cardinal and mutable bring a fixed quality into being. Imagine the Moon in Libra and the Moon in Sagittarius in the alembic. Together their union makes the Moon in Scorpio: two masculine energies create a feminine one. In this way the combined chart replicates the alchemical nature of relationship. This technique is useful in ascertaining patterns, challenges and timing in the relationship, but it does not describe individual needs. This is reflected in the natal horoscopes with their interaction symbolized by the chart comparison. The combined chart is the horoscope of the new entity: the relationship.

A combined chart may describe an intense synergy between two people. But what happens when only one of the two desires intensity? Or only one commits to the relationship? Conflict may occur or the relationship might simply dissolve or continue on functionally, but not necessarily intimately. Alchemists never worked alone; a partner was essential to complete the work. The alchemist's partner was the *soror mystica*, the sacred sister. The decision to pursue the 'alchemical gold' in each relationship is a shared choice.

Combined Horoscopes

There are two main types of combined charts: one is known as the composite chart and the other is known as the relationship chart or the Davison chart, named after the astrologer who developed the concept. Both of these methods use midpoints to generate the single horoscope. The composite chart uses the midpoints between the same two planets, points or angles while the Davison chart uses the midpoint between the two individuals' birth times and places. Both techniques became of interest to the global astrological community in the latter part of the 1970s. Another combined chart, called the coalescent, was introduced in 1992 by Lawrence Grinnell and David Dukelow, who focused on harmonics to merge the two horoscopes. However, this type of chart is not as widely used as the composite and Davison charts.

It is uncertain when the composite chart was first used in astrological practice. The method was researched early in the twentieth century in Europe and introduced to American astrologers by John Townley. But it was not until *Planets in Composite* was published in 1975 that the technique became widely known. In this book, the author Robert Hand enthusiastically endorsed the composite chart:

> I have found the technique of composite charts to be the most reliable and descriptive new astrological technique that I have ever encountered.[117]

German astrologers had referred to the method at least fifty years earlier than Hand, but it was with this publication that the technique of combining horoscopes became popular with astrologers. Michael Meyer described the composite chart in this way:

> A composite chart can be understood as a chart of the relationship, revealing its quality and focal areas more or less independently of the personal perspectives of the individuals involved. It is a map describing the various qualities, potentialities, temperament, etc. of the relationship itself.[118]

In 1977 British astrologer Ronald Davison released his book *Synastry* which introduced a new combined technique. The Davison relationship chart is also a midpoint chart determined by the midpoint between the couple's dates and times of birth. This creates the time of the chart while the geographical midpoint of their places of birth generates the longitude and latitude of the horoscope.

Unlike the composite chart the Davison relationship chart exists in time and space; therefore, other astrological techniques can be applied to this horoscope. The composite chart is a hybrid; therefore there are anomalies which occur beyond the traditional framework of an astrological horoscope. One method is not better than the other. It is a matter of personal choice. The decision swings towards the Davison chart when the astrologer wants a chart that has a birth time and place, as this chart can then be progressed or relocated and other techniques such as Astro*Carto*Graphy, fixed stars and solar arc directions can be applied. Those who accept the premise that a relationship is made, not born, may be more inclined towards the composite chart. Astrological techniques are designed to help us see through the horoscope's symbols and images into a deeper understanding, not as a literal or prescriptive truth. The astrologer uses whichever technique does this.

I use the composite chart, using midpoints for the house cusps. Being representative of the meeting points of each partner's astrological archetypes and images, the composite chart is not 'real' per se. This does not distract me, as relationship itself is a construct of two individuals. Let's examine each method before we look at delineating combined charts. While the detail behind the construction of the combined chart may not be of interest, it is important to understand how the charts are constructed in order to be confident when using them.

The Composite Chart

Planets in the composite chart are calculated by taking the nearest midpoint between the same planets in each individual's horoscope. In the circle of the zodiac, there are always two midpoints that exist between any two planets or points. Both these midpoints are opposite one another, but one will be closer to both planets than the other. When calculating the composite planet, the shorter arc between the two planets should always be used to determine the midpoint.

For instance, Angelina has her Sun at 13Ⅱ25; Brad has his Sun at 25♐51. The two Suns are opposed by sign and there are two zodiacal midpoints between these two placements: 19♍38 and 19♓38. Pisces is the closer midpoint between these two placements; therefore the Sun in their Composite chart will be at 19♓38. The table following the horoscope below shows the planetary placements in their natal horoscopes and how they combine to form the composite chart.

The composite chart is not a chart created using time or place; therefore there may be astronomical irregularities when generating this unique chart. For instance, retrogradation is not used; therefore, retrograde planets do not exist in a composite chart. On page 326 is the composite chart for Brad and Angelina generated by Solar Fire. At first glance there are some astronomical abnormalities such as the Vertex being conjunct the Ascendant and the Sun quincunx Venus. As suggested, the synergy of relationship creates unimagined possibilities.

	Angelina Natal	Brad Natal	Composite nearest midpoint	Notes
☉	13♊25	25♐51	19♓38	A's Sun is in the 11th while B's Sun is in the 1st but the composite has the Sun in the 6th conjunct the South Node; therefore the polarity of the 6–12th houses are important to take into account
☽	13♈05	22♑49	2♓57	
☿	22♊19R	16♑06	4♈13	
♀	28♋09	23♑28	25♎48	
♂	10♈42	10♑01	25♒22	
♃	17♈25	9♈50	13♈37	
♄	17♋23	19♒08	3♉15	The Sun and Moon are both in Pisces in a Balsamic phase
⚷	26♈46	10♓34	3♈40	
♅	28♎47R	10♏04R	4♎26	Mercury, Jupiter, Chiron and Uranus become angular
♆	10♐20R	16♏48	28♏34	
♇	6♎31R	14♏13R	25♏22	
☊	0♐53	11♋09	21♏01	
ASC	28♋53	11♐54	5♎24	Venus should be considered in the Aries/ Libra polarity as it is close to the Aries midpoint as well
MC	17♈52	26♏58	7♋25	
Vx	11♐05	27♋22	4♎14	The Vertex cannot be conjunct the Ascendant astronomically, but is consistent with their chart comparison

In some cases, Mercury and Venus can be in the opposite sector to the Sun, which is geocentrically impossible. In a natal chart Mercury is never more than 28° from the Sun; Venus is never more than 48°. However, a composite chart, especially when the Suns are in opposite sectors of the horoscope, can yield anomalies such as a Sun–Venus or Sun–Mercury opposition, even a Mercury–Venus opposition. In these cases both midpoints should be noted. This occurs with Venus in the above composite chart; therefore, the Venus polarity of Aries–Libra should be considered. Note that Angelina's Venus is 28♋09 opposite Brad's Venus at 23ß28, creating the midpoint at 25♎48 which squares both their Venuses. However, their Sun is 19⋇38 and since Venus is seen within an arc of 48° from the Sun, the placement should read 25♈48. Using the polarity of 25♈48–25♎48 reiterates their natal Venus opposition. Their different approach to values is again highlighted in their relationship.

Before proceeding it is important to reflect on this incongruity to sense how you respond to these inconsistencies. If one accepts the symbolic nature of the chart then this will be good enough; however, if you are dismayed at the astronomical abnormality then this may inhibit your ability to work with the symbols in the chart. I have noted that when these abnormalities occur they often highlight something else that is significant in the relationship. This is a dilemma that escapes the computer programmer and throws us back on our own imagination.

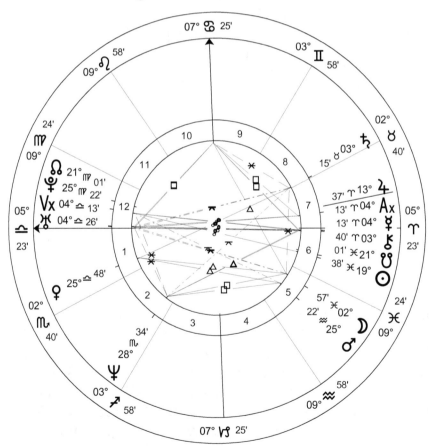

The Composite Chart: Angelina and Brad

For moderate latitudes the Vertex falls in the western hemisphere of the horoscope, generally between the 5th and 8th houses. But when combining the midpoints of two charts, the Vertex might fall in the eastern hemisphere of the horoscope, as in this example. Brad and Angelina each have their Vertex conjunct the other's Ascendant; therefore this Ascendant–Vertex conjunction flows through from their chart comparison into the composite chart. In actuality the Vertex, as derived from the Midheaven, should be in Aries, not Libra. Nonetheless, in terms of synastry this is noteworthy and highly significant, bringing the symbol to the forefront of their relationship. Interestingly, both these anomalies are in the Aries–Libra polarity of self and other.

Angles on the Relationship
Angles in the composite chart can be calculated in one of two ways:

1. Deriving the Ascendant and house cusps from the MC, or
2. Using the midpoint of the Midheavens, Ascendants and other house cusps.

The Derived Ascendant: All the house cusps, the Ascendant–Descendant and the Vertex–Anti-Vertex axis are derived from the composite Midheaven using the Table of Houses for the latitude where the relationship takes place. The MC will always be the same but the Ascendant will change if the relationship moves, according to the latitude of the new location. Using this method the Ascendant will be slightly altered when the relationship relocates to different places.

Midpoints: The midpoint of each house cusp and angle is calculated and used. This chart will not change even if the couple relocate or move overseas.

The composite charts used in this book are calculated using the Midpoint method. Over time I have come to prefer this technique. A dilemma with the Ascendant can occur in a small percentage of cases. What follows is an exception which should be noted when calculating the composite chart. This occurs in the charts of Diana and Charles, as noted in the following explanation. However, I would reiterate that this irregularity may in itself be significant, pointing to the conflicts in their relationship concerning their individual orientations to life.

When both Midheavens are in a close opposition to one other, then the near and far midpoints will also be close in opposition. For instance, the midpoint between 1♈ and 5♎ is 3♑ because the arc between ♎ and ♈ is shorter than the midpoint of 3♋, although this is very close as well. The angles between the MC and Ascendant may vary in each chart. For instance, a trine between the MC and Ascendant could exist in one chart, yet in the other horoscope there may be a sextile. When these two conditions occur, the Ascendant–Descendant axis in the composite chart may not always faithfully reflect the two charts from which they are derived. For instance, the MC of Diana's chart is 23♎03 and Charles's is 13♈18, with the near midpoint being 18♑10. Using this MC, the computer generates the composite horoscope Ascendant at 11♈54.

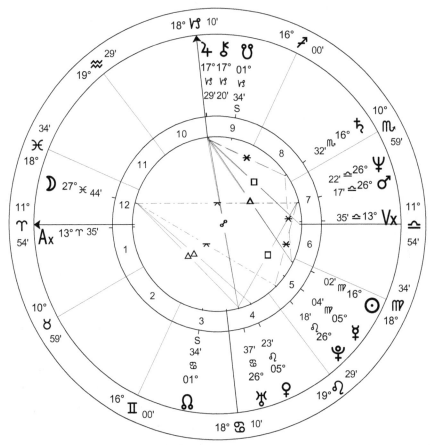

The Composite Chart: Charles and Diana

Diana's Ascendant is 18♐24 (a sextile to her MC) while Charles's is 5♌24 (a trine to his MC), yielding a composite Ascendant of 11♎54. However, the MC combination of 18♑11 and Ascendant of 11♎54 is impossible. The computer generates the composite chart using the near midpoint for the MC, but the far midpoint for the Ascendant.

Ironically, the Chiron–Jupiter conjunction on the MC is very apt for their royal relationship. This horoscope does not reflect each individual chart's orientation from the Ascendant. One solution is to use the opposite midpoint as the MC (18♋11), which would be compatible with the composite midpoint Ascendant of 11♎54. The other solution is to work with the horoscope as it is, being cognizant of the interplay of polarity in all the houses.

The Davison Relationship Chart
Ronald Davison's book *Synastry: Understanding Human Relations through Astrology* details the basics of synastry and introduces the technique of the relationship chart. Like others working with the composite chart he agreed that one horoscope could symbolize a relationship:

> The essential quality and the potentials of a relationship between any two people can be symbolized within the framework of a single horoscope.[119]

He explains that the relationship chart was born out of his working with progressions and it has proved a valid technique for him. I have also heard from astrologers worldwide who use this method effectively. The inherent averaging of the charts is still used, but the calculations are done for the midpoints of time and space. The relationship chart is formed by first finding the midpoint in time and space between the two charts; that is the halfway point on the globe by longitude and latitude and the midpoint between the GMT birth dates and times. Then a chart is calculated for this position and time. This horoscope exists in time and space, unlike the composite chart.

	Brad Pitt	Angelina Jolie	Davison Relationship Chart
Longitude of Birth	35N20	34N03	34N41
Latitude of Birth	96W56	118W14	107W35
Date and Time of Birth	18 December 1963, 12.31 p.m. GMT	4 June 1975, 4.09 p.m. BST	10 September 1969, 2.20 p.m. GMT

While the time and place of the chart is manipulated, I always suggest it may have some significance to the couple. The following table compares the relationship chart positions with the composite chart. Note the differences between the two planetary positions in each of the charts.

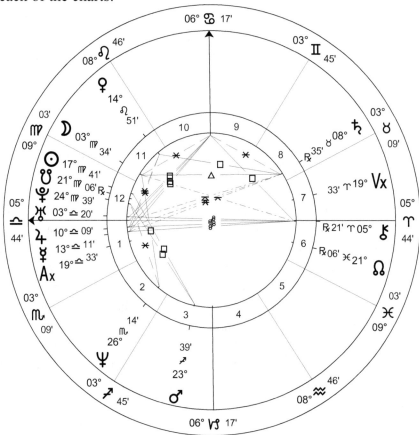

Davison Relationship Chart Angelina and Brad, 10 September 1969, 2.20 p.m. GMT, 34N41 107W35

	Angelina Natal	Brad Natal	Davison Relationship Chart	Composite Chart
☉	13♊25	25♐51	17♍41	19♓38
☽	13♈05	22♑49	3♍35	2♓57
☿	22♊19ᴿ	16♑06	13♎11	4♈13
♀	28♋09	23♑28	14♌51	25♎48
♂	10♈42	10♑01	23♐39	25♒22
♃	17♈25	9♈50	10♎09	13♈37
♄	17♋23	19♒08	8♉35ᴿ	3♉15
⚷	26♈46	10♓34	5♈22ᴿ	3♈40
♅	28♎47ᴿ	10♍04ᴿ	3♎20	4♎26
♆	10♐20ᴿ	16♏48	26♏15	28♏34
♇	6♎31ᴿ	14♍13ᴿ	24♍39	25♍22
☊	0♐53	11♋09	21♓06	21♍01
ASC	28♋53	11♐54	5♎44	5♎24
MC	17♈52	26♍58	6♋17	7♋25
Vx	11♐05	27♋22	19♈33	4♎14

What is interesting to note are the differences between the positions of the planets in the composite and the relationship charts.[120]

- Note that the composite Sun and Moon are opposite the Sun and Moon in the Davison chart. In my experience this is often the case *or* the Sun and Moon can be similar in both charts. Since the Sun and Moon travel through the zodiac at a fairly regular speed the composite and the relationship charts generally have their signs conjunct or opposed.[121] The Balsamic lunation phase is kept intact in both methods.

- There is no real relationship between Mercury, Venus or Mars as these planets travel irregularly through the zodiac.

- Brad and Angelina were born twelve years apart and their Jupiters are in Aries. Therefore in the composite chart Jupiter is also at the midpoint in Aries, but in the Davison chart it is in Libra as the chart is cast when Jupiter is only halfway through its cycle. There can be a difference between Jupiter's placement in the composite and the Davison charts. Similarly to Jupiter, the nodes are opposite each other in the two charts due to Brad and Angelina's age gap. The outer planets will remain relatively close together as they are slow moving, unless there is a much larger age gap.

While we are able to explain logically the difference in planetary positions between the two charts, nonetheless from an astrological point of view they are quite different. However, what each demonstrates is the necessity to be aware of polarities in the horoscope. In my experience, while the charts can be quite different there are often some similarities in the important aspects of the chart. For instance, the Ascendant is often close to or opposite the composite Ascendant. This is the case in the relationship chart for Pitt and Jolie. The Suns are generally near the same degree of a polarity although the Sun in one chart can be opposite the Sun in the other. The Moons are generally close in longitude or opposite one another. The three essential components of the Ascendant, Sun and Moon generally are aligned in both techniques.

Following is Charles's and Diana's Davison chart. Of interest is that even though the MC is different, Jupiter is culminating, which is similar to the composite chart. This time it is conjunct Uranus, unlike in the composite chart when it was conjunct Chiron.

The Davison chart brings the near midpoint of Libra to the Ascendant. The Sun is now in Pisces opposite the composite Sun in Virgo while the Moon in Libra makes an out of sign opposition to the composite Moon in Pisces. The Full Moon lunation phase is kept intact in both charts. Venus in the Davison chart is opposite the composite Venus. Both are in the 4th house; in the relationship chart Venus is conjunct Chiron. Since Charles and Diana are nearly thirteen years apart in age, their Jupiters are opposite each other, as in the previous example. This couple also have the Vertex axis aligning with their partner's Ascendant axis and the composite chart shows this clearly, being on the Descendant.

Even though the composite and the Davison charts are manipulated in some ways, they both symbolize one relationship.

Both are inspired by cosmic images, like any other horoscope. The composite chart is created out of each natal chart, which suggests that this chart is a synthesis of the couple, merging the components of each chart. It symbolizes the union as its own separate entity. Being incarnate in time and space, the Davison chart is more visible in and affected by the world at large. I think of the composite chart as private while the Davison relationship chart is more public. Robert Blaschke suggests:

> a composite chart symbolizes the life force energy of a couple as if it were a third personality, a separate relationship entity; whereas the Davison chart, because it exists in both time and space, symbolizes forces working on a couple from outside of their relationship, be they from the family, from children,

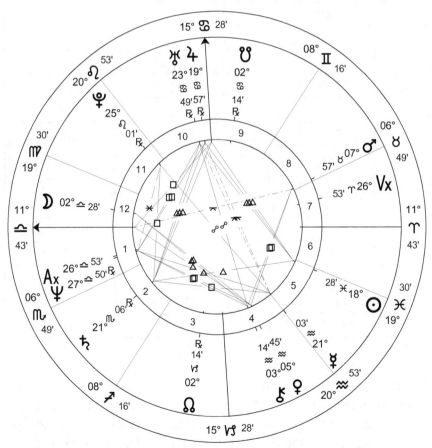

Davison Relationship Chart Charles and Diana 9 March 1955, 7:59 p.m. GMT, 52N10 0E11

from financial pressures, or from past life factors that are creating present karma.[122]

Perhaps until you find your own way, you may experiment with both. I generally recommend starting with the composite chart using midpoints to calculate the Ascendant and getting used to one method before you try another tactic. Many astrologers use both types of chart as it is apparent that each is imaginative and encourages separate metaphors and distinct intuitive descriptions.

	Diana Natal	Charles Natal	Davison Relationship Chart	Composite Chart
☉	9♋40	22♏25	18♓29	16♍03
☽	25♒02	0♉26	2♎29	27♓44
☿	3♋12℞	6♏57	21♒04	5♍05
♀	24♉24	16♎23	5♒46	5♌24
♂	1♍39	20♐57	7♉57	26♎18
♃	5♒06℞	29♐53	19♋58℞	17♑29
♄	27♑49℞	5♍16	21♏07℞	16♏32
⚷	6♓28℞	28♏13	3♒14	17♑21
♅	23♌20	29♊56℞	23♋49℞	26♋38
♆	8♏38℞	14♎08	27♎50℞	26♎13
♇	6♍03	16♌34	25♌01℞	26♌18
☊	28♌11	4♉58	2♑15	1♋34
ASC	18♐24	5♌24	11♎43	11♈54
MC	23♎033	13♈18	15♋28	18♑10
Vx	4♋17	22♐53	26♈53	13♎35

From Natal to Composite: Flow-through

Flow-through suggests that themes recognized in the natal charts or chart comparisons are imported into the composite chart. We have already noted some of these themes but I will review these as they highlight an important relational statement. When analysing the composite chart I find it of great value to visualize the process of synastry as continuous, looking for themes of importance throughout all the steps of the analysis.

Planet/ Angle	Natal	Chart Comparison	Composite Chart	Notes
☉	Brad's Sun is 25♐51; his South Node is 11♑09; the eclipse after birth was 14 January 1964 at 23♑43 ♂ his Venus. Angelina's Sun is 13♊25 and the South Node is 0♊53		The 6th house Sun is conjunct the South Node, both were born in an eclipse season with the Sun near the South Node	Both eclipses being at the South Node bring images from the past into the present. This also alerts us to their sensitivity as a couple to eclipse cycles
☽	Brad has the Moon and Mars in Capricorn while Angelina has the Moon and Mars conjunct in Aries	A's Moon in Aries squares B's Mars in Capricorn	The Moon and Mars are in an out-of-sign conjunction. Mars rules the Descendant, the Moon, the MC	Interchanges of Moon and Mars represent the themes of individual needs, ambition, desire and the expression of anger
☿	B has Mercury in Capricorn trine Uranus and sextile Chiron. A has the same aspects to Mercury	Their Mercurys are quincunx by sign, a separation of 6°	Mercury is on the Descendant conjunct Chiron opposite Uranus rising	Unusual, yet unique, innovative, therapeutic ways to communicate could develop through relating

♂	A has Mars opposite Pluto; B has Mars trine Pluto	A's Mars is quincunx Pluto while B's Mars is square Pluto	Mars is exactly quincunx Pluto to the minute	Each bring their forcefulness and power to their relationship
♃	Both have Jupiter in Aries due to being born twelve years apart	Jupiter is conjunct Jupiter	Jupiter is in ♈ in the 7th house	Compatible social and philosophical beliefs are essential to their partnership
♅	A and B both have Uranus square the Ascendant	A's Uranus is square B's Moon; B's Uranus is quincunx A's Moon	Uranus conjunct the Ascendant and quincunx the Moon in the 5th	Independence and uniqueness need to be nurtured or these partners might go their separate ways
Vx	B has the Vertex at 27♋22 in the 8th house while Angelina has the Vertex at 11♐05 in the 5th	B's Vertex is conjunct A's Ascendant; A's Vertex is conjunct B's Ascendant	The Vertex axis is aligned with the Ascendant axis	A powerful sense of destiny, mystery and intrigue is experienced by each partner

As you begin to analyse the horoscopes you may find continuity of other themes. For instance, both have the Part of Fortune in the 11th house; therefore, this is repeated in the composite chart. The Part of Fortune is linked to the lunation cycle; therefore it draws attention to Brad being born under the New Moon phase while Angelina was born under the Last Quarter phase. Together, the composite chart creates a Balsamic phase with both luminaries in Pisces.

The amount of information generated often feels overwhelming. We can be led in all directions; therefore it is important to trace and amplify one theme at a time. This theme might be determined by the agenda of the couple whose charts you are comparing or a specific relationship question about a motif that is prominent from the beginning, as in the following case.

Freud and Jung: Mars in the 11th

Let's return to the collegial rivalry of Freud and Jung. When we look at their composite chart, the Mars theme that we have identified as the theme of rivalry and competition in this relationship is again highlighted in the 11th house of friendship. The composite Mars is also dignified in Scorpio and rules the IC, the base of the chart. Neptune is conjunct the IC and quincunx Mars.

Freud Natal	Jung Natal	Composite Chart
Mars in 11th in Libra	Mars in 11th in Sagittarius	Mars in 11th in Scorpio
Mars is waxing quincunx Pluto	Mars is waning quincunx Pluto	Mars is opposite Pluto

Composite Mars is in its home sign of Scorpio opposite the sign's modern ruler, Pluto. It is interesting that the rising degree in this chart is 22♐10 and Jung's Mars is 21♐22. The degree culminating is 12♎22 and Freud's Mars is 3♎22. Each one's Mars is conjunct an angle of the composite chart, bringing their individual Mars out into the open in this relationship. The Martian archetype of competition and rivalry continues through the charts in what I have referred to as a 'flow-through'.

Each has Uranus and the Sun in the same sign; in the composite chart Uranus and the Sun are in a wide conjunction. The Sun is on the Descendant of both charts and this repeats in the composite chart conjunct Mercury along with Uranus in the 7th house. Maintaining their individuality, but also the need for mutual admiration and recognition of their creative ideas is important. The Sun on the Descendant reminds us that it is not the individual who shines, but the working relationship or the amalgam of both men's creative fire and ideas. By remaining singular and competitive in their psychoanalytic circle the potential of their composite chart could not be developed.

The outstanding interaspect of their Sun–Moon conjunction (Freud's Sun is 16♉19 conjunct Jung's Moon at 15♉35) rearranges itself in an interesting way. Freud's Moon in Gemini and Jung's

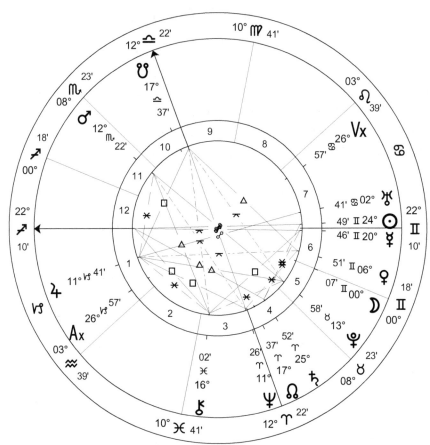

The Composite Chart: Freud and Jung

Moon in Taurus become the composite Moon at 0♊07. Jung's Leo and Freud's Taurus Sun generate the composite Sun, also in Gemini at 24♊49 on the Descendant. All the inner planets except Mars are in Gemini, another image suggesting that their rivalry may stem from incomplete sibling issues that are replayed in the 11th house arena.

When considering what the planets, signs, houses and aspects of a composite chart may represent, it is necessary to always keep in mind that the chart does not represent an individual but an amalgam of individuals. It is important to be aware of the specifics of this relationship, as the astrological images will have a different nuance according to whether you are looking at a mother–child, business or marriage relationship. Before you begin to use this technique you must be consistent in your choice of chart, as each technique is different. As in all astrological methodology, it is important to feel comfortable with the technique being used. We will explore the angles, planets, houses, signs and aspects in a composite chart. However, this can also be modified for use with the Davison chart.

Angles on Relationship
The Midheaven of the composite chart is similar to the natal chart in that it represents the aspirations and goals of the couple in the world and the potential achievements and status of the relationship. The MC symbolizes images of the contributions and purpose in the world for the relationship. While the MC represents the fruits of the world tree, the IC symbolizes the deep roots that secure the worldly experiences. The IC is the foundation stone, the deep-rooted security systems and familial support mechanisms that are available to the relationship. Gathered at the IC are the most intimate and personal symbols for the couple's security and home life.

The Ascendant is an image that the couple use to interact with their environment. It is the energy that is most easily seen by others and a symbol of the personality of the relationship. The Descendant is the energetic representation of the couple as they relate to the world together. This characterizes where, as a couple, they meet and greet others: not as individuals but as a unit, a union and a duet. The Ascendant–Descendant axis informs us of the level of mobility and ease with which the couple faces life challenges. It suggests the quality of resources available to meet these challenges as well as the most efficient and comfortable method of facing life together.

The Vertex–Anti-Vertex axis is the third axis and in a way it stretches us into a three-dimensional view of relationship because it focuses on the unknown qualities that we experience through the relationship, transforming who we are. When the Vertex is involved it seems these relationships have a lifelong effect and often change the course of our lives. Planets on this axis in the composite chart develop over the course of the relationship and transform the nature and direction of the relationship. The house polarity that the axis occupies will be significant for the couple to explore in terms of an environment that may reveal unknown aspects of their relationship. Of all three angles, the Vertex–Anti-Vertex is the most likely to be ignited unexpectedly or mysteriously.

Planetary Fusion: Combining the Planetary Archetypes
The planets in a composite chart hold the same archetypal resonances, but these are now sounded through a relationship, not a single individual. Therefore it is important to try to conceive of how the planetary energy might express itself when two individuals blend together, compromise and commit to the well-being of their partnership.

Composite Sun
There is only one Sun in our solar system and it is the central focus. We could use this image to suggest that in any system there is only room for one Sun; yet in every relationship there are two, as each person brings their own Sun into the partnership. This might generate too much heat in the relationship unless a way is found to moderate and focus the intensity. This is the nature of the composite Sun, which blends the two temperaments and shifts the centre of gravity away from an individual to centre attention on the relationship. As an image of father or authority, the composite Sun also suggests how the relationship is cultivated and promoted. When the couple begin to forge their commitment to the relationship the focus shifts from I to We, and from individuality towards mutuality. At the heart of every relationship is the central point which keeps the relationship alive and radiant. This is the composite Sun.

As an image, the composite Sun is the heart of the relationship, the planetary organ that provides the power and vitality to the relationship. It symbolizes how the relationship remains vital and how the couple can be more animated and lively. The Sun is also a symbol of identity and represents what is unique and especially characteristic of the relationship. It symbolizes initiatives and goals for the relationship, and as the heart centre of the composite chart the Sun reveals the essence and purpose of the relationship. The encompassing question might be 'For what purpose has this relationship been created?' On a more pragmatic level it suggests factors that are important to identify as well as core issues in the relationship. The house position of the Sun will shine light on which areas are of interest and importance to the couple, and aspects to the Sun highlight challenges to the vitality and resilience of the relationship while identifying other energies that need to be acknowledged in the relationship.

Like all composite planets, there is often an irony in the quality of the composite Sun which is important to reiterate. The composite Sun is often at odds with one or both partners' Sun signs. For instance, a Sun in Sagittarius involved with a Sun in Aquarius may have their composite Sun in Capricorn. As individuals, their mutual recognition of freedom and wider vistas may need to find a more conservative focus in their relationship. When a couple locates their composite Sun the relationship shines; therefore, the house of the composite Sun will suggest where the couple might metaphorically find more sunshine.

Composite Moon

As the indication of attachment and the barometer of emotional security, the Moon is especially important in composite charts where dependence and mutual concern are highlighted, such as mother–child relationships, couples with children and/or long-term committed partners living together, even flatmates. In your relationship, the composite Moon's house position suggests where you both might build the foundations for your emotional well-being and where you share in the shelter of each other. Your composite Moon signifies the emotional comfort levels and what is needed to help secure your relationship. It is where you find the feelings of belonging and even the atmosphere and ambience needed in your home and private spaces to nurture and grow your relationship together. Since the Moon also represents the literal home it indicates whether there might be many moves or if a permanent address would be more comfortable. Could you live interstate or overseas?

The Moon is instinctual; in your natal chart it suggests the habits and familial themes that you both bring into the relationship, but in the composite chart it suggests the innate patterns and rituals that are natural to your relationship. Do you fit together easily, ride the ups and downs of life in tandem or does the relationship falter in times of stress and difficulty? Is the relationship familiar and safe? These are reflective questions addressed by your composite Moon. However, it is also important to recognize the layers of emotional patterning and family behaviour that we bring into relationship. You are already sensitive to certain manners, reactive to ways of being and attached to particular things. You already have your patterns and preferences for relaxing, eating and sleeping. What happens when they are overlooked, especially by the person you love? These clashes are found in the comparison of your natal charts; the composite chart reveals emotional needs, security and well-being together and what feels habitual and natural for the partnership.

The Moon reflects the many aspects of living in rhythm together. In a particular house it describes which areas of life need cultivation in order that you both feel safe and secure together. By aspect it suggests other forces that challenge and strengthen the security of the relationship. Ultimately, the Moon is about emotional security and safety, and its position in the composite chart addresses these levels of your relationship.

Composite Mercury

Mercury moves faster than any other planet in our solar system; therefore, the ancients likened it to their fleet-footed god Mercury. Similarly, the alchemists named the element known for its quickness of movement after him. Mercury is never static, always in motion and it is a priority when comparing horoscopes: without adequate communication and interchange, a relationship can falter and ultimately fail. Composite Mercury describes the intellectual aspect of your partnership; it is the meeting of minds and your ability to both brainstorm together and discuss important issues. For the alchemy to have an effect in your relationship, both communicating and listening are important. Each of you will bring your own ways of thinking into the conversation; therefore, whether you exchange a few words or many, what is important is that you each remain connected to the dialogue. We have forged the way we learn and listen earlier in life but if we respond habitually to a tone in the voice, body language or facial expressions from these entrenched patterns we might miss a great discussion.

Composite Mercury shows your tête-à-tête as a couple, the natural lines of communication and conversing as a duet. Planets in aspect to Mercury influence the nature of communication and the feelings of being heard and understood. Its house position tells us about the areas of life where communication for your relationship is natural and most effective, where you learn and converse together and what skills you might develop to improve your communication. Basically, Mercury is your language as a couple, how you speak and commune together, the ideas that you share as one, your joint understanding or the disagreements that you need to focus on. When addressing Mercury in the composite chart, the astrologer is concerned with how the ideas, communication, language and plans of the relationship can be effectively shared and understood. Being dualistic by nature and willing to see both sides, Mercury relates skilfully and is honoured in relationship through interaction, movement, humour and the expression of ideas.

Composite Venus

Venus speaks of the facility of relationship, the ease of affection and the power of love. A core trait of Venus in the composite chart is the couple's personal value system, what they appreciate, like, admire and what they judge to be important. It also indicates how much worth they place upon certain objects and social graces. As the ruler of Taurus, Venus is interested in material values, but as the ruler of Libra she pays attention to spiritual ones; therefore, Venus helps to identify where the relationship could become more cherished or treasured. For instance, Venus in Leo may like the theatre; Venus in Libra might prefer a quiet dinner for two; perhaps composite Venus in Pisces enjoys dancing together.

Venus values the power of love and in the composite chart it addresses the area of the relationship where love and things of value can be discovered. Aspects to Venus point out the challenges and concerns but also the supportive energies that can be consciously used to help nurture the love in the relationship. By nature, Venus suggests the physical and material pleasures that are natural to the relationship, being an indicator of the sexual and financial ease and experience of the couple. Composite Venus is the pleasure principle of the relationship, how the couple find their sensual compatibility in sharing the worlds of music, food, affection, visual or fragrant delights; for instance, this might refer to the tastes of the relationship, not only culinary, but decoratively, artistically and socially. Therefore, composite Venus illustrates how the couple might prefer to socialize, how they can agree on decorating their home, what music to listen to and how to source the best food and wine. At its core, Venus turns her face towards love and in the composite chart she suggests how this may be expressed by the couple. Venus makes every effort to find beauty and harmony in her environment and the composite chart shows where this can be best experienced in the relationship.

As the barometer of values, Venus also represents money and the composite Venus is a guide to negotiating this tricky territory. For business associates and partners it is an important image to acknowledge as it will indicate how effortless or difficult money issues might be. For intimate partners it represents the potential of resources and assets. Its house position is where the prosperity of the relationship may be revealed.

Composite Mars
In the composite chart Mars suggests where the couple needs to focus their energy, apply their will and assert their desires. Composite Mars symbolizes the objectives, goals and ambitions of the relationship; therefore, it is wise to consider what this archetype invites you to aim for as a team. Mars by house points to areas in life where your relationship could take action, strive to achieve, where you need to invest your energies and act on instinct. It locates an area where you can combine your forces to become a competitive and dynamic duo. However, it might also reveal areas of conflict or where together you face disagreements and disputes from others in your environment. Astrologically, Mars symbolizes anger and libido, emotional and sexual expression, and coaches

you to reflect on ways your relationship might express these desires more functionally.

By aspect, Mars indicates other forces that need acknowledgement when expressing the desires and goals of the relationship. Therefore Mars is important to consider when reflecting on your relationship goals, drives and ambitions as well as expressing frustration, anger and negative feelings in your partnership. Mars also suggests how much life force is available to light the fires of your partnership and how much fuel is available to drive it forward. On the other hand, Mars suggests the need to conserve and monitor your energetic output. Mars is the expression of vitality and life force and suggests how, as a team, you harness these energies to your best advantage.

Composite Jupiter

Expansion and inflation are astrological attributes that are associated with Jupiter; on the one hand, this might be largesse, yet on the other it could be extravagance. By its placement in the composite chart Jupiter illustrates the couple's outlook and attitude towards freedom and expansion, generosity and faith as well as their mutual perspective on morality and human values. In relationship it constellates issues to do with religious ideals, philosophical beliefs and cultural mores. Composite Jupiter is an amalgam of the couple's way of life; how their different social backgrounds, spiritual beliefs and optimism combine together as a comfortable philosophy. It highlights an image of where the couple can educate themselves to move beyond their family of origin's beliefs to create their own. As an archetype it speaks to cross-cultural experiences and in the composite chart it will show where the couple will stretch themselves beyond their comfort zone. Jupiter governs growth and indicates where this is emphasized; therefore, its house position is a key to understanding where this happens.

Travel, generally overseas, or journeys afar is Jupiter's domain. The travel may not always be physical, perhaps emotional or intellectual. In the composite chart Jupiter gives a clue as to where new adventures may take place. Concerned with education, Jupiter also leads the couple into new avenues of exploration and learning, expanding their convictions and opinions on life matters. Wherever we find Jupiter, we find faith, and this is its great gift in the composite chart. Its house position is where the couple might begin to find greater meaning in their relationship and the world at large. Jupiter is often equated with good fortune, the great benefic of traditional astrologers, and in the composite chart it shows where the couple find these blessings.

Composite Saturn

In a composite chart Saturn indicates the structure and backbone of the relationship, the need for agreed-upon rules, regulations and boundaries. Saturnine boundaries can be consciously constructed to contain the relationship; at other times they might feel restrictive and rigid, so it is prudent to be aware of Saturn's significance in relationship. Saturn helps to illustrate the constraints and limits placed on relationship through social and cultural conditions. Its presence suggests where boundaries are important, which areas of shared life feel restrictive or controlled as well as where insecurities and pressures may originate. Couples born within a short period of each other may have the same Saturn sign, belonging to the same sub-system of their generation, sharing similar experiences of trends and fads, but also the same internal moral compass regarding laws, rules and what is socially acceptable.

Saturn, symbolic of the chart's backbone where structure and organization need to support the relationship, indicates which traditions and rules need to be respected. It also points to where responsibility, maturity and authority may become problematic when everyday tasks are not equally shared. However, it also illuminates the areas where solidity, stability and longevity can be forged by the couple. By nature, Saturn represents the outermost limits of what is still within our control and jurisdiction. While it is often experienced as limitations, it is the maturing force within the relationship that helps to secure and structure the relationship in the 'real world', bringing lasting success and achievement. Saturn symbolizes the area of your life together where hard work, determination, resolution and responsibility pay off.

Chiron and the Outer Planets

Forces beyond our control are symbolized by Chiron and the outer planets. When looking at the composite chart these planets represent larger patterns that may come into being because of the alchemy and nature of the individuals. What happens when two souls with a familial and cultural past, two characters with patterns and life experiences, two personalities with will and desire, merge in the alembic of relationship? Often something beyond their known experience is shaped and this is personified by the outer planets.

Composite Chiron

Chiron in the composite chart represents where the relationship may feel awkward, marginal or vulnerable. The aspects to Chiron help to address the energies in the relationship that feel wounded or unable to be voiced or expressed. This might represent the place where there are patterns or aspects of the relationship that feel unable to be healed, irreconcilable differences or conditions beyond their control. And while this may be the feeling, the truth is that this is also the place where the relationship finds its humility and spirituality. Paradoxically, what feels wounded also has an energetic pulse that allows the couple to accept the difficulties: not to seek to fix or replace this aspect of their relationship, but to acknowledge and work with it as it is. Composite Chiron is a key to understanding where your relationship is beyond the bounds of the system or where as a couple you feel marginal, possibly excluded. It is the interplay between belonging and not belonging.

Chiron differentiates feelings of dislocation. Perhaps the couple feel excluded from their families of origin, neighbourhood or even society, but through mutual acceptance of one another they find a place to belong. Chiron becomes the healing balm that allows the couple to feel at home, belonging to each other through their commitment. When the energy of Chiron is adopted by the couple, they find themselves forging alliances with many different and varied individuals, other couples and groups. Composite Chiron points to the wound that is apparent in the relationship, but also reveals the path for healing. It locates where the relationship can find its own space, exclusive of the world and its demands. Therefore it often represents the spiritual hub that unites the couple, a private place of intimacy or a meditative or remedial retreat that brings a sense of restoration and healing. In a way, composite Chiron is the mentor and therapist embedded within the relationship.

Composite Uranus

Depending on the nature of the relationship, Uranus may be in the same zodiacal sign as that of the two individuals; for instance, schoolmates, siblings, first boyfriends or girlfriends probably share the same sign. But wherever it is, it is energy not easily integrated into relationship, as Uranus's urge is to be separate. The more restricted it feels, the more it rebels against what has become habitual. Therefore, composite Uranus suggests where the couple can find the space and freedom to be themselves, unfettered by the pressure to conform. Put simply, the composite Uranus shows where the unusual, the extraordinary as well as the rebellious inclinations of the couple might be found. This area suggests where there needs to be fewer rules and more spontaneity. Imagine the twelve houses of the horoscope as the rooms of your house. The house that Uranus is in is the room that needs more light, more openness, more technology and innovation, as well as more space. It is the place where each partner in the relationship does their own thing without it being detrimental to the overall partnership.

Uranus is a key to what is unexpected and unpredictable. It addresses what is distinctive about this relationship and what the merger has created that is unique. However, it may also be the area where the couple feels most polarized, torn apart or split. Therefore, it is important to be aware that composite Uranus speaks about where the couple needs to feel separate. By aspect and house position it describes where freedom and individuality are paramount. The paradox of separateness and belonging is found wherever Uranus is placed. Here is where individuality and freedom support and energize the relationship. Composite Uranus invites the couple to be more adventurous, alert to all the opportunities, and to participate with what it brings into the relationship.

Composite Neptune

Neptune spends fourteen years in a sign and therefore many of the same generation share the same sign placement. The planet Pluto does not travel uniformly through the signs, but since 1940 it has averaged a similar speed to Neptune's and the two planets have been travelling about two signs apart. Therefore Neptune and Pluto will probably be in compatible elements. You may have a sextile between the two in both your natal and composite charts. In a way, both planets are associated with the world beyond our everyday awareness.

What dreams and expectations have been created through the merging of this relationship? Something greater can be born through the fusion of those in this relationship and Neptune points to where this might be. That something is not easily known but the couple could have an inkling. Composite Neptune conjures up unspoken dreams, the potentialities and fantasies of the couple. But it also points to where illusion and deception may occur. By aspect it suggests energies that might be susceptible to being lost, chaotic or misplaced, as this is where boundaries between the real and the imagined become blurred and veiled. It brings the issue of surrender and acceptance to the relationship and also addresses larger patterns of addiction and loss of direction that could be unleashed in the relationship from the familial past.

While Neptune addresses the areas that may be idealized, it also suggests areas of creativity and spirituality for the couple. Its house position is where the imagination is located, helping to address the larger dimension of where the couple can be more soulful and visionary. Composite Neptune is where both ideals and disappointments gather; therefore, it is good to address the ideals, dreams and fantasies that are part of the relationship, as well as to name any disappointments without blame and judgement. In honouring Neptune the couple becomes more aware of any delusions that might erode the foundation of their relationship, as well as the dangers of misreading responses or overprotecting insecurities. Neptune in the composite chart is where there is sensitivity, sometimes helplessness, but this vulnerability is shared so it is not weak but, ironically, robust and potentially healing. The planetary position may also point to where misunderstandings and taking things for granted can occur. In this place it is always wise to have reality checks about what has been said and what has been agreed upon.

Composite Pluto
Pluto, the underworld god, is focused on what lies beneath the surface of relationship. In the composite chart it addresses the issues that may be buried, patterns that are hidden or pressures from the past that haunt the present. Composite Pluto suggests where the

relationship may be drawn into difficulty; yet, on the other hand, it also represents the transforming and life-altering experiences that are available. There is a soulful side to the archetype of Pluto as it anchors relationship in a deeper and more authentic place.

Pluto illustrates how the power of relationship might be best expressed. Planets in aspect to Pluto can be either empowered or disempowered, depending on how the relationship is able to handle the high voltage of the energy. While the house position of composite Pluto might address areas of relationship where loss and emotional confrontations may be experienced, it also locates the area where the relationship can be rebuilt and reborn through trust and intimacy. Composite Pluto transforms, like an alchemical opus. Alchemical texts depict the process of submerging two individuals in the cauldron of their relationship. When immersed in the alembic together, alterations and revelations occur. In the context of relationship, each of you will begin to become more vulnerable to one another in this area of your life. As well, greater patterns from both your families of origin may begin to heal past hurts, encourage authenticity and honesty and bring you both closer on a soul level.

Signs of Relationship
The role of the signs as being descriptive of the qualities of planetary archetypes is not as pronounced in a composite chart as it is in a natal chart. Agreement among astrologers does not exist about the validity of the signs in the composite chart. Some feel the signs are not valid since they are abstractions due to the manipulation involved in creating the composite chart. These astrologers prefer not to use the signs because they do not represent the true zodiacal positions.

However, elements and sign qualities are descriptive and useful in ascertaining an emphasis or a lack of an element or an overabundance of a particular modality. Signs are also useful to focus on when discussing core placements, such as the rising sign, the Sun and the Moon signs. They may not be as effective as they are in the natal chart at describing a particular planet, yet at times they are still of value. If you are using signs to describe the planets or angles in the composite chart then I would encourage you to use the polarity of the signs because of the way the sign has been created in the composite chart. As we saw in the comparison between the relationship and composite charts, the Ascendant, Sun and Moon could be opposite one another in each chart. Polarity is important as this is the inherent nature of relationship: *twoness*. Therefore if you work with signs, keep in mind the polarity of signs, not just the sign itself. For instance, any planets in Aries should be examined through the spectrum of their Aries–Libra polarity.

Sign	Polarity	Sign	Nature of Polarity
♈	♈ ♎	♎	Self and other; me and you; personality and relationship
♉	♉ ♏	♏	Mine and yours; mine and ours; sharing material and emotional attachments
♊	♊ ♐	♐	Ideas and meaning; making sense of the world we share
♋	♋ ♑	♑	Private and public; our inner and outer worlds and how our domestic and work lives interact
♌	♌ ♒	♒	Creativity and community: participating in social life as a couple, the community and friends we share
♍	♍ ♓	♓	Order and chaos: the focus on physical and mental well-being and sharing our everyday lives together

Inhabiting the Relationship: Composite Houses

The descriptions of the houses in a composite chart are similar to those in a natal chart except that they reveal environmental influences for two or more individuals. The personal focus is yielded for the enhancement of the relationship. For instance, the 6th house generally refers to work, health and the daily regime. In a composite chart, it would describe the daily regimen of the couple, not the health of an individual, but perhaps the health of the relationship – how could it be improved or understood? This does not describe a partner's work, but the daily tasks, duties and effort needed for the relationship to function well. Therefore, when considering the houses of a composite chart it is important to keep the context of the relationship in mind. I feel the sign on the cusp of the house does not play such an important role as it does in a natal chart; however, the impact of planets in the houses must be delineated in terms of the relationship.

As with the signs, it is important to remember polarity when examining the houses; for instance, in examining 6th house planets in the composite chart, the 12th house also needs to be considered.

The First House themes of persona and vitality are applied to the relationship; therefore, this house could suggest:

- The first impression that the couple projects
- The type of impact that the relationship makes on others
- The personality of the relationship and how others might see the couple
- How the two individuals function as one unit
- The vitality and outreach of the relationship

The Second House themes of resources and values are applied to the relationship; therefore, this house could suggest:

- The finances and possessions of the relationship
- Attitudes, habits and expectations that the couple has towards their resources and assets
- The combined values of the relationship and the role these play in the security of the relationship
- Material security and the issues around money, finances, spending and saving
- The ease or difficulty in sharing resources

The Third House themes of communications and mobility in a composite chart could suggest:

- Communication patterns in the relationship. How the couple is able to discuss both the trivialities and the concerns of their relationship and daily experiences
- Habitual communicative patterns; what is taken for granted or left unsaid
- Relatives, neighbours and others present in the day-to-day environment

- The ease of mobility, change and adaptability in the relationship
- The meeting of minds, sharing ideas, attitudes towards education

The Fourth House themes of home and emotional security are applied to the relationship; therefore, this house could suggest:

- Innermost emotional life of the couple; depth of relationship, emotional security
- Imprints of the family of origin; roots and background of the couple
- Real estate holdings or the home environment
- The home, belonging, where relationship feels at home
- Domicile and the nature of home and family
- The importance of family and familial connections to the relationship

The Fifth House themes of self-expression, creativity and children in a composite chart could suggest:

- The freedom to take risks in their relationship or as a couple, the greatest risk to be themselves in the relationship
- The children or mutual creativity of the relationship
- Self-expression and the enjoyment of playing and expressing themselves in each other's company
- Playfulness, sexual pleasure and enjoyment, and fun in the relationship
- The attitudes towards both the inner and outer child and creativity

The Sixth House themes of work, health and daily routines are applied to the relationship; therefore, this house could suggest:

- How the partnership is able to work together. How the relationship is of service and how each individual within the relationship is able to serve the other
- The duties and responsibilities of the relationship; the daily routine

- The give and take aspect of the relationship
- The day-to-day habits and rituals of the relationship
- How the couple is able to debrief and share the personal experiences of their day

The Seventh House theme of others is applied to the relationship; therefore, this house could suggest:

- We/us
- One-to-one encounters with others, especially other couples
- How the partners feel as a team; the quality of interaction within the relationship
- The couple's adversaries and rivals
- Agreements, documents and contracts signed as a couple

The Eighth House themes of intimacy and privacy in a composite chart could suggest:

- The forces that create the transformational aspects of the relationship
- Which inheritances and resources impact the joint property and resources
- The psychological impact that the relationship exerts on others
- Emotional sharing and the potential for intimacy
- Attachment and bonding; the level of trust inherent in the relationship
- The sexual life as a mirror of intimacy and closeness

The Ninth House themes of philosophical beliefs and values are applied to the relationship; therefore, this house could suggest:

- The shared philosophy and the intellectual pursuits of the relationship
- The world view of the couple
- The idealism and search for greater meaning in the partnership
- Travel abroad and the contact with foreign places, cultures and ideas

- Cross-cultural experiences shared in the relationship
- The potential for sharing spiritual practices and meaning

The Tenth House themes of status, vocation and worldly pursuits in a composite chart could suggest:

- The intention of the relationship
- The purpose and prestige of the relationship
- How the relationship supports the individual to achieve their goals in the world
- How the unit functions in the world
- How the world perceives and acknowledges the relationship

The Eleventh House themes of group participation, friends, hopes and wishes are applied to the relationship; therefore, this house could suggest:

- Friendships made by the couple, social situations and the ability to feel part of a wider community
- Shared hopes and wishes
- The ability and facility to receive love
- The relationship's role in the larger community, communal projects and the impact on the society which embraces them

The Twelfth House theme of what is hidden or repressed is applied to the relationship; therefore, this house could suggest:

- What might be repressed and invisible to the partnership
- Dealing with the hidden behaviour patterns that each partner is facing due to the impact of the other and their heritage
- The impact of each partner's family history on the relationship
- The potential of telepathic communication between partners or sensitivity to each other's emotional states

Composite Dialogues: The Aspects
As with the natal horoscope, potent aspects are important for understanding the alchemy of any relationship. However, in my experience composite aspects, especially difficult ones, are not

easily recognized or even apparent in the early life of a relationship. When the couple becomes settled in a committed relationship, then the aspects are more lived and, therefore, more obvious. My experience has been that difficult aspect patterns such as T-squares and Grand Crosses are often overlooked by individuals at the onset of a relationship. Perhaps this could be an instinctive defence mechanism until the relationship has developed resources to deal with the difficulties or developed greater trust in the viability of the partnership.

Aspect theory is similar to that of natal charts except that you will be delineating the aspects for a relationship, remembering that the aspect is not operating between two individuals but rather is an aspect of the relationship itself.

The *conjunction* is highly subjective and may be a blind spot in the relationship, especially when incompatible planetary energies are combined.

The *opposition* could polarize the relationship and become an area of splitting. This could suggest that the couple may hold different values and attitudes about theses energies than others. The opposition points to the need for compromise and agreement in the relationship, otherwise there is a tendency to separation and polarization.

The *square* is dynamic and points to an energetic pattern within the relationship that could cause tension and discord. This is where the couple may feel pulled apart, so strategies to help resolve conflict and tension around these issues would be helpful.

The *quincunx* pulls the relationship in different directions; however, there can be more consciousness and ability to reflect rather than to act out. Be aware of the difficult combinations in the quincunx and remain alert for any covert patterns due to this combination.

As in a natal chart, look to the *trines* and *sextiles* to support the relationship and determine where energies are likely to flow and become opportunistic. These aspects also offer strategic and helpful outcomes when the relationship is exploring ways to change habits and patterns.

I look for the flow-through from the natal charts or aspect grid to determine if a theme is imported into the composite chart or if it is a unique expression of the relationship itself. Notice how the standout aspects in the natal chart comparison may have been reconfigured because of the combination of the two charts. While studying the composite chart, keep all the synastry images in mind. I am alert for angular planets, strong aspect patterns, difficult combinations between inner and outer planets as well as any rearrangements of planetary energies created by the composite chart.

For instance, Angelina (A) has the stellium of Mars, the Moon and Jupiter in Aries in the 9th house, with Jupiter exactly on the MC. Brad (B) shares the Jupiter in Aries, but in his 4th house almost 13° from his IC, and Jupiter squares his Mars in Capricorn. B's Mars squares A's stellium while A's Jupiter squares B's Moon, which is also in Capricorn. In A's natal chart the Moon, Mars and Jupiter stand out. In chart comparison B's Moon, Mars and Jupiter are also brought into the picture. In the composite chart these planets are rearranged: Jupiter is angular in the 7th house while Mars and the Moon are in an out-of-sign conjunction in the 5th house. Jupiter is semi-square the midpoint of this conjunction. The entanglement of these three energies is rearranged, but still evident. Therefore the Moon, Mars and Jupiter themes will be significant in this relationship; this highlights that the paradoxical needs of emotional security, stability, safety and individuality, and of freedom and independence, will be set in opposition in this relationship.

Delineating the Composite Chart

Commencing the analysis of any chart is often overwhelming, and the composite chart even more so due to its nature and composition. However, in the composite chart you have already analysed two natal charts and compared these two charts, so you are already aware of many of the patterns and themes of the relationship. The composite chart can be seen as a continuation of this process and as such you are looking for repeated patterns that flow through from the previous chart analysis. At the same time you will be alert to new themes and patterns formed because of the alchemical composition created when these two individuals become one unit. This chart can be used to examine themes and patterns in the relationship by considering the planets in the way we have above. Like any horoscope, there are some important points to consider. Try also to keep in mind the anomalies that are contained in a composite chart: there will be a few stand-outs to look for.

The Angles and Angular Planets

As in any horoscope, angular planets dominate. For instance, in Angelina and Brad's composite chart, Uranus is on the Ascendant so space, distance, freedom and adventure are in the driver's seat in this relationship. The couple appear electric, interesting and avant garde, but unexpected events and surprises may just be around corner. Opposite Uranus are Mercury and Chiron on the Descendant, suggesting the need for clarity of communication and understanding in their shared way of life. This theme stands out and suggests the relational opposition between independent action and the need to communicate and discuss mutual goals. Each partner has a Mercury–Uranus trine in their natal horoscope and the challenge to communicate effectively is brought to the surface.

Important Aspects and Aspect Patterns

Evaluate which aspects are dominant in the chart. I would be looking for strong links between inner and outer planets, strong conjunctions, oppositions and squares. For instance, in the Jolie–Pitt composite chart, the Sun is on the South Node opposite Pluto on the North Node. The Sun–Pluto opposition might address power struggles within the relationship and the need to identify working together as a way of facing strong opposition and challenges from others. However, the couple may also be identified as a power couple, as together they may appear to be influential and charismatic. As mentioned above, the opposition of Uranus to Chiron–Mercury speaks of the necessity for clarity of communication. The chart is like a see-saw swinging back and forth.

   I would also be very aware of a major aspect pattern in the horoscope. Even though the couple may not be aware of this energy in their relationship, it is potentially around the corner when the relationship develops.

House Emphasis

Houses that are strongly inhabited point to central areas where the couple will become engaged and occupied. In the composite chart the polarity must be taken into account as well. For instance, in the Pitt–Jolie horoscope the 5th, 6th and 12th houses have two or more planets. Children and creativity (5th), daily routines and working together, lifestyle and maintaining order (6th), and spirituality and imagination (12th) all play a major role in the relationship. The 6th–12th polarity stands out as the most important. This suggests that the overall theme of order versus chaos is highlighted in this relationship. Although there are no planets in the 11th, it is brought into play because of its polarity to the 5th. Therefore the community at large, colleagues and friends play a role in the couple's focus on children and creativity.

Transits to the Composite Chart
It is always important to bring the composite chart into the present. By examining the transits you are able to infer which areas of the relationship may be more stressed or pressured during the current period. For instance, one transit of importance from 2009–2014 would be Neptune as it transits the Mars–Moon conjunction in the 5th house of Brad and Angelia's composite chart. During 2009, Jupiter and Chiron were also close to Neptune. Chiron continued to transit this conjunction until 2012 while Neptune transited this until early 2014, bringing the confusing themes of children and creativity into the forefront of their relationship.

Comparing the Composite Chart to the Natal Charts
Chart comparison is also possible between each natal chart and the composite chart. Each partner's chart can be compared to the composite chart to consider which partner may be more or less comfortable with certain aspects and parts of the relationship. This comparison reveals the connection that each partner has with the relationship itself. For instance, Angelina's Mars at 10♈42 conjoins the Chiron–Mercury conjunction on the Descendant of the composite chart. She may be more forward in bringing difficult agendas and relational conflicts to the table for discussion than Brad, whose Mars at 10♑01 squares this position and Angelina's Mars as well. She may also be the one to initiate action on contracts, legalities, agreements and partnership issues.

CHAPTER 20

NODAL POINTS
Meeting and Marriages

Our word 'node' has various meanings. One of its definitions suggests a point of intersection. Astronomically, this describes where a planetary orbit crosses the ecliptic. It is the Moon's orbital path across the ecliptic that defines the North and South Nodes of the Moon, an indispensable astrological image for meeting points. Allegorically it represents a crossroad of Heaven and Earth, Soul and Spirit, Sun and Moon; therefore, the nodal axis has come to symbolize important junctures, rendezvous and turning points in both spiritual and mundane terms.

Nodal Points

There are other intersecting or nodal points in the horoscope. The angles of the horoscope mark the two points where the ecliptic, the path of the planets, crosses one of the great astronomical circles. For instance, the Ascendant–Descendant axis occurs where the horizon meets the ecliptic and is an axis which marks the meeting of self with other. The MC–IC axis is found where the meridian meets the ecliptic and where the relationship with the parents and familial others is focused. The Vertex–Anti-Vertex is the plane where the Prime Vertical crosses the ecliptic, where we engage with deeper yet concealed aspects of the self that often appear as alter egos and other selves. Therefore, these three axes plus the nodal axis are like roads or paths through the horoscope and where they intersect with others' planets or points is where a soulful encounter is likely.

In relationship astrology we could use the expression 'nodal point' to characterize the meeting point or intersection of two individuals in time or space. When potential partners first cross paths and recognize their connection it is felt as a powerful moment. This nodal point in their relationship can be memorialized through other charts such as a meeting, engagement or marriage chart. When two people meet, the possibility of a new world opens up.

Crossing Paths

An oft-quoted phrase of Sufi mystic and poet Rumi is: 'Lovers don't finally meet somewhere. They're in each other all along.'[123] When lovers meet, they may not recognize each other right away. But some do.

When poet Rainer Maria Rilke met Lou Andreas-Salomé at a friend's apartment in Munich on 12 May 1897, he knew. He had met her before through her writing; but now this encounter was in person. The next day he sent her a letter by messenger describing spending yet another 'twilight hour' with her. He was twenty-one, she was thirty-six, and for the rest of his life she would be his 'most intense and enduring friendship' as well as his passionate lover for the next three and a half years.[124] Virginia Woolf met Vita Sackville-West on 14 December 1922. When she learned that Vita was also a writer, Virginia offered to help publish her work. On that day Virginia had no inkling that Vita would ever be her lover. It was not until three years later that they began their passionate affair. On the day they first met, Venus was retrograding across Vita's Scorpio MC and about to station in a few days. She was thirty and Virginia was forty. Where paths cross in time and space, seeds of future relationship are sown; some germinate immediately, some take their time and others lie barren.

What is this force or fate that brings two people to meet at the same crossroads at the same time? How is this arranged? So often this moment of meeting seems providential or destined in some way; therefore, we would imagine that important synastry themes would be inherent in the meeting chart if the seeds have germinated. This moment of recognition of connection becomes the meeting chart. The first imprint that the relationship makes upon the individuals can be charted; the horoscope of the moment becomes a witness and a testament to the potential of the merger. While this moment may not have been written down or noted it is often still very alive in the feeling memory. Time and again, couples have told me the story of their meeting. When paths cross it is an eternal and sacred moment. The meeting chart is a significant chart in itself, but is also the transits to the natal and composite horoscopes. If the connection develops, the significant transits at the time of meeting are guideposts to the consolidation of the relationship.

In Chapter 12 we referred to the destined meeting of Grace Kelly and Prince Rainier which was arranged by *Paris Match* magazine. I suggested that the approaching Full Moon was a cosmic herald for the future royal couple. Even though their meeting was brief and arranged for publicity, a connection was made, as within a year they were married. Grace returned home to do a film *The Swan* in which she prophetically played a princess. Rainier and she wrote to each other and in December 1955 he visited the US and met Grace and her family. They celebrated New Year in New York, where he proposed. Below is their meeting chart in Monte Carlo; I have set this for 2.30 p.m. because reports seem to suggest that they spent the later afternoon in the palace gardens. As he arrived late, I have settled on this speculative time of meeting at 2.30 p.m.[125] Grace was twenty-five; Rainier was thirty-one.

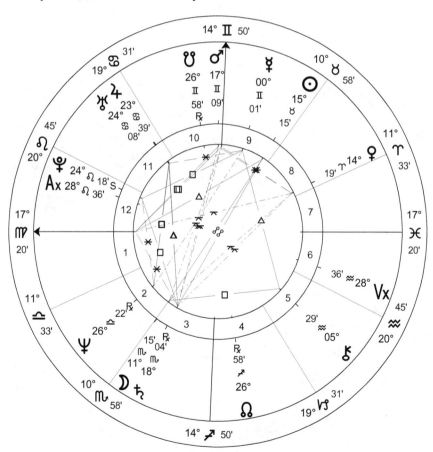

Meeting of Grace Kelly and Prince Rainier III of Monaco, 6 May 1955, 2.30 p.m., Monte Carlo, Monaco

Note that Mercury moved into Gemini at 2.05 p.m. that day. Virgo rose between 1.00 and 3.35 p.m. while Gemini culminated between 1.27 and 3.35 p.m.; therefore, Mercury ruled both the Ascendant and MC between 1.27 and 3.35 p.m. Perhaps we might credit Mercury as their intention to remain connected through letter writing. Mercurial images were also plentiful around the time of their meeting:

- Grace changed her mind about keeping the appointment
- Her car had a minor collision with one of the photographer's vehicles on the way to the palace
- Rainier was late
- The meeting had been arranged by *Paris Match* magazine

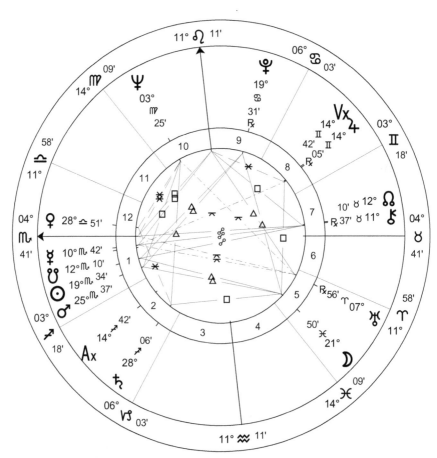

Grace Kelly, 12 November 1929, 5.31 a.m., Philadelphia, PA, USA

Mercury is a messenger of the gods. His herald's wand, the *kerykeion*, signals the god's approach. Something is afoot. This is one moment in many, but in retrospect it is a moment with deep significance and great meaning. Mercury's ingress into its ruling sign as the two met is propitious and an interesting image to amplify; not particularly significant in the continuous movement of the cosmos, but for this one moment when paths crossed it is of interest symbolically. A communion occurs. At the crossroads of the soul, time is not linear but often elongated and eternal.

Grace Kelly's time of birth is recorded on her birth certificate whereas Prince Rainier's time of 6 a.m. is not verified.

Transiting Neptune was retrograde, but when direct would approach Grace's Venus at 28♎51. It would be exactly conjunct Grace's Venus for the first time later in the year and would continue its passage across her Venus throughout 1956. This is a classic transit

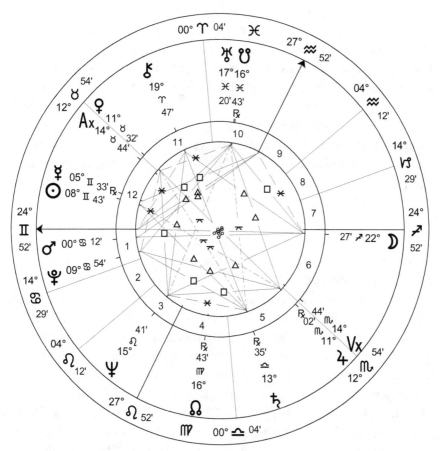

Prince Rainier III of Monaco, 31 May 1923, 6:00 a.m., Monaco

that is equated with falling in love, being swept away or engaged in a momentous shift in values and love. Prince Rainier's Venus at 11♉ is opposite his Jupiter at 11♏ and squares his Neptune at 15♌. His T-square aspects Grace's chart: his Venus is conjunct her North Node in the 7th house, his Jupiter is on her South Node, and his Neptune is on her MC. Meeting the Prince would alter her life direction significantly. Transiting Venus that day was opposite the Prince's Saturn. Note too that Grace's Jupiter–Vertex conjunction in Gemini is conjunct the MC of the meeting chart.

As we do not have Rainier's verified time of birth we can look at the range of the Moon that day and use it to estimate the couple's composite Moon. However, the meeting chart along with their marriage chart can serve as a viable symbolic map of their partnership as well.

As mentioned previously, the Moon was approaching its full phase, conjoining Grace's South Node and the Prince's Jupiter. This meeting would lead to a major cultural shift for Grace in language and culture, a shift indicated by her Jupiter–Vertex conjunction in the 8th in Gemini. Rainier's Sun in Gemini was conjunct this. The pain of dislocation due to the relationship is also echoed by Chiron's conjunction to her 7th house North Node, also conjunct Rainier's Venus. Transiting Saturn was retrograde in Scorpio, having transited Grace's Sun twice in its series of three passages. By the end of the year it had completed its transits of the Sun and Mars, consolidating the direction that began the day Grace met the Prince of Monaco under the auspices of the messenger-god Mercury.

Royal engagements seem far away from pedestrian life, but in many ways they serve to remind us of the enchantment of meeting one's mate. Every relationship will have its conception story, perhaps not as well documented as a royal one, but nonetheless a storyline where destiny played its part. On an August day in 1957 in Tokyo, Michiko could never imagine that she would cross paths with Crown Prince Akihito on a tennis court and eventually become the Empress of Japan. And when Mary Donaldson from Hobart, Australia, shook hands with a young man in a pub in Sydney on 16 September 2000 she did not know that he was the Crown Prince of Denmark. When she found out later that evening, she still had no idea that in four years she would become the Crown Princess. The day she met

Frederick the Sun was exactly opposite her Venus, but the bigger picture showed Neptune transiting her North Node resonating with a time when Mary was at an auspicious and unimagined crossroads. For Frederick, the transiting North Node was exactly conjunct his Descendant and he too stood at a crossroads in relationship.

The meeting chart and its transits to the natal charts can articulate the soulful narrative that brings two individuals to the same crossroads.

Transits and Progressions at Times of Meeting

Not all relationships have a specific meeting chart because the relationship may evolve over time or a relationship may not be possible at the time. There may be a mutual moment of recognition, an engagement or later public declaration which can be used. But when a relationship builds over time, it is also of interest to reconstruct the transits and progressions to understand the influences that were and may still be operational. Let's look at another royal rendezvous. Although Charles and Diana were in each other's company when she was young, Diana's first grown-up encounter with Prince Charles occurred in November 1977 when she was sixteen and her sister Sarah was dating Charles.[126]

Planet	Transits on 1 November 1977	Comments
♃	6♋03℞; went ℞ on 24 October and would remain ℞ until February 1978	Jupiter is transiting Diana's 7th house having already transited Mercury, the ruler of her 7th. It would retrograde back to conjoin Mercury once again. It is also close to her 7th house Sun
♄	29♌04; enters ♍ in December and goes ℞	Saturn is transiting Diana's North Node in the 8th house and would repeat in February and July 1978. Saturn is returning in Charles's chart
♅	11♏53	
♆	14♐32	Neptune is approaching Diana's Ascendant
♇	15♎02	Pluto is transiting Charles's Neptune–Venus conjunction

♆	3♉11℞; Chiron was discovered on 1 November 1977	Chiron is transiting Charles' Moon–North Node conjunction in the 10th house
☊	13♎47	The North Node has just transited Charles's Neptune–Venus conjunction and is conjunct his IC

Diana and her sister were invited to Prince Charles's thirtieth birthday party in November 1978. Interestingly, his solar return Ascendant that year was 14♎22 conjunct his Neptune–Venus that had just been transited by Pluto. The image of relationship was on the horizon of his life.

It was not until July 1980, when they met again, that Charles seemed to take an interest in Diana. He invited her to Balmoral, which seems to be the beginning of their romance. On 6 February 1981 Charles proposed and their engagement was announced publicly on 24 February. Charles and Diana were married on 29 July 1981, twenty-five years after the other 'wedding of the century' of Grace Kelly and Prince Rainier. The transits from November 1977 to July 1980 may be significant as destiny draws them together at this time. I would note the major transits as the seeds of themes that are being worked out and replayed throughout their relationship.

Planet	Transits on 1 July 1980	Comments
♃	6♍03: enters ♎ in October	Jupiter is transiting Diana's Pluto in the 8th Jupiter is transiting Charles's 2nd house Saturn
♄	21♍29: enters ♎ in September	Saturn is approaching a trine to Diana's Venus, repeating the Venus–Saturn trine in Diana's natal chart. Saturn squares Charles's Mars–Vertex conjunction in the 5th house
♅	21♏52℞	Uranus has opposed Venus and squared Diana's Moon, igniting the natal T-square with the same three planets. Uranus has conjoined Charles's Sun and will conjoin it once again

♆	20♐48R	The transit of Neptune over Diana's Ascendant is in its last phase. Neptune is transiting Charles's Mars
♇	18♎58	Pluto is finishing the reconstruction of Charles's Neptune–Venus conjunction and Pluto is approaching Diana's MC, symbolizing her encounter with power in the world
⚷	17♉01	Chiron is approaching Diana's T-square of Uranus opposite the Moon square Venus. Charles is approaching his Chiron opposition but also its opposition to his Sun
☊	20♌44	The nodal transit across Diana's Uranus–Moon opposition has just been completed

Between their initial meeting and their visit to Balmoral, transits illustrate the powerful dynamics affecting each of their charts. For instance, Charles has the Sun at 22♏ opposing Diana's Venus at 24♉ and squaring her Uranus–Moon opposition. Transiting Uranus had been triggering this dynamic. Diana's Ascendant at 18♐ is closely conjunct Charles's Mars–Vertex conjunction; Neptune was transiting both these angles. Pluto had transited Charles's Neptune–Venus conjunction.

The transits are revealing. Diana's world of 'other' is opened up by the transit of Jupiter through her 7th and 8th houses, while Saturn consolidated her destiny with its transit to the North Node–Mars. July 1, 1980 was Diana's 19th birthday. Jupiter was closely conjunct the solar return Ascendant, while the solar return Venus at 16♊39 was retrograding near her natal Descendant. A week later it would turn direct and conjoin her Descendant for the third time during this Venus sub-cycle. At 19 the returns of the lunar nodes and solar return Moon would be embedded in the solar return horoscope. Therefore the solar return repeated the Moon – South Node conjunction in Aquarius in proximity to her natal Moon – South Node conjunction in Aquarius.

Charles's ideal of love is being transformed with the Pluto transit to his Neptune–Venus while the Chiron transit to his Moon–North Node signifies the opening of an emotional wound. The transits to the charts illustrate the first seeds of the relationship being sown and what might later be harvested. Progressions will also be of interest, but I shall look at these for the time of their marriage.

Mr and Mrs Smith

Brad Pitt met Angelina Jolie on the set of *Mr and Mrs Smith*. They played a married couple who each had a secret. Brad was married; Angelina was divorced. Certainly we will not find the truth of their relationship from the celebrity pages and gossip columns. But we do know the film began production in 2003 and was released in 2005, the year Brad announced he was seeking a divorce. Transits from mid 2003 to the end of 2004 would be significant as these were preparing the groundwork for their relationship. I find reviewing the transits to the natal and even composite charts helpful in setting the stage for a couple's life together. The major transits for this period are below:

Planet	Position 1 July 2003	Position 1 Jan 2005	Comments
♄	3♋29	24♋56R	♄ is moving through Jolie's 12th during her ♄ return. In 2005 it will cross her Venus and Ascendant. ♄ is in Brad's 8th house opposing his stellium in ♑ which includes the Moon and Venus. They meet as ♄ transits the MC of their composite chart
⚷	15♑39R	25♑33	Chiron is opposite transiting Saturn affecting the ♋/♑ planets
♅	2♓36R	3♓55	Uranus hovers in the early degrees of Pisces exactly conjunct their composite Moon
♆	12♒40R	13♒51	♆ trines Angelina's Sun
♇	18♐03R	22♐43	Pluto makes a dynamic square to the composite chart's Sun and nodal axis

As the above grid shows there are dynamic transits at the time of meeting which are important to consider. The strong Saturn transits illustrate that time is important while the transits to the composite chart suggest that, even before their connection is acknowledged, the relationship is undergoing its challenges.

The Tropics of Erotica: Anaïs and Henry

Anaïs Nin and Henry Miller were both writers of erotica, sometimes verging on the pornographic. Miller was well known for his novel *Tropic of Cancer*, banned in the USA, while Nin's writings explored sexual taboos including incest. Their paths crossed in December 1931 when Henry arrived at Anaïs's home in Louveciennes, France, having been invited by her publisher. Anaïs was already married and at twenty-eight was on the cusp of her sexual exploration; Henry was seeking creative invigoration. Their passionate and complex affair began early the next year. Anaïs felt that Henry initiated her into an erotic and creative way of being,[127] while it is obvious from the numerous impassioned love letters he wrote to Anaïs that Henry was obsessed with her.[128]

Henry Miller's time of birth is often quoted as 12.30 or 12.45 p.m., but Erica Jong in her chronicle of his life, *The Devil at Large*, quotes 12.17 p.m.[129] A hand-drawn horoscope in Arthur Hoyle's blog on 'The Astrological Henry Miller' also shows 12.17 p.m.,[130] which is the time used for the following chart. In 1930–31, Henry Miller was 'an American in Paris'. Uranus was transiting his Ascendant. In December 1931, Uranus would turn direct at 15° Aries, preparing to transit Henry's Ascendant for the final time, having crossed it twice previously. Visible on his horizon was the archetype of experimentation and the unexpected. Embodying the transit for Henry was Anaïs Nin, atypical of her time and a woman on the verge of self-exploration and sexual abandon.

It is not surprising that Anaïs was also encountering Uranus as it moved across her South Node and opposed Mars on her North Node. The South Node conjoins her Vertex in the 7th house. She too was restless, searching for adventure, liberation and a bohemian lifestyle. Her retrograde Mars in Libra rested on Henry's Descendant and, for this moment in time, he embodied this archetypal image that was being transfigured in her soul. Her Vertex–South Node conjunction conjoined his Ascendant; something deeply known, yet mysterious, perhaps from the past, was stirred. This opposition, which sits across Henry's Ascendant–Descendant axis, brings two planes of existence into the same space. Both interconnected axes are being transited by Uranus, awakening an erotic connection between the two. But her Mars is also square Chiron in the 4th house, a symbol that her desire may also act as a compensation for earlier wounds from her family experience.

Reciprocally, Henry's Vertex also sits on Anaïs's Ascendant, an aspect we have met with our other couples and a powerfully mutual image of paths crossing in time and space. But it is also a compelling connection that anticipates self-discovery and revelation with another, in this case Anaïs. Having this interaspect between the two charts means it will be repeated in their composite horoscope with the Vertex conjunct the Ascendant. The Vertex axis crossing the Ascendant–Descendant axis suggests that two paths are intersecting, and at this crossroads each person will be radically altered.

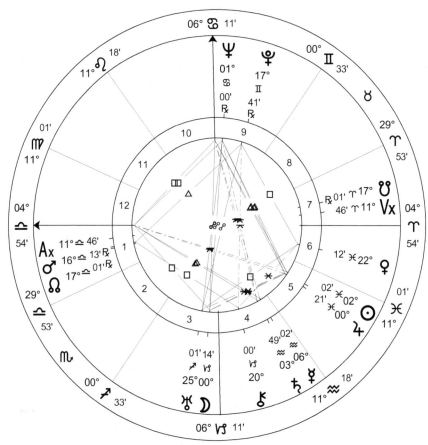

Anaïs Nin, 21 February 1903, 8:25 p.m., Neuilly sur Seine, France

Henry's Sun in Capricorn falls on Anaïs's IC and is also conjunct her Moon, strong images of a familial connection. Being opposite Neptune and conjunct Uranus, Anaïs's Moon indicates that her moods may move back and forth between feeling enmeshed and in love to needing space and separation, a swing that Henry's Sun may ignite. Saturn, the ruler of his Sun, is also squaring Anaïs's Moon, which she may feel as criticism, especially of her writing and the discipline of this craft, echoing her Saturn conjunct Mercury in the 4th house.

Henry also has a Moon–Uranus conjunction, and his is part of a triple conjunction with Mars in Scorpio.[131] Being in the 7th house, it may be easier for Henry to know the untamed erotic feminine in his outer experience of women rather than in his own interior life. Certainly this is descriptive of both Anaïs and June, his wife at the time. When Anaïs met June she became intrigued and infatuated

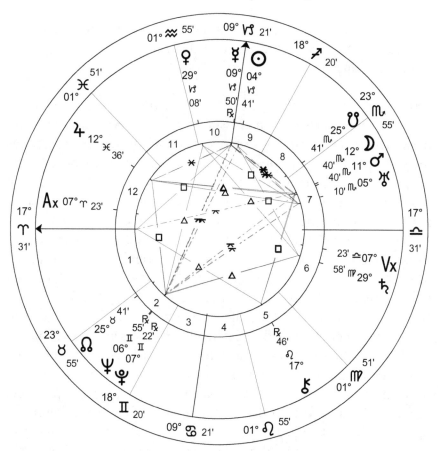

Henry Miller, 26 December 1891, 12:17 p.m., Manhattan, NY, USA

with her, which led to a sexually romantic relationship between the two women. Anaïs's Venus in Pisces forms a T-square with Uranus and Pluto, an astrological image of her provocative and magnetic erotic character. This aspect pattern may have been personified by Henry, finding its expression and liberation through Henry's Mars in Scorpio trine Jupiter, an archetypal image of a powerful and erotic masculine figure.

Born over eleven years apart, they both have Jupiter in Pisces. Anaïs's Jupiter is conjunct her Sun in Pisces in the 5th, an apt metaphor for the search for the idealized and larger-than-life father. When Anaïs was ten, her musician father abandoned the family for a beautiful young piano student. Anaïs has Neptune trine the Sun, so both rulers of her Piscean Sun are in aspect to the symbol of her essential self. The archetypes of Jupiter and Neptune are embedded in her being as a poetic and symbolic thinker:

> The Symbolic interpretation is the only one which expands, enlarges the world, and makes it boundless, illimitable. All others reduce it.[132]

Anaïs identified with poetry and the imagination, seeing its reflection in artistic and charismatic men. She was a muse who engaged with these artistes on the 5th house stage of creativity and sex. As Uranus transited in opposition to her 1st house Mars–North Node, Henry Miller embodied the awakener. Henry's progressed Moon in that month of meeting Anaïs was opposite his 7th house Uranus, so in a way his feeling life would be aroused too, albeit unpredictably.

While their relationship did not or could not last, their story is forever woven together through Nin's diaries and novels. Both were unorthodox writers who lived outside the conventions of their day and engaged in all aspects of an erotic life. Anaïs Nin and Henry Miller were also exponents of astrology. Nin was introduced to astrology by her therapist René Allendy, who was also an astrologer and homeopath. In turn, she introduced Miller to Conrad Moricand, a famous Swiss astrologer living in Paris.[133] In 1939 Miller read Rudhyar's *The Astrology of Personality*. The book's inspiring effect lasted a lifetime, with Miller cataloguing it as one of the hundred books 'which influenced me the most'.[134] Astrology and Anaïs were muses for Miller, while Nin's inspiration was influenced not only by Henry Miller but by analysts such as Allendy and Otto Rank. It was in this era of self-exploration and discovery that their paths crossed and forever altered each other's course of life.

When paths of the soul cross and connect, each one is altered infinitely.

The Marriage Chart

The marriage chart is traditionally the horoscope of the exchange of vows, the 'I do' of the wedding ceremony or the declaration of marriage. A marriage chart could also be a commitment ceremony or the time when a ritual bonds a couple together. The marriage chart is arranged, unlike the meeting chart which is serendipitous. Both partners choose a time or agree on a time of marriage. The conscious process that takes place on the way to the wedding[135] can

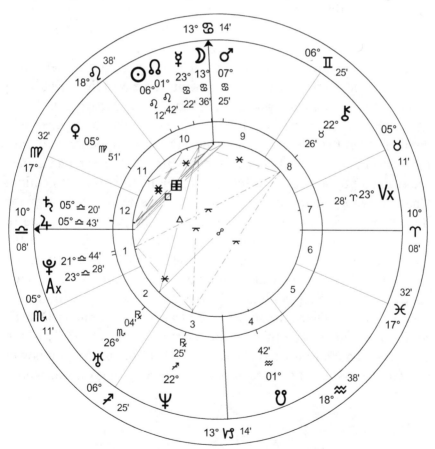

Diana and Charles's Wedding, 29 July 1981, 11.30 a.m., St Paul's Cathedral, London, England

be amplified through the transits and progressions leading to that moment. We might expect more social, traditional or public images in this chart, rather than in the meeting chart which might have more personal, private or momentary imagery that is important.

Diana and Charles were married on 29 July 1981 in what was described as a fairy tale wedding; however, as we know, the fairy tale did not have a happy ending. According to the BBC, Diana arrived almost on time for the 11.20 a.m. BST ceremony at St Paul's Cathedral and took 3½ minutes to walk up the red-carpeted aisle. Shortly after this, the ceremony began. The exchange of vows and then the declaration by the Archbishop of Canterbury of marriage took nearly 4 minutes. After a brief private signing ceremony, the Prince and Princess of Wales walked back down the aisle together. I have set the chart for 11.30 a.m. which is an estimation of the time of the declaration of their marriage.[136]

Libra is rising in nearly the same degree as the composite Descendant and relationship Ascendant. At the time of the wedding Jupiter and Saturn were conjunct, heralding a new societal and cultural cycle. Both were rising at the time of the wedding, bestowing an eminent national and social importance on this marriage.

The Sun is near the nodal axis, suggesting that an eclipse will happen when the Moon conjoins the Sun: this happened two days later on 31 July at 7♌51. The Moon is eclipsing the Sun and Diana, the Roman goddess of the Moon, is symbolically poised to eclipse Charles, whose rising degree is 5♌24, close to the degree of the Sun in the marriage chart and the eclipse degree. This theme of Diana obscuring Charles in the public eye is also mirrored in the marriage chart with the Moon culminating in Cancer very close to Diana's Sun. The marriage luminaries are aligned to their natal charts with the Sun conjunct Charles's Ascendant and the MC–Moon conjunct Diana's Sun. Mars by transit will conjunct Diana's Sun in three days. The ruler of the chart is Venus at 5♍51, which conjoins Diana's Pluto and Charles's Saturn, foreshadowing power and control issues in their relationship. The ongoing transits were:

Transiting	Aspects to Charles's Chart	Aspects to Diana's Chart
Jupiter at 5♎43	Both Jupiter and Saturn are approaching the IC and the Neptune–Venus conjunction over the next four months	Both Jupiter and Saturn are approaching the square to Diana's 7th house Sun over the next month
Saturn at 5♎20		
Uranus at 26♏04 R	Uranus is transiting Chiron having just completed the transit to his Sun	Uranus is opposite her Venus, square her Moon and igniting her T-square
Neptune at 22♐25 R	Neptune is conjunct his Vertex but also transiting in proximity to his Mars	Neptune is beginning the transit of her 1st house
Pluto at 21♎44		Pluto is transiting her MC
Chiron at 22♉26	Chiron is exactly opposite Charles's Sun. Natally he has a Sun–Chiron conjunction; Chiron is approaching its opposition	Chiron is conjunct Diana's Venus and Uranus is playing havoc with the T-square
North Node at 1♌42	The North Node had just transited his Ascendant	The North Node has just transited her Vertex and is about to enter her 7th house

After the wedding the newlyweds took the open-top state landau to Buckingham Palace. They emerged on the palace balcony with the extended family at 1.10 p.m. BST and kissed in front of the world. At this time the Sun was on the MC, whereas during the wedding the Moon was on the meridian. Leo had culminated and the Sun was conjunct the MC. Both luminaries had culminated in their ruling signs during this highly public time. During the marriage, in front of their families and guests, the Moon was on the MC, but now on the public balcony, the symbol of the king or Charles was above. However, an eclipse would soon occur.

Examining the houses of the wedding chart would be valuable in locating areas of activity, stress, concentration and conflict for the couple, depending on the planets in these sectors. With the Sun and Moon in the 10th house, the marriage is public and its goals and needs are to work together in the world. I take note of themes in the wedding chart that are similar to the natal charts, the chart comparison or the composite chart. For instance, Charles has the Moon and North Node in the 10th house of his natal horoscope and this is repeated in the marriage chart, but now the Sun is aligned with the Node.

Progressions

Marriage or a public ritual of commitment in relationship marks a potent passage in the course of one's life. This union is an archetypical event in life's calendar and as such secondary progressions will be revealing of the development that leads to this. Traditionally, the progressed Sun to Venus indicated marriage; however, since marriage is such a unique moment for each partner there will be different progressions which reveal their inner maturity on the way to the wedding. While an archetypal experience, relationship is also highly personal in its timing.

I am alert to lunar progressions in synastry as the aspect between each partner's progressed Moon will generally remain the same throughout their relationship because the progressed Moon's movement of 12–15° a year is similar for both individuals.[137] At the time of the wedding Charles and Diana's progressed Moons were trine one another. I am also interested in the relationship between the couple's progressed lunation phase as a barometer of the phase of life they are moving through and whether this will be compatible throughout their lives. Charles is experiencing his Full Moon phase and Diana is in her First Quarter. From this perspective he is ready to fulfil his destiny while she may still be searching for new paths of endeavour.

The progressions can help to modify difficulties inherent in the chart comparison. However, this will depend on the level of conscious development of each partner. It is of interest to compare the progressed planets in the same way as the natal ones. Here are the progressions ('P') for Diana and Charles on their wedding day.

Prog. to 29 July 1981	Charles	Comments	Diana	Comments
Sun	25♐34	In the years before the marriage, Charles's P Sun conjoined Mars and the Vertex	28♋49	Diana's P Sun had been exactly opposite Saturn during the year.
Moon	11♋07	Each Moon has progressed into the sign of the other's Sun. Charles's P Moon is in his natal 12th house	9♏22	Diana's P Moon is conjunct Neptune. Currently the progressed Moons are trine
Lunation Phase	**Full Moon**	Charles has reached the midpoint of the cycle, a fulfilment and realization, a more objective time	**First Quarter**	Diana is in an action-orientated phase. Each may be looking for different outcomes at these times in their lives
Mercury	28♐14	P Mercury is approaching Jupiter in the 5th house	8♋48	P Mercury is conjunct the Sun in the 7th
Venus	26♏37	P Venus is approaching Chiron	15♊45	P Venus is approaching the Descendant
Mars	15♑51	P Mars squares Neptune–Venus	13♍43	

A Saturn Cycle Later

On 29 April 2011, Diana and Charles's eldest son, Prince William, married Kate Middleton amidst much celebration and optimism. The wedding was scheduled to begin at 11 a.m. and the following chart is set for 11.20 a.m., the pronouncement of their marriage.

Their wedding took place nearly thirty years after the marriage of Diana and Charles; Saturn had returned to Libra and another generation of hopeful Britons celebrated the union of their prince with a beautiful 'commoner'. However, the memory of Diana still lingered over the ceremony; Diana was a mere twenty years old when she married Charles, who was thirty-two. William and Kate are both from the next Saturn in Libra generation, as echoed in their composite chart. Saturn in Libra conjunct the IC is a vital part of their wedding chart. Their marriage celebration marks their coming of age into the second Saturn cycle of their lives. Saturn is on the lowest angle of their wedding chart while, in William's parents' marriage chart, it is rising.

Diana and Charles had Jupiter rising; William and Kate have Jupiter in the 10th house of the marriage chart conjunct Mars, ruler of the MC. Prince William also has Mars ruling the MC with Jupiter conjunct the MC. In his parents' marriage chart Jupiter was conjunct Saturn while in William's marriage chart the Jupiter–

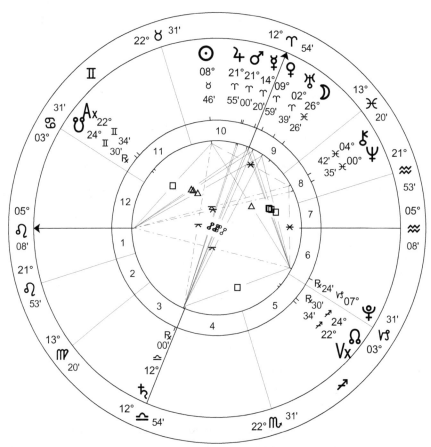

William and Kate's Wedding, 29 April 2011, 11.20 a.m.,
Westminster Abbey, London, England

Saturn opposition had occurred the previous month. The Jupiter–
Saturn cycle speaks about the social responsibilities inherent in
the marriages; Diana and Charles's cycle was entwined with the
personal axis of the Ascendant–Descendant, whereas William and
Kate's is aligned with the MC–IC axis. In this chart Jupiter is in a
powerful stellium in Aries which may be more effective in directing
their social needs.

Prince William was born on 21 June 1982 at 9.03 pm in London,
shortly after the New Moon in Cancer. With the Node at 13♋, this
New Moon was an eclipse. Saturn squares his nodal axis. Saturn
at the bendings with the South Node in Capricorn symbolizes
deeply felt responsibility, already part of the blueprint of their royal
wedding. How they satisfy the Saturn archetype that has such a
strong design in their synastry is their challenge. And this puzzle
will become more apparent as their children grow and the cardinal
demands of self-fulfilment, family ties, relationship needs and
social duties need to be woven together.

Kate Middleton's time of birth is not yet known at the time of
writing. She was born in Reading, Berkshire, on 9 January 1982;
therefore, her Moon will be between approximately 6♋21 and
21♋46. Kate was born on the day of a total lunar eclipse which
occurred at 7.54 that evening at 19♋14; therefore her nodal axis
is in the same polarity as her Sun and Moon, with Saturn squaring
this axis. Kate shares this instinctive sense of responsibility with
William. Like Diana, both will be sensitive to the eclipse cycles
throughout their lives.

(Note: While in the final production stages of this book, *The
Astrological Journal*, Sept–Oct Vol. 59 # 5, page 11, reported
Catherine, the Duchess of Cambridge's birth time as 7 pm. The
Moon is 18♋41 and Leo rises, within eight degrees of William's
Vertex. Their MCs are conjunct the other's ICs. As discussed, these
intersecting angles appear frequently in synastry. At present the
time has yet to be confirmed.)

Kate and William's Composite Chart
We must be cautious about their composite chart as Kate Middleton's
time of birth is unknown. Therefore a noon chart is used for her,
which means the angles and houses cannot be used. The Moon that
day was in Cancer; therefore her Moon will be in Cancer, and when

382 From the Moment We Met: The Astrology of Adult Relationships

William and Kate's composite chart is formed, the Moon is also in Cancer with the Sun, Venus and Mercury all in Aries.

Aries is also well represented in their wedding chart with Mercury and Venus again in the sign, along with Mars, Jupiter and Uranus. Kate and William both have Mars in Libra which forms a composite Mars as part of a T-square between the Sun in Aries and its ruler Mars exactly opposite in Libra, square to the Moon. The T-square confirms that a more conscious effort is crucial in the relationship to identify its needs, urges and goals. The Arian and cardinal emphasis suggests that abundant activity might be at the cost of emotional security and home life.

While sharing the Moon in Cancer suggests that there is recognition of each other's moods, needs and emotional characters, this can also suggest the couple might get caught up in the same emotional atmosphere, making it difficult to comfort or be available for the other. Or with similar placements one partner may polarize; in this case it may be Kate, as she already has the Sun in Capricorn. We saw this similar aspect with the Emperor and Empress of Japan who both have the Moon in Pisces.

Electing a Marriage Chart

Because the marriage time can be chosen, couples often consult astrologers for the 'best' time to be married. But is there ever a best time? Astrologically there may be advantageous times, but because of the many restrictions in electing a horoscope, this good time might end up being a work day or 4 a.m. or during a holiday or an inappropriate anniversary. If the couple wants to be married in June on a Saturday between 2 and 4 p.m., the options for choosing the right time are severely limited. This aspect of astrology is called electional astrology, as the astrologer uses astrological premises to elect the best time. However a 'best time' at the best of times is always subjective and very personal.

Each couple is unique. A standard set of rules for every wedding chart suggests that everybody should be married when certain astrological windows of opportunity open. However, this type of approach does not take into account the uniqueness of each couple and their needs. In my practice I have elected many marriage charts for couples, developing my own approach based on my experience and beliefs. For me it is not just a matter of arranging the right astrological symbols, but it is also necessary to have the couple participate in the process. This shifts the focus from choosing a time to participating with time. For instance, while we might not choose to have Venus retrograde in a wedding chart, it might be unavoidable in the time frame given. Therefore the discussion might focus on what this means, how it might symbolize an aspect of their union. Perhaps one of the partners has this aspect in their natal chart or they met when Venus was retrograde. I am alert for patterns and repetitive themes in a relationship even if they are astrologically difficult.

I do not believe the 'right' chart will change a 'wrong' relationship. Therefore, the first step for me in electing a marriage chart is to consult with the couple on their chart comparison and composite chart to highlight areas of compatibility and conflict, shared and separate areas of life, as well as significant themes that underpin the relationship. My experience is that any difficult aspect patterns in the composite chart are not generally known to the couple until they are more entrenched in their relationship; therefore, the possibilities of these patterns are worth exploring with the couple. Out of these sessions I hope to facilitate the process of consciously recognizing patterns and behaviours in their relationship.

After this process I engage them in thinking about what they want out of their relationship, what they feel is most important in their marriage and what expectations and dreams they harbour. I encourage them to speak about their goals and fears, their creative process, lifestyle and living arrangements. Then working with the parameters of the times and dates they have supplied, I start to look for charts that reinforce their natal chart comparison and the composite, taking advantage of the current planetary pictures to fortify the strengths of their relationship and what they have signified as important. And, most importantly, I place what I am responsible for in perspective, having listened to, discussed, reflected on and taken into account the couple's desires and concerns. I feel my responsibilities are to do my best to delineate the landscape of time, illuminate the archetypal images and symbols at the moment and consider the possibilities inherent in them. I cannot know how the gods at the time will literally manifest, but I can contemplate the archetypal images of the horoscopes for this moment in time.

I clearly remember electing my first marriage chart and the responsibility I felt to get it perfect. It was a long time ago and I was still quite naive in my astrological understanding. My client, 'Bonnie', had consulted me several times between 1978 and 1980. Neptune was about to transit her Venus in Sagittarius. We talked about its symbolic possibilities and especially the idea of falling in love, which was of great interest to her. But we also spoke about the idealization, deception and illusions that often accompany falling in love under a Neptunian spell.

As it turned out, Bonnie did meet a man and fall in love. Two years passed, and they asked me to choose their wedding date. May, early afternoon, and outdoors were the parameters, so there was not a lot of choice, but we settled on a date. Since Bonnie believed that I had played an important role on the way to their wedding, I was invited to the ceremony. I accepted. I awoke on the morning of the wedding and it was pouring rain. I thought of the wedding being held outside and felt responsible for not getting the date or the weather right. I felt sick, wanted to cancel, but reluctantly got ready to go. Just before I got into my car, the rain stopped. As I approached the venue, the sun came out and it was beautiful. The grass sparkled in the sunlight, the air was fresh, and the smells were pleasantly intense. The wedding took place in a gazebo. As the guests spilled out onto the lawns, Bonnie mingled among us, looking exquisite and radiant with her dress trailing behind her on the glittering grass. Bonnie and the sun were glowing. Many remarked what a beautiful and perfect day it was, to which Bonnie replied, 'My astrologer chose the time.'

'Beginner's luck,' I thought. I reflected on what were my responsibilities and capabilities. From that point I began to develop a participatory model using astrological principles which included consultation with partners on the 'way to the wedding'. There are a few rules which I try to abide by; however, if there is already a pattern in the comparison or composite charts, then I accept that this pattern, even if astrologically difficult, is repeating in the marriage chart, and work within those strictures, highlighting this in the discussion with the couple. Some astrological hardship which reveals itself in the marriage chart may already be embedded in the relationship, aspects inherent to the dynamic of the couple. Every astrologer will develop their own unique way of electing a marriage time.[138] Since I am focused on the individuals, I try to listen to their needs rather than be formulaic about a 'right' time.

There are many significant times during a marriage ceremony, such as the beginning of the service, the exchange of vows and the declaration of the marriage celebrant. Therefore it is important to be consistent with your timing, as each service will have its own progression. I prefer to elect the chart for approximately the time of the declaration of marriage; therefore it is important to know the sequence of the ritual so one can also work back to the time when the ceremony would begin.

As one works within these parameters the astrological changes around the angles becomes evident. Here are some considerations I try to honour, although they are not always available during the times specified. However these images are a way of thinking about what might be included in the marriage chart.

- The Sun and Moon in harmonious aspect, trying to avoid squares between the Sun and Moon. The waxing phases after the First Quarter to the Full Moon work well for first marriages. However, if it is the second or a later marriage, or if the couple have been together for some time, then a waning Moon would be reflective of their previous experience. I try to reflect on the phase of the Moon as a metaphor of the couple's union.

- The Ascendant–Descendant axis of the marriage chart is important. Tradition states that fixed signs on the Ascendant–Descendant axis are good for consolidation and longevity, as is having the rulers of both angles in good aspect to one another and being careful of placing critical degrees on either the rising or setting degree. Outer planets, including Saturn, on either angle may also be problematic. However, it is difficult to fulfil all this criteria and the degrees, signs and angular planets will also depend on the aspirations of the couple. Once an Ascendant is chosen it can always be modified using techniques such as Sabian symbols, fixed stars, etc. I have found that repeating the composite Ascendant for the marriage chart can be effective.

It is good to remember that while the time of the wedding may be planned to arrange for a particular degree to rise, there may always be delays and complications that alter the time of the exchange of vows and declaration of marriage.

- I am aware of the planets that will rise across the horizon or culminate during the marriage ceremony. Twelfth house planets in the marriage horoscope have just risen while 9th house planets will have culminated; therefore, these will be strong placements as they will have become prominent during the ceremony. I have found that planets rising or culminating during the lead-up to the vows can be very influential. They often signify an important archetypal consideration for the philosophy and spirituality of the relationship, something perhaps overlooked in the couple's agenda.

- Scrutinize the inner planets' sign positions for detriment or fall; check whether Mercury, Venus or Mars is retrograde and if so, what stage of its retrograde cycle it is in. While these times are best avoided this may not be possible, in which case I return to the natal and composite charts to see if the position is repeated. If the wedding date cannot be changed I would amplify the potential meaning of the retrograde planet with the couple to see how they experience this energy in their relationship.

- The house position of the Sun is dependent on the time of day so it is interesting to consider that mid-morning marriages may have the Sun in the 11th house, while those just after sunset will have the Sun in the 6th. Few marriage charts will have the Sun in the 2nd, 3rd or 4th house unless couples are happy to be married between about 10 p.m. and 4 a.m. Be aware of what the Sun shines light on. Mercury and Venus will be close by and from Mars outwards retrograde planets will be in the opposite hemisphere; therefore, the Sun at the time is a key to the chart structure and hemispheric emphasis.

- Aspects that the Moon is making during the ceremony may be felt strongly and will become a significant symbol for the life of the marriage. It is important to be aware of the difficult aspects that will become exact after the exchange of vows. I would also take into account the lunar aspects in the natal and composite charts to see if there are repetitions and patterns. The needs of the relationship will help to differentiate between which lunar aspects may be appropriate and which ones not.

• Venus and Mars in a good aspect consolidate the two relationship archetypes in the marriage chart. It is best to avoid their retrograde periods, unless they are also retrograde in the partners' horoscopes. If difficult aspects between Saturn, the outer planets and Venus and/or Mars are unavoidable then these can be mitigated through conscious participation and awareness of the archetypal dynamic.

I try to keep the variants as simple as possible, incorporating the goals of the relationship into the marriage chart if that is achievable. For instance, if family is important, lunar aspects and the 4th house would be a consideration. If children are a high priority the 5th house and its extensions would be taken into account. If finances are important then 2nd house considerations, etc., take precedence. If the couple is people-orientated then Air and Water signs could be more appropriate.

Once one factor is chosen, another important one may disappear; therefore, it is difficult to maximize all the important factors. I often try to avoid the void of course Moon, as this suggests that a change of Moon sign is imminent. Under this stage of the Moon there may be some confusion or uncertainty. However, by waiting until the Moon enters the next sign the angles may have changed, creating a new ambience. Therefore, discerning what is important and what is not is a high priority. Note that Kate and William's marriage chart has a void of course Moon.

Most marriages are not planned astrologically. If you are looking at the synastry of your own commitment or marriage, or that of a friend or client, then it is of interest to look at the marriage chart in tandem with the chart comparison and composite horoscope. If called upon to be part of the wedding plans, then I look at the election of the marriage chart as a rite of passage, highlighting the groundwork and encouraging the couple's conscious preparation on the way to their public commitment and endorsement of their union.

Mergers

A committed relationship is a merger of two separate entities who bring their personalities, their resources, their ideas and their past into an amalgamation. As in any union, the everyday routines and details are essential to maintain a healthy merger. However, with a personal relationship the domestic, familial, financial, social and relational concerns can often erode a buoyant and erotic partnership when an underlying and meaningful layer of connection is not acknowledged. It is essential in an ongoing committed relationship for the mundane desires to be wedded to the spiritual. This deeper connection of any relationship is ultimately the unification of souls. It is the soul that can reach past the mundane, the trivialities of the everyday, the inconsistencies and incompatibilities, into the source of life that binds two people together.

But it takes work and commitment; it takes the binding style of Saturn to shape a vessel that can hold the multiplicities of two individuals in one space. More so, it takes the intention of love.

Relationships are nodal. They not only represent the intersection of two sentient beings but the meeting of two souls on both the mundane and spiritual levels. The primitive force of Eros mingles these two souls together to craft their legacy as one. This occurs as the relationship moves through time.

– CHAPTER 21 –
COUPLES AT THE CROSSROADS
Timing and Transition in Relationships

Astrological timing features quantitative and qualitative approaches, including both literal and symbolic qualities of time. It embraces objective and subjective observations of time. For instance, Pluto in Capricorn could symbolize an economic downturn, an era of governmental transformation, a period of being controlled, held hostage by underworld forces, or a time of restructuring large-scale corporations and administrations. This is an imaginative view of the character and quality of Pluto in Capricorn time. If an individual had an angle or inner planet in Capricorn then the timing of this image would be personally applicable to them, both imaginatively and literally. From a quantitative perspective an astrologer can also measure this time as beginning in 2008 and lasting until 2024. We can be even more precise, listing the first ingress of Pluto into Capricorn as 26 January 2008, Universal Time. Forecasting involves the marriage of these two ways of timing in a considered and thoughtful way.

Consistent with the ingress of Pluto into Capricorn, the world economy did falter and a long period of economic re-evaluation and restructuring began. Did astrology predict this period? Can astrology be predictive? Or is this synchrony, magic or chance? These are important questions that each practising astrologer must ask themselves to formulate their own beliefs and philosophy, which in turn inform their approach to their practice.

Astrology is based on time and we need to feel comfortable with working with time. My experience has taught me to work with timing symbolically: to respect the planetary cycles and their timeframes, as symbols, not facts. In doing so, clients are more able to participate with their own understanding of the situation. I have experienced this way of working to be more revelatory and revealing. Rather than making closed-ended statements about possibilities, an interactive presentation of the horoscope's images and symbols, along with perceptive questions to the client, encourages them to be reflective and imaginative. For instance, discussing the imagery and symbolism of Pluto in Capricorn transiting the Midheaven at a given time allows the client to focus their own ideas and feelings on their vocational goals, to reflect on potential changes in the structure of their careers and to consider what hierarchal shifts in their familial or worldly environs might then arise. This also creates the psychic space for revelations and insights to occur.

This orientation to astrological timing is especially helpful in relationship astrology as the possibilities are multiplied due to the involvement of others. Timing techniques can be applied to each partner's horoscope as well as to the composite chart. Astrologically, we are always moving between each partner's individual and collective experience, their separateness and their involvement in a partnership. When considering relationship we are faced with stories and images of two individuals from two different family backgrounds and life events. The time before they met is invested with memories, emotions, traumas, opinions, sentiments and experiences which may infiltrate the present and future of the relationship. The past that each one brings into the relationship is highly subjective and personal and often unknown to the other, yet this history influences the present-day relationship and will be there in their own transitions.

Astrology is also a remarkable self-help tool for reflecting upon timing in our own intimate relationships and friendships. My experience is that couples take advantage of astrology at decisive moments in their relationship: either at the beginning, when the relationship is forming and there are questions about compatibility and commitment, or when there is a significant turning point in their relationship, whether due to a change of employment, birth of a child, an affair, exposure of a secret, illness, etc., or when the couple is considering a separation.

Attachment through Time

In *The Family Legacy* we looked at Mary Ainsworth and John Bowlby's attachment theories based on the premise that feelings of emotional security led to a stronger capacity to explore relationships beyond the family.[139] While original attachment theory focused on early childhood, it was also proposed that attachment was a natural human experience throughout the life cycle. By the later quarter of the twentieth century, research began to focus on attachment in adulthood by examining the bond that develops over time between adults in emotionally intimate relationships.[140]

The emotional connection between intimate adults is similar to the bond between a child and their caregiver. Parallels indicated that feeling emotionally secure and safe when in the proximity of the other, establishing affection and body contact, and sharing play and mutual language all created attachment. What develops over time in adult relationships is akin to early attachment: first physical attention and care, feelings of safety when nearby, responsiveness, sharing and discovery. In adult intimacy, sexual closeness peaks at the beginning of the relationship but over time caregiving and attachment develop and become stronger. Similar to infant attachment, there are different approaches to adult relating that are recognizable, such as feeling secure, anxious, ambivalent, disconnected or self-reliant. All styles of attachment shape the ability to balance separateness with commitment in relationship.

Astrologically we can identify all the inner planets at work in developing adult attachment. First and foremost is the Moon, as it underpins the sense of safety, feeling loved and cared for. It is the foundation for the primary sense of feeling loved. From this secure base the archetype of Venus can develop in adolescence and adulthood. Before fundamental security is cultivated in an adult relationship, the sense of physical attraction and discovery, affection and body contact, is often more obvious. Desirability and magnetism bring the archetypes of Venus and Mars to the fore. Aspects to Venus and Mars are significant when reflecting on the early stages of adult connection and the capacity for attachment. Mercury also plays his role sometimes in recreating the partners' 'baby talk', but more in establishing relational communication and language. The Sun develops individual confidence. Self-expression and identity through relating grow with the partner's fostering, support and encouragement. As with infant attachment, adult attachment encourages individuation. But by adulthood all the inner planets are more established, recognized and acknowledged; therefore they play a large role in adult attachment.

Attachment between adults develops over time. Attraction, desire and longing may be immediate, but attachment is nurtured and worked upon. It matures through the challenges and hard times that the couple face during the construction of their relationship. It is tested as the couple reaches a crossroads in their relationship. And it is strengthened through openness, sincerity and trust over time. An astrological chart comparison brings the assets and liabilities of the couple to light, but it is the passing of time that reveals their trials and setbacks. How the partners manage to work together through these times reinforces the core of the relationship and their attachment. With the development of each partner's sense of security and caretaking in the relationship, the composite Moon is secured. It is during these critical times that the composite chart is often most insightful because it is a symbol of the soul of the relationship. The composite aspects remind the couple of the inherent composition of their relationship and encourage consciousness of acceptance in their relationship and its continuing evolution.

Cycles and Relationship
There are two distinct ways to consider astrological timing in relationships. One is from the perspective of the individual, looking at the transits and progressions to each partner's horoscope. The other is from the view of the relationship, looking at the transits to the composite chart as well as combining the progressed planets. Let's begin by considering the individual charts in the context of times and timing within relationship.

Each partner enters the relationship at a certain point in their life cycle. If the partners are close in age, they have crossed the threshold of their relationship at a similar time and will experience the same planetary cycles throughout their life together. For instance, Prince William and Kate Middleton were born six months apart and share most of the social and outer planets' positions. In fact, all the planets from Mars outwards are close, as tabled below. Therefore their composite chart will also reflect these shared positions. As they journey through their lives individually and as a couple, they will experience the same planetary life cycles within a similar timeframe.

Planet	Kate	William	Comments
♂	10♎21	9♎12	Mars went R from 20 February 1982 to 11 May 1982; hence Kate and William have Mars in Libra conjunct, even though they were born six months apart
♃	7♏14	0♏29℞	In the six months between their births the planets have turned direction; therefore, where one has the planet direct, the other may have the planet retrograde. The exception is Saturn which each has direct. Saturn turned direct two days before William was born. The planets are in close proximity and will also be repeated in the composite chart
♄	21♎49	15♎30	
⚷	18♉03℞	25♉16	
♅	3♐06	1♐29℞	
♆	25♐27	25♐32℞	
♇	26♎48	24♎29℞	
☊	22♋26	13♋19	They share the nodal axis; each was born in the eclipse season

Generation Gaps and Age Differences
William's parents came from very different age groups. His father was over twelve years older than his mother and each had the social and outer planets in different signs, signalling their citizenship of different generations. Growing up in different times suggests unconnected memories of current affairs and global events, dissimilar peer groups, exposure to different fashions, music and social trends, perhaps diverse political and economic views or independent values in a social context.

	Charles	Diana	Composite	
♃	29♐53	5♒05℞	17♑29	Charles was 12 years and 7 and a half months older than Diana. She had just turned 20 when she married, while Charles was 32. Charles had his Saturn return two years previously; by the time Diana would have her first Saturn return, Charles would be 41 in the throes of midlife, experiencing his Pluto square Pluto and Neptune square Neptune
♄	5♍16	27♑48℞	16♏32	
⚷	28♏13	6♓28℞	17♑20	
♅	29♊55℞	23♌20	26♋37	
♆	14♎07	8♏38℞	26♎17	
♇	16♌33	6♍02	26♌18	
☊	4♉57	28♌10	1♋34	

As the table above shows, Charles and Diana will experience the initiations of the life cycle at very different times. Their composite chart's generic cycles have not yet happened for Diana, suggesting the relationship challenges her to respond and act beyond her experience. For instance, when they were married Charles had already experienced his Saturn return. Diana would experience her Saturn return 9½ years later, while the composite chart would have its Saturn return three years later. When Diana was experiencing her exact Saturn return, Charles was experiencing his exact Neptune square. This was in early 1991. Charles had already experienced his Uranus opposition and would experience transiting Pluto square to his natal Pluto later that year. By this time rumours of their marriage difficulties abounded, yet the details of their affairs had not yet emerged. No doubt this lack of synchrony in their individual life cycle development would be a stressor to the relationship; however, the management of this crisis is in the hands of the couple at the crossroads. The balance between each partner's individual freedoms and relationship needs, as well as the strength of their attachment, are decisive factors in how the crisis is handled.

I find it helpful to consider the life cycle stages indicated by the placement of the outer planets in the context of each individual. While one partner might be in a difficult life transition such as the Pluto square Pluto, the other may be in a completely different life segment, like a Jupiter opposition. It is significant to note the timing of these different life cycle stages, especially when there is an age difference, since life goals, experiences and interests may vary widely at times. Roles may also shift due to the demands of the life stage and its accompanying circumstances such as the birth of children, creative and educational pursuits, career changes, retirement, illness, etc.

Cycles of Synchrony

I am always on the lookout to see if one partner's cycles are brought into alignment with the others. For instance, I have often seen this occur with the progressed Moon. Even though couples may have a difficult aspect between their natal Moons, this is mitigated by their progressed Moons. For instance, many couples whose natal Moons are conflicting may have them conjunct or trine by progression.

We have already witnessed Diana and Charles's progressed Moons forming a trine.

This is the case in Grace and Prince Rainier's progressed horoscopes. As noted, Rainier's time of birth is not verified, but at noon on the day of his birth the Moon would be 26♐06, hence his Moon would be within approximately 6° either side. Grace's Moon was 21♓50 and potentially squared Rainier's Moon. Her progressed Moon on the day they met was 28♒47 while Rainier's, using the noon time, was 27♒49, bringing their progressed Moons into alignment. Due to the nature of the progressed Moon's movement of about 1° a month, the synchronization of the partners' progressed Moons will remain close during their relationship, moving in and out of this progressed alignment. Even being in the same sign at the same time suggests the capacity to understand the emotional landscape of each other and the relationship.

Another interesting consideration is each partner's solar return chart. Year after year there are continuous cycles embedded in solar return horoscopes, such as the eight-year pattern of Venus and the nineteen-year pattern of the Moon.[141] Due to the nineteen-year cyclical pattern of the Moon, the partners' solar return Moons may synchronize. This is the case in Diana and Charles's solar return charts. Note below how their Moons synchronized in the solar return charts year after year.

Year of Solar Return	Diana's Moon in Solar Return	Charles's Moon in Solar Return
1988	29♑48	22♑48
1989	18♊13	14♊42
1990	0♏18	26♎55
1991	3♓24	0♓22
1992	20♋06	14♋14
1993	8♐55	4♐36
1994	19♈57	17♈07
1995	23♌48	20♌09
1996	10♑38	5♑49
1997	29♉58	24♉50

In their natal charts, Diana's Moon is on the South Node while Charles's Moon is on the North Node in the challenging square between the signs Aquarius and Taurus. The synchrony of their solar return Moons at least for 7½ months each year might temper the natal variance. It is not a pattern that I encounter often, but when I do I honour the partners' emotional complexity and involvement by paying more attention to the lunar archetype on all levels of their relationship. This is not a technique, but one of the numerous ways that astrological imagery can reveal patterns we are asked to consider and reflect upon.

Because there will be so much information and detail generated, I am alert for imagery that repeats similar themes and patterns. It is important to think outside the box when analysing this amount of information. While there are priorities when assessing time techniques, it is also important to be mindful of recurring images that confirm the patterns emerging from your analysis. In this way you begin to develop your own unique approach.

Individual Times and Cycles

Each individual's chart will record different transits and progressions during a similar period. This is important to note in terms of the individual's experiences, which may affect the partnership. Each partner lives through their own transits and transitions during the course of their relationship. When there are interaspects between the couple then the transit will affect both horoscopes but the transits will still be personal and individual. When in a relationship, all personal transits will have some bearing on the relationship itself. Having an image and name for the experience is often very helpful for the partner, who may then be more able to witness the transition rather than feel responsible or drawn into it.

For instance, starting in late 1983 and throughout 1984 Prince Charles experienced Pluto transiting his Moon. His son Harry was conceived and born during this time.[142] It is a powerful transit for a man in reshaping his relationship with his inner and outer feminine figures. We can imagine it would have an impact on his relationship with both his mother and his wife, even his perception of his wife's relationship with his mother. His wife Diana could become the living embodiment of his own Plutonic dynamics and become drawn into displaying the turbulent and darker feelings that might be stirring in Charles's feeling life. How Charles experiences the transit will make an impact upon the safety and continuity of the relationship. For Diana it may also exacerbate any of her own private feelings at the time. With the naming of the transit and the awareness of the change, Charles's transformation has a greater possibility of being honoured and understood, not just in the context of his intense feelings, but in its impact on his partner and the relationship.

Secondary Progressions

When considering the secondary progressions there could be significant developments which are very important to one partner's maturity, yet challenging to the other partner who may be in another phase of development. Therefore it is useful to compare the progressed charts to see if there might be developing dissimilarities. Let's contemplate some major scenarios:

- The Progressed Moon. We have already considered the progressed Moon by sign and whether it is compatible with the partner's progressed Moon. The progressed Moon's house position is also important, as this suggests an emotionally sensitive area of life that may preoccupy our thoughts and feelings for the next 2–2½ years. As an environment that demands more focus and attention, how might this impact the relationship? For instance, if one partner's Moon is in the 12th while the other's is in the 7th house, feelings of isolation or the need for retreat might feel at odds with their partner's urge for contact and connection. Assessing each partner's progressed Moon and its emotional and psychological phase symbolizes moods and life rhythms in the context of their relationship.

- The Progressed Sun. Take note of the progressed Sun's degree and sign for each partner. Are their progressed Suns in aspect with each other? If so, this will last throughout their relationship, as the progressed Sun moves fairly evenly between 57' and 61' a year.[143] The progressed Sun symbolizes the evolving identity, but is each partner's self-development progressing in the same direction? Diana and Charles both have their natal Suns in Water. But Charles, being twelve years older, had his progressed Sun move into Fire by the time Diana was born and their progressed Suns remained in signs quincunx to one another throughout their relationship.

- The Progressed Lunation Cycle. What is the progressed lunation phase of each partner? This is important to contemplate as each partner may be undergoing a different chapter in their life; a partner experiencing the Full Moon phase will feel very different from a partner who may be experiencing their Balsamic phase. As we see below, Charles and Diana's progressed phases do not synchronize well. When Charles is in the last phase of the cycle, Diana is disseminating and when Diana is in the waning Last Quarter phase of the cycle, Charles is beginning a new one. While each partner is moving through the same period of time, they are identified with different concerns and goals, orientated in an opposing direction.

- Planets changing direction or signs. When a planet changes direction by secondary progression the natural appearance of the archetypal energy slowly begins to shift. While the issues and concerns associated with the planet are the same, their development and expression are being felt and sensed in a different way. This might feel unsettling to a partner. Similarly, when one of the inner planets, especially the Sun, Mercury, Venus or Mars, changes signs by secondary progression the individual's field of experience begins to broaden in perspective of that archetype. Therefore, if any of these progressions are current or about to happen, it is always worthwhile bringing these images to light for the partners to contemplate.

What follows is a snapshot of Charles and Diana's progressions at four different times in their lives. The first time is the progression of Charles's Sun and Moon to the day of Diana's birth. I always find it of interest to progress the older partner's horoscope to the day when the younger was born. Here we see the first dynamic of the Sun and Moon in their progressed charts. In this case we see the progressed Suns moving through signs that are quincunx one another while the progressed Moons are in trine to one another. I am also looking to see if any other inner planets or angles are making major aspects to the other's horoscope. But what I find most helpful is the dynamic interplay of each one's phase of the progressed lunation cycle. I find it helpful to have a discussion on the parallels and dissimilarities of the phases the couple are moving through.

Prog. Date	Charles P ☉	Diana P ☉	Charles P ☽	Diana P ☽	Charles Prog. Lunation Phase	Diana Prog. Lunation Phase
Diana's Birth 1 July 1961	5♐10	9♋39	22♎54	25♒02	Balsamic	Disseminating
Marriage 29 July 1981	25♐34	28♋48	11♋07	9♏22	Full Moon	First Quarter
Divorce 28 August 1996	10♑56	13♌14	7♒14	12♊21	New	Last Quarter
Diana's Death 31 August 1997	11♑58	14♌11	19♒35	24♊49	New	Last Quarter

Since the major transits to each individual's chart are heralds of change and evolution, all significant transits are important to consider in context of the impact that the individual's transition will have upon the relationship. However, in terms of relationship themes, it is important to take note of key transits and progressions to relationship zones and other planetary significations of relationship.

Across the Ascendant–Descendant Axis
In terms of adult relationships, transits to the Ascendant–Descendant axis are consistent with relationship themes. Transits to the Ascendant are more focused on changes in the self or self-image, yet it is these changes that are often evident in relationship. For instance, the transit of Neptune to Diana's Ascendant in the year before her engagement, or Saturn crossing Angelina's Ascendant mid 2005 just as she and Brad begin to come out about their

relationship, are astrological examples of personal transitions in the context of a developing relationship. I have often experienced the slower moving planets across the Ascendant as emergent aspects of the self that become visible through relationship. For instance, as Uranus transits the Ascendant it symbolizes a turnaround: what emerges is something unexpected or unlived. Henry Miller was experiencing Uranus transiting his Ascendant when serendipitously he was introduced to Anaïs Nin. A disowned aspect of the self materializes. I have seen singles, who say they would never marry, get engaged as Uranus transits the Ascendant. Uranus presents us with the path we have not walked down.

Transits across the Descendant and into the 7th house are indicative of changes occurring in the individual's attitudes towards relationship. For instance, if Saturn crosses into the 7th house, new structures, contracts and commitments in relationship may be necessary. As a planet of restructuring, it suggests that the relationship needs reorganization and a new framework. It does not necessarily signal an ending of the relationship, but perhaps an ending of the way the individual has been in the relationship. For approximately 2½ years Saturn will move through the 7th house and then travel into the 8th. This will be the time when the relationship is tested for its emotional strength and honesty. For those in a new relationship this might suggest the time for consolidation and commitment, a planning phase for anchoring the relationship. For those not in a relationship, this could suggest coming to terms with their sense of aloneness or a commitment to the self to be more dedicated to the possibility of relating. Saturn transiting the 7th opens the door to a new arrangement and composition in relationship.

Uranus takes approximately seven years to go through the 7th house and signals new forms of independence in relating. It makes its greatest impact during the time it transits the Descendant and for the following year. Uranus is separation; it signals a disconnection from the patterns and models of relationship that are no longer supportive. Separation does not suggest breaking up, but it does imply relinquishing worn-out patterns and practices in the relationship. For a couple unable to resolve their differences or stuck in a disappointing cycle, the Uranus transit may indicate the time when the relationship shatters. For an individual not in relationship this might signal an unexpected encounter or an exciting or life-altering event that leads to the possibility of relationship. Underpinning the transit is a separation from what is no longer viable towards a reconnection with what is erotic and life-enhancing. Uranus's transition is an ongoing balancing act of separateness with partnership.

Neptune takes approximately fourteen years to transit the 7th house and during this time the ideals, dreams and fantasies of relationships are tested. By transit, Pluto too is in this house for a long period, focusing on the transforming and repairing of relationship patterns, intimacy issues and trust. While these planets are in the relationship sector for a long period of time, it is the transit across the Descendant that is the most likely time when these archetypes manifest in the context of altering the relational patterns. Both are potent images of initiation in relationship and are potentially life-altering and transforming. In both cases, relationship becomes the vehicle that brings the individual into a deeper relationship to their inner self: Neptune offers the experimentation with creativity and spirituality while Pluto evokes the descent into the self. Relationship becomes the agent of immersion and therapeutic change.

Transits through the 7th house eventually cross into the 8th. This period of our lives is focused on others and our patterns of relating. Whether we are in a committed relationship or not, they speak about the deep changes in our understanding of relationships, our patterns with others and our intentions in and expectations of relationships. Jupiter and Saturn transits through the 8th are more perceptible than those of the outer planets; nonetheless, the transits of the outer planets into the 8th house are worthy of examination.

The Moon's progression through the 7th and 8th houses is also important to note. Since the progressed Moon is the barometer of our feeling life and the heart of our emotional presence and security, its passage through the 7th marks a time of focus on the authenticity of feeling involved, secure and loved in the relationship. It is a time of sensitivity to the other and suggests the need to be emotionally present on a level that nurtures and feeds the soul. It seeks to feel loved in a way that brings emotional security and satisfaction. If this is not present there is an awareness of the need to change the habits and ritual of the relationship. If the individual is single there is a growing need to feel involved with others and the individual's psychological awareness is focused on developing their capacity to relate.

The progressed Moon through the 8th house brings the deeper feelings of loss and grief to the surface. It is a time of many endings. Without a deeper and more intimate connection in relationship, the individual feels as if they are in the closing stages of their emotional bond. Something is dying at a deep level. It is a time of mastery and confrontation with one's deeper feelings, often accompanied by aloneness, loss and grief. However, this progression is soulful and full of meaning, as it evokes soul-searching and honesty in relationship. The deeper sense of betrayal and lack of trust is being worked through. Whether in a relationship or not, an individual's attachment style and relational patterns will become perceptible through this period of deep therapeutic change.

Transits to Venus and Mars

Of course we will be very interested in transits to Venus and Mars in the context of transition and developments in the sphere of relationship and desire. We have already mentioned that Bonnie, a client early in my career, met the love of her life as Neptune was transiting her Venus. Princess Grace had transiting Neptune conjoin her Venus synchronous to becoming engaged to Prince Rainier. Angelina Jolie had transiting Saturn conjunct her Venus as she consolidated her relationship with Brad, while Diana had Uranus opposite her Venus in the year before she and Charles were married. In that year Charles had transiting Neptune conjunct his Mars. Ironically, in the year before Charles was married to Camilla transiting Pluto was conjunct his Mars. His son William had Saturn transit his Mars in the year before his wedding. No doubt transits to these archetypes awaken the erotic quality of relationship.

Transits to Venus and Mars impact the way an individual understands their inner values and desires, which has a bearing on their status in relationship. Each transit will find its own unique expression in an individual's life. The slower-moving transits to Venus reveal alterations to an individual's perception of their worth and personal values. In turn this will be reflected in the outer world through relational changes. Transits to Mars suggest the modification of goals and desires and what the individual goes after and chooses. Mars is action-orientated, risk-taking and explorative, and the slower-moving transits motivate the individual to pursue their desires and take risks in relating. Individually we need to assess these transits in the context of the whole chart and the individual's life stage and circumstances.

Transits of Venus and Mars

The transits of Venus and Mars move relatively fast; therefore, their influence on timing is more fleeting. However, there are some exceptions. The transits of Venus or Mars may act as a trigger to the larger cycles that are already operating. This is especially so when the outer planet is reflected by the transit of an inner planet in a similar combination. For instance, a Uranus transit to natal Mars can last about fifteen months using a 1° orb. However, within this time frame, transiting Mars will also aspect natal Uranus. Here we have the transiting combination both ways and this could be helpful for recognizing when the larger pattern may be revealed.

I am aware too of the Venus retrograde period every nineteen months as well as the Mars retrograde period approximately every two years. By transit their effect during these times is extended. I take note of the area of the chart that the transit impacts as it is this area where relational experience may be turning around. I am cognizant of any planets that will be aspected, mainly by conjunction or opposition, three times during the retrograde phase.

An early client taught me to be aware of the fast-moving transits of Venus and Mars. When Ben first came for a consultation, he was enormously animated at having just met someone who was not only attractive, passionate and exciting, but whom he was sure would become his long-term partner. They had only met the week before. There were no major transits that to me would indicate the preparation for a long-term partnership, but transiting Mars was opposite natal Venus and transiting Venus was conjunct Uranus. Certainly those were exciting transits. When I saw Ben three months later we concentrated on his work issues. He never mentioned relationship. When I picked up the threads from our last consultation, he did not say much except that the relationship did not last, and that it was not for him. It seemed to end as quickly as it began. I learnt to be alert for longer-term relational images to back up the Venus and Mars transits.

Other Considerations

We develop our own way to assess the transits and progressions in terms of relationship but I am also alert to transits to the Vertex–Anti-Vertex axis as well as the nodal axis. As discussed, these angles symbolize meeting points, so transits to these angles often synchronize with the entry or exit of significant others in our lives. These points are like portals exposing crossroads where significant encounters may occur. Whether they are partners, rivals, friends or adversaries, they meet us at the crossroads and often contribute appreciably to our course in life.

Transits to the luminaries and Mercury are also important to note. As the Sun, Moon and Mercury are vital to ego development, transits to them provide us with opportunities for growth, maturity and consciousness. Therefore, as we become more individuated the possibility of relationship also increases. While transits to these planets may not speak directly about adult relationship, they concern authentic and independent growth which is often mirrored through relational exchange.

Now let's turn to the second way of reflecting on relationship timing by considering how the composite chart is influenced through time.

Composite Timing and Relationship

The Davison relationship chart exists in time and space; therefore it can be progressed. Transits to this chart represent aspects to planets and points situated in a matrix of time and space. The composite chart is derivative of the partners' natal charts, assembled together; therefore it is not bound by time and space. Timing involving the composite chart is qualitative and symbolic, and I am more inclined to imagine the transits to this chart as initiatory images rather than literal events.

Transits to the Composite Chart

Using transits to composite charts can be an effective timing technique. Since the planets in the composite chart have been created by midpoints, the transits to these planets bring the combined energy of the couple to life. As the couple settles into their relationship, the composite chart becomes more embodied. The imagery of the current transits might come to life more than they did at the beginning of their time together. Transits to the more difficult or energetic parts of the horoscope bring issues to consciousness, of which the couple may have previously been unaware.

Again, it is the slower-moving transits that are of most significance. Jupiter and Saturn symbolize the social changes and challenges for the couple. They mark communal time in the couple's life as well as the natural transitions in the development of the relationship. In terms of the direction of the relationship, transits to any of the four composite angles are highly significant. These demonstrate directional changes in the course of the relationship.

Transits to the inner planets speak about changes to the core of the relationship; for instance, transits to the Sun evoke the themes of confidence and recognition as a couple or being identified as 'We' such as we are, rather than I am. Transits to the composite Moon bring security and care to consciousness, issues that will be reflected through living conditions and rituals, the home and family, as well as domesticity and nurturing. Mercury's focus is on the voice of the relationship; therefore transits to this composite planet will highlight the communication style of the couple and their connections and affiliations. Transits to composite Venus focus on the resources, assets and values of the relationship and may bring the issues of affection, sharing, love and money to the attention of the couple. Mars is desire; therefore, we might imagine transits to this composite archetype involving the couple's longings and aspirations, their sexuality, energy and the way they resolve conflict as well as their ability to strive together towards common goals.

As there is so much information gleaned from the individual's transits and progressions, I generally focus more on the 4th harmonic aspects by transit: the conjunction, opposition and square. The transiting conjunction has the highest priority, the opposition and squares are secondary. Below is a way of thinking about transits to the composite chart. However, since these scenarios are generalized, they could also be applied to transits to the Davison chart.

Jupiter transits might signify journeying together, whether that is a physical or spiritual voyage. It marks periods of growth and movement forward, the impact of new beliefs, ideologies and information on the couple. It would also relate to their experience of expansion and freedom in the relationship. When Jupiter transits are highlighted, this marks the time when the ideals of the relationship are challenged to grow, the horizon of the couple's future is under development and a new faith and optimism is needed for the next phase of their life together.

Saturn, on the other hand, points to consolidation and structure in the development of the relationship. Perhaps this is the right time for a long-range plan for the couple, the time to take responsibility for its future direction or the time for commitment and accountability. Saturn transiting the composite chart is akin to the maturation process of the relationship. As the harvester, Saturn brings the consequences of past actions, but it also carries the report card of what is lacking so the next cycle can incorporate this growth. Saturn signifies an ending or a door closing, often the end of a particular chapter of life together. This needs to be acknowledged, but with every ending a new chapter requiring maturity and confidence in the future opens. Saturn prefers stability and certainty; this does not come through control or rigidity but through dedication and hard work, accountability and sensibility. Whatever planet or part of the chart Saturn is transiting is the key to what needs strengthening and structuring.

Transiting Chiron and the outer planets represent atmospheric changes that the couple may be unprepared for. The transiting nature of these planets is to bring the unresolved past into the present, the unknown into consciousness and what we deny into the open. From the ego's perspective this is quite fearful, yet from the perspective of the soul this is liberating and welcomed. Therefore, if we consider what the soul of the relationship is seeking through the changes mirrored by the transits we might be better able to put these changes into the context of the evolution of the natural relationship. These transits do not need to be judged nor feared, but accepted as initiatory developments in the ongoing life of the relationship.

Chiron by transit reveals the times when feelings of despondency or complaint might challenge the relationship. This might be due to a setback suffered by the couple or the pain of daily living becoming too difficult to bear. Perhaps something did not work out in the way the couple intended, or sadness permeated a difficult period or maybe there is heartbreak from facing loss that affects the relationship. In Chiron's realm, suffering is situated alongside healing and in his cave we develop the profound respect for the uncertainties of life. When Chiron's transit to the composite chart is highlighted, there may be an episode of pain, but there is also a period of acceptance. It is an important transition during which the couple have the opportunity of pulling together, even though they feel the times are pulling them apart.

By nature the transits of Uranus awaken and enliven; however, a separation or distancing from old patterns and ways of being is usually needed for the process to be successful. Uranus calls for change and movement, and by nature catches the relationship by surprise. Astrologers always suggest 'expect the unexpected' with Uranus. Once the nature of the crisis reveals itself, the couple needs to work consciously towards the required change. It may be a period of restlessness, which can be exciting or anxiety-provoking. Things are changing, moving fast towards the creation of more freedom and opportunity in the relationship. The planet affected by Uranus's transit is the energy that wants to awake to new possibilities in the relationship; therefore, the couple would be wise to find new avenues of expression and creativity for this energy. It is important to recognize that Uranus seeks to be disengaged from the past; therefore, being mindful of moving forward needs to accompany this time.

Neptune conjures up illusions, glamour and visions. When the transit is emphasized, it is important to acknowledge that all may not be as it seems during this period. At this time there could be a tendency to idealize or spiritualize any difficulties to defend against negative feelings or disappointments. However, every relationship will experience the cycle of highs and lows, expectations and disappointments, as well as closeness and separation. When things are not working, it does not mean that the whole relationship is wrong. But under Neptune transits this often feels so. On the other hand this is also the time to dream, not as a means of escaping the difficulty or the past, but as a means of invoking the future. Under Neptune transits, the relationship is shifting from one way of being to another; therefore a vision statement is needed. The couple might feel that what kept them together is shifting, disappearing or dissolving. There is movement, but it is not yet known, not even imagined; therefore, what is called for is faith and vision, not fantasy and deception. When the force of the transit passes, the couple find themselves in places they never knew were possible. What is necessary during the period is that the relationship allows the process to take place, supported by the strength of their union.

Inherent in Pluto transits is the cyclical nature of relinquishment and renewal. Pluto points to what needs to be released for new energy to be available. Its process is the lived experience of endings; therefore, it suggests where closure is necessary to ensure the renewal of this feature of the relationship. Pluto encourages integrity and honesty, focusing on whichever part of the relationship needs to be more transparent and out in the open, even though it feels vulnerable or shameful. By transit it confronts the partners to be more trusting and intimate. This generally occurs during difficult passages when truth and integrity are the only allies that can create the necessary changes. Pluto's transit to the Composite chart portrays the human inevitability of change and loss, but also encourages partners to use their deepest resources of love, trust and integrity to confront the necessary process to move forward with greater strength and resolve.

It is also important to recognize the transits of the lunar nodes as well as the accompanying eclipses. The house position being transited by the North Node indicates the area where the relationship can develop over the next eighteen months. The opposite house, where the South Node is transiting, becomes the area where embedded resources need to be liberated in order to encourage developments at the North Node. The transits of the nodes point to aligning the material and spiritual dynamics of the partnership.

Due to the averaging of the couple's outer planets, the transits might show specific generational passages that one individual may have already experienced while the other may not. This transit is significant to the relationship as it addresses both the age difference as well as an important transition for the couple. What is necessary to note is how each partner, from their perspective of time, understands the nature of the transition.

For instance, the composite Uranus for Angelina and Brad is 4♎26. Uranus opposed this position in June 2011 for the first time. In a natal chart this transit generally occurs between the ages of thirty-eight and forty-two, depending on the speed of Uranus in the first half of its cycle. At this time Angelina was thirty-six, several years before this transit would occur for her personally. Brad was forty-seven, having experienced the transit personally in 2005–6, as he divorced and began his relationship with Angelina. The qualitative timing in the composite chart suggests that the relationship is undergoing a shift and there needs to be more room, separateness and space. For Brad this experience might have had resonant or familiar tones, whereas for Angelina she had not yet had this experience to draw upon.

My experience is that the composite chart is responsive to transits and has been valuable in amplifying and exploring important themes for couples at the crossroads. Like individuals, relationships grow over time. Through honouring and participating with the energies of the transition a more secure and stable base for the relationship is cultivated.

The Composite Progressed Chart
As noted previously we can progress the Davison chart; however, we cannot progress a composite chart as it does not represent a moment in time. But we can use a technique known as the composite progressed chart, which uses the midpoints of each partner's progressions at the same date. And again, as with a natal composite chart, there will be anomalies.

This technique can be fairly cumbersome at first due to the amount of data available; however, I do find that the composite progressed Sun, Moon and their lunation phase are always worthy of note. Therefore, I routinely calculate the composite progressed Sun and Moon and reference their positions back to the composite chart. I am alert for any progressions of note, especially the other inner planets. I have often seen that those progressions reveal the development of archetypal themes in the relationship, symbols of interest and importance for the couple. If we imagine that progressions are soul portraits then any stand-outs or strong progressed statements will signify creative, poignant and emotional times and themes worth considering.

Let's return to Virginia and Vita, whose natal charts were introduced in Chapter 11. They met on 14 December 1922 but did not become intimately involved until three years later. Before their romance blossomed, they shared a mutual love of writing. Virginia had a small publishing press and offered to bring out one of Vita's novels. These images are reflective of the composite Moon in Gemini in the 3rd house and the rulership of Jupiter, situated in the 1st house, of the composite Ascendant and MC. Note the composite Sun and Mercury conjunct the North Node and Mercury's square to the Moon, which it disposits. The last minutes of mutable signs on the angles of the composite horoscope seem to say that a new season is about to emerge on all relationship fronts, as all the angles will progress to 0° of a cardinal sign, with Aries being on the Ascendant.

To create the composite progressed chart we progress each horoscope to 14 December 1922. From these two charts, a new composite chart can be created, which is the composite progressed horoscope. The progressions are contemplated in the context of the evolution of their relationship. But since this composite progressed chart is timed to their meeting, it could also be considered in light of the possible themes that may emerge throughout the course of their relationship. We might ponder what brings them together,

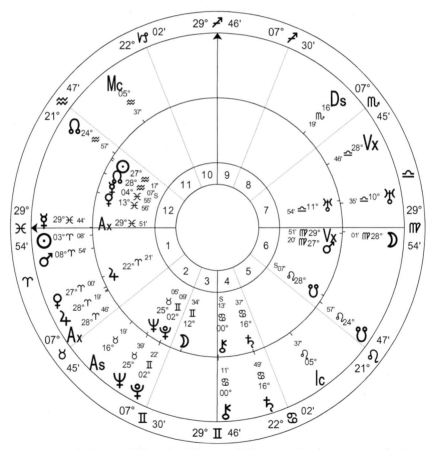

Bi Wheel: Inner Wheel – *Vita and Virginia's composite chart;*
Outer Wheel – *Vita and Virginia's composite progressed chart to first meeting on 14 December 1922*

which motifs are prominent and what indications there may be for attachment. Below is a biwheel with Virginia Woolf and Vita Sackville-West's composite chart midpoints on the inner wheel and the composite progressed horoscope at 14 December 1922 on the outer wheel.

What is immediately noticeable is that Mercury has progressed to the Ascendant opposite the progressed Moon that is about to conjoin the Descendant and enter the 7th house. The composite progressed Moon is also conjunct natal Mars and the Vertex. The progressed Vertex is opposite progressed Jupiter, making it conjunct the progressed Anti-Vertex. This highlights the progressed archetypes of the Moon, Mercury and Jupiter in the composite progressed chart. Progressed Venus is also on the progressed Anti-Vertex alongside progressed Jupiter. It is making a quincunx to the natal Mars; therefore the progressed Moon and Venus are quincunx each other, bringing this powerful progressed aspect into alignment with natal Mars. Staying with these images we begin to weave these archetypal threads through the fabric of Virginia and Vita's relationship.

Being conjunct the Ascendant, progressed Mercury symbolizes an essential and soulful component of their relationship that has come into focus at this time. Aligned with the Ascendant, the Mercurial archetype is coming out of the 12th house into a more visible place, able to be seen by themselves and others through their writing, letters and commentary. Throughout their relationship they were both writers who corresponded intimately with each other.[144] They met when each one's progressed Mercury was changing direction: Virginia's natal Mercury went retrograde by progression when she was nineteen and stationed direct at age forty-one, a year after she met Vita, while Vita's natal Mercury was stationing going retrograde in her progressed chart at that time of meeting. Virginia died on 28 March 1941. Throughout the time that Vita knew Virginia, her progressed Mercury was retrograde.

	Natal Mercury	Prog. Mercury 14 Dec 1922	Prog. Mercury 1 Jan 1928	Prog. Mercury 1 Jan 1934	Prog. Mercury 28 Mar 1941
Vita	21♓48	4♉29S	3♉25R	29♈48R	25♈22R
Virginia	18♒03	24♒59R	26♒10	0♓11	7♓36
Composite	4♓55	29♓44	29♓48	0♈00	1♈29

These mutual Mercury stations are highly significant as they symbolize a turning point in the way each one composes the record of their lives. And since each partner's Mercury is stationing and moving in opposite directions, the composite Mercury will also be slow-moving, lingering on their composite Ascendant of 29♓54 for well over a decade, as shown in the table. The symbol is a profound indicator of the face of their relationship being shaped by their mutual love of letters and writing. One of Woolf's famous novels, *Orlando*, was born out of her relationship with Vita.

The progressed Moon is not only opposite the progressed Mercury, but it conjoins the composite Descendant and Vertex. It is about to enter the relationship sector of the 7th house where it will remain for three years. During this time Vita and Virginia became acquaintances and developed their friendship. As the Moon progressed through the last degrees of the 7th house and into the 8th house of the composite chart their relationship became sexual, intense and intimate. Synchronously, the composite progressed Moon was in the 8th house for the period that they remained sexually intimate. When their sexual love came to an end, their attachment was strong enough to survive the ending of their love affair and they remained friends until Virginia's death. Each woman had Jupiter as the ruler of the 11th house.

At this time of meeting, progressed Jupiter was at 28♈19 opposite the progressed Vertex at 28♎46. The ruler of the Vertex is Venus which is progressed nearby at 27♈00. This speaks of the crossroads at the time in their development of beliefs, values and ideals. Also of interest is that Vita's natal Venus is intertwined with this, being at 28♈48, while Virginia's natal Moon is 25♈19, as follows:

Virgina	Vita	Composite	Comment
☽25♈19 □ ♀29♑04	☽29♋49 □ ♀28♈48	☽12♊34 □ ♀13♓56	Virginia and Vita share a Moon–Venus square which is recreated in their composite chart. Natally these planets form interaspects as Virginia's Moon is conjunct Vita's Venus, while Vita's Moon is opposite Virginia's Venus. When they met their composite progressed Venus was at 27♈00
♂27♊23℞	♂27♐17	♂27♍20	Mars is opposite in the natal charts and its composite position is conjunct the two angles of the Descendant and Vertex

The shared cardinal Moon–Venus square is potentially a strong psychic connection. This is carried forward into their relationship through the similar symbol in their composite chart, now blended with different qualities, yet the archetypal composition remains the same. Composite progressed Venus amidst the natal placements is illustrative of the feminine values and personal fondness that is potentially ready to be valued in their relationship.

As we saw previously, Virginia's and Vita's Mars are exactly opposite. The composite Mars is conjunct the Descendant and the Vertex, and when they met the progressed Moon was conjunct Mars. Having their natal Mars opposite each other, as well as Mars being angular in the composite chart, conjures images of passion and desire. The composite progression of the Moon to the composite Mars suggests that a felt experience of this becomes imprinted upon the relationship, while the images of natal and composite Venus and Mars in contact with the Moon and progressed Moon document the potentiality of attachment.

Given so much information I am inclined to stick to the astrological images that speak to the nature of adult attachment, such as Venus and Mars, the 7th and 8th houses, etc., as well as the Moon and inner planets. However, I am also mindful of other zodiacal alignments that are prominent. For instance, in Virginia's natal chart the Sun is at 5♒29 conjunct the MC at 5♒54, squaring Saturn at 5♉52. The composite progressed MC when she met Vita was at 5♒37, aligning her natal MC with the composite progressed

MC at the time of meeting. I am not inclined to interpret this image but rather hold it as a powerful symbol of synchrony and connection.

In a similar way I note that in Vita's progressed horoscope on the day she met Virginia, the progressed Moon and the progressed Descendant were conjunct, echoing the composite progressed Moon on the composite Descendant. Serendipitously, Vita's progressed Moon and progressed Descendant were both opposite the composite Venus. Again, rather than interpreting this, I reflect on the potent synchrony taking place in both the lunar development in Vita's life and in her potential relationship with Virginia. I am in awe of these cosmic synchronies but these images do not have a meaning until we assign that meaning to them. Therefore, I hold these images and their potentialities until I am able to discuss them with the individuals, even though as an astrologer I can see their significance and possibilities.

Using astrological timing techniques for relationships has more possibilities and anomalies because two or more individuals are being considered. I follow my format of studying the natal charts with their transits and progressions, then the composite chart. Due to the amount of information I make notes and tables and am always alert for repetitions, patterns and images that feel profound and resonant. It is these images that I try to stay with to amplify and develop their meaning and influence.

By the Sea
As I was finishing this book, Angelina Jolie filed for divorce from Brad Pitt. They had known each other for twelve years. They were married on 23 August 2014 at their Château Miravel in the south of France. In 2015 they both starred in a film, written and directed by Angelina, about a married couple living in France whose relationship was in difficulty. Unlike *Mr and Mrs Smith*, their first film together, *By the Sea*, their last film, was not popular. Although any similarity to 'real life' was denied, the film captured a couple at a crossroads. Ironically, the only two films the couple collaborated on bookended their Jupiter cycle together.

Media reports and astrological blogs were highly speculative about the separation. However, like any couple, the basic reasons for the separation are often private and personal, sometimes incomprehensible and mysterious. Blame and recriminations so often accompany a relationship breakdown that we overlook the soulfulness, the deeper meaning and significance, of the split.

I have not changed any of the astrological commentary on their case study throughout the book, but our approach to reading the material will now have shifted due to their split. It serves to illustrate how subjectively we read the symbols depending on their context. Rather than use astrology to legitimate the breakdown, let's return to their horoscopes to review the astrological symbols that were in effect at the time. We will be confronted with our astrological beliefs: can astrology reveal the ending of the relationship or is it best employed as a means of being more conscious and reflective? How might we respect the soul of the relationship and honour the ending as an initiatory rite in each one of the partner's lives?

Mid September 2016, when Angelina filed for divorce, the couple stood at the crossroads. The path that led here was now at a critical turning point. As suggested, the angles and nodal axes of the horoscope are sensitive to directional changes, entrances and exits, so I would imagine transits to these angles would be emphasized. Saturn was in the 11th degree of Sagittarius completing its third transit across Brad's Ascendant and Angelina's Vertex. This transit that stressed both their angles began the end of 2015 and was complicated by its square to Neptune, which was exact that month for the last time. Therefore, Brad also had transiting Neptune squaring the Ascendant while Angelina had transiting Neptune in her 8th house squaring her Neptune–Vertex conjunction. During this same time frame Angelina had transiting Uranus conjoin her MC. The transit was active during the filming of *By the Sea*. Its retrograde transit to her MC synchronized with the release of the film in November 2015, while its final transit of the MC began to wane in 2016. By the end of 2015 and the beginning of 2016 the transiting nodal axis was on Brad's MC–IC axis. Transiting Chiron was approaching his IC. Jupiter had entered Libra and would transit their Vertex–Uranus–Ascendant conjunction in their composite chart in the next fortnight.

In Chapter 18 I mentioned the couple's sensitivity to eclipses since both were born with the Sun near the South Node. Their composite chart has the Sun at 19♓38 and the South Node at 21♓01. The eclipses of 2016 were significant, falling across the 6th–12th polarity of their composite chart. The solar eclipse of 9 March at 18✶56 conjoined the composite Sun while the solar eclipse of 1 September at 9♍21 opposed the composite Moon. The lunar eclipse of 23 March at 3♎17 was on the composite Vertex–Uranus–Ascendant while the lunar eclipse on the day after Angelina filed for divorce was 24✶20, again close to their composite Sun. The lunar eclipse of 16 September 2016 fell across the MC–IC axis of Brad's horoscope, already sensitized by the transit of the nodes earlier in the year.

The eclipses to the composite Sun, Moon and Ascendant symbolize something in the relationship being obscured or brought to light, while the transits to the personal angles are suggesting that each partner's direction is shifting. Neither of these suggests a break-up, but both highlight the need to be watchful. It is significant transits to the natal and composite inner planets that will underline the substantial changes occurring in each partner's private life (natal chart) and their partnership (composite chart). As this is both a marriage and family relationship, and we are focusing on adult relationship, transits to Venus and the Moon will be of significance. Since each partner's identity and future plans will be affected, transits to the Sun and Mars will also be of interest.

In context of the life cycle, Angelina was nearing the final stage of her Neptune square Neptune phase. Natal Neptune is opposite the Sun and transiting Saturn had been opposing the Sun and conjoining Neptune throughout 2016, bringing reality to bear on her expectations and dreams, especially concerning the masculine or literally the men in her life. In 2017 the square of transiting Neptune to her Sun is exact. During her two-year marriage Uranus had transited Mars, the Moon, Jupiter and the MC. In 2016 it completed the square to her 12th house Saturn, the ruler of her Descendant. In 2017 it opposes itself; natal Uranus is involved in a T-square opposite Chiron and square Venus. During the two years following Angelina's divorce petition, the Uranus transit will reawaken this T-square to Venus. In 2015 Pluto had squared the Moon, her chart ruler. At the time she filed for divorce, Pluto was squaring Jupiter and the MC. Within the period before and after filing for divorce, Angelina's Sun, Moon, Venus and Mars had received significant transits from the planets of alteration and transformation, Uranus and Pluto.

Brad too had potent transits to his Sun and Moon. Transiting Chiron had begun its square to his Sun, which would last throughout 2017. Natal Chiron in the 3rd house was already sensitized by the transit of Neptune conjoining it. Transiting Uranus was retrograde and in its second square to his Moon–Venus when Angelina filed for divorce. Transiting Pluto had conjoined Mercury, the ruler of his Descendant, twice. As for Angelina, the transits to the Sun, Moon and ruler of the Descendant were intense.

In 2016, transiting Chiron finished its opposition to the composite Sun and was still completing its transit across the composite South Node in the 6th house. Brad had begun his Uranus transit to Venus while Angelina was about to begin hers; therefore in the composite chart transiting Uranus was poised to oppose Venus in the coming year, a fitting symbol in all three charts for separation. Brad's progressed Sun at 19≈31was conjunct his natal Saturn while Angelina's progressed Sun at 22♋50 was conjunct her progressed Saturn, focusing attention on the developmental themes of autonomy, reliability, responsibility, parenting and control. Brad's progressed Moon had just entered Capricorn in the final degrees of the Last Quarter phase while Angelina's progressed Moon was at 24♎34 in the 4th, approaching her Uranus–Chiron–Venus T-square. She had just entered her progressed First Quarter phase, an action-orientated time of life, unlike Brad who was approaching his Balsamic phase, a time of inner contemplation and withdrawal.

Astrologically, the time in each chart reveals an intense change, a time of initiation and soul-searching. But how this is acted out is up to the partners and the spirit of the relationship. I do not consider that these astrological symbols suggest separation or divorce; however, they do reveal a crossroads in relationship, which can be articulated by the astrologer and then contemplated and considered by the couple to assist them in navigating the difficult crossing.

CHAPTER 22

AN ASTROLOGICAL ANATOMY OF RELATIONSHIP
Alchemical Analyses

We are at the Balsamic phase of our journey into relationship astrology, a time of closing, when quiet moments for reflection are needed. As the cycle closes, the essence of what has past becomes embedded in the seeds planted for the next round. This chapter in the cycle is a time of mindful waiting. Throughout the book we have considered some case examples to illustrate various aspects of relationship astrology, not just as factual evidence, but also as a way to imagine the archetypal possibilities that are offered through the study of horoscopes. With every horoscope we are examining two kinds of history: one is factual, referring to what has literally happened in the life of the individual; the other record is the story of the soul. We also foresee two types of possibilities: one exists in the outer world, while the other is present to the inner life.

Astrological work is constantly shifting in and out of different realities, but the two realities it constantly moves between are the literality of the day and the imagination of the night. Each one of these worlds can inform the other through the wise use of astrological images. We can ensoul our literal world by understanding the symbols of our horoscope, as well as animate our inner world by acknowledging their connections to outer events and relationships. Therefore an astrological case study not only embraces the facts of the outer world but also the fiction of the soulful spheres. Now, the best case study is concentrating on your own relationships. Hopefully, as you do so, the seeds of your study will begin to flourish into greater meaning and understanding.

Once two individual horoscopes are examined they can be merged into one, rearranging their elements and constituents to create a new horoscope that is a metaphor for their relationship. This is astrological chemistry. And now with three horoscopes and a plethora of detail, it is time to review the complete process.

This process could also be likened to a forensic examination. The skeleton of each horoscope is analysed and the anatomy of each natal chart reveals patterns, preferences, experiences, wounds, strengths and weaknesses. Placing two horoscopes side by side or over one another brings the interconnected and disjointed features of each horoscope to light in the context of an 'other'. A combined chart can reveal the alchemical changes that take place when both frameworks act together as one. But what is crucial in this examination is a study of the heart. The science of the examination can reveal the potentials and pitfalls of each individual in relationship. But it is through each partner's love, attachment and sympathy for the other, as well as their level of self-awareness, that the astrological revelations can be applied successfully by the partners. Relationship astrology is remarkable in its findings, but it is through our intention to participate with their images and apply them that the course of our relationships benefits.

Let's review the process we have begun throughout the book and connect this to our own horoscope and that of our partners and friends.

The Anatomy

Below is a step-by-step approach to use when beginning the process of relationship analysis. Eventually, relationship astrology and synastry will become natural and you will find your own way to process all the details. When beginning to work astrologically, techniques and frameworks help to structure an approach to the astrological data; however, over time your individual style and methodology begins to emerge out of your own beliefs and biases.

This checklist was developed for students beginning to practise relationship astrology, but it can be adapted for your own personal use. Most of the questions are reflective, encouraging a way of thinking about approaching a chart. There is a vast amount of information when two horoscopes are studied; therefore, I find it valuable to have a checklist of areas of focus and priority. There are many avenues to explore, so I encourage you to adapt this to suit your methodology. But to start, we need to be aware of some background details.

Significant Details and History

- Ascertain the agenda, issues, concerns and questions that are foremost in the couple's minds. Because there is so much information, focusing on certain themes or timing throughout the process promotes continuity and a deeper understanding of the patterns and issues at hand.

- What is the nature of the relationship: a current or past relationship, marriage, business partnership, friends, colleagues, siblings, parent–child, co-workers, or employer–employee? Each type of relationship will have slightly different astrological elements that need to be considered.

- Note the difference in age and any astrological cycles that may be similar or divergent. Which trans-generational themes might become more significant because of the age differential?

- When did the relationship begin? How long has the relationship lasted? Take note of the first meeting time or the first time the partners became conscious of the other, as well as the date of any other significant events. Note any periods of transition in the relationship that the couple feel were or are decisive to sustaining their union.

- Where did the couple meet? Are there cultural, familial, racial, religious, social, economic, educational or other differences that might impact upon the relationship?

- If possible, gather images about the family background, such as each individual's birth order, the family of origin and parental marriage, the number, gender and names of their siblings, their familial role and grandparents. Note any traumas, deaths, divorces, re-marriages, etc. Relationship themes in each partner's family background are helpful in classifying and understanding astrological themes.

Preparation of Natal Charts and Grids

- Two or more natal charts have been prepared and thoroughly analysed in the context of relationship themes, taking into account the nature of the relationship being considered. What are the individuals' needs, desires, aspirations, values, motivations, longings and capacity for sharing and being in relationship? What are their primary goals and orientation to life? Where are their weaknesses and strengths, their dreams and ideals?

- Transits and progressions have been computed and recorded for each individual at the same date, such as the present date, the date of the consultation or a special time or anniversary in the relationship. Take notes of the major transits and the positions of the progressed Sun, Moon and the lunation cycle.

- The two charts are superimposed on one another: each individual's horoscope has been presented with the other's planets placed around the rim of the horoscope or two bi-wheels have been generated to examine where the partner's planets fall in the other's horoscope.

Natal Charts Themes

- Contemplate the houses of the horoscope that are appropriate for the type of relationship that you are examining.

- Ascertain the important horoscope 'lacks'; for instance, consider any element or quality that is lacking or emphasized. Note interceptions and duplications, chart shapes, any lack or abundance of a particular type of aspect. Is there a particular hemisphere emphasis or a lack or abundance of retrograde planets? You are looking at the lacks in a horoscope as potential unconscious hooks where the partner may fill this lack for the other. Which images are the individuals open and receptive to, and which areas of their own chart may they be avoiding?

• Are there difficult aspects or aspect patterns? Do any planets appear dysfunctional? These planets may be identified by their difficult astrological signification, weakened by their placement in the chart or involved in challenging aspects. Reflect on whether the partner may embody this energy for the other. Does the partner fulfil any planetary urges, for instance the needs of the Moon, the communicative style of Mercury, the assertion of Mars, or the authority of Saturn?

• Consider the 'hooks' in the chart: any area or energy where projection or projective identification can occur, such as the Descendant or planets on the Descendant.

• Take into consideration the other angles of the horoscope: the Ascendant, MC–IC and Vertex–Anti-Vertex, as well as the nodal axis. Do any of these angles overlap?

• What is your overall impression of the relationship? What are the astrological signatures that contribute to your thoughts and feelings about their partnership? Consider each partner's planets and aspects to imagine patterns or tendencies that they bring into the relationship.

• Reflect on the images of the horoscope from a psychological perspective. Are there astrological patterns that suggest sacrifice, dependency or disassociation? Are there any indications of reactive patterns such as 'freedom versus attachment' or an 'approach-avoid' pattern? Or any indicators that suggest themes such as symbiosis versus separateness or an urgency to forge commitment versus the need to take time?

• Consider the astrological statements that may suggest lack of clarity or grounding. Is there a tendency to idealize or romanticize the other or the relationship? What is revealed about values and communication styles, each partner's basic day-to-day needs and security issues?

• Since there are many ways to approach the analysis, develop your own way of thinking about how different relationship issues reveal themselves when analysing planets in signs, houses and by aspect.

Transits and Progressions

- How are the transits and progressions indicative of relationship themes and developments at this time? What are the main transits affecting the stability and direction of the relationship?

- Where is each individual in their own life cycle development? Is this synchronous with their partner? If not, contrast the differing life cycle stages or transitions; for instance, one partner may be experiencing a Uranus transit while the other might be undergoing a Pluto transit, or one may be having a nodal return while their partner is undergoing a Saturn opposition. How might any major transits at the moment influence the individual and their relationship?

- Besides individual transits, what are the progressions of the Sun, Moon and phase of the progressed lunation cycle revealing? How does this natural unfolding in their personal lives impact the shared life of the relationship? Where are each partner's inner planets by progression? Do the progressed interaspects modify the theme that the natal charts reveal?

- Thoroughly analyse the impact that each individual's transits and progressions might have on the relationship. It is helpful to make tables and notes of the quantitative timing of these passages, using some images and metaphors that come to mind.

Chart Comparison

- Create two bi-wheels or superimpose one partner's planets onto the other's horoscope and vice versa. Note the houses that the planets inhabit in their partner's chart. For instance, in which house does the Moon fall in the other's horoscope?

And Saturn? Are there planets falling on the partner's angles? If one partner has a stellium, where does it fall in the other's chart? Which houses do the partner's planets strongly impact?

• Summarize one partner's planets in the other partner's houses and the significant aspects that are made between both charts. How is the individual impacted by the other's energy?

• Does their orientation to life coincide, dovetail or conflict? Are there aspect patterns in one individual's horoscope that place stress on the other partner's houses?

The Synastry Grid

• Create a synastry grid between the two individuals in relationship. Define your parameters as far as the type of aspects you will be using as well as the orbs used for each aspect.

• Analyse the aspect grid. Is there an abundance or shortage of aspects? Is there any type of aspect not represented or one that is dominant?

• Note any interaspects that focus on the mutual aspects of two planets. This will bring a potentially dominant theme to the relationship. What are these two planets, and which themes might be indicated by the combination of these two archetypal aspects between the couple? Are there any planetary aspects repeating from the natal charts?

• Break down the grid; for instance, highlight the boxes where the personal planets are in relationship to each other. Of the potential four aspects between the Sun and Moon, how many are there? Of the potential four aspects between Venus and Mars, how many are there? What are the aspects between one partner's outer planets in relationship to the other partner's inner planets? Use the synastry grid as the focus of the dynamic lines of interchange and interaction between the couple.

- Depending on the presenting theme, use the interaspects to define the areas of potential mutuality, support, conflict and rivalry.

The Composite Chart

- Generate a composite chart. Be mindful of whether you are using a composite midpoints, a composite derived Ascendant or a Davison relationship chart. Try to be consistent with the combined chart that you are using. Analyse the horoscope considering the planets in the houses, major aspects, angular planets, etc.

- When examining the composite chart, what are your first impressions? What are the potentials that are forged by the couple becoming defined as one system or one entity rather than two individuals?

- Which patterns are repeating from the natal charts and in the comparison of these two charts? Which new themes emerge because of the alchemy in their relationship?

- How does this chart help you to guide the couple to address some of their basic issues and themes that have been presented?
  What are the strengths and weaknesses embedded in this horoscope?

- Where can this couple best direct their energies and their relationship?

- Are there any themes in the composite chart that follow on from the themes in their personal charts, the synastry grid or the chart comparisons? If so, where do you see these themes operating in the life of this relationship and how could you best articulate this recurrent theme in the context of the evolution of this relationship?

Transits and Progressions to the Composite Chart

- What are the areas of the chart that the transits are stressing? Which areas and themes are in need of focus at this time and in the times ahead?

- Where are the composite progressed Sun and Moon and what is their lunation phase?

- How do the transits and progressions to the composite chart help the couple to understand the deeper implications of this moment in time?

As suggested, this checklist is to help you contemplate the fullness of the process, as well as begin to collate some of the charts needed and ways we might start to think about the different horoscopes in context of a relationship analysis.

Other Considerations

If you are beginning to do relationship analysis for others, either as an apprentice or a professional, it is important to be mindful of other considerations that may affect the outcome of your consultation. While you may be focused on a relationship between two other people and have prepared carefully for the consultation, there are subtle factors that may also be at play.

Your Chart and the Chart You Are Studying

Synastry is quietly in play in the relationship between us as astrologers and our client or friend. It is present every time we read another's horoscope. When preparing a consultation, synastry between you and the person whose chart you are reading is immediately accessible and of great value.

Implicit in synastry is how we engage and experience relationship. Although we might not consider this, we are in a type of relationship with the person whose horoscope we are reading or the student we are teaching. No matter how objective, impartial or nonjudgemental we are, we respond to their personal stories and horoscope symbols from our own images and experiences. Even if the person whose chart we are reading is not present, the horoscope symbols still engage us in our own patterns, prejudices and narratives. Therefore, one of the first unspoken considerations when reading an astrological chart is to take into account the synastry between us and our client or the person we are reading for to see how this may highlight some of our potential reactions.

Experience has shown me that in preparing for any chart consultation, awareness of difficult interaspects between my chart and the client's helps to flag potential areas of concern and complications that might arise between us. It is as if the interaspects are the playing field where transference and projection are more liable to surface. Hence, synastry is not just the compilation of astrological techniques for analysing relationship, but an art. Skill in the art of astrological consultation highlights our participation with others, both as astrologer and personally.

Personal Checklist and Biases
Another important consideration is any relationship biases and experiences that may affect the way we approach and interpret certain aspects of the horoscope. We hold our own preconceptions and understanding about certain relationship issues; therefore it is important to be aware of where we may be influenced by these. In order to participate more fully with the dynamic of synastry, reflect on your own experiences of and attitudes toward relationship by considering the following. Most importantly, what are your experiences of relationship?

- Any personal prejudices that you carry about relationship
- How did your familial and personal experiences shape your attitudes towards relating
- Beliefs, ideals and disappointments that you carry about relationship
- Your relationship comfort zones:
    - What biases do you bring into the session?
    - What issues are 'loaded' for you, in terms of relationships?

It is important to be mindful of our relationship comfort zones, opinions and biases when reading a horoscope or consulting with others. These shape the way we interpret the astrological symbols. There are many relational concerns that could be part of a relationship analysis; therefore, it is wise to be aware of how we react to contentious issues in relationship. Reflect on the following issues and how you might feel if these entered into one of your consultations. This is only a partial list of some issues that could arise – consider other matters not on the list with which you may be uncomfortable.

- Abortion
- Addiction, alcohol and/or drug or substance abuse
- Bisexuality, homosexuality or sexuality in general
- Blended families, stepchildren
- Co-dependency
- Debt; other issues concerning money
- Depression, grief and loss
- Divorce or separation
- Domestic violence; child abuse
- Gender inequality
- Infidelity
- Mental illness
- Pornography

How comfortable do you feel about exploring intimate and personal details with others?

Ethics

Synastry is a natural feature of all astrological work. Inevitably, clients ask a question about their partner: 'Are we compatible?' or 'Can you look at my partner's chart for me?' Concerned parents seek insight through their child's horoscope so they can better understand their relationship. Or a client wants to know about the transits to a friend's chart to find out what's going on between them.

In applying the art of synastry we are faced with finding an ethical framework that honours the complexity of the process. Engaging in the act of chart comparison for a couple or the creation of their composite chart brings in another relational dynamic, which is the formation of a triangle with the astrologer and the possible collusion with one of the partners that excludes the other. This is emphasized if we have already consulted with one of the partners and forged an alliance. It can be especially complicated if we are seeing only one partner, yet are working with the horoscopes of both. Unintentionally, we may become complicit with the partner we are seeing. When our own horoscope is taken into account in the context of each of the partners and their composite chart, it can flag many issues for consideration, such as how we feel more aligned with one partner than the other, or where our own relational history might be stirred.

A composite chart can exist between us and anyone we choose, but experience has taught me that, while the composite chart is enormously valuable in portraying the dynamics of a relationship, it is only brought to life when two individuals combine and are committed to the bond. It is a map of a merger and shows possibilities and patterns; when the connection is mutual, then the composite energies become potential opportunities.

Consider how you will conduct your synastry sessions. Reflect on the ethics of examining a partner's chart without their permission or when they are not there. How can you maintain an ethical perspective when only one partner is present?

Referrals and Summary

When working with relationship astrology there will be many suggestions and strategies that you can offer the couple. However, there are also many issues that arise that are beyond our expertise. Therefore a referral list of relationship counsellors and other practitioners is indispensable. For instance, I try as much to keep my referral list as current as possible in case it is appropriate to refer one of my clients to another professional. On my list of referrals I include:

- Family therapist
- Financial advisor
- Grief counsellor
- Health practitioners: herbalist, homeopath, masseur and naturopath
- Legal advisor
- Psychiatrist
- Psychologist
- Relationship counsellor

Astrological data is not static, it needs to be applied in the context of a particular situation or question in order to bring it to life. In relationship astrology, we apply the astrological images to analyse the relating patterns and potentials of an individual. This can then be expanded into synastry, the art of using astrological analysis to assist two people to be more aware of the patterns and dynamics in their relationship.

Relationship astrology encourages us to become more mindful of our interactions, more tolerant of others and more accepting of ourselves. It invites us to reflect on the soul of relationship, not as a goal or an ideal but as an inspiration for us to participate in an authentic relationship. It is not just a project about compatibility and possibility; it calls us to honour the mysteries of our attachments, not for what we want them to be, but for how they truly are. Relationship astrology helps to ensoul our connections through the recognition and revelation of our true self in love and relationship.

The following appendixes supplement techniques and themes discussed throughout the text. Some are designed to tabulate and focus the vast amounts of information generated in an astrological analysis of relationship.

APPENDIX 1: Aspects to Venus and Mars (Chapter 4)

	Venus by Sign and House	Aspects to Venus	Comments
Whitney Houston	11♌12 in 6th	☌☉ △☽ ⚹♂ ☍♄ □♆	Whitney's Venus–Sun is in a T-square, in opposition to Saturn and square to Neptune, illustrating a tug of war between her personal dreams and the reality of her feelings of self-worth. Whitney's Venus–Sun is opposite Bobby's Sun which sits on her Saturn, echoing and reiterating the critical inner voice.
Bobby Brown	3♈04 in 2nd	⚹☿ ☍♃ ☌⚷ ☍♅ △♆ ☍⚷ ☌☊	Bobby's Venus is conjunct the North Node and Chiron, opposite Jupiter and Uranus which fall on Whitney's Mars stimulating an attraction between each other, but also bringing Bobby's conflicted feelings of self-worth to the surface. In the astrology of relationship each one's complex self-worth issues are emphasized by the other.
Brad Pitt	23♑28 in 2nd	☌☽ ☌☿	Angelina's Venus is in a T-square with Chiron and Uranus and she has become a strong advocate for women's rights and the disenfranchised, echoing her own challenges with self-worth. Brad's Venus is in the Capricorn stellium, opposite her Venus and on her Descendant, perhaps offering ballast for Angelina's capricious Venus aspects.
Angelina Jolie	28♋09 in 12th conjunct ASC	□⚷ □♅ △☊	

	Mars by Sign and House	Aspects to Mars	Comments
Whitney Houston	8♎29 in 7th	☍☽ ⚹♀	Although conjunct the IC, Venus in the composite chart is unaspected when using the defined orbs. In the composite chart Mars has few aspects and is in Libra, the sign of its detriment.
Bobby Brown	20♏24 in 10th	□☉ ⚹☽ ♂♆ ⚹♇	In Whitney's chart Mars is also in Libra in the 7th house, while Bobby has it in the sign of its rulership, squaring Whitney's Sun–Venus and Saturn.
Brad Pitt	10♑01 in 1st	♂☿ □♃ △♅ △♇ ♂☋	Because Brad and Angelina's Mars are square each other, they will repeat the 4th harmonic aspects to the planets that Mars aspects in each other's charts. Interestingly their Venus' are also opposed, but in the composite chart Venus is trine Mars.
Angelina Jolie	10♈42 in 9th	⚹☉ ♂☽ ♂♃ □♄ △♆ ☍♇	Each partner's Mars is strongly aspected; therefore we would imagine each being strongly focused, independent and forthright. Brad's Mars aspects Mercury and Jupiter so he is challenged through ideas and visions whereas Angelina's Mars aspects both luminaries and finds her contests in the realm of family and the personal.

APPENDIX 2: Temperamental Associations (Chapter 13)

Element	Quality	Humour		Season	Lunar Phase
Fire	Hot & dry	Yellow bile	Choleric	Summer	First Quarter to Full Moon
Earth	Cold & dry	Black bile	Melancholic	Autumn	Full Moon to Last Quarter
Air	Hot & wet	Blood	Sanguine	Spring	New Moon to First Quarter
Water	Cold & wet	Phlegm	Phlegmatic	Winter	Last Quarter to New Moon

Element	Platonic Type	Alchemical Stage	Tarot Suit	Psychological Type
Fire	Imagination	Calcinatio	Wands	Intuition
Earth	Demonstration	Coagulatio	Pentacles	Sensation
Air	Intelligence	Sublimatio	Swords	Thinking
Water	Opinion	Solutio	Cups	Feeling

Elemental Considerations

Many factors could be taken into account when weighting the elements. We can start weighting the elements to determine planetary imbalances as well as to reflect on how our life experiences may have shaped or altered our natural temperament. Temperamentally, we can also consider the planets and houses.

Planets can also be associated with an element. For instance, all the planets could be seen through the eyes of the elements:

Sun	Fire
Moon	Water
Mercury	Air (secondary Earth)
Venus	Air and Earth
Mars	Fire
Jupiter	Fire
Saturn	Earth
Uranus	Air
Neptune	Water
Pluto	Water

Mars is fiery; when placed in a fire sign, it becomes even fierier. Uranus is airy and perhaps in aspect to another airy planet like Mercury would add an element of Air to the chart. Combinations of planets would add elemental influences to the horoscope. Since there are a multitude of astrological combinations possible, each horoscope needs to be evaluated by a competent astrologer before a firm diagnosis of elemental strengths and weaknesses is determined.

The houses of the horoscope may also be categorised elementally: We could also consider the houses in terms of the elementary trinities; for instance, houses 1, 5 and 9 being Fire; houses 2, 6 and 10 being Earth; houses 3, 7 and 11 being Air; and houses 4, 8 and 12 being Water.

Throughout the tradition of astrology there are differing views and correspondences to temperament. These are ways of thinking about astrological temperament, not fixed rules.

APPENDIX 3: Temperament Worksheet (Chapter 13)

Temperament Worksheet

NAME _____

Planet or Angle	Sign	Points	Fire Yang	Earth Yin	Air Yang	Water Yin	Cardinal	Fixed	Mutable
					ELEMENT			QUALITY	
Ascendant		4							
Ruler of Ascendant		4							
Moon		8							
Dispositor of Moon		2							
Sun		8							
Mercury		5							
Venus		5							
Mars		5							
Jupiter		3							
Saturn		3							
Uranus		1							
Neptune		1							
Pluto		1							
		50							

TOTAL: Fire + Earth + Air + Water + Cardinal + Fixed + Mutable = 100

Temperament Worksheet

NAME _____

Planet or Angle	Sign	Points	ELEMENT				QUALITY		
			Fire Yang	Earth Yin	Air Yang	Water Yin	Cardinal	Fixed	Mutable
Ascendant		4							
Ruler of Ascendant		4							
Moon		8							
Dispositor of Moon		2							
Sun		8							
Mercury		5							
Venus		5							
Mars		5							
Jupiter		3							
Saturn		3							
Uranus		1							
Neptune		1							
Pluto		1							
		50							

TOTAL: Fire + Earth + Air + Water + Cardinal + Fixed + Mutable = 100

APPENDIX 4: Temperament Examples (Chapter 13)

Temperament Worksheet

NAME: BRAD PITT

Planet or Angle	Sign	Points	ELEMENT				QUALITY		
			Fire Yang	Earth Yin	Air Yang	Water Yin	Cardinal	Fixed	Mutable
Ascendant	♐	4	4						4
Ruler of Ascendant	♈	4	4				4		
Moon	♑	8		8			8		
Dispositor of Moon	♒	2			2			2	
Sun	♐	8	8						8
Mercury	♑	5		5			5		
Venus	♑	5		5			5		
Mars	♑	5		5			5		
Jupiter	♈	3	3				3		
Saturn	♒	3			3			3	
Uranus	♍	1		1					1
Neptune	♏	1				1		1	
Pluto	♍	1		1					
		50	19	25	5	1	30	6	14

Temperament Worksheet

NAME: ANGELINA JOLIE

Planet or Angle	Sign	Points	ELEMENT				QUALITY		
			Fire Yang	Earth Yin	Air Yang	Water Yin	Cardinal	Fixed	Mutable
Ascendant	♋	4				4	4		
Ruler of Ascendant	♈	4	4				4		
Moon	♈	8	8				8		
Dispositor of Moon	♈	2	2				2		
Sun	♊	8			8				8
Mercury	♊	5			5				5
Venus	♋	5				5	5		
Mars	♈	5	5				5		
Jupiter	♈	3	3				3		
Saturn	♋	3				3	3		
Uranus	♎	1			1		1		
Neptune	♐	1	1						1
Pluto	♎	1			1		1		
		50	23		15	12	36		14

Temperament Worksheet

NAME: VIRGINIA WOOLF

Planet or Angle	Sign	Points	ELEMENT				QUALITY		
			Fire Yang	Earth Yin	Air Yang	Water Yin	Cardinal	Fixed	Mutable
Ascendant	♊	4			4				4
Ruler of Ascendant	♒	4			4			4	
Moon	♈	8	8				8		
Dispositor of Moon	♊	2			2				2
Sun	♒	8			8			8	
Mercury	♒	5			5		5	5	
Venus	♑	5		5			5		
Mars	♊	5			5				5
Jupiter	♉	3		3				3	
Saturn	♉	3		3				3	
Uranus	♍	1		1					1
Neptune	♉	1		1				1	
Pluto	♉	1		1				1	
		50	8	14	28		13	25	12

Temperament Worksheet

NAME: VITA SACKVILLE-WEST

Planet or Angle	Sign	Points	ELEMENT				QUALITY		
			Fire Yang	Earth Yin	Air Yang	Water Yin	Cardinal	Fixed	Mutable
Ascendant	♑	4		4			4		
Ruler of Ascendant	♍	4		4					4
Moon	♋	8				8	8		
Dispositor of Moon	♋	2				2	2		
Sun	♓	8				8			8
Mercury	♓	5				5			5
Venus	♈	5	5				5		
Mars	♐	5	5						5
Jupiter	♓	3				3			3
Saturn	♍	3		3					3
Uranus	♏	1				1		1	
Neptune	♊	1			1				1
Pluto	♊	1			1				1
		50	10	11	2	27	19	1	30

	Fire	Earth	Air	Water	Cardinal	Fixed	Mutable
Brad	19	25	5	1	30	6	14
Angelina	23	–	15	12	36	–	14
Signatures	Brad is Cardinal Earth = **Capricorn**; Angelina is Cardinal Fire = **Aries**						

	Fire	Earth	Air	Water	Cardinal	Fixed	Mutable
Virginia	8	14	28	–	13	25	12
Vita	10	11	2	27	19	1	30
Signatures	Virginia is Fixed Air = **Aquarius**; Vita is Mutable Water = **Pisces**						

APPENDIX 5: Synastry Worksheet 1 • Assessing the Natal Horoscope – Lacks and Resources (Chapter 14)

Chart A: _____   Chart B: _____

Horoscope Lack/Emphasis	Chart A	Chart B	Comments
Elements: Fire			
Elements: Earth			
Elements: Air			
Elements: Water			
Modes: Cardinal			
Modes: Fixed			
Modes: Mutable			
Vulnerable Planet/s			
Angular Planets			
Aspect Patterns			
House Emphasis			
Hemisphere Emphasis			
Retrograde Planets			
Lunation Cycle			
Interceptions Duplications			
Other Considerations			

APPENDIX 6: Synastry Worksheet 2 • Assessing the Natal Horoscope – Relationship Themes (Chapter 15)

Chart A: _____   Chart B: _____

Feature	Chart A	Chart B	Comments
7th House: Sign Ruler & Planets			
8th House: Sign, Ruler & Planets			
Relationship Houses			
Nodal Axis			
The Vertex			
Animus: The Sun			

Anima: The Moon			
Anima: Venus			
Animus: Mars			
Communion: Mercury			
Ethics & Morals: Jupiter			
Commitment: Saturn			
Generational Influences: The Outer Planets			

APPENDIX 7: Synastry Worksheet 3 • House Sitting – My Planets in Your Houses (Chapter 16)

Chart A Planet/ Point	Falls in Chart B's House #	Notes
Sun		
Moon		
Mercury		
Venus		
Mars		
Jupiter		
Saturn		
Chiron		
Uranus		
Neptune		
Pluto		
North Node		
MC		
Ascendant		
Vertex		

Chart B Planet/ Point	Falls in Chart A's House #	Notes
Sun		
Moon		
Mercury		
Venus		
Mars		
Jupiter		
Saturn		
Chiron		
Uranus		
Neptune		
Pluto		
North Node		
MC		
Ascendant		
Vertex		

APPENDIX 8: Using Your Solar Fire Program for Synastry

1. Generating two bi-wheels
- Open the two natal charts that you are analysing
- On the top menu under <u>View</u>, click on BiWheel
- In the box that opens, under Selected Charts, Inner Wheel will be highlighted. Under the charts click on the partner # 1. Now Outer Wheel is highlighted. Choose the chart of the other partner.
- Click on View in the bottom right hand of the screen
- The chart that is presented has partner 1 in the inner wheel and partner 2 in the outer.
- Reverse the process and create a bi-wheel with partner 2 in the inner wheel and partner 1 in the outer.

On the first bi-wheel note the planets of partner 2 and in which houses they fall in partner 1's chart. Note planets that fall on the angles of partner 1's chart or those that are conjunct planets in partner 1's horoscope. Make similar notes for the second bi-wheel.

2. The Synastry Grid
- Open the two natal charts that you are analysing
- On the top menu under <u>Reports</u>, click on Synastry
- In the box that opens, under Selected Charts, Chart Across will be highlighted. Under the charts click on the partner 1. Now Chart Down is highlighted. Choose the chart of the other partner.
- Click on View in the bottom right hand of the screen
- The chart that is presented has partner 1's planets across the top of the grid and partner 2's planets down the grid. The box will highlight the aspect using its glyph as well as the degree of orb of the aspect and whether it is <u>A</u>pplying or <u>S</u>eparating.

When using Solar Fire software, you can choose your parameters for the aspect grid by selecting the planets, aspects and orbs you would like to use.

- To choose the planets for your Synastry Grid, go to <u>Chart Options</u>, click on Displayed <u>Points</u> and choose <u>Planets and</u>

Chiron (or if you prefer make your own file called Synastry Grid). Then click on the edit button and choose the planets and points you want to include. Save these changes and then click Select.

- To choose your aspects go to Chart Options, click on Aspect Set – choose Planets and then click on Synastry. Then click on the edit button and choose the aspects and the orbs you want to include. Use the same orb for the luminaries and other planets as well as the same orbs for applying and separating. When you are familiar with how these might operate you can change the parameters later. Save these changes and Select.
- Now you are ready to generate the aspect grid. Go to Reports, click on Synastry. Then choose the two charts – Chart Across and Chart Down. Your synastry grid will then be generated within these parameters.

3. Creating a Composite Chart
- Open the two natal charts that you are analysing
- On the top menu under Chart, click on Combined
- In the box that opens:
  - Under Chart Type to Generate choose Composite-Midpoints
  - Under Combined Chart Title add the two charts. Click on your first chart. Then use the ctrl button & mouse to click on partner 2 who will appear under Title 2. Once both are highlighted under Combined Chart Title, click OK at the bottom.
- Your Composite Chart will appear under Calculated Charts

At this point I would save the composite chart to your files. On the top menu choose Chart and click on Save to File. I would save to a file called Synastry. If you do not have a file called Synastry then I would create one by clicking on the Create button on the right.

You will also be able to generate other types of composite charts such as the composite-derived Ascendant or the Davison relationship chart using the same procedure.

APPENDIX 9: Birth Data Used in Text

Whitney Houston	9 August 1963, 8.55 p.m. EDT, Newark, NJ, USA	Birth Certificate Chapter 4
Bobby Brown	5 February 1969, 5.21 a.m. EST, Boston, MA, USA	Birth Certificate Chapter 4
Angelina Jolie	4 June 1975, 9.09 a.m. PDT, Los Angeles, CA, USA	Birth Certificate Chapter 4
Brad Pitt	18 December 1963, 6.31 a.m. CST, Shawnee, OK, USA	From Memory Chapter 4
Janet (Client)	25 October 1944, 4.45 p.m. AWST, Perth, WA, Australia	From hospital record Chapter 9
Ella Fitzgerald	25 April 1917, 12.30 p.m. EST, Newport News, VA, USA	Birth Certificate Chapter 11
Marilyn Monroe	1 June 1926, 9.30 a.m. PST, Los Angeles, CA, USA	Birth Certificate Chapter 11
Fred Astaire	10 May 1899, 9.16 p.m. CST, Omaha, NE, USA	Birth Certificate Chapter 11
Ginger Rogers	16 July 1911, 2.18 a.m. CST, Independence, MO, USA	Birth Certificate Chapter 11
Sigmund Freud	6 May 1856, 6.30 p.m. -0.57.44, Freiberg, Moravia (Czech Republic)	Family Bible – place of birth is now Pribor, Czech Republic Chapter 11
Carl Jung	26 July 1875, 7.32 p.m. LST -0.29.44, Kesswil, Switzerland	From daughter. Gret Baumann Chapter 11
Diana, Princess of Wales	1 July 1961, 7.45 p.m. GDT, Sandringham, England	Charles Harvey from Queen's assistant press secretary Chapter 12
Charles, Prince of Wales	14 November 1948, 9.14 p.m. GMT, Buckingham Palace, England	News announcement Chapter 12
Akihito, Emperor of Japan	23 December 1933, 6.39 a.m. JST, Tokyo, Japan	Sy Scholfield from newspaper article Chapter 12

Michiko, Empress of Japan	20 October 1934, 7.43 a.m. JST, Tokyo, Japan	Astrology Institute of Japan Chapter 12
Virginia Woolf	25 January 1882, 12.15 p.m. GMT, London, England	Frances McEvoy quotes friend Chapter 13
Vita Sackville-West	9 March 1892, 4.15 a.m. GMT, Knole, England	Mother's diary Chapter 13
Kurt Cobain	20 February 1967, 7.38 p.m. PST, Aberdeen, WA, USA	Birth Certificate Chapter 14
Courtney Love	9 July 1964, 2.08 p.m. PDT, San Francisco, CA, USA	Birth Certificate Chapter 14
Grace Kelly	12 November 1929, 5.31 a.m. EST, Philadelphia, PA, USA	Birth Certificate Chapter 20
Prince Rainier III	31 May 1923, 6.00 a.m. BST, Monte Carlo, Monaco	6 a.m. time is often quoted but is not substantiated Chapter 20
Anaïs Nin	21 February 1903, 8.25 p.m. -0.09.20, Neuilly sur Seine, France	Birth Certificate Chapter 20
Henry Miller	26 December 1891, 12.17 p.m. EST, Manhattan, NY, USA	Biography 'Always Bright and Merry' by Jay Martin, page 3 Chapter 20
Prince William	21 June 1982, 9.03 p.m. BST, London, England	News announcement Chapter 20
Kate Middleton	9 January 1982, Reading, England	No verified birth data Chapter 20

For the most comprehensive data source consult Astro-Databank, pioneered by Lois Rodden: http://www.astro.com/astro-databank/

– BIBLIOGRAPHY –

Arroyo, Stephen. *Relationship and Life Cycles*, CRCS Publications, Vancouver, WA: 1979

Blaschke, Robert P. *Astrology A Language of Life Volume IV: Relationship Analysis*, Earthwalk School of Astrology, Port Townsend, WA: 2007

Clark, Brian. *The Family Legacy*, Astro*Synthesis, Stanley, Tasmania: 2016

Davison, Ronald. *Synastry: Understanding Human Relations through Astrology*, ASI Publishing, New York, NY: 1977

Forrest, Jodie & Steven. *Skymates*, Seven Paws Press, Chapel Hill, NC: 2002

Greene, Liz. *Astrology for Lovers,* Red Wheel/ Weiser, San Francisco, CA: 2008
   — *Relationships & How to Survive Them,* CPA Press, London: 1999
   — *Relating: An Astrological Guide to Living*, Samuel Weiser, New York, NY: 1977

Greene, Liz and Sasportas, Howard. *The Development of the Personality,* Samuel Weiser, York Beach, ME: 1987
   — *The Inner Planets,* Samuel Weiser, York Beach, ME: 1993
   — *The Luminaries*, Samuel Weiser, York Beach, ME: 1992

Hand, Robert. *Planets in Composite: Analyzing Human Relationships,* Para Research, Gloucester, MA: 1975

Idemon, Richard. *Through the Looking Glass*, Samuel Weiser, York Beach, ME: 1992

Jung, C. G. *The Collected Works of C. G. Jung*, trans. R. F. C. Hull et al. (20 volumes), Routledge & Kegan Paul, London and Princeton University Press, Princeton, NJ: 1953–79

McEvers, Joan (Ed.). *Intimate Relationships*, Llewellyn Publications, St. Paul, Minnesota, MN: 1991

Moore, Thomas. *Care of the Soul*, Harper Perennial, New York: 1992
   — *Soul Mates Honoring the Mysteries of Love and Relationship*, Harper Collins, New York: 1994
   — *The Planets Within*, Lindisfarne Press, Great Barrington, MA: 1990

Sargent, Lois Haines. *How to Handle your Human Relations*, A.F.A., Phoenix, AZ: 1958

Thornton, Penny. *Synastry,* The Aquarian Press, London: 1982

Townley, John. *The Composite Chart: The Horoscope of a Relationship,* Samuel Weiser, New York, NY: 1974

– ENDNOTES –

[1] Brian Clark, *The Family Legacy, Astro*Synthesis, Stanley, Tasmania: 2016.*

[2] These booklets are available as e-booklets through Astro*Synthesis – see www.astrosynthesis.com.au/

[3] The Kindred Spirits Report is published by Esoteric Technologies; see http://www.esotech.com.au/product/solar-writer-kindred-spirits-download/

[4] See Brian Clark, *The Family Legacy.*

[5] I first heard this expression used by Isabel Hickey when describing Saturn in a class on synastry in 1978. See Isabel Hickey, *Astrology, A Cosmic Science*, Alteri Press, Bridgeport, CT: 1970.

[6] Adolf Guggenbühl-Craig, *Eros on Crutches*, Spring Publications, Dallas, TX: 1980, p. 27.

[7] Hesiod, *Theogony*, translated by M. L. West, Oxford University Press, Oxford: 2008, p. 6.

[8] Lyrics from *Love Changes Everything* by Andrew Lloyd Webber from his musical, *Aspects of Love.*

[9] For instance, Sappho mentions Eros as the son of Ouranus and Gaia. Other poets and authors list his parents as Zephyros and Iris or Ouranus and Aphrodite.

[10] Of interest is that Homer, in the great heroic epics *The Iliad* and *The Odyssey*, does not include Eros. He is concerned with heroic triumphs and Eros, who is often considered anti-heroic, seduces the hero away from battle. Eros is a lover, not a fighter. He mingles the gods together rather than separating them; therefore he is not of interest to Homer.

[11] Marie-Louise von Franz, *The Golden Ass of Apuleius*, Shambhala, Boston, MA: 1992. In Chapter 7, p. 136, she states: 'If you think of Psyche as the archetype of the anima and of Eros as the archetype of the animus...'

[12] C. G. Jung, *Dream Analysis: Notes of the Seminar Given in 1928–30*, ed. William McGuire, Bolligen Series XCIX, Princeton University Press, Princeton, NJ: 1984, §172.

[13] C. G. Jung, *Collected Works, Volume 7: Two Essays on Analytical Psychology*, translated by R.F.C. Hull, Routledege & Kegan Paul, London: 1953, 'The Eros Theory' §32.

[14] Plato in *The Symposium* suggests that Eros's mother is *Penia* or Poverty.

[15] The asteroid belt contains tens of thousands of small rock formations up to 1,000 kilometres in diameter, mostly orbiting between Mars and Jupiter. The first asteroid was discovered in 1801 and named Ceres. The first four were discovered between 1801 and 1807 and named after the four potent Olympian goddesses: Ceres (Demeter), Pallas (Athena), Juno (Hera) and Vesta (Hestia).

Four asteroids are connected with the Erotes. Eros, asteroid 433, was discovered on 13 August 1898. It has been linked to passion, intensity and attraction in emotional and sexual relationships. Cupido, asteroid 763, was discovered on 25 September 1913. It has been associated with vanity. Amor, asteroid 1221, was discovered on 12 March 1932 and has been suggested as the capacity for compassion or spiritual love. Anteros, asteroid 1943, was discovered on 13 March 1973 and suggests requited love or love returned.

[16] Sigmund Freud, *An Outline of Psychoanalysis*, translated by James Strachey, London, 1949, pp. 5–6.

[17] Marie-Louise von Franz, *The Golden Ass of Apuleius*, p. 82.

[18] For more on the Corinthian Aphrodite, see my article at: www.astrosynthesis.com.au/wp-content/uploads/2017/11/The-Corinthian-Goddess-Brian-Clark.pdf

[19] From a speech of Hyperides (fr. 205 Jensen) quoted in Mark Golden, *Children and Childhood in Athens*, Johns Hopkins University Press, Baltimore, MD: 1990.

[20] See 'The Hymn to Aphrodite', *The Homeric Hymns*, translated by Michael Crudden, Oxford University Press, Oxford, 2001.

[21] Hesiod portrays this birth in *Theogony,* translated by Dorothea Wender, Penguin, Harmondsworth: 1984, pp. 189–199.

[22] Homer, *The Iliad,* translated by Richmond Lattimore, University of Chicago, Chicago: 1961, 5:889-891.

[23] C. Kerenyi, *The Gods of the Greeks*, Thames and Hudson, London: 1951, p. 176.

[24] 'The Hymn to Ares', *The Homeric Hymns*, 79. Because of the reference to the planet, it has been suggested that this does not belong to the Homeric hymns and has been incorrectly included.

[25] For a thorough examination of the anima and animus, see Chapter V 'The Inner Partner', Liz Greene, *Relating*, The Aquarian Press, London: 1986, pp. 110–154.

[26] I am using the term 'inconjunct' to encompass both the semi-sextile (30°) and the quincunx (150°). Both are 12th harmonic aspects; the semi-sextile is 1/12 while the quincunx is 5/12 of the circle. These were not aspects recognized by traditional astrologers. Inconjunct suggests not being connected, referring to their lack of connection to the Ascendant. Eighth harmonic aspects are the semi-square (45°) and the sesquiquadrate (135°).

[27] For the Venus cycle refer to http://www.melaniereinhart.com/ Articles: Venus Queen of Heaven and Earth.

[28] For students beginning their journey into astrology, I highly recommend Sue Tompkins, *Aspects in Astrology*, Element Books, Shaftesbury, UK: 1989.

[29] For instance, Venus in Capricorn has a 'critical' dialogue with Mars in Aries at the ending of their cycle, as they form a waning square with one another. It is 'critical' in that they are three-

quarters through this particular cycle, and form a square to each other which impedes the way they see one another.

[30] For an excellent examination astrologically of the different facets of love see Richard Idemon, *Through the Looking Glass*, Samuel Weiser, York Beach, ME: 1992, pp. 117–176. For instance we could associate the first four facets of love with the fixed signs: *Epithumia* as Taurus; *Philia* as Leo; *Eros* as Scorpio; *Agape* as Aquarius. Idemon considers these associations.

[31] See Oprah Winfrey's interview with Whitney Houston at: http://www.dailymotion.com/video/x1aa5re_whitney-houston-on-oprah-2009-day-1_people

[32] By 'strong aspect' I refer to the five Ptolemaic aspects, along with the quincunx.

[33] See Appendix 1 for a summary of aspects to Venus and Mars in our case studies.

[34] This was reported in many media stories. For instance, see http://www.dailymail.co.uk/tvshowbiz/article-2172189/Angelina-Jolie-mortified-Brad-Pitts-mother-writes-anti-Obama-anti-gay-marriage-letter.html

[35] J. E. Cirlot, *A Dictionary of Symbols*, translated by Jack Sage, Routledge & Kegan Paul, London: 1981, p. 153.

[36] Brian Clark, *The Family Legacy.*

[37] For an examination of the progressed Moon cycles through the horoscope see Brian Clark, *Secondary Progressions*, Astro*Synthesis (Melbourne: 2002), available from Astro*Synthesis www.astrosynthesis.com.au/

[38] For an amplification of the astrology, see Glennys Lawton, 'Leaving Home', www.astrosynthesis.com.au/articles/articles.html

[39] For a popular version of this myth see Ovid, *Metamorphoses*, translated by Mary M. Innes, Penguin, London: 1955, Book 3, pp. 83–87. Quotes are from this translation.

[40] For the etymological connection to Hestia as the goddess of hospitality, hence host and ghost, see Barbara Kirksey, 'Hestia: a Background of Psychological Focusing', in James Hillman (ed.), *Facing the Gods*, Spring, Dallas: 1980, p. 110.

[41] Howard Sasportas, *The Twelves Houses*, Aquarian, Wellingborough: 1985, p. 68. (Reprinted edition, Flare, 2007.)

[42] See Liz Greene, *Relating*, Aquarian Press, London: 1990, Chapter V, pp. 110–154.

[43] Carl Jung, 'Marriage as a Psychological Relationship', *Collected Works Volume 17: The Development of the Personality*, § 331.

[44] In *The Family Legacy* this was also explored in terms of the Houses of Relationship.

[45] Ray Soulard Jr. (ed.), *Letters to a Young Poet by Rainer Maria Rilke*, translated by Stephen Mitchell, Scriptor Press, Portland, OR: 2001, p. 26.

[46] There are no bad houses in astrology, but the ancients defined the 2nd, 6th, 8th and 12th houses as 'bad' because they did not make a Ptolemaic aspect to the Ascendant. These four houses are semi-sextile or quincunx the Ascendant; therefore they are categorized as not being in a harmonic or in harmony with the Ascendant. This is a quantitative way of illustrating the houses and by no means is qualitative or descriptive of the nature of these houses. The language of traditional astrology needs to be seen in context.

[47] For instance see Brian Clark, 'The 8th House: The Sacred Site of Eros' and Sandy Hughes, 'The Soul's Plunge into the 8th House' from *Intimate Relationships*, edited by Joan McEvers, Llewellyn Publications, St. Paul: 1991.

[48] Jeff Jawer, 'The Paradoxes of Intimacy', *Intimate Relationships*, edited by Joan McEvers, Llewellyn Publications, St. Paul: 1991, p. 70. This union is also the composite chart. While a composite chart expresses the potentialities of a relationship, it becomes animated and erotic from the fusion of the partners.

[49] A 7th house relationship is a one-to-one counselling session between a client and therapist, perhaps working on a particular issue, dealing with behavioural strategies and problem-solving. In an 8th house relationship, the therapist is working with transference. A deeper exploration is taking place. The client and therapist are involved in an intimate exchange of trust and are reawakening childhood trauma for release and transformation. In a business partnership, an 8th house relationship begins when the partners' resources are shared and merged. There is one bank account and each has free access. Trust is paramount as the partners are called upon to share their livelihood.

[50] For an excellent treatise on intimacy and relationships, see Thomas Moore, *Soul Mates*, Harper Collins, New York: 1994.

[51] Dane Rudhyar, *The Astrological Houses*, Doubleday & Company, Inc., New York: 1972, p. 108. The other two basic 8th house factors were management and responsibility.

[52] An unexpressed Mars is synonymous with a lack of insight or clarity. When anger and libido are blocked, so is the ability to discern. Potentially, a Mars in Scorpio has tremendous insight and emotional clarity. However, when this becomes bound up with withheld anger and rage, a lack of insight into the self may prevail. For a woman this unexpressed Mars may feel like imprisonment and entrapment.

[53] T.P. and P.T. Malone, *The Art of Intimacy*, Prentice Hall Press, New York: 1987.

[54] Brian Clark, *The Family Legacy.*

[55] Traditionally, the planets were said to rejoice in certain houses. Planetary joys described the houses the seven planets enjoyed inhabiting. These were:

The 1st house	**Mercury**
The 3rd house	**Moon**
The 5th house	**Venus**
The 6th house	**Mars**
The 9th house	**Sun**
The 11th house	**Jupiter**
The 12th house	**Saturn**

[56] Graham Little, *Friendship Being Ourselves with Others*, The Text Publishing Company, Melbourne: 1993, p. 251.

[57] Carl Jung, *Memories, Dreams, Reflections*, translated by Richard and Clara Winston, Pantheon Books, New York, NY: 1973, p. 5.

[58] Marsilio Ficino, *The Letters of Marsilio Ficino, Vol. 2*, Fellowship of the School of Economics, London: 1978, p. 52.

[59] Anaïs Nin, *The Quotable Anaïs Nin*, collected and complied by Paul Herron, Sky Blue Press, San Antonio, TX: 2015, p. 10.

[60] From the official website of Ella Fitzgerald, http://www.ellafitzgerald.com/about/index.html

[61] From the official website of Ella Fitzgerald, http://www.ellafitzgerald.com/about/index.html

[62] See *Scientific American* article by Adrian Ward, 'Men and Women Can't Be "Just Friends"', 23 October 2012, http://www.scientificamerican.com/article/men-and-women-cant-be-just-friends/

[63] See http://www.gingerrogers.com/about/quotes.html

[64] Duane Schultz, *Intimate Friends, Dangerous Rivals: the Turbulent Relationship between Freud and Jung*, J. P. Tarcher, Los Angeles, CA: 1990, p. 216. This was referring to the 'brutal, sanctimonious Jung and his disciples'. The letter was written on 26 July 1914, which happened to be Jung's thirty-ninth birthday. Jung shared the birthday with Freud's wife, Martha, who was born on 26 July 1861.

[65] Sigmund Freud, *The Standard Edition of the Complete Psychological Works of Sigmund Freud, Volume V*, translated by James Strachey, Vintage, London: 2001, p. 483.

[66] This discussion of Freud's friendships continues on from the examination of his sibling relationships in *Family Astrology*.

[67] William McGuire, ed., *The Freud/Jung Letters*, translated by Ralph Manhein and R.F.C. Hull, Princeton University Press, Princeton, NJ: 1974, p. 539.

[68] J. M. Ashmand, *Ptolemy's Tetrabiblos*, Symbols and Signs, North Hollywood, CA: 1976, p. 124.

[69] Jung, 'Synchronicity: an Acausal Connecting Principle', *Collected Works Volume 8*, § 869 footnote.

[70] Thomas Moore, *Soul Mates, Honoring the Mysteries of Love and Relationship*, Harper Collins. New York: 1994, p. 93.

[71] In 1978 Stephen Arroyo released his groundbreaking book *Astrology, Karma and Transformation*, CRCS Publications, Vancouver, WA, which approached astrology from a more conscious and spiritual perspective.

[72] When referring to karma, Carl Jung used the term 'psychic heredity' which included things like our predisposition to disease, character traits, special gifts as well as the 'universal dispositions of the mind' or archetypes. See Carl Jung, *Collected Works Volume 11, Psychology and Religion*, § 842–846.

[73] For instance in 1975 Martin Schulman founded Karmic Astrology and published volume 1 of his series on this in his book called *The Moon's Nodes and Reincarnation*, which had a strong impact on the way the lunar nodes were seen as indicators of past lives. In 1987 he released his astrological book *Karmic Relationships*.

[74] Dane Rudhyar, *The Astrology of Transformation*, The Theosophical Publishing House, Wheaton, IL: 1980, p. 71.

[75] Brian Clark, *Vocation: The Astrology of Career, Creativity and Calling*, Astro*Synthesis, Stanley, Tasmania: 2016.

[76] 'Vertex' is derived from the Latin *vertere*, meaning 'to turn'. It has many synonyms which congregate around the image of the highest point or apex, such as the crown of the head, a pinnacle or mountaintop.

[77] L. Edward Johndro was an engineer, as well as an astrologer, who equated astrology with an electromagnetic field of influence; hence why he coined the term Electric Ascendant.

[78] The Prime Vertical is one of the Great Circles which pass through the zenith, the point directly above the observer; the nadir, the point directly below the observer; and the east and west points of the horizon.

[79] Janet Booth, 'The Vertex, Cosmic Appointments', *The Mountain Astrologer*, June/July 2003.

[80] Because the Vertex has this 'fated' quality, it is useful in synastry and chart comparisons, especially among bonded relationships that 'last a lifetime': parent–child, siblings, soulmates, etc.

[81] http://scandalouswoman.blogspot.com.au/2008/11/grace-kelly-americas-princess.html

[82] Because the data is not verified the Vertex cannot be confirmed. However he will have Jupiter opposite Venus on Grace's nodal axis.

[83] See Jeffrey Wolf Green, *Pluto the Evolutionary Journey of the Soul*, Llewellyn Publications, St. Paul, MN: 1985.

[84] The lunar nodes retrograde through the zodiac about one sign or 30° every 18–19 months.

[85] Pluto's official discovery date is 18 February 1930, discovered by Clyde Tombaugh. Fifteen years earlier Percival Lowell captured two faint images of Pluto when searching for this unknown planet dubbed 'Planet X'. An eleven-year old schoolgirl proposed the name Pluto for the new planet, which was unanimously chosen by the members of the Lowell Observatory. The other suggestions were Minerva and Cronus. Astrologers had also speculated on its discovery: see http://www.astrolearn. com/articles/astrologers-on-pluto-1897-1931. In 2006 Pluto was reclassified as a minor planet.

[86] Isabel Hickey, *Astrology, A Cosmic Science*, CRCS Publications, Sebastopol, CA: 1992, p. 283. When this edition of the book was published, 'Pluto or Minerva' was included as Part Two.

[87] See http://schoolofevolutionaryastrology.com/school/

[88] Liz Greene, *Relating*, xii.

[89] Brian Clark and Kay Steventon, *The Celestial Tarot*, US Games, Stamford, CT: 2006.

[90] See Appendix 2 for tables.

[91] C. G. Jung, *Psychological Types, The Collected Works, Volume 6*, translated by H. G. Baynes and R. F. C. Hull, Princeton University Press, Princeton, NJ: 1971, §933.

[92] C. G. Jung, *Psychological Types, The Collected Works, Volume 6*, §933.

[93] For a diachronic understanding of the development in the ways of thinking about temperament in astrology, I highly recommend Dorian Gieseler Greenbaum's *Temperament: Astrology's Forgotten Key*, The Wessex Astrologer, UK: 2005.

[94] C. G. Jung, *Psychological Types, The Collected Works, Volume 6*, §703.

[95] C. G. Jung, *Psychological Types, The Collected Works, Volume 6*, §724.

[96] C. G. Jung, *Psychological Types, The Collected Works, Volume 6*, §640.

[97] C. G. Jung, *Psychological Types, The Collected Works, Volume 6*, §934.

[98] June Singer, *Boundaries of the Soul*, Anchor, New York: 1972, p. 206.

[99] This refers to a planet that is confined by malefic forces such as the planets Mars, Saturn, even Pluto. For instance, the Moon

might be separating from a conjunction with Mars but applying to a conjunction with Saturn. This is a traditional technique but is of interest in terms of the planet's containment.

[100] The Via Combusta is between 15 Libra and 15 Scorpio and considered a difficult part of the zodiacal pathway, especially for the Moon. This is a traditional technique which could be considered.

[101] See Brian Clark, *Planets in Retrograde*, Astro*Synthesis, Melbourne: 2011. Available from www.astrosynthesis.com.au/

[102] Richard Idemon, *Through the Looking Glass,* p. 197. Idemon refers to the interpersonal signs as social and transpersonal as universal.

[103] Carl Jung, *Modern Man in Search of A Soul*, translated by W.S. Dell and Cary F. Baynes, Routledge & Kegan Paul, London: 1953, p. 57.

[104] Thomas Moore, *Soul Mates, Honoring the Mysteries of Love and Relationship*, p. 61.

[105] Richard Idemon, *Through the Looking Glass,* p. 9.

[106] In 1958, *How to Handle Your Human Relations* by Lois Haines Sargent, published by the American Federation of Astrologers (APA) was subtitled 'Comparison Astrology'. In 1982, Penny Thornton's book *Synastry*, Aquarian, Wellingborough: 1982 outlined a framework for synastry.

[107] Liz Greene, 'Chart Comparison and the Dynamics of Relationship', *The Jupiter/Saturn Conference Lectures*, CRCS Publications, Reno, NV: 1984, p. 16.

[108] Stephen Arroyo, *Relationships and Life Cycles*, CRCS Publications, Vancouver, WA: 1979, Chapter III, pp. 145–155.

[109] Solar Fire was developed in Australia by Esoteric Technologies. See http://www.esotech.com.au/

[110] For a meaningful exploration of the anima and animus, see Liz Greene, *Relating*, pp. 110–154.

[111] For a deeper understanding of these houses, see Brian Clark, *The Family Legacy.*

[112] See Appendix 8, 'Using your Solar Fire Program for Synastry'.

[113] Stephen Arroyo in *Relationships and Life Cycles*, CRCS Publications, Vancouver, WA: 1979, p. 80, states that his 'philosophy of comparisons is based on the fact that human beings are functioning energy fields; we're composites of many energy fields that are functioning simultaneously in an interrelated way'. I was first introduced to swapping the houses in a chart comparison by Stephen Arroyo in this book, pp. 145–155.

[114] Ley lines refer to an alignment of significant and spiritual places in the geography of an area. These are tracks that link together sacred land forms. As a metaphor the aspect lines link together the different parts of the soul and between people these are the tracks that the relationship travels down.

[115] J. Ashman. *Ptolemy's Tetrabiblos,* Symbols and Signs, North Hollywood, CA: 1976, p. 124.

[116] Thornton, Penny. *Synastry,* p. 93.

[117] Robert Hand, *Planets in Composite,* Para Research, Rockport, MA: 1975, p. 3. A year before this book was published John Townley released his book *The Composite Chart* published by Samuel Weiser, New York.

[118] Michael Meyer, *The Astrology of Relationship*, Anchor Books, New York: 1976, p. 182.

[119] Ronald Davison, *Synastry*, ASI Publishers, New York: 1977, p. 244.

[120] When researching the Internet I located this article by John Townley that also uses Brad Pitt and Angelina Jolie's combined charts: http://www.astrococktail.com/compositedavison.html

[121] Robert P. Blaschke in *Astrology A Language of Life, Volume IV – Relationship Analysis*, Earthwalk School of Astrology Publishing, Port Townsend, WA: 2004 on p. 62 notices that: 'One

difference between a Davison chart and a composite chart is that births that are an even number of years apart often have close to identical Suns in both charts. But, if the births are an odd number of years apart, it is likely that a Davison Sun will be opposite from the composite Sun.'

[122] Robert P. Blaschke, *Astrology A Language of Life, Volume IV – Relationship Analysis*, p. 62.

[123] See http://www.wordsof.net/va/rumi/

[124] Rilke and Andreas-Salomé, *A Love Story in Letters*, translated by Edward Snow and Michael Winkler, W.W. Norton & Company, New York: 2008, pp. ix–xiii.

[125] One of the photographers was Edward Quinn who tells his story of photographing the pair that day, including literally bumping into Grace on the way to the palace: http://edwardquinn. com/Text/Texts/First%20Meeting%20Grace-Rainier.html/

[126] Similarly Sisi, who was sixteen when she became the Empress Elisabeth of Austria, met her future husband with her sister Helene who was to marry the Emperor Franz Joseph. Destiny decided Sisi's path when the emperor chose her over her sister.

[127] See Anaïs Nin, *Henry and June*, Penguin, London: 2002.

[128] Gunter Stuhlmann, ed., *A Literate Passion; Letters of Anais Nin and Henry Miller, 1922–1953*, Harcourt, New York, NY: 1987.

[129] See http://www.exeterastrologygroup.org.uk/2016/05/henry-millers-phlegmatic-temperament.html

[130] See http://www.huffingtonpost.com/arthur-hoyle/the-astrological-henry-mi_b_5397661.html

[131] There is controversy over the number of planets in a stellium. Since aspect patterns usually have a minimum of three planets I am comfortable with the term 'stellium' referring to three or more planets in a sign. Donna Cunningham uses the expression 'triple conjunction' which is another good description when only three planets are involved in a stellium. See *The*

Stellium Handbook by Donna Cunningham at http://www.
londonschoolofastrology.co.uk/doc/Stellium.pdf

[132] Anais Nin, *Diary of Anais Nin, 1939–1944*, Harcourt, Brace,
Jovanich Publishers, Orlando, FL: 1969, p. 77.

[133] See http://www.huffingtonpost.com/arthur-hoyle/the-
astrological-henry-mi_b_5397661.html

[134] Henry Miller, *The Books in My Life*, New Directions Books,
New York, NY: 1966, p. 319. This book was digitized by the
Internet Archive in 2005.

[135] *On the Way to the Wedding* by Linda Schierse Leonard,
Shambhala, Boston: 1986 is an excellent Jungian exploration of
the expectations, idealizations and fantasies in relationship.

[136] Penny Thornton in her book *Synastry*, The Aquarian Press,
1982, p. 157, sets the wedding chart at 11 a.m. which was the time
published on the wedding invitations. Guests were asked to arrive
on time and be seated for Diana's arrival. BBC News says Diana
arrived close to the scheduled time of 11.20 a.m. suggesting the
service allowed for this time difference between the guests and
Diana arriving: http://news.bbc.co.uk/onthisday/hi/dates/stories/
july/29/newsid_2494000/2494949.stm
   Astrodatabank suggests the time of 11.17.30 a.m.: http://www.
astro.com/astro-databank/Diana,_Princess_of_Wales.

[137] Over time the progressed Moons will move in and out of
sync as one moves faster than the other.

[138] For instance, see Robert P. Blaschke, *Astrology a Language
of Life Volume IV – Relationship Analysis*, pp. 145–158.

[139] Brian Clark, *The Family Legacy.*

[140] See Michael B. Sperling and William H. Berman, eds.,
Attachment in Adults, The Guildford Press, New York, NY:
1994, or work done by other researchers such as Cindy Hazan
and Phillip Shaver: http://adultattachmentlab.human.cornell.edu/
HazanShaver1987.pdf/

[141] See Brian Clark, *Dynamic Solar Returns*, Astro*Synthesis, Melbourne: 2009, pp. 11–12.

[142] Prince Harry's Pluto is 0♏33 opposite his father's Moon at 0♉25 and paternal grandmother's Sun at 0♉12.

[143] The Sun travels at different speeds throughout the zodiac, travelling fastest through the sign Capricorn and slowest through the sign Cancer. The average daily movement of the Sun is 59'8$^{1}/_{3}$". In Capricorn its daily movement averages 1° 01' 07", while in Cancer the daily movement averages 57'16".

[144] Louise DeSalvo and Mitchell Leaska, eds., *The Letters of Vita Sackville-West to Virginia Woolf*, Cleis Press, San Francisco, CA: 1984.

Astro*Synthesis

Astro*Synthesis was founded in Melbourne in 1986 as an astrological education programme. Since that time Astro*Synthesis has consistently offered an in-depth training programme into the application of astrology from a psychological perspective. The foundation of the course has been constructed to utilize astrology as a tool for greater awareness of the self, others and the world at large.

From 1986 to 2010, Astro*Synthesis offered its dynamic four-year teaching program in the classroom. Astro*Synthesis now offers the complete program of 12 modules through distance learning.

For a detailed syllabus or more information on Astro*Synthesis E-Workbooks, E- Booklets or reports please visit our website:

www.astrosynthesis.com.au

CPSIA information can be obtained
at www.ICGtesting.com
Printed in the USA
BVHW042028091019
560665BV00002B/54/P